# Contractors' Handbook

The expert guide for UK contractors and freelancers

Second edition

# Praise for the first edition

*Don't even think about embarking into freelancing without ordering a copy of the Contractors' Handbook by Dave Chaplin. You could easily spend years finding out the hard way, what this highly focused and relevant book tells you and, after reading it, you will know exactly how to handle all the pitfalls and joys of contracting.*
David Colom
D J Colom & Co Chartered Accountants


*I'm finding the handbook to be very interesting and useful, especially as I'm rewriting my CV to a more high impact format. The best part so far has been the recent 'contract renewal' which, having read the handbook, I referred back to my agent to get it redrafted as a new contract with a change of title, and took the opportunity to get an increased rate as well!*
Paul Gardner, UK Contractor


*Whatever stage you are at with your career in contracting or freelancing, the Contractors' Handbook is an invaluable source of information and hints and tips. The author Dave Chaplin's successful career as a contractor means that he's now able to pass on the secrets of his success. And as a former contractor, I can really relate to the subjects Dave covers in the book; having this available during my contracting career would have been a big help. The Contractor's Handbook lays out everything you need to know about working as a contractor, in a clear and concise fashion, and the format of the book, with Dave's real life examples, make it an easy and enjoyable read.*
Rob Crossland
CEO, Parasol Group


*Rarely do you pick up a book that answers all the questions. Not only does the Contractors' Handbook answer them in detail, but it also goes into areas I hadn't even thought about – despite creating and running several successful businesses. Whether you are a freelancer, contractor, interim, freelance consultant or locum, regardless of the years you have been working, this comprehensive book is an absolute gem. Get one and I promise you it will remain on your shelf for reference and get used regularly. Highly recommended!*
Darren Fell
Managing Director, Crunch

*To order more copies of this book or to obtain further information about ContractorCalculator's future publications, please contact:*

Marketing Department

ContractorCalculator

An imprint of Byte-Vision Ltd

112c Roman Road

Basingstoke

Hampshire RG23 8HE

Tel: 01978 368808

Fax: 01978 368809

Email: office@byte-vision.com

Web: contractorshandbook.co.uk

# Contractors' Handbook

The expert guide for UK contractors and freelancers

Second edition

Dave Chaplin

CONTRACTOR
CALCULATOR.CO.UK
your expert guide to contracting

First published in 2008 by ContractorCalculator
Reprinted in 2009 (three times)
Reprinted in 2010 (twice)
Reprinted in 2011 (three times)
**Second edition published 2012**

ContractorCalculator
An imprint of Byte-Vision Ltd
112c Roman Road
Basingstoke
Hampshire RG23 8HE

British Library Cataloguing in Publication Data:

A catalogue record for this book is available from the British Library

ISBN 978-0-9560745-2-2

Dedicated to my parents and my dear wife,
for all their love and support.

# Acknowledgements

There are many people to whom I am grateful for advice, ideas and encouragement offered during the development of this second edition of the *Contractors' Handbook*. In particular, I would like to thank the contractors, from every sector, who have contributed to this book in one way or another: some because I've had the pleasure of working alongside them and developing friendships for life, and others whose brave fights with HMRC and HM Treasury have established important principles that have helped all contractors.

The impetus for first edition came from the hundreds of contractors who have sent in queries – from the basic to the bizarre – to the Contractor Doctor on ContractorCalculator.co.uk. Their regular questions help shine a light on current contracting, legislation and tax issues. They have also helped us illuminate some of the darkest corners of contracting legislation, 'worst practice' and even lifestyles! Many people who successfully used the first edition to start or develop their contracting careers have contributed to the second by providing invaluable feedback, which has been duly incorporated into these pages.

Numerous experts within the contracting sector have generously given of their time and freely offered their advice and opinions on the wealth of guides developed on ContractorCalculator.co.uk, and which form the backbone of this book. Some are 'inside sources' who wish to remain anonymous, but my public thanks go, among others, to:

James Abbott, Baker Watkin

John Brazier and Simon McVicker, PCG

David Colom, D J Colom & Co

Rob Crossland and Derek Kelly, Parasol and ClearSky

Tony Harris, Contractor Financials

Adrian Marlowe, Lawspeed

Seb Maley and Andy Vessey, Qdos Consulting

Roger Sinclair, Egos.

Many others have also contributed, not least the dedicated team at Copestone.

My wife, father, other loved ones and friends deserve special mention, for their unfailing support and incredible patience during the creation of the second edition.

**To all of you, my heartfelt thanks.**
Dave

# Contents

# Foreword to the second edition

By John Brazier
Managing Director
PCG

The strategic importance of contractors and freelancers to ensuring that the UK remains highly competitive in a global economy continues to increase, as has the size and influence of the UK's freelance and contracting sector – both in the UK and the rest of Europe.

PCG research conducted by Kingston University's Small Business Research Centre shows that, since 2008, the UK's flexible workforce has grown by 12% to 1.56 million. Contractors and freelancers now account for one in twenty of the working population. By providing additional skilled labour to increase the capacity of organisations and to bring them fresh insights, contractors and freelancers are making a disproportionately large contribution to rebalancing the UK's economy towards investment and exports.

As their numbers have increased, so has the influence of this vital group of uniquely skilled and flexible knowledge workers. Through the PCG, contractors and freelancers have secured representation at the highest levels of Government and policy making in Westminster through the All Party Parliamentary Group (APPG) on the Freelance Sector. This group is tasked with highlighting the contribution contractors and freelancers make to the UK economy, as well as with drawing attention to the challenges they face and the barriers to their growth.

The UK's knowledge workers are highly mobile. Many UK-based contractors and freelancers deliver their services to clients outside the UK, making their own contribution to Britain's exports. Within Europe, a critical mass of pan-European contractor and freelancer organisations are placing flexible workers at the heart of the policy agenda – both at the European Commission (EC) in Brussels and the European Parliament in Strasbourg.

As well as increasing in number, contractors and freelancers are themselves evolving, adopting new skills and working practices to ensure they maximise the benefits of new technologies and access to new markets. The flexible workforce's stakeholders, including clients, are becoming increasingly aware of the benefits that contractors and freelancers can bring to their organisations.

Alongside this growth comes a thirst for knowledge on how to flourish as a contractor and maximise the opportunities of the freelance lifestyle. This knowledge comes from representative industry bodies, such as PCG, as well as through websites like ContractorCalculator.co.uk, plus, of course, publications like the *Contractors' Handbook*. And this second edition is particularly timely, as it expertly details the May 2012 changes to how the IR35 tax legislation is administered – perhaps the most significant changes since IR35 was introduced in 1999.

By accessing this knowledge, contractors and freelancers can unleash their true potential, building a firm foundation for launching and managing successful freelance and contracting businesses.

**John Brazier**

# Preface to the second edition

Three years on from the first edition of the *Contractors' Handbook* and the contracting sector has not only survived the worst economic downturn since the end of the Second World War, but also continued to grow and further support UK Plc.

But it has been far from 'business as usual' – much has changed. Indeed, since the Coalition Government came to power in 2010, IR35 (the 'contractor tax') has never been more active. First the government set up the Office of Tax Simplification, for which I and ContractorCalculator consulted extensively. And then the IR35 Forum came along, adding a further layer of complication for limited company contractors to deal with from May 2012, in the form of HMRC's new business entity tests and guidance. Before then, the Agency Workers Regulations (AWR) came into force in Autumn 2011, resulting in changes for many contractors and their recruiters.

But despite these dramatic shifts, much has not changed in the last three years. The hard work, cutting-edge skills, broad experience and flexibility of the key members of the UK's workforce remain the drivers of economic recovery and success – contractors are still the pathfinders of growing businesses and economies. Vital to the success of UK Plc for centuries, highly skilled and flexible contractors have always been found in every sector – from science, engineering and medicine, through crafts and trades, to education, the arts and media.

Research from PCG confirms that the number of contractors in the UK continues to grow; it reached 1.56 million in 2011, up from 1.4 million in 2008. And anecdotal evidence, combined with a 50% rise in ContractorCalculator.co.uk readers since the first *Contractors' Handbook* was published, points to this growth continuing.

This second edition of the *Contractors' Handbook* remains the expert guide for all contractors and freelancers in the UK – whether you're just considering the move into contracting, or have many years of experience, this book can help you. It's a resource that pulls together in one place: my first-hand experience; the wisdom of many successful contractors built up over nearly two decades; the specialist knowledge of dozens of expert contributors; ContractorCalculator's numerous contractor-focused calculators; plus of course the site's 650+ carefully researched and regularly updated guides.

Independent ABC audits show that in the last three years the readership of ContractorCalculator.co.uk has grown 50% to over 150,000 unique visitors each month. Readers keep coming back, which is not surprising since we have added a huge amount of new material to the website, including our new and very popular Online IR35 Test. This new material is reflected in the size and composition of the second edition of the Handbook, which has been updated with almost 50% new material. Alongside guidance on navigating HMRC's new IR35 administration framework, there is a new chapter on AWR, updates to tax and legislation, new solutions in the 'what to do when things go wrong' chapter and extensive guidance to help contractors from overseas.

So, for those of you who have longed to take control of your destiny and move into contracting, I offer you encouragement and practical 'how to' guidance for your journey. More and more people are choosing contracting as a career choice because of the flexibility it allows. And, regardless of the economic landscape, the best time to go contracting is "right now". For experienced contractors, you'll find information on advanced techniques to really 'up your game'. And should things go wrong along the way, I'll share with you solutions that have been effectively used by me and others.

Most successful contractors remain successful because they recognise that their market is always moving, and maintain their skills accordingly. This book provides another opportunity to do just that, but for the skills that feature less highly on most contractors' radars, but can be even more important than the letters after your name when it comes to winning the best contracts: things like CV writing, contract law, negotiation techniques and key sales and marketing skills. This second edition also features guidance on adopting the contracting mindset, providing clear lessons on how to move on from being an employee and apply the new rule book of contracting to how you manage your finances, how to work with clients and how you resolve challenges.

As a graduate with a maths master's degree, my ambition was to become a teacher; but the lure of the City and its rewards to IT contractors have ensured my goal remains unrealised. However, through ContractorCalulator.co.uk and the *Contractors' Handbook*, I have found other channels to pass on what I have learnt. If you find this second edition helpful, I shall be delighted. And if you don't find what you're looking for, would like to take issue with anything I've written, or have any questions about contracting, then please do get in touch with me through www.contractorshandbook.co.uk.

**Dave Chaplin**
London, June 2012

# 1
# Why go contracting?

## 1.1 The main reasons people do it

The decision to move from being a permanent employee to becoming a contractor seems to have been endlessly dramatised. In fact, it's not that big a decision at all. Choosing to become a contractor ranks well below decisions like getting married or deciding on which career to choose.

In fact, if you are reading this, you've probably already made some fairly important decisions about your career, which is why contracting sounds attractive. You may be a programmer with years of experience and already earning good money in a job. Or you may be a recently qualified engineer and wondering whether you should give contracting a try.

After reading on, the choice can only be yours. The question is, do you always want to be asking yourself 'what-if?'. Don't forget that you can always return to the permanent workplace if contracting doesn't suit you. But if you don't take the plunge, you'll never know what you've missed!

Most contractors go down the contracting road for three typical reasons:

- To do the things they really want to do, and this includes taking more time off

- To avoid the things they really don't want to do

- For the money.

### 'It's not what I want to do anymore'
Actually, it is the second reason that drives many wannabe contractors into the sector, and then keeps them happily embedded in the contractor lifestyle. In their last role as a permanent worker, or permie, something happens to make them think: 'Surely there must be something better out there?'

Many of us get to the stage in our careers when we become as experienced, skilled and technically proficient as we are likely to get in our chosen skill set. This could be in programming, engineering, medicine, marketing or many other disciplines.

## The catalyst

**DAVE SAYS:** My decision to go contracting didn't happen overnight. It's the same for most contractors. The final decision is normally made after a 'right that's it!' event. Common ones are false promises that fail to materialise, like not being promoted or receiving a smaller than deserved rise in salary or receiving no rise at all.

I was working for a consultancy firm that sold me on to various banks at twice what they were paying me. Before I finally decided to go contracting I had a frank chat with my firm and told them I was not happy and what I expected from them, which was more money and more training. They promised it, it never happened; so I left.

I was basically a contractor already, but with one agent that I gave 50% of my money to each month. Cutting out the middleman was a no brainer. I made a few enquiries, handed in my notice, and within two weeks had secured a contract that saw my take home pay double overnight.

The common theme, however, is that for most the next stage of progression after reaching a professional or technical pinnacle is into management, which tends to raise two big questions:

1.  Do I really want my future career progression to be on the management track? It typically means doing a lot less of what you have previously enjoyed doing, and doing a lot more managing and progressing your career, which becomes an all-consuming end in itself.

2.  Having become the most qualified person at what I do, would I want to start at the bottom again, learning a new skill set and being the smallest fish in a bigger pond?

So many potential contractors find themselves being promoted, or not being promoted, either of which can prove frustrating. And typically many highly qualified professionals find themselves sidelined into 'special projects' or doing tasks they really don't enjoy.

This then makes them think about what it is they really want to do.

**Now, what can I do that I have always wanted to?**
So, having been given a reason to think about taking the contracting route, we then think about the first reason – contractors who go contracting because they get to do what they want to do.

Here is a really important point: contractors are not employed by the organisation that pays them for what they spend their time doing. There is a big difference between being paid as an employee to perform a task and being paid to do a task without being employed. This will be explained in more detail in section 1.3.

## Been there, done that!

### True flexibility

**DAVE SAYS:** Cash was the initial front-runner when I was thinking about reasons to go contracting, but the flexibility was what made me never go back to being a permie.

My initial view of contracting was that I'd basically get paid much more for doing pretty much the same thing. But, as you soon learn after you've been contracting for a year or, so there are many more benefits than just the extra cash. Being able to take off much more time, and having the cash to take more holidays are real bonuses.

I love travelling and took many long weekends in places like New York, Las Vegas, Paris and Moscow, often indulging my love of golf along the way. And I still had money left over each month for savings.

The other great bonus was the training. I sent myself on lots of courses and got certifications. I'd been begging my previous employer for this for ages, but it never happened. The director even said to me after I left that the problem with spending money on training people up is that they then leave.

Within a year of leaving I achieved a recently launched Microsoft Certification, and was one of the first 500 in the UK to get it; that never would have happened if I'd stayed at the firm.

The major point of difference is that, as a contractor, as long as you perform, you can do a lot more of what you want to do. It varies between different types of clients and different sectors, but the common theme is that you take control of your work and your work-life balance.

If you are a software developer and have been allocated specific sections of software to develop during the week, and you finish early on Thursday, you could take Friday off. The developer sat next to you who is an employee has to find something else to do to finish their week. Or, to be more precise, they will either be found something else to do or will try and stretch out the job to last the week.

However, it does not always work like that. If a contractor is an offshore safety specialist working on an ongoing drilling project, for instance, they can't just leave for the weekend until their safety role is covered. But you can bet that what they are being paid more than compensates them for working some weekends!

Contractors have a level of flexibility that permanent employees simply do not have. If they can afford it – and many can – contractors can take long periods of time away from work, or they can choose to work particularly hard for a few years to earn enough to retire early. The keyword is **choice;** a contractor really can choose what work to do, when to do it, and how to do it.

This can also work well for contractors with families who want to be able to choose to spend more time with them, particularly if they have young children or perhaps they want to spend time as a carer for a parent or other relative. The increased money contracting brings can make flexible working possible for many with family commitments who might otherwise not be able to work at all.

**For the money**
In addition to the flexibility contracting gives, and the ability to leave behind the world of office politics, another important reason people choose to become contractors is for the money. And that's not surprising, because contractors typically earn between 20% and 150% more than permanent employees.

Why do they get paid so much more? It is generally because they are not employees but also because they may, particularly in some key sectors and disciplines, be highly skilled and very rare, in which case market forces contribute to their high rates. As an employee with such skills, even if they're well rewarded, it is not often that an employee's true market value is paid to them, particularly if they have been with a company for a long time.

Employees are expensive and a high risk to employers. They insist on having reasonable wages, pensions and a whole raft of benefits, yet even if they become too ill to work or the work itself dries up for a while, they still have to be paid. Employers also have to pay additional National Insurance Contributions on top of everything else.

Contractors are cheap by comparison and almost always highly cost-effective to use. They are not employed by the company they are contracting for, so don't have the overheads associated with permanent employees. And if they don't work, they don't get paid, whatever the reason. So the result is that contractors get paid more for taking the risk of not being employed. And, as we'll see in later chapters, that need not be much of a risk at all.

But contractors also have a bit of a trick up their sleeves that makes the contracting option so rewarding for so many. As they are not employees, contractors can pay much less tax, meaning that more gross income finds its way into the contractor's bank account. The tax advantages are explained in greater detail in section 1.3.

## Been there, done that!

## It's not just about the money

**DAVE SAYS:** Sadly, and unjustifiably, contractors can get a bit of a reputation as being 'money grabbing'. The fact is that whilst they expect to be paid the going market rate, many would rather work on an interesting project that pays less than on a frustrating project that pays more.

Once, two of my friends jacked in high-paying contracts because the firms needing the work done were simply no fun to work for! The first one was a bank that suffered from heavy bureaucracy, making it impossible to move forward quickly. The second was a consultancy whose expectations were unrealistic – they expected to build Rome in a day and it was the contractor's fault if that miracle couldn't be achieved.

Contractors typically go contracting because they hate politics and/or working for bad bosses. Most of them just like to get things done, achieving the goals of the project and adding value to companies along the way.

Contracting can be a great way of life and, with the help of this book, you too can pick up the tips and tricks to make a real success of it.

# Why do contractors choose the contracting lifestyle?

- They want to earn more.

- They love the hands-on work they do and want to carry on doing it.

- They have become disillusioned with permanent work.

- They don't like office politics, have heard one too many false promises, and are fed up working for sometimes unappreciative management.

- They don't want to move up the ladder by going into management and finding themselves doing a job they do not enjoy.

- They don't want to move into a role they don't want.

- After many years working really hard, obtaining their valuable skills, they would like to have more holiday than the 20-25 days a year they currently get.

- They'd like to have more time to pursue other interests, hobbies and business opportunities outside of the 9 to 5, including spending more time with families and children.

- They see contracting as a way of earning more money, taking more holidays, and continuing to do what they love doing.

## 1.2 Profile of the typical contractor

Actually, there is no such thing as a typical contractor. But there is a collection of skills, experience and attributes that makes it possible for people to choose to become a highly successful contractor.

Firstly, there are the hard skills a person must have before they consider going contracting. A successful contractor needs to have a transferable skill that has a proven market demand from clients who need this skill on a one-off basis to complete a specific project.

### Been there, done that!

### What does a contractor look like?

**DAVE SAYS:** Not all contractors are the same, but all of the successful contractors I've met have the same traits: first and foremost, they're highly skilled and passionate about their work. They're not afraid to work hard, but they do expect to get paid handsomely for it. They aren't interested in climbing corporate ladders. Contracting gives them a way to do the same thing as they were doing as an employee, but with loads more benefits and the opportunity to earn six-figure salaries.

Most IT, engineering, construction and technical skills, for example, are transferable. So too are those skills, particularly in engineering, surveying, architecture and medicine, where a professional qualification is required to practice.

Although less common now, many IT professionals in the past became highly skilled at developing major organisations' legacy systems. You can be sure that this made them highly respected within their business. But their skills were not in a common computer language and thus not transferable to wider industry.

So the potential contractor's skills must also be in demand by a wide market. In other words, there must be plenty of potential clients out there who need that skill and are therefore prepared to pay well for it.

A budding contractor must also have some hard business skills, although these can be developed, not least through reading books like this one.

However you go about contracting, and however you feel you dislike the thought of it, as a contractor you have to make some business choices for yourself, otherwise you might just as well remain as a permanent employee.

A grasp of marketing, sales, finance and taxation are needed to be a successful contractor, but they are remarkably easy to pick up. We'll cover all of these subjects later in the book.

Softer skills, such as managing and motivating people, also start to become more important, because as a contractor you have to:

- Act as 'account manager' to your client

- Hit the ground running when starting a new contract

- Work with employees of the client, some of whom may feel the higher wages and better conditions contractors enjoy are not deserved

- Work with other contractors, who may well become your best friends and a great source of future contracts.

Most importantly, you have to want to be a contractor. There are so many benefits to the contracting lifestyle, and sometimes hard work is required to maintain those benefits. But there are several hundred thousand people in the UK who have chosen to work as contractors and wouldn't go back to being a permie. Not all of them can be wrong!

# 1.3 Contracting compared to being a permanent employee

Contracting as we know it today had its roots in the IT boom of the 1980s, although it has now spread to cover virtually every sector. Back then it was typical for someone to leave work on the Friday as a salaried employee and return on the Monday as a full-blown contractor. They could be doing exactly the same job, at the same desk and for the same company, but finding themselves being paid three or more times as much as they had been the week before!

Nowadays the same happens, but the contractor should be working with a different company. That's because contracting with a former employer immediately after leaving them puts the contractor at risk of still being seen by the taxman as 'employed', with the risk of being caught by nasty tax legislation called IR35. This is explained in greater detail in chapter 8.

But there are some important differences when comparing the situations of contractors versus permanent employees, as can be seen in table 2. The contractor may get paid a larger sum, but the permanent employee enjoys a range of benefits that have a hidden cost to the employer. At a glance, table 2 does not appear to greatly favour the contractor. But in the key categories of pay, hours, holidays and tax, being a contractor can far outweigh all the other benefits combined.

## Pay
Contractors are paid a gross sum, usually weekly or monthly, and by the hour or day. Day rates can be typically up to £500 per day, increasing to £1,000 per day at the top end of the market. Some very specialist roles can be even more.

## Type of contract
The difference between the types of contracts an employee has with their employer and the contract a contractor has with their client is significant:

| | Permanent employee (permie) | Contractor |
|---|---|---|
| Pay | Standard market rates – much less than contractors or consultants | 20% - 100% more than employees |
| Type of contract | Of service, as an employee The employer is required to supply paid work during the contract of service and the employee is obliged to accept it | For services as a company. The employer is not required to provide paid work; the contractor only has to do work previously agreed to. |
| Hours | Usually fixed or limited flexibility | Flexible |
| Holidays | Paid, 28+ days | Unpaid, flexible |
| Notice | Usually weeks | No, subject to contract |
| Redundancy | Minimum statutory | No |
| Benefits Sick pay | Yes/statutory | No |
| Maternity | Yes/statutory | No |
| Pension | Yes/stakeholder | No |
| Private health | Potentially | No |
| Company car | Potentially | No |
| Mileage allowance | Potentially | No |
| Health club | Potentially | No |
| Staff canteen | Potentially | No |
| Crèche | Potentially | No |
| Social events | Potentially | No |
| Company politics | Yes | No |
| Promotion worries | Yes | No |
| Tax and expenses | PAYE, NIC, few allowances | Salary, dividends, high allowances |

*Table 2 Permanent employee versus Contractor*

- An employee-employer contract is a *contract of service*

- A contractor-client contract is a *contract for services.*

Basically, the contractor's contract is just the same type, one for services, as if the client were hiring, say, a grounds maintenance company.

They come in, cut the grass, get paid and move on to their next client's site. The contractor is just another service provider and, as long as the work is completed to the agreed standard, according to budget and schedule, they get paid.

---

## Been there, done that!

## No need to work for free

**DAVE SAYS:** One bank I worked for was in real trouble, having set some crazy deadlines that we were never going to be able to achieve. They pressed hard for the contractors and permies to work twelve-hour days and weekends, which started becoming the norm.

As contractors on daily rates, this wasn't ideal. So the contractors got together and said we weren't going to work for free, and that they had to pay us extra money for the extra work. Given their position and the huge market demand for contractors they had no choice but to pay up.

The permies were promised 'bonuses' after the software was released, which were nowhere near what the contractors were paid. You won't be surprised to hear that quite a few of them went contracting after that!

---

An employee, with a contract of service, on the other hand, is controlled by their employer. Most permanent employees would not consider themselves as controlled by their employer, but in practice they have signed a contract that says they will do a job, which the employer, within certain limits, can change. They also have to be present at a specific place between certain hours and for certain minimum days of the year.

Another crucial difference is that the employer has what is called a 'mutuality of obligation' with their employees, but not with their contractors. What mutuality of obligation, or as it is referred to in the contracting sector 'MOO', means is that if the employee keeps their part of the bargain and turns up to work, the employer has to find them some work to do and pay them regardless.

This often means that the permanent employees get a great deal of the less exciting and satisfying work, because contractors rightly refuse to do the work as it was not in the original agreement with the client. An employee can't do this, even if it's not in their job description, because in the real world employees do what they must to secure their next promotion or pay rise, or perhaps even to keep their job.

## Been there, done that!

### Saying 'no'

**DAVE SAYS:** During a project for a client, when I was effectively a permie, I was asked to learn some bizarre old programming language for an existing client requirement. Apparently, as my employers put it, knowledge of this tool 'was a great opportunity and would look good on my CV'.

After some research it turned out that it was an almost defunct language that the client required to update some old system they had. Hardly a CV-enhancing skill set to learn. I expressed my dissatisfaction at having to do this, but still had to do it anyway. It was the dullest six months of my career.

During my contracting years I was often asked whilst on site using my up-to-date skills to 'have a look' at some legacy system to quickly help the client out. I always politely refused. I didn't march backwards in my contracting career.

Whilst it might seem odd to be going into these nitty gritty details so early in this book, it is necessary because these key contract points are of vital importance for establishing a contractor's tax status and therefore how much more or less tax they may be liable for.

## Hours

Employees are required to work at a specific place or places for a specific number of hours on specific days. Although many employers operate some form of flexi-time, in practice, for most employees, there is little flexibility.

Contractors have no set hours, although there are reasons why contractors may be restricted to working certain hours on some contracts. If for example, key members of the client team were only present during traditional office hours, then the contractor might have to be present during some of those hours to get their work done.

## Holidays

Employees, and even temporary workers, have a statutory right to holiday pay. It can vary above the statutory minimum, depending on the generosity of the employer, but is rarely more than 30 days. Contractors, on the other hand, do not enjoy holiday pay; in practice, most simply save some of the extra money they earn as contractors to tide them over the periods they choose not to work, or may not be able to work through illness.

## Been there, done that!

### Cheap deals are yours for the taking

**DAVE SAYS:** Getting away is much easier for contractors, because you don't have to worry about managing a fixed holiday allowance. If the project is quiet and you fancy a long weekend, you can take time off. You can then qualify for all those last minute cheap deals.

Contractors may have to plan their holidays around the requirements of clients, particularly workflows associated with the contracts on which they are working. With some planning, this is very easily done; we cover holidays for contractors in chapter 12. Without a doubt contractors, if they choose, can take off much more time than permanent employees.

## Notice and redundancy

Neither applies to contractors, although they do to employees. But many contractors would not want the loss of flexibility that comes with being an employee, and therefore entitled to notice and redundancy. Conversely, many employees feel the need to have the cushion of a redundancy payment – no matter how small – if they lose their job. The key lesson for contractors is to put by enough to survive the usually short periods between contracts.

## Benefits

As they are not employed by the client, contractors receive no employee benefits. This should not matter, however, as the contractor's extra pay is more than enough to cover these benefits. It also means contractors get to choose the benefits they want, whereas many employees find themselves paying tax on benefits, such as cars and gym membership, that they don't particularly want or need.

Providing some financial cover for periods of sickness is a sensible approach, and not an expensive one, for a contractor to take, and we cover this topic in chapter 12.

## Company politics

Every organisation, whether large or small, has politics. If you're a part of that organisation as an employee, you can't help being dragged into office politics. From minor disputes over the right brand of coffee in a small business, to trans-corporation battles between departmental leviathans over billions in capital investment, for most of us politics are a pain that causes untold stress inside and outside work.

Contractors, of course, do not work for the company and, except for minor things like understanding job requirements and getting timesheets signed, do not take orders from, or come under the thumb of, the company's management.

During the research for this book, company politics was one of the most common reasons cited by contractors as to why they left their full time permanent job to become a contractor.

## Getting ill

**DAVE SAYS:** In all my years of contracting I think the longest time I took off ill was 3 days, when I had to go into hospital for an operation. I still would have gone into work if it wasn't for the fact that the op' was on my leg, so I couldn't physically get into the office!

You'll see more contractors at work with various sniffles and ailments than permies because they don't get paid if they don't go in to work. I rarely called in sick, but was once ordered home to rest after falling asleep at the desk when a virus zapped me of energy for a week!

It's not that contractors have to work when they're feeling unwell, it's more to do with the fact that they're likely to be doing work they enjoy, and that they'd rather do that and get paid than watch daytime TV.

**Promotion worries**

Most organisations base pay and benefits on some form of rank within their infrastructure. Promotion for most employees is often the only way to improve their lot. But there can never be more managers than workers, so promotion opportunities are generally hard-fought contests, frequently with good doses of constant pressure and unpleasantness.

Why should contractors worry about promotion if they don't work for the client? They'll be off to the next higher paying contract in a few months anyway, so there is no need at all to get involved in anyone's power play or disputes. Contractors who want to promote themselves can simply take the opportunity to win a contract with a better rate, and buy the 'manager's perks' with the difference.

**Tax**

Employees generally work on the Pay as You Earn (PAYE) tax scheme with their employer arranging to deduct their income tax and National Insurance Contributions at source. There are very few deductions employees can claim to reduce their tax payments, so they often face the double whammy of not only earning less than contractors, but also paying more tax than them.

One of the major advantages that most contractors enjoy is that they do not collect pay taxed at source under a PAYE scheme. Contractors who opt to provide their services through a limited company can divert the income from the company in a variety of beneficial ways, such as dividends for themselves and payments into their pension funds, which employees are unable to do.

Another major advantage for contractors using their own company is that they can charge expenses against the business, which means that technically they make less profit, but as a result they also pay less tax. Plus, if they earn enough, which most do, they can register for VAT and claim VAT back on their costs.

**Tax advantages**
Here's a classic example of the tax advantages of buying work equipment as a contractor:

To buy £2,400 (including VAT) of new computer equipment, the cost to the contractor's company would only be £2,000, because the VAT can be reclaimed. The remaining £2,000 would be tax deductible so a contractor on higher rate tax would only see a net reduction in take home pay of £1,200.

If the £2,400 of computer equipment was bought and paid for with a contractor's net pay, the extra earnings would need to be £4,000. That's because corporation tax at 20%, £800, should be added, and dividend tax of 25%, £800, on the resulting £3,200 dividend should also be paid.

The net result is that buying equipment via a company ex-VAT with pre-taxed income is much more tax efficient and cost effective.

Some contractors find themselves better suited to working through what are known as umbrella companies, which give them official 'employee' status and therefore deduct tax and National Insurance Contributions at source. Such contractors do take home less net income than they might otherwise, but there are some tax advantages with expenses, which means they're still better off compared to permies.

Chapter 6, How to set up and run your business, takes you through your trading options in detail. It also gives example calculations showing how financially better off contractors can be compared to employees.

## 1.4 Common contracting myths

Not surprisingly for a sector that has grown so rapidly in such a short time, there are many myths about contracting and contractors that might discourage a permanent employee from taking the plunge. However, like most myths, they can be debunked. Here are some of the more common contracting myths:

### Contractors' income is not much higher than permanent workers receive

The fees earned by contractors should always be more than permanent employees earn; much more. Provided you take a professional approach to finding contracts you will avoid gaps between contracts and should, if you follow the steps in this book, make considerably more money than you could in permanent employment.

If your skill set is heavily in demand then you could at least double or even triple your current take home pay by going contracting.

### Your skills will become outdated

A common fear is that after a year or so your skills will become outdated or even redundant. Some worry that without the training an employer might arrange for an employee, it will not be possible to update the contractor's skills and that contractor will then find it hard to get work. Some contractors do have this problem, but no more so than permanent employees who also don't invest time in training.

Plus, of course, contractors have all the benefits of having developed their skills at a number of different companies, so they often have knowledge and abilities way in advance of permanent employees who have mainly worked for one or two companies for a long time. Permanent employees who have had only one or two jobs over many years are the ones who find it hardest to make the transition to contracting. Change is very healthy, for contractors and permies alike.

## Skills don't become outdated

**DAVE SAYS:** When I worked at a consultancy that 'body-shopped' me out and made a nice profit, this was the standard line they told us: "Sure, you'll make lots of money in the short term, but when your skills become out of date no one will hire you."

Well, this proved to be inaccurate. You learn new skills on the job, and many of them are timeless and transferable. For me in IT, sure I had to learn new versions of software, but provided you jump onto the ship before it sails you'll be fine.

Remember that the permanent people tend not to get much training from their firms, so even if you send yourself on a course you are still a valuable commodity whilst the industry is transferring to the new product.

A common strategy to learn new skills is to learn them on your existing contract, so that you have actual commercial experience which you can take to the next one. Treat your contracts like stepping stones. This might require sending yourself on a training course, and a bit of midnight oil burning at home getting up to speed, but it's not the whole time and you are rewarded very well for it.

Contractors who work hard to keep their skills updated rarely experience problems finding work. Contractors also have the luxury of being in complete control of their professional development. They can attend as many courses as they wish, in addition to investing regularly in the latest professional books and manuals, whereas permies frequently have to beg managers for training with all sorts of restrictions and payback clauses added to their contracts in the event they leave their employer.

**You are given all the boring work to do**
It is true, there are some contracts that nobody would want to do, but the simple solution is not to apply for the contract, or not to accept it when it is offered to you. Remember, contractors aren't told what to do by the manager, like permanent employees. On the contrary, contractors choose what projects they want to work on.

Should a contractor be asked during a contract to complete something that is outside the bounds of the original contractual agreement, then the contractor is not obliged to do it and, in most cases, shouldn't even think about doing it. If things become untenable (which is very rare) the contractor can simply leave, then sue the client for breach of contract, which is not as difficult or expensive as it sounds (see chapter 10).

### You do not get benefits – sick pay / holidays / health insurance / company cars

We've already covered this topic and we know that it is true. However, as their own employer, contractors can buy all the benefits they want. And, interestingly, many contractors find themselves taking fewer days off sick; not because they're working through their illness, but because they're enjoying what they do and don't tend to feel the 'Monday blues'.

Health insurance is available for contractors, and can guard against long periods of time off work due to sickness. Company cars benefit employees who would not normally be able to afford such a model themselves, and therefore cost significant amounts of extra tax. But it is much cheaper for an individual to purchase and fund their own car, and most contractors very quickly amass the disposable income to buy exactly the model they want.

### You cannot get a mortgage without two years worth of accounts

Contractors can access specialist financial services products, such as mortgages, created specifically for them. In fact, because some lenders recognise the earning potential and higher net pay of the contracting model, contractors often secure better deals than those available to permanent employees. Plus, with the additional money contractors are earning, they can also make overpayments and clear mortgage balances in less time.

### You are liable for costly errors in your work.

It is true that contractors, as service providers, are liable for any errors they make, but so are professionals like lawyers and accountants. To mitigate this risk, most limited company contractors simply purchase their own professional indemnity (PI) insurance, whilst umbrella company contractors are generally covered by their umbrella's PI insurance (the differences between these contracting styles is described later in the book). Just like any other insurance, it is there to protect the contractor in case a client makes a claim against them.

## It's a hassle setting up a company and doing all the accounts

A contractor can buy a new company online in less than half an hour for around £20. Most contractors work with accountants or umbrella companies that handle the vast majority of record keeping, accounting and tax return preparation online.

Contractors usually only have to keep accurate invoicing, timesheet and expenses records, not much more than they would as a permanent employee. In fact, some contractors might find running their own company simpler and less painful than extracting expenses from their former employer!

The hardest part about contracting is making the decision to leave the perceived comfort and security of permanent work to go and get that first contract.

Once that decision has been made, most wonder why they didn't choose to become a contractor years before. Perhaps they were waiting for this book to be published!

## Been there, done that!

### Guest house heaven

**DAVE SAYS:** One of my friends was sensible enough to save his money when he was contracting, a hard task for any young and single person working in London, where there is plenty of opportunity to party.

After five years he gave up the rat race, moved to Scotland and bought a guest house. He now spends the morning attending to guests, the afternoons playing golf and the evenings with his family. If you plan well you, too, can buy yourself out of the daily grind.

# Contracting lessons from this chapter

- Contracting offers you choice. You can choose what contracts you wish to accept and you can choose to avoid work that does not interest you.

- Contracting enables you to earn more money. Often much more.

- Contractors have much greater control over their careers.

- You can become a contractor if you have a recognisable transferable skill set that is in demand.

- Many contractors chose to go contracting because they can continue doing what they enjoy most for more money, without climbing the management ladder and moving away from their skill set.

- Your increased earnings and company structure should more than make up for the lack of employment benefits.

- Not only can you maintain your skills when contracting, but you can also greatly enhance them.

- Office politics are minimised for contractors.

- Contractors can take much more holiday than permanent employees.

- Contractors don't work for promises. They just get paid. Simple.

# 2
# Markets for contracting

## 2.1 Why do clients like contractors?

The UK has traditionally had a more flexible labour market when compared to many other European Union member states, and that remains true today. The last decade has seen a wealth of new employment laws, including the Agency Workers Regulations – some argue these empower employees; others see them as reducing the UK's flexibility and competitiveness on the world stage.

There has been a mixed impact on the lot of the contractor as a result of legislation but, on balance, contractors still compare very favourably to employees when organisations are looking for highly skilled, task-based work to be completed. That's because:

- Contractors do not have to be employed and therefore

  - Contractors are cheaper and more cost effective over time

  - Contractors are more flexible

  - Contractors are the low risk option.

In addition, contractors also bring other benefits to an organisation, such as:

- New skill sets (although contractors are not normally there to train the company's employees)

- Lessons from other organisations

- The ability to focus entirely on completing the project, without getting sucked into other areas

- Greater productivity and motivation to get the job done

- Objective viewpoints, untarnished by office politics.

Different client organisations place a different emphasis on how they use contractors compared with their employees. The contracting sector has matured since it took off in the 1980s, with contractors having proved their worth time and again. There are a lot of organisations in the marketplace that not only like using contractors, but also see it as a long-term business model, basing their future development and growth on actively encouraging the greater use of contractors throughout their businesses.

Many companies use contractors as a flexible workforce and might have a ratio of permanent employee headcount to contractors of 80/20. This allows them to shed staff when times are tough without the expense of redundancy.

However, contractors in these kinds of firms need to be careful not to become 'tail-end charlies' and take any 'random' work assigned to them by the client – which is called work 'coming down the pipe' – rather than specific projects as detailed in their contracts, as this may impact adversely on their tax status.

It has been known for contractors to stay with client firms for ten or more years, earning the nickname coined by ContractorCalculator, 'permtractors'. Contractors who work like this are clearly employees and have strong cases to claim employment rights; they will also be subject to the taxation employees pay.

### 2.1.1 Saving money and paperwork

Organisations always have tasks that need to be completed, but which only have to be done once – so they naturally don't want to take on someone permanently to do the task. Contractors are there to complete such projects, and when the project is finished, they go on to another one at another company.

On an annual basis, working with contractors also costs less. Hiring a permanent employee costs the salary plus many hidden costs (see table 2.1). With contractors the situation is much simpler and cleaner, without the strings attached. The client can pay the contractor what will generally be more than the salary for a permanent employee, but they get a highly skilled and motivated expert who can hit the ground running.

| Permanent employee | Contractor |
| --- | --- |
| Visible costs<br>Salary | Visible costs<br>Fee |
| Invisible costs<br>Holiday<br>Benefits/pension<br>Employer's NIC<br>HR<br>Training<br>Sickness<br>Employment rights<br>Risk | Invisible costs<br>None |

*Table 2.1 Total costs of employees versus contractors*

From the client's perspective, if the contractor does a bad job they can be taken to court for breach of contract, or not paid, which is not the case with a permanent employee. In practice, though, the client knows their contractor will almost certainly deliver the goods, because they've brought on board an expert who has every motivation to get the job done, get it right and get it finished on time.

In some organisations, the invisible costs of employment, as shown in table 2.1, can be as high as the employee's gross salary, particularly if they are a senior employee with many benefits. Employees also attract employment risk, which we cover in the next section, and that is another key reason why clients like contractors.

Permanent employees also need to have their benefits administered, which requires a whole functional department, human resources management, or, in a smaller business, takes up the time of senior managers and directors. Canny clients recognise this as an overhead – the purely process management element of an HR department is not a productive, business generating, fee earning part of an organisation. Employees also expect to be trained, and not only to be trained, but also to have the course fee paid for by their employer, plus the costs of their time whilst training, plus travel, sustenance and accommodation expenses.

Is it any wonder that client organisations prefer contractors?

## 2.1.2 Flexibility

Permanent employees of the typical grade and skill levels that contractors work at are generally not very flexible. Of course it is not that most well paid, highly skilled workers and professionals won't work long hours, weekends and travel great distances. They are not flexible in the sense that they cannot be recruited very quickly, in a matter of days or weeks, and they cannot be 'divested', asked to leave the organisation, very quickly either.

Contractors can be recruited within a matter of days, complete a project over a few weeks or months and then leave. No baggage and no risk, no redundancy, no golden handshakes or parachutes, and no endless negotiations over benefits. All the company gets is a series of invoices from the contractor or the agency that is acting on the contractor's behalf. Easy, simple and quick.

Employees also come with employment rights. These have certainly enormously improved the lot of most workers and labour relations in general over the years. Unfortunately, they have also removed a great deal of flexibility from the labour market; the sort of flexibility that allows companies to adapt quickly and take advantage of new opportunities.

Contractors are not employees and therefore do not have employees' employment rights. So they can start and finish specific contracts very quickly.

Why does this help? Well, it offers companies enormous flexibility. For example, when a portion of IT security needs to be rapidly overhauled at a bank, it simply calls in a squad of specialist contractors who do nothing else until the job is done. And when it's finished, they go away and the company doesn't have to worry about them anymore.

Similarly, when a nuclear power station needs a rapid and specific repair; a specialist contracting engineer comes in, identifies the fault, rectifies it and goes away. Their highly expensive skills do not need to be paid for over 52 weeks of every year, just to make sure they are on hand for the few weeks every couple of years that their skills might be needed.

The Confederation of British Industry (CBI), the employers' group that includes most major companies with a base in the UK, has completed study after study showing that the ability of contractors to provide flexibility offers savings of 30% – 40% in costs over comparable employment.

As can be seen in table 2.2, there are a significant number of financial and legal barriers to hiring and firing permanent employees. With the exception of short notice periods, contractors do not have any of the barriers that permanent employees have, which makes them particularly attractive to client organisations.

|  | Permanent employees | Contractors |
|---|---|---|
| **Starting** | Notice from previous job – months | Notice from previous job – Days or a few weeks |
|  | Agency fee – up to 40% gross salary | Agency fee – included in fee |
|  | Joining bonus – possible | Joining bonus – no |
|  | Joining costs – yes (new car, etc) | Joining costs – no |
| **Leaving** | Notice – several weeks to months | Notice – maximum weeks |
|  | Redundancy – usually months | Redundancy – no |
|  | Golden parachute – possibly | Golden parachute – no |
|  | Gardening leave – possibly | Gardening leave – no |

*Table 2.2 Hiring and firing – a comparison between employees and contractors*

## 2.2 Contractor markets

There is a market for contractors wherever a client needs a highly skilled and flexible worker to achieve a particular task in a specific time. A 2011 report by Kingston University's Small Business Research Centre and PCG* (formerly known as the Professional Contractors Group) estimated that there are 1.56 million contractors in the UK, about 1 in 20 of the UK workforce. This has increased from 1.4 million in 2008.

These workers tend to be IT and telecoms specialists, engineers, oil and gas and energy experts, marketing, media and management freelancers, technicians, and in the construction-related professions and trades. But the contractor net spreads much wider, too, taking in the arts, media, training, teaching, medicine and virtually every skilled sector.

Not surprisingly, the 'hottest' contractor markets tend to be found in these sectors:

- IT and telecoms
- Engineering
- Construction
- Oil and gas and energy
- Management
- Marketing
- Arts, literary and media
- Other sectors requiring highly skilled, flexible workers.

The research by PCG and Kingston University shows that interim managers represent the second largest contracting group in the UK (numbering 161,000), whilst IT and telecoms contractors are the fourth largest (93,000). The top spot is held by freelancers in arts, literary and media occupations (265,000), with teaching/education in third place (110,000).

* Kitching J. and Smallbone D. Exploring the UK Freelance Workforce Kingston University Small Business Research Centre, 2011.

It is not just commercial companies that use contractors: the public sector is also a major consumer of contractors' services. This includes HM Revenue & Customs, as well as the behemoths of health and defence. The latter both spend huge sums on all of the major contractor skills areas. Styles of work may differ with public sector clients, but as they are in a seller's market, where contractors are generally holding the balance of power, they have to pay market rates, just like private sector clients.

Various government initiatives designed to increase the percentage of public sector contracts won by small to medium sized enterprises (SMEs), such as contractors, have been launched. The jury is still out on how effective these initiatives might be, although in theory the focus of public sector procurement should be on value, which contractors can provide in great quantities.

## Been there, done that!

### The simplest test of your marketability

**DAVE SAYS:** The simplest test for asking yourself whether or not there is a market for your skills, is to look around and see if someone in your office, who has a similar skill set, is a contractor. If you can spot such a person, and you feel that you have better skills and experience than them, start writing your resignation letter!

Contractor clients are looking for a specific type of worker. At one end, they do not want consultants who spend a few days a week lending advice but not generally completing major tasks on an ongoing basis for a single client. At the other end, contractor clients do not want low skilled workers, or 'temps' or 'agency workers' as they are often called, who can perform a wide variety of low skill roles, albeit on a flexible basis.

And that's a key point to bear in mind, because contractors are neither consultants nor temps or agency workers – they are contractors. Contractors tend to work for one client at a time on one project, then move onto another contract with a new client.

Contractors are different from consultants because they tend to work for only one client at a time, rather than many, and actually perform ongoing tasks to complete a project, rather than just offering advice.

Contractors are different from agency workers because they are highly skilled, so require little or no supervision or control by their clients, earn well above mean incomes, and tend to work in a particular sector. They don't move from one lower skill occupation to another in a different sector, and don't work under the direct supervision, direction and control of the client.

## Been there, done that!

### Contracting can be long term

**DAVE SAYS:** I contracted for eight years and always found work. And I know contractors who have been doing it for 20 years and never been out of work. Whatever the economic climate, firms will always have one-off jobs that need doing for which they cannot justify hiring an employee.

The market does sometimes fall, but it never gets wiped out. Instead, the market forces of supply and demand come into play: you're likely to always be in work, but you may have to take a drop in fees during the hard times. But the flip side is that you can charge more in better times. Another way to look at it is, even when you're earning less than you did on previous contracts, you're still likely to be earning more than a permie.

Sectors like film, music and journalism are generally not considered to be contracting areas although, confusingly, many in this sector do work on a contract basis. But whilst, for example, creative professionals in the film industry work on a project basis, often for a fee rather than being employed or hired on a fixed-term contract, these sectors are much more specialised and work to their own rules.

## 2.2.1 IT and telecoms

The market for IT contractors in the UK is very large for two reasons:

- There is a major shortage of skilled workers in this area

- Businesses can't neglect their IT departments, because their companies simply won't run without them!

There are simply not enough IT workers in the UK to go around. The British Computer Society (BCS) and the e-skills UK information and communications technology sector skills council maintain a close watch on how many school leavers and university students take up computing, and year after year both report that there are never enough to meet demand. According to e-skills UK, the UK will require a further half a million IT workers by the end of the decade and current levels of IT graduates will be unable to meet this demand.

Despite the substantial rewards a career in computing offers, fewer and fewer young people choose it. That means most of the time, UK organisations can't recruit the IT people they need. And, perhaps more controversially, it is also likely to mean that those with mediocre or even poor IT skills are able to find permanent employment. Companies that employ them then often have to rely on highly skilled contractors to come in and clean up the mess.

There is a great deal of media coverage about offshoring to help solve this problem. But after the first great wave of interest in outsourcing to India, Eastern Europe and elsewhere, organisations rapidly discovered that a large part of the work simply cannot go abroad.

Why? Well, the offshore centres can do the rote work, but not the higher level development work. That is when managers need to work closely with IT departments and it is just not practical to do this when your IT department is abroad. We won't go into a detailed look at how offshoring works, but most of the experts agree that it will not have a major impact on IT contracting in the UK. The proof is in the pudding, and the pudding is the resiliency of the UK contracting sector for IT professionals.

Much of the demand for IT and telecoms contractors in the UK comes from one square mile: The City. Financial services in London account for a substantial proportion of IT and telecoms contracts in the country. Work in banking and insurance is tremendously demanding and not all contractors can take the pressure, but the rewards are considerable.

After financial services, service companies of all types engage the largest groups of IT contractors. Companies that offer extended marketing and delivery tend to need great IT support to help them keep costs down.

In the high-tech sector, demand tends to remain high no matter what the wider economic picture is. And demand tends to remain steady for contractors in manufacturing business in the UK, which is still the ninth largest manufacturer in the world by value.

## 2.2.2 Engineering

Engineering contractors can be as diverse as the disciplines within engineering. The very nature of many engineering projects is that they are just that – projects, with a beginning, a middle and an end. And that is ideal for engineers who want to work on a flexible basis.

In fact, if it were not for engineering contractors, who, many would argue, have been around a lot longer than IT contractors, very little engineering would actually be done. There is an ongoing, desperate shortage of engineers worldwide, not just in the UK. There are, therefore, many overseas contract opportunities for engineering contractors who want to spread their wings and explore the world.

Although all engineers tend to be in demand all of the time, there are peaks and troughs of availability, according to the types of projects ongoing at any one time, and their geographical spread.

Unlike many IT contractors, nearly all engineers require a professional qualification in order to practice. There are levels within these; for example an incorporated engineer does not have quite the same professional status as a chartered engineer, regardless of how well they do the job. Pay rates tend to reflect this.

The requirement for incorporated and chartered status means that the professional institutions play an important role in the engineering market. Engineering contractors who gain and then maintain their professional status through continued professional development (CPD) effectively obtain a 'passport' to work with virtually any UK client, and for many clients worldwide.

## 2.2.3 Construction

Contractors in construction have, in many respects, separate rules to other areas of contracting, and there are also special conditions that apply to the industry. Legislation is often specific to the sector, and there is even a special court for construction issues. The construction sector experiences periods of great demand and periods of relative stagnation, with opportunities for contractors following these trends.

Where there is any kind of demand for construction, there are also contractors – whether it's for building railways, schools, office blocks or retail units. The industry completely depends on its 'contingent workforce' – small companies and even single workers who are available whenever they are needed.

Construction is a sector that is particularly sensitive to the economy. In fact, the sector is notorious for shedding tens of thousands of workers when times are bad, although when things pick up there are generally skills shortages and fantastic opportunities for contractors. Feast or famine!

## 2.2.4 Oil and gas and energy

The UK is a global centre of excellence in the oil and gas and energy sectors. As a result, it has a thriving contracting sector supporting these industries. The UK also exports a sizeable chunk of its expertise in these sectors, so there are ample opportunities for contractors seeking assignments overseas.

Even though the UK's North Sea oil fields are mature, exploration is still highly active, particularly in deep-water exploration, in which UK-based firms and contractors have developed unique capabilities. Contractor rates in the UK are among the highest in the world, and UK projects attract some of the best talent from within and outside the UK.

UK-based contractors also operate globally, and there are opportunities on every continent and for every specialism – from exploration geologists and geophysicists to offshore and marine engineers.

Opportunities for contractors in the UK's energy sector are significant and encompass thermal, nuclear and renewables. Both the nuclear and renewables sectors are set to grow in the next decade and are good strategic markets with long-term potential for contractors to target.

Contractors from all disciplines can find roles in the oil and gas and energy industries, including engineers and scientists, safety and risk management professionals, IT contractors and a wide range of management, marketing, legal and other support professionals.

### 2.2.5 Interim management

Interim managers or executives can be found throughout the private, public and not-for-profit sectors. Although the interim management field is often considered to comprise just senior executives and board level managers in major turnaround or change projects, it actually encompasses a huge range of skills and levels of seniority.

In addition to managing director and business unit leadership roles, interim management contractors can be found in every functional area within an organisation — anywhere where a flexible and highly skilled worker is required to work on a project, cover a period of high workloads or act as a temporary replacement for employees on maternity leave or long-term sick leave.

Roles can be found in finance and accountancy, legal and human resources, marketing and sales, procurement and all areas of operations.

### 2.2.6 Other highly skilled flexible workers

There are other types of contractor in the marketplace who work for periods of time on a contract for a single client and on a flexible basis. They typically include:

- Teachers and lecturers
- Arts, literary and media freelancers
- Scientists
- Medical personnel
- Financial analysts and actuaries
- Coaches and trainers

- Other workers with specialist, niche skill sets.

Although from a diverse range of sectors, all these types of contractors do share the same profile: they are highly skilled at what they do and prefer to work on a flexible basis, earning more than their permanent contemporaries and making the most of the flexibility the lifestyle affords. In other words, they are typical contractors!

## 2.3 Contractor earnings

When it comes to gross earnings and take home pay, contractors have a number of advantages over their permanent employee equivalents:

- Payment is gross, pre-tax and much higher

- Contractors can factor in business expenses and items like pensions

- Contractors can use various perfectly legal techniques to become more tax efficient, i.e. paying less tax and having more cash in their pocket.

You should consider how much more of the money earned will come to you through tax efficiency, rather than being taken in deductions like income tax and National Insurance Contributions.

### 2.3.1 Rates

As a general rule, the rates a contractor can expect to command are significantly higher than those of a permanent employee in an equivalent role. Almost certainly, the extra percentage they're earning should be in double digits.

Rates range from £15 per hour for more junior roles up to £175 per hour and even higher for technical consultants with years of in-depth experience in a particular specialism or product. Experienced project managers receive around £75 per hour, although once you start earning more than about £30 per hour, rates are often quoted on a daily basis.

But again, those rates are purely indicative and, by the time you read this, will be out of date. No matter what your skill, if a client needs you urgently, or others in your field are busy on a major project elsewhere, you could find the rates you are offered rising sharply.

Hourly and daily rates fluctuate across sectors and in each area rates can vary depending on level of experience and the current market demand for that skill. Like most jobs, the general rule is that if your skills took a long time to master and are in short supply, then you will command more money than someone who acquired their skills relatively easily and in a much shorter space of time.

## Tax avoidance is legal

Over the last few years, particularly after the 2008 recession, UK Governments involving all three major parties have voiced concerns over "tax avoidance", saying that they want to clamp down on it.

Their stances are as politically motivated as they are economically naive. Politicians know this, but have been 'playing to the gallery' during tough economic times, largely to create 'noise' and distract attention from the parts they and their parties played in generating economic turmoil.

But let's be clear: tax avoidance is of course perfectly legal and part of any well-functioning taxations system. On the other hand, tax evasion is a criminal offence and should be dealt with as such. By politicians, including senior cabinet ministers, speaking of legal tax avoidance as if it were a crime, they can only damage the UK economy.

Everyone is entitled to plan their affairs in a legal manner in order to minimise their taxes. And when you are a contractor running your own limited company, rather than an employee, many avenues open up to enable you to do that. Perfectly legally.

## Been there, done that!

## Making the most of the dot-com crash

**DAVE SAYS:** When the dot-com bubble of the 1990s burst, I'd been earning very well for several years and putting money aside. Rather than accepting projects on much lower rates, or not working at all, I chose to ride out the recession by taking a year off, travelling around Asia. Living in Asia for a year cost far less than being in London without a job.

When I chose to come back, I'd missed the worst of the crash. I quickly won a contract through my network, but rates were half what they'd been before. They then took another two years to fully recover. So my advice to contractors is to try and save money and not rely on earning the highest fees all the time. And if rates drop considerably and you fancy a spot of travelling, then an economic downturn is just the time to go.

### 2.3.2 Tax efficiency

Everything changes when you become a contractor and bill your client using your own limited company. In chapter 1, we explained that employees pay income tax and National Insurance Contributions (NICs), which are taken out of their salary, usually monthly, by their employer.

Contractors working through a limited company don't work this way. Tax is paid, but in significantly reduced amounts. This is what is known as tax efficiency. Do not mistake tax efficiency, which is a perfectly legal practice of mitigating tax liabilities (or reducing your tax bill) with tax evasion, which is illegal and involves defrauding HMRC, the government and your fellow citizens who pay tax legally. Tax evasion can, in the worst case scenario, land you in prison, and at the very least is likely to wipe you out financially when you are caught.

There are alternatives to using a limited company, particularly if you have a contract that is judged by the taxman to be inside the IR35 legislation, which is covered extensively in chapter 8. One alternative is to trade through an umbrella company, which, although not as tax efficient as working through a limited company, for those contractors working inside IR35 it can still be more tax efficient than permanent employment.

You can also contract as a sole trader, but the vast majority of clients and agencies won't offer work to a sole trader because of the risk that the contractor may try to claim employment rights. It is also possible to trade via offshore solutions, which are generally tax avoidance vehicles of some description and are only for contractors with a healthy appetite for risk. Most UK contractors use limited companies or umbrella companies. Your trading options are covered in greater detail in section 6.2.

There are a number of ways limited company contractors can pay themselves and a wide range of tax payment timings. Generally, instead of being paid a monthly salary that gets taxed at source, contractors pay tax after their end of financial year accounts have been completed and tax returns filled in. After the first year of contracting they may be required to make an interim payment on account once the taxman can estimate how much tax you should pay each year.

After calculating the profits in their limited company, and setting aside the money for corporation tax, contractors will then typically pay themselves:

- A small salary that attracts either no or very little income tax and little or no employee's and employer's NICs

- Dividends, which often form the bulk of a contractor's earnings; these can only be paid out of profits, and although they attract income tax, there are no NICs to pay.

In addition, whilst expenses do not form a part of a contractor's income, contractors are often better off because they are allowed to claim certain travel, subsistence and other expenses that permanent employees cannot. Plus, these are deducted before tax is calculated, helping reduce contractors' tax bills.

All of this amounts to considerably more than contractors would have been paid if their gross earnings were paid as a salary and taxed at source.

| | |
|---|---|
| Permie salary | £50,000 |
| Cost to employer | £55,866 |
| Employers NI (13.8%) | £5,866 |
| Employees NI | £4,337 |
| PAYE | £9,883 |
| Net income | £35,779 |
| Net income % of cost to employer | 64% |
| | |
| Contractor revenue | £55,866 |
| Salary | £9,000 |
| Employers NI | £208 |
| Employees NI | £169 |
| PAYE | £179 |
| Corporation tax | £9,331 |
| Distributable profit | £37,326 |
| Further tax on dividends | £1,718 |
| Contractor takes home | £44,259 |
| Net income % of revenue | 79% |

For the same monetary cost to the employer of £55,866, the contractor takes home nearly £8,480 more per year.

But beware…

Don't skip chapter 8 about IR35, which we mentioned earlier; it might sound dull, but it is important to get your head around IR35, because understanding it is the best way to ensure your take home pay is as high as it possibly can be.

**CONTRACTING MINDSET TIPS:**

Flexible contracting income allows a choice when paying tax

When you were a permanent employee, you paid a fixed amount of tax via Pay As You Earn (PAYE) each month, and probably focused on your take-home pay without giving too much attention to payslip deductions like 'employee NI' and 'employer NI'. Contracting income is much more flexible, allowing you greater choice over when and how you pay tax.

Would you rather pay up to 60% tax now, or save for early retirement?

Out of each £1,000 you earn, what would you rather do? Pay the taxman £400 and put £600 in your pocket or pay no tax now and invest in a pension you can draw down when you retire?

Let's say you earned £100,000 in contracting fees but have been offered a dream permanent job. Do you bung the taxman £40,000 and walk away with £60,000, or would you prefer to pay just £10,000 in tax and keep £90,000?

Or let's assume you have built up a cash pile of £100,000 in your contracting company. Would you rather declare a single dividend and pay 40% of that in tax, or drip feed yourself an income over several years, varying your dividend according to how much personal allowance is left after other earnings?

Employees have much less control over their tax affairs

As an employee, you probably paid the same amount each month into your pension and may not have had the excess income to choose to add additional voluntary contributions; or if you did, you may have found the associated admin and pension plan inflexibility off-putting.

When you were employed and changed jobs, perhaps with a lump-sum severance package or 'golden handcuff' sign-up bonus, you could not choose to defer payment of the cash until your tax situation was more beneficial or hold it in reserve for a rainy day. Your former or new employer would pay you via PAYE and tax you accordingly.

If you had a good year and were paid a bonus, then chances are you were not given the option of stashing that cash away tax-free until you had a lower-earning year, or fancied a long break, and so couldn't eke out the bonus to use when it suited you.

Contractors have choices that employees don't

Employees can't choose when to pay tax, but contractors can. In fact, as a contractor you can choose to sacrifice a substantial proportion of your annual earnings into a pension scheme tax-free, thus allowing you to retire early with a potentially substantial retirement income.

If you decide to take a break from contracting and take a permanent job then, rather than keeping your limited company dormant, you can exercise legislation from HMRC, Section 1030A, which allows you to remove excess cash up to £25,000 as 'capital', rather than income, paying tax at 10% and not 40% or even 50%.

Contractors can choose when and how to disburse the money they've generated in their contractor limited companies. So you could take a year off and pay yourself a dividend up to your personal allowance, or drip feed dividends as your other income varies: the choice is yours.

**Contractors control their tax affairs and can choose when and how to pay themselves according to their income and tax situation.**

## 2.4 Contractor skills

A contractor has to have something specific to sell. In the job market, that something is a skill or set of skills, with the accompanying experience of putting those skills into use for relevant employers or clients. The skill could be highly specialised and technical, like thin film section analysis or finite element modelling; or it could be a management skill, like project or programme management, which has to combine a detailed knowledge of the technical with knowing how people and projects tick.

So, to become a contractor you have to have a skill to start with. However, as later chapters in the book will reveal, it is not just possible, but in many cases easy and worthwhile, to develop your skills and make yourself even more of a hot property than you already are!

Concern that their skills will quickly date is what keeps many employees from making the transition into contracting. But, in practice, most contractors not only have no problem maintaining their skill set but find that contracting offers opportunities to learn new skills on the job. Because you will be earning more money and can claim the expense of training courses from your contracting business, you'll find that your financial investment is not as painful as you think, and the financial benefits of up-skilling can be significant.

Best of all, you'll be choosing to learn skills in the disciplines that excite and interest you the most, and/or where you feel there are or will be contract opportunities. Of course, if you are a chartered professional, such as an engineer, accountant or marketer, your professional institute will require you to conduct so many hours of continued professional development (CPD) each year. As long as the courses you select qualify according to your professional institute's CPD rules, you can maintain your professional qualifications and learn new skills in areas that interest you, not your employer.

To be successful and stay in contract, contractors also have to acquire 'contracting skills'. These skills are what this book is all about. Contracting skills are those skills and capabilities that a contractor needs to run a successful and profitable contracting business. They include basic sales and marketing skills to secure lucrative contracts, through to company administration and financial and time-planning abilities.

### The Trick to Hot IT Skills – insights from an IT contractor

The shifts of demand in IT contracting depend less on economics and more on the specific skills required. Some skills areas, like .NET and Java, for example, are really hot and seem to stay that way. Others, like the entire app development and mobile and online retail area, have seen a massive increase in rates of pay and demand. These have been driven by the huge increase in smartphone use, and, without doubt, new areas in web development will constantly occur.

The trick to keeping on top of the job is to make sure that you have at least a handle on the hottest skills. This can be challenging as a contractor, when you are your own 'HR department' and responsible for your own training and development. So you need to use downtime on the job to study and stay at the cutting edge, or to find other ways to keep from slipping back.

But the real point to remember in all this is that businesses need IT contractors, regardless of economic conditions. So contractors don't really have to worry about shrinking IT departments. Indeed, when they shrink, the companies call in contractors to fill in the gaps.

To give another example in the IT sector, during the booming dot-com era between 1995 and 2001, everyone who could became a contractor, even those with poor IT skills or only one year's experience. Many of these contractors were getting paid £100,000 a year and it didn't matter if they had two heads, dressed like a tramp, and hadn't washed for a month – someone would hire them.

As reality dawned and the bubble burst, those who should not have entered the contracting market in the first place were soon forced back into permanent employment. As a general rule, those with the top skills continued to win work.

However some did not and an interesting observation and powerful lesson was that those who continued to find contracts were not always the ones who were most suited to the roles, but the ones who were better at securing contracts – which means better at marketing themselves. Self promotion, marketing and sales are core contracting skills that are covered in greater detail in chapters 4, 5 and 11.

## 2.5 The future of contracting

One thing is quite clear: most of the contracting industry is not cyclical. With the exception of many but not all parts of construction, there are no real boom and bust times for contractors in the UK. Certainly there have been periods of unbelievably intense demand, like during the dot-com boom. But, so far, we haven't really seen periods of very low demand that equate to spikes in unemployment of the wider UK workforce. There are a few good reasons for this, described below.

### 2.5.1 The UK economy and contractors

Whether business is booming or slack in the UK, businesses need to make their IT departments work, utilities need engineers to keep supplying essentials and machines still have to be kept running. Our public services will not be allowed to shut down and the international financial markets keep dealing, no matter how rosy or ropey the economy is looking.

There is, at all times, a shortage of skilled high-technology workers and engineers in the UK. Each year the media mourns the shrinking graduate intake figures in subjects considered to be 'difficult': engineering, IT, physics, mathematics, etc. In fact, according to a 2010 report by The Royal Society, British universities produce fewer than 10,000 science graduates each year. As highlighted earlier in the chapter, IT and engineering workers are in desperately short supply and the situation is not improving. Yet both the private and public sectors are increasingly dependent on IT and engineering for their critical infrastructure.

So the inexorable laws of supply and demand will kick in and contractors who can work flexibly to fill gaps at short notice and patch up what may start to become an increasingly leaky machine will find themselves in high demand. Probably very high demand.

The caveat, and to an extent paradox, to the supply and demand equation is that in major economic downturns the demand for engineers and IT contractors tends to be at the very least maintained, but perversely rates can drop; in some cases dramatically.

## 2.5.2 Insulated from trends

Contractors have, for the most part, been insulated from economic trends. The research by PCG and Kingston University's Small Business Research Centre published in October 2008[2] concluded that there were 1.4m contractors and freelancers in the UK. The preliminary results of the second study published in November 2011 revealed that the sector has grown by 12% to reach 1.56m contractors and freelancers. The market would not be steadily growing unless there were paying clients to drive continued growth.

There is continued demand in the IT sector. There were 65,000 contractors in 2008, growing to 93,000 in 2011, according to PCG/Kingston University. And anecdotal evidence suggests that these are conservative estimates. This continued demand is largely down to the fact that businesses have to stay competitive and technology is an ever-increasing component of that competitive edge. There was a time when you still met executives who didn't know how to log on or needed their PAs to print out their emails for them, but that time has long gone. Nowadays, IT and technology experts

[2] Kitching J and Smallbone D. Defining and Estimating the Size of the UK Freelance Workforce Kingston University Small Business Research Centre, 2008.

sit on the board alongside finance and sales directors, and they play an integral, often central, part in developing corporate strategies.

There are parallels in the engineering sector. The shortage of engineers in the UK is so acute that non-EU engineers are allowed to come and work in the UK with significantly fewer barriers than most other job roles. The Migration Advisory Committee, an agency of the UK Home Office, maintains up-to-date lists of occupations that cannot be filled by UK and EU workers. This list is consistently populated with a wide range of engineering, technical and scientific occupations.

But what about the companies that engage the services of contractors? Contractor clients do experience the peaks and troughs of business alongside the economic cycles. Labour market surveys and the market demand in those times suggests that contractors are needed as much during economic downturns as during prosperous years. Sometimes more.

So, why is this? Because companies have to stay competitive, and if investment in key areas falls, then, in most sectors, so does business. There is one other piece of business logic worth noting. When times are bad, companies downsize employees. But they still need the jobs done, so contractors are called in to do them. And during times of economic uncertainty, when large organisations are fearful of making investment decisions in case the economy goes the wrong way, labour market surveys confirm that contractors are used as a low-risk option to manage growth and increase capacity.

### 2.5.3 How might contracting evolve?

There is an increasing body of evidence to suggest that both the number of contractors operating in the UK contracting sector and the demand for contractors by clients will continue to grow:

- The 2011 data from PCG and Kingston University shows that the number of contractors and freelancers grew by 12% over the three years to 2011; the research published in 2008 showed that the sector had grown 14% in the previous decade

- According to labour market data from the Office for National Statistics (ONS), during the final quarter of 2011, the number of self-employed workers in the UK reached record-breaking levels of over 4m people

- Eurostat labour force data from 2011 estimates that 32.6m European workers are self-employed – that's 15% of the European workforce. And 23m of these self-employed workers are freelancers or contractors working in one-person companies.

Surveys conducted and sponsored by industry bodies, trade associations, recruiters and service companies consistently highlight the difficulty of recruiting and the ongoing demand for contractors in the core contracting disciplines of IT and engineering. The rapid growth of the sector since 2008 suggests that the use of 'contingent' workers, such as contractors and temps, is likely to increase, driven by the need to improve labour market flexibility to maintain the UK's global competitiveness. These surveys include the:

- Monster Employment Index
- Reed Job Index
- Recruitment and Employment Confederation (REC)/ KPMG Report on Jobs
- Bank of Scotland Report on Jobs.
- The Chartered Institute of Personnel and Development (CIPD)/Hays Resourcing and Talent Planning Survey
- Manpower's Talent Shortage Survey
- The CIPD/KPMG Quarterly Labour Market Outlook
- The Manpower Employment Outlook Survey
- The Confederation of British Industry/Harvey Nash Employment Trends Survey.

You can keep up to date with the latest market supply/demand data by signing up to the ContractorCalculator newsletter, which always includes the latest monthly market statistics and analysis.

So there is little doubt that contracting will grow, and that an ongoing stream of well motivated and highly skilled contractors with well developed contracting skills will be required to meet this demand.

# Contracting lessons from this chapter

- There is a market for contractors wherever a client needs a highly skilled flexible worker to achieve a particular task in a specific time.

- There are many organisations in the marketplace that like using contractors.

- Organisations always have tasks that need to be completed, but which only have to be done once – so they don't want to take on someone permanently to do the task.

- Contractors can be recruited within a matter of days, complete a project over a few weeks or months and then leave. No baggage and no risk, no redundancy, no golden handshakes or parachutes.

- Contractors are not employees and therefore do not have employees' employment rights. So they can start and finish specific contracts very quickly.

- Contractors tend to work for one client at a time on one project, then move onto another contract with a new client.

- As a general rule, the rates a contractor can expect to command are significantly higher than those of a permanent employee in an equivalent role.

- There are a number of ways limited company contractors can pay themselves and a wide range of tax payment requirements and timings.

- Most contractors not only have no problem maintaining their skill set, but also find that contracting offers opportunities to learn and develop new skills on the job.

- To be successful and stay in contract, contractors also have to acquire 'contracting skills'. These skills are what this book is all about

- There is an increasing body of evidence to suggest that both the number of contractors operating in the UK and the demand for contractors by clients will continue to grow.

# 3
# Making the transition

# 3.1 Preparation – an introduction

When you're ready to make the move from being a permanent employee (or 'permie') to becoming a contractor there are a number of steps that could give you a flying start. The process recommended here is tried and tested – it has worked again and again, been refined over years and led to many successful careers in contracting.

Parts of the process will also tell you if you're not ready for contracting. For example, if you can't make the numbers add up at the start, maybe now is not the right time to move into contracting. Perhaps you need to spend a couple of months saving some more money to ensure the transition goes smoothly, and also to ensure that you have a financial safety net in place in case things don't go exactly to plan.

This chapter is just an overview of some of the key topics. We include creating a curriculum vitae (CV) here because it is an important part of the transition process, but it is also such an important part of successful contracting that we dedicate the whole of chapter 4 to the subject. Similarly we touch here on the tax issue of IR35; but, as it is so fundamental to anyone considering becoming a contractor, it is also covered more comprehensively in chapter 8.

## 3.1.1 Market research

The first thing that any prospective contractor should do is to get online and visit the job boards that cover their target industry. Professional market researchers use the phrase 'desk research', although most of us think of it as surfing the net!

Job boards, LinkedIn and other social networks have really become the place to find new work. The chances are you're probably already very familiar with them – maybe you secured your last permanent job through a job board or via a contact on LinkedIn. Browsing the job boards and relevant LinkedIn groups, as well as other professional social networks, will give you a sense of what's out there and how you fit in. Are your skills marketable? Do you see lots of demand for people who do what you do? Answer a few of the ads on the job boards and see how long it takes for a response. Don't be discouraged if you aren't getting calls; just continue looking and, instead of just searching for your specific area of expertise, try looking for something similar to what you do. This is all about testing how marketable your skills are.

Of course you need to create a CV and post it on relevant job boards, plus keep your LinkedIn and other social media profiles updated and relevant. These are your primary 'sales and marketing' tools. You should also upload your CV to any online databases that your market research has shown are used by agencies and clients who have the types of contracts you want.

## Been there, done that!

## Market research comes in many forms

**DAVE SAYS:** My market research consisted of a conversation with a contractor at the same firm, who had exactly the same skills and who told me the market was "on fire". I also spoke to an agent would said he could get me a contract immediately. I wouldn't recommend this as your only research, but do spread your research net as far as you can.

One word of warning – because you're looking for a job and you're a first timer you may well receive lots of agents 'phishing' by calling you on the premise that they have a position you might be interested in. The truth is they probably haven't, and are just trying to find out who your last boss was and the name of key people in other companies where you've worked.

Recruitment advertisers are increasingly using social networking sites as a source of jobs, including contracts. Check out all the most popular sites and join relevant forums – you may get feedback from other site members, although take care not to place too much trust in unsubstantiated claims.

### Advice you get from forums
It pays to be very careful about the advice you take, particularly legal advice. Forums are notorious hangouts for people who want to have a view on everything regardless of whether or not they are

experts. Taking advice from someone who isn't an expert could land you in lots of trouble. Particularly in legal and accounting areas lots of people have opinions about how they think things should work, often based on their own moral principles and their views of 'fairness', but typically their opinions don't actually align with the law.

*Golden rule*: Make sure you take expert advice from qualified people.

The other major source of information about jobs and your sector is the trade media. Most sectors have a huge range of niche websites and trade magazines. Plus many professions and disciplines have their own professional bodies, producing their own media, which can sometimes be the best source of market data.

There are also a number of sites dedicated to contracting professionals. Whilst these vary considerably in the quality of information available, there are some that are likely to become essential to your contracting. Probably the best place to start is the independent site run by this book's publisher, contractorcalculator.co.uk, which produces a monthly market report on the current state of the UK contracting sector.

### 3.1.2 Setting rates

The next stage in the transition to contracting process is to establish rates for your skills, so you have a starting point for negotiations with a client or agency. Again, browsing the job boards, and the internet generally, will help you research rates, which is the next stage in the transition process.

For first-time contractors it is hard to know what rate to quote for your skills. Many first-timers are nervous about asking what they're worth, because their new rates seem so high when compared to previous permanent roles. But all successful contractors learn to better understand their value in the marketplace as their contracting career builds. The following, in addition to the research you have done, will help you get it right.

## Getting Started: The Minimum Rate

Remember that contracting pays more than permanent employment, because you generally not only get a higher gross income, but will also benefit from lower tax payments. You can determine a minimum starting point for your contracting rate based on what you are paid as a permanent employee, by using ContractorCalculator's free web-based services.

To do this, start with your permanent salary and add in your benefits, such as healthcare and pension contributions, until you get to a 'total package' figure. Put that figure into ContractorCalculator's Permanent to Contracting Calculator to determine your minimum starting rate. The calculator can be found at:

 contractorcalculator.co.uk/PermanentToContractingCalculator.aspx

For example, if you type in a total package of £50,000, the results show that you need a minimum rate of £28 per hour outside IR35, or £37 per hour inside IR35 (IR35 is explained briefly later in this chapter and then in more detail in chapter 8).

Table 3.1 shows some basic comparisons between what hourly rate would be required to match annual gross salary and benefits.

| Salary | Hourly rate | | Daily rate | |
|---|---|---|---|---|
| | Outside | Inside IR35 | Outside | Inside IR35 |
| £25,000 | £15 | £19 | £118 | £152 |
| £30,000 | £18 | £24 | £138 | £178 |
| £35,000 | £21 | £27 | £159 | £206 |
| £40,000 | £23 | £30 | £179 | £232 |
| £45,000 | £26 | £34 | £197 | £256 |
| £50,000 | £28 | £37 | £216 | £292 |
| £75,000 | £42 | £56 | £322 | £429 |
| £100,000 | £57 | £79 | £436 | £597 |
| £125,000 | £71 | £93 | £540 | £702 |
| £150,000 | £85 | £111 | £643 | £836 |
| £175,000 | £101 | £135 | £764 | £1,019 |
| £200,000 | £113 | £150 | £854 | £1,139 |
| £250,000 | £144 | £183 | £1.082 | £1,378 |

*Table 3.1 Minimum hourly and daily rates*

Although you need to be aware of your likely IR35 status within a contract, it is not the basis for negotiation. You state your daily, or hourly, rate and talk about IR35 issues later. The inside IR35 rate is ideally the minimum rate to accept, for your desired annual salary.

Minimum rate is the operative word, because for example most contractors earning £75k per year are senior enough to command rates of £500 per day, and these are generally rounded-up during negotiations to the nearest £25. Hourly rates tend to be rounded-up to the nearest £5. Over £35 per hour and you will generally be working on day rates anyway.

Whilst not recommended for IR35 reasons (discussed in later chapters), some formerly permanent employees have their first contract with their existing employer. So the employers often focus on negotiating a rate based on the employee's current salary. But negotiating fair and market-based contract rates with clients that are based on equivalent permanent employee salaries and tax calculations is a red herring, as the two costs are not directly comparable.

However, you may find that clients use the cost of what they see as equivalent employees as part of their negotiating position. The comparison is invalid, as contractors are business-to-business services providers supplying their specialist skills to clients on projects with a defined duration and outcome. Permanent employees have a totally different and long-term relationship with their employer, and enjoy a range of benefits that contractors do not. These include both the financial, such as employer-funded pension plans, and the intangible, such as employment rights.

If as a contractor you base your rate on your salary, then you are losing out, because you are not taking into account the full cost to the employer of hiring you.

**Search the internet**
During your market research, you should have found some sites that offer useful survey results stating what rates certain skills can command in the current market. While these figures provide some good overall guidelines they can be a little limited, since they do not take into account combinations of skills, the level of experience, and market sectors. Use your current salary as the baseline for the rate you should expect and ask your colleagues.

The other thing to accept is that on a few occasions you may discover that the agent has been less than fair with the rate they are paying you out of the gross fee from the client. Don't take this personally – agents are there to make money and you must ensure you negotiate at the next contract renewal or new contract.

## Ask Other Contractors

'Human intelligence' is generally the best source of information. Make sure you talk to as many colleagues and friends as you can, although be careful to manage relationships in the workplace of your current permanent employer. Existing contractors and permanent employees who have worked with contractors will know the work and will understand the value of specific skills. Simply ask an experienced contractor you know or work with who has similar skills and experience to your own.

## Been there, done that!

### Better than you

**DAVE SAYS:** Some contractors worry about whether they are good enough to be contractors, assuming all contractors to be experts. Contractors don't have to be experts, but they certainly can't be novices. Requirements are driven by the flexible needs of the market, not by the need for experts.

I was working on a client site for a consultancy who took half my fees, and sitting two desks down from a contractor who used the same skill set as me. After weeks of working with him and teaching him how to use the advanced aspects of the product, I figured that if he was a contractor then I could be too!

It is highly unlikely, although not impossible, that you will be able to charge the same amount as the contractors you talk to. Their experience and skill sets will differ from your own. You should establish a range by talking to a few contractors, and then try it out in negotiations. Establish a minimum, for example £400 per day and a maximum like £500 per day. Aim for £450, and the £25 less or more is likely to be the agent trying to increase their margin rather than the client's limit.

### Different Markets – Different Rates

Some markets can pay more than others, although you can never be certain that this is the case. There may be regional variations or timing factors that can skew rates both up and down. In IT contracting, banking is generally known to pay higher rates. But in the same way that not all bankers earn those eye-watering City salaries we hear about, your particular part of the banking market may differ too. Talking to friends and colleagues who do very similar work to your own is a good method of benchmarking variations.

### What Kind of Rate: Hourly Rate or Daily Rate?

Varying types of contracts with different types of clients tend to use different pay periods. In anticipation of talking to potential clients and agencies that might have all types of expectations, you need to have a rate proposal prepared for each scenario. Rates tend to be on an hourly or daily basis. Payment is weekly or monthly.

## Been there, done that!

### Efficiency gains

**DAVE SAYS:** I've been on projects where, because of my niche development strategy, it means I've never struggled to finish on time and leave the office by 6pm. Developers in other teams have struggled on through until midnight. And we were both paid the same.

It took a couple of months before the boss enquired how I managed to achieve this level of productivity. After telling him he paid me to train the other 20 developers so that they could achieve the same results!

**The Hourly Rate** – You are paid for the number of hours you work. This type of rate is more common than the daily rate and is normally for rates below £30 an hour. The hourly rate can be better than the daily rate. Both the client and the contractor know exactly where they stand. Clients may cap weekly hours accumulated to avoid problems, but may demand more hours at busy times.

**The Daily Rate** – You are paid for the number of days you work. This type of rate tends to be favoured by clients in the finance sector and is more commonly offered to those earning rates of about £300+ per day. Many clients like the 'day rate' because they can keep tighter control of budgets. They might occasionally ask you to work late to hit a deadline without adding the extra hours and cost they would if you were on an hourly rate. But typically you would get the hours back another day when work was not so busy and you could leave the office early. That's the theory, anyway!

Most contractors should be prepared to put in the occasional long day or week to get something finished, provided it is not being demanded all the time. However, the willingness of professional contractors to do this is sometimes abused by clients – we cover this issue in chapter 10.

Weekly, monthly and calendar month periods tend to be negotiated as a package, with a contract schedule detailing hours per week, and days of the month to be worked.

### 3.1.3 Crunch the numbers

This is the stage of the transition process when you find out whether you are kidding yourself about wanting to become a contractor. The key question is: can I afford to go contracting?

It is always best to err on the side of caution. So work on the assumption that it might take between one and six months for you to win your first contract. This might seem like a long time, but when you are up and running as a contractor, all your fellow contractors will tell you to build up a fund of six month's living expenses to cope with the unexpected. And of course because you are earning twice as much, saving six months money will only take you, six months!

If you work in a high demand sector, you could find a role within days or weeks. Ideally, you should always start working on finding a contract in the final weeks of your permanent job or current contract. Calculate your monthly outgoings and be honest with yourself, making allowances for the luxuries you enjoy over and above the basics like housing costs, utilities, food, clothing, transport costs and so on.

## Make the numbers work for you

**DAVE SAYS:** When I took the leap into contracting I made some money just from the transition. My firm paid me at the end of the month as usual, and I also received ten days paid holiday that I had accrued. Then I started my contract straight away and was paid weekly. I was lucky, but you should make sure you've saved enough to make a smooth transition into your new life as a contractor.

Set aside a budget to pay for professional advice from accountants and solicitors. This may be needed for things like contract reviews (typically around £100 for a basic review), accounting advice and starting up a company. Add to this some costs for travel and subsistence, including for hotel accommodation, as you may need to travel for interviews. Although remember these costs can be claimed back as expenses once you have started trading as a contractor (see chapter 6 on pre-incorporation expenses).

Work out how much cash you have in the bank and do the calculation – if you left your permanent employment tomorrow, could you exist for long enough to secure your first contract? Take into account any holiday not taken that the firm will also have to pay you when you leave. If you don't yet have enough, would three to six more months of saving make the difference? If so, consider deferring the transition to contracting while you save up the cash you'll need to make the switch comfortably, with minimum risk.

Also, bear in mind the timings of payments. You might finish work with a month's money, and when you get a contract you could be paid weekly. This will certainly help the cash flow. But it might not always go so smoothly and having savings can help tide you over. If you are paid monthly on your first contract, remember you'll have to work the thirty days and then invoice. Most agents pay within five days of the invoice, and they shouldn't drag it out thirty days.

## 3.1.4 Timing the transition

Each element of the contracting market, whether it's IT, engineering, construction or something else, has its own cycles you need to become aware of. It also has two annual cycles, driven by the financial year and holiday seasons.

**January to February** – after the Christmas holidays, clients are spurred into action. New budgets are approved and hiring starts. This is the equivalent of *spring*.

**March to April** – this is the equivalent of *summer*. Arguably the best time to look for a new contract.

**May to June** – As the summer holidays approach, this is the equivalent of the *autumn*. If you can secure a three-month contract in March, you'll be in a strong negotiating position in June.

**July to August** – Holidays break the rhythm of the market, and hiring becomes a low priority. If you're not in a contract by the end of June, you may end up unemployed until September – contractor's *winter*.

**September** – *spring* again! After the summer holidays, children return to school, decision makers are back at their desks and the human resources department awakens from its slumber.

**October to November** – another contractor *summer* brings better paid contracts. This is a good time for contractors to be monitoring job boards and calling contacts looking for contract opportunities.

**December** – *autumn* and *winter* come around quickly. Many projects are scheduled to deliver in the week before Christmas, which means that this is the perfect time to renegotiate. By 24th December, the market goes dead until the New Year.

The key is to ensure you don't finish a contract in November or December and June to August as you could find yourself out of work. By juggling initial contract periods and renewal timings, you can ensure your contracts do not end during those months. In addition, shorter renewal periods mean greater opportunity to renegotiate and the right to add renewals to your CV, LinkedIn profile and other professional networking sites. The importance of this is covered later in this book.

### 3.1.5 Handing in notice

If you're still working in a permanent job, it's time to hand in your notice. Hopefully your employment contract does not require you to wait out an excessively long notice period before you can move on to something else. Legally, there is almost nothing you can do to challenge a long notice period. You do not want to breach your contract by violating the notice period terms, especially as your employer could hold you responsible for any losses incurred because of your early departure. So, when handing in your notice, you may find yourself in one of two situations:

**A good relationship with your employer**
If you're in this happy position, you are likely to be able to constructively negotiate an earlier departure date. The employer may be willing to do this for several reasons. Some employers who are good managers will not want personnel who are leaving working on their projects. Management experts say that this employee is the most liable to be careless, and not likely to be motivated to provide their best work. In addition, departing employees can be security risks. Your employer may be sorry to see you go, but may wish to see you leave without delay.

It may also be possible to offer your employer a deal involving remuneration or benefits that will allow you to depart early. Knowing that you are about to depart, employers may be happy to save a little money on your pay and benefits, as they will no longer have their intended effect of motivating you to work.

**A poor relationship with your employer**
If you find yourself in this situation, there may be other possibilities for leaving your job early. An employer who does not like you may, of course, be glad to see you leave. In this case make sure that all the formal details involving your termination have been checked and respected, so that the firm can never come back to you with demands or liabilities in respect of your early departure.

Sadly, but quite often, your unfriendly employer wants to keep you, because replacing you is a nuisance, even though the employer has made it clear that you are not liked. In this case, ask yourself if there is any way in which your employer has not respected the terms of your contract? Have all of your holiday benefits been paid?

Have the conditions in terms of the workplace been respected? Is there any area in which the employer has been remiss? If so, you could claim breach of contract and terminate the contract immediately. You could even sue for constructive dismissal if the breach is a serious one.

Unfortunately, this happens much more often than one might expect. It is wise to take professional advice if you choose to pursue the breach of contract route, for, as we highlighted earlier, leaving early without justification could cost you a great deal.

### 3.1.6 Preparing a Curriculum Vitae

Unless you're fortunate enough to be recommended directly to a client, the next key stage in the transition process is to create a good Curriculum Vitae (CV), to be sent out to prospective clients and agencies and uploaded onto relevant sites and job boards.

You'll also need to update your LinkedIn profile, as well as your profile on relevant professional social networking sites. The latter is important. According to LinkedIn, contractors who have completed their online profile are 40 times more likely to receive opportunities. And when you're applying for contracts, it's important that agents and clients get a similar 'story' from both your CV and online profiles.

We will be covering writing your CV and updating your profiles in more detail in chapter 4, but here we cover some suggested approaches for contractors. Under no circumstances should you ever, ever lie on your CV or in your online profiles. You will be found out, lose the contract, damage lots of work relationships and quite possibly never work in the sector again. However, it is possible to emphasise the positive elements of your background to help you attract the attention of the agent or client.

A good CV will immediately grab the attention of the reader, who is probably looking for any excuse to delete your CV and go on to others on their screen. So the trick is to make the first thing visible exactly what the reader is looking for, saving them a miserable hour trawling through dozens of poorly presented efforts.

To ensure that you grab that attention, you need to tailor each CV you send out so that, right at the top, you maximise the value of the experience and skills you have that makes you right for the contract being offered. What you want to avoid is a laundry list of what you've been doing since you left full-time education.

The ideal CV, of course, would be one where you seek position X and, right at the top, you can say that you've been working at X for the past ten years. If only life were that simple! When applying for position X, explain right at the top of your CV the experience you have that makes you right for position X. You can do this in a short profile at the beginning, which you can then follow up with a list of your directly relevant work experience.

Each CV you upload or send out should be tailored with the idea of matching your work and education to exactly what the agency or client is looking for. This really is very important: the agent or client will not spend much time in saving the few useful CVs and deleting rejected ones. Even if you have the ideal background, if you haven't spent enough time on your CV, it is very likely to find its way into the recycling bins of every agent who looks at it.

An example: if you worked on more than one type of skill in your past job, you can list just the one that the agent or client is looking for first in your profile. You can mention the others later. You have most definitely not told a lie on your CV; you have simply presented the pertinent information in the best light and helped the agent or client to identify you as a likely candidate. If you are applying for a contract through an agent, it is the agency's job to send your CV to the end client, once you have agreed to allow them to do so. Some agents frequently abuse this privilege and send out your CV without your permission.

Others will even obtain your CV without your permission and you will be surprised to find that a client you have never heard of is considering you for a job you've not asked to be considered for! Chapter 10 details what you should do in either of these scenarios, but you should know that you own your CV. No one, under any circumstances, has the right to view it or send it out without your permission.

## CONTRACTING MINDSET TIPS:
### Your CV is your marketing brochure and a key sales tool
Contractors supply a business-to-business solution to their clients. That means a contractor's CV is not a CV as employees understand it, but a marketing brochure for a sales professional (the contractor) to use to make a sale. So, as with any effective marketing material, the CV must highlight the features and benefits a contractor can offer a potential client.

### Are you interested in how your accountant got on at school?
You want a conservatory built and ask a couple of builders to send you relevant information and examples of their work. Do you need to wade through 20 years and 50 pages worth of detailed design specifications, including the builder's first-ever project?

When you are attending a networking event, and you ask the stranger sitting next to you 'tell me about what you do?', you don't expect a blow-by-blow account of their school career, including exactly what exams they passed and at what grade?

When you're looking for an accountant, are you most interested in the one who once went on a course to design spreadsheets, or the one who saved another client £30,000 a year through better tax planning?

### You client wants to know how you can solve their problem, fast
Clients seeking contractors to work on a specific project have the option of choosing from multiple potential business solution providers, not potential employees. They base their decision on the many CVs they receive in response to an advertisement.

If you present your client with a life history containing irrelevant details of qualifications you gained at school, old projects you completed as a junior using different skills in a different sector, your potential client will remain just that – a potential client.

Unless the client can find out quickly from your CV that you can solve their problem, the client will choose another contractor who has used their CV correctly as a marketing and sales tool.

### Use your CV for what it is – your marketing brochure and sales tool
Your CV is your marketing brochure to be used as a key sales tool. It must present the features of the skills and experience you can apply to the client's objective, challenge or problem, and the benefits you will bring to the client's organisation if they hire you to provide your services.

Because the client can choose from multiple suppliers, your brochure must succinctly communicate only focused information relevant to the task required, demonstrating that you not only have the necessary skills, but have also achieved the same impressive outcome for other clients in the recent past.

**Clients want your CV to be a short, relevant marketing brochure showing you can effectively provide the solution they require.**

## 3.2 Securing a contract

Having done all your market research, prepared your rates and handed in your notice, the next vital stage in the process, and the ultimate reason for embarking on this exercise, is to secure a contract. Searching for a contract, compared with finding a permanent position, is a very different process. Recruiting a contractor typically takes only one interview, compared to sometimes up to five or six for a permanent position.

The timescales are much shorter, too; a contractor is usually hired within a week of the interview and there are few, if any, contractor candidate tests. Applicants to a permanent post may endure weeks or even months of waiting and intensive candidate testing before they are awarded a position. The motivation behind this very different recruitment process is that the decision by the client to hire a contractor is typically made only a few weeks before they are needed, so the contractor is wanted on-site 'yesterday'.

Plus, as we have mentioned earlier, contractors are not employees and have no employment rights. So, if the client doesn't like the contractor for whatever reason, the contractor can be fired immediately, subject to the terms of the contract; and it is the contractor's responsibility to prove they delivered according to specification, not the client's. Trying to remove a permanent employee, on the other hand, can be a lengthy, stressful and expensive process, and the heavy and process-driven burden of proof is on the employer. That means employers want to be as sure as possible that they have the right candidate before they employ them.

For first time contractors it is advisable to only commit to a maximum of a three to six month contract, so that you can see what it is like on the job, talk to other contractors, and learn how to determine what you really have a right to ask for.

### 3.2.1 Applying for contracts

If you have handed in your notice but are still working out your notice period, you may have time constraints, but keep to as much of the following process as you can during your spare time. Whilst it might be tempting to start applying for contracts during working hours, don't do it if you can avoid it. You will, however, find yourself dealing with agents early, late and during lunch.

But always do this in your own time. Not to do so is unfair to your current employer (who may at some point think of hiring you back as a contractor); is probably against the terms and conditions of your contract of employment; and might have an adverse effect on your reputation, which is a key tool in any contractors' marketing toolbox.

So, once at home and totally devoted to finding work, make applying for contracts your 'other' full time job until you've won your first contract. We devote the whole of chapter 5 to finding and securing contracts, but what follows is a useful overview that will help you put in context some of the other information you'll be reading.

**Initial Activities**
You should register with and upload your CV to all the relevant agencies you've found during your market research, so that you are entered onto their databases and become a prospective candidate. Agents make use of huge databases of contractors when attempting to match someone to a position; if you're not on it, you'll never be contacted for a potential interview.

Lists of key agencies can be found online – JobServe is usually a reliable starting point, and a good place to first upload your CV. There are many other sites that offer this functionality. Some of them serve niche recruitment markets, so if you are in IT, engineering, oil and gas or finance, or another specialism, there will be a specialist recruitment site you can access. Upload your CV a minimum of one month before you're planning to start contracting, as it can take a few days or weeks for your CV to filter through to all the major agency databases.

**Daily Activities for Securing a Contract**
Having prepared to enter the market, and left your full time position, following the daily schedule below will ensure you are optimising your job search activities. It also means you have a routine – being at home after years of the structured life of permanent work can be disorientating, but working at finding your contract is your job, for now.

Morning:

- Call agencies that you applied to yesterday afternoon.

- Chase up any other positions you have applied to and have not yet spoken to the agent about

- Search the job websites for suitable positions that have been added since yesterday

- Send off email applications.

Afternoon:

- Call agencies that you made applications to in the morning

- Chase up any other positions for which you have applied and have not yet spoken to the agent about

- Search the job websites for suitable positions that have been added since you last looked

- Send off email applications.

Unfortunately, the contract search process can be quite dull and often frustrating, but the harder you work at it, the sooner you'll get a position.

### Locating Positions – using online job boards

As the job boards are such an important source of potential contracts, it is vital you monitor these websites regularly. Most contracts are advertised on the internet via job boards. There are many specialist job boards for specific sectors, but at the time of writing some the most important job boards are:

- CWJobs

- TotalJobs

- Jobsite

- JobServe

- Monster.

These are so dominant in the recruitment sector that agencies will frequently post the same position on all boards.

The main jobs boards have a free alerts facility that you can set up to automatically email you when a new job is advertised that matches your specified criteria, for example, "C# Developer London". You can set up multiple alerts with different criteria, and with a bit of tweaking should find a way to refine the results. But don't 'refine' them so much that you miss potential opportunities – it's better to have to delete a few emails through the day than to not get an email for a contract you're perfectly suited to.

Make sure you keep a log of what roles you have applied for. It's a good idea to maintain the log using a cloud service, so that you can call it up instantly on your smartphone, tablet, laptop or PC when an agent or client calls. That way you will know instantly which role the call refers to. A log will also prevent you from submitting multiple applications for the same role through different agents.

**Targeting your Application**
It is likely that you will be applying for different roles that might focus on different aspects of your skill set. As we explained in section 3.1.6, to give yourself the best chance of success you need to target your application and your CV accordingly. Remember to:

- Tailor your CV to the position

- Write a targeted email or covering letter to accompany your uploaded CV for the position.

Writing many different versions of your CV can be time consuming to start with, but you'll soon build up a collection of different versions. For example one might paint the picture of you being a great C# Programmer, while another might focus on you being an experienced Project Manager.

## 3.2.2 Staying with your current firm but as a contractor – warning!

A common occurrence when permanent employees decide to become contractors and they have a good relationship with their manager is for the manager to offer the new contractor their first contract. This is of course very tempting. You know the work, the people and the workplace. You could suddenly be earning a lot more money for doing the same work you did before.

There is, unfortunately, one very serious problem with this arrangement. You will almost certainly fall into the tax law constraint, which is loosely referred to as 'IR35'. It's a term you will become very familiar with as a contractor, because it makes such a difference to how much you can potentially earn as take home pay, after tax. That's why there's a whole chapter about IR35 in this book.

But for now, here's what you need to know: HM Revenue & Customs (HMRC) will almost certainly assume that if you move from being a permanent employee one week, to doing exactly the same job as a contractor the next, you are really an employee disguised as a contractor.

That means that you will have to pay PAYE, income tax and National Insurance Contributions on your pay, and that will considerably reduce what you would earn if you were contracting 'outside' IR35, even through your own limited company. You could try to claim you are 'outside' IR35, but you would find it difficult to prove.

It is possible for a contractor to remain outside IR35 when contracting for a former employer, but you have to work that much harder to prove you are not a disguised employee. Not only do you have to avoid falling foul of the standard tests of employment that HMRC will apply if it investigates you, but you also have to clearly identify and demonstrate how your relationship with your former boss and working practices from when you were an employee have changed since changing status from employee to contractor.

The safest route – and often the best for your future CV and career development – is to politely decline. Explain why you are doing so, because you never know when you might come across your manager again. Then move on to another company where you will be able to benefit fully from your new contracting lifestyle and increased earnings.

And also remember you decided to leave your last employer for a reason that is unlikely to have gone away simply because you have changed status – old habits die hard; especially ex-bosses' old habits!

### 3.2.3 Working with agencies

Recruitment agencies are responsible for brokering most of the work in contracting, and can account for as much as 95% of all contract vacancies in some sectors. The agencies working in many sectors tend to treat it as volume work. As such, they aim to place as many contractors with as many clients as they can, because that is what drives their business models and generates maximum revenues and profits.

So bear this in mind and be cautious when dealing with appeals from agents who may appear to be on your side, or claim they want to help you. All they really want is your signature on the contract and the agency margin that comes with it. As we will show in chapter 5, you should always be fair to the agent, but never fall into the trap of believing that the agent is your friend. Think about who pays the agency; it's not you, it's the client. So although you are an essential part of the process, remember that all agencies work for clients, and not for you.

A good agency, and there are many, won't beat around the bush with you. They will ask if they can send your CV out to a given client. They probably won't know very much about the nature of the work; they simply can't because they deal with all sorts of contracts and skills sets. They may try to make sure you have the right profile, and you should help them to do so. But be cautious: agencies that claim to do more than these few simple steps may not, unless there is strong evidence to the contrary, be being totally honest with you.

Recruitment is generally a high volume 'bums on seats' game. Some agencies will try and justify higher margins to their clients based on them doing extra-special candidate selection and the like. This is questionable; most agencies do the same. That's not to say agents don't work hard for their money. The truth is they work very hard to close deals. They have to make plenty of calls and line up plenty of interviews for candidates before someone says yes. And that's just for starters.

Many contractors don't understand how hard agents work, and think they just do CV matching. That's true to a certain extent, but the hard work is creating the opportunities with a steady stream of clients and making it all happen.

So, whilst they may not be your best friends or always have your best interests at heart, there's every reason to be professional, friendly and fair with agents when dealing with them. After all, agencies are providing you with a cheap commission-only outsourced sales force – that's not to be taken lightly.

### 3.2.4 Going direct to the client

It is highly unusual for contractors to deal direct with clients when securing a contract, apart from at the interview stage. That said, contractors who are many years into their contracting career may find themselves dealing direct with clients, because it suits their relationship and the contractor is sufficiently in demand that they can dictate terms.

However, clients generally use agencies because they want to distance the client company from the contractor, so that there is no possibility of there being the slightest suggestion the contractor is an employee. Clients do not want a contractor claiming they are an employee and claiming employment rights, which is something both clients and contractors want to avoid.

In addition, clients use recruitment agencies to find candidates that match their requirements because that is what agencies do – they match people with work opportunities. A client, who may be a busy project manager, does not want to sit down at a computer, post adverts, wait for the responses and then sift through them to try and identify likely candidates. Especially as, along the way, they'll probably also be contacted by salespeople from trade magazines and other job sites trying to sell them recruitment advertising space, as well as by recruitment agencies selling their services.

A rule of thumb is not to sign anything before an agency sets you up with an interview, because that will allow you flexibility if offered the opportunity to go direct as a result of your own networking and not the agent's. The client will have an agreement with the agency which prevents them from taking you on direct if the agent has introduced you.

### 3.2.5 Attending interviews

This, like every part of the transition process, is crucial. If you do not perform at this stage then you will not win the contract. We cover interview techniques in chapter 5 and advanced interviewing and sales techniques in chapter 11, but the key points are also given below.

Preparation for the interview is hugely important. Find out why the client needs you, research the background of the client company, check you understand and have the skills they are looking for, and prepare your own list of questions. The basic do's and don'ts for contractor interviews are the same as when interviewing for permanent employment. Dress properly, take an umbrella if it is raining, make sure you know where you are going, and if you are driving make sure you can park.

Never be late. This, unless you have called ahead with a very good excuse, will almost certainly lose you the contract. Know the names and titles of the interviewers – the agency should be able to tell you these. The interviewer(s) will be looking for a number of attributes during the interview. They will want to know if you are articulate and a good communicator; are you going to get on with the team; is the chemistry there? When talking about the technical aspects of the contract, the interviewer will be able to tell very quickly if you have a good grasp of the subject.

Be sure to ask your questions when invited, or during the interview, if appropriate. These will demonstrate to the interviewer that you have thought about the contract, prepared and hopefully asked intelligent questions to better communicate your expertise and suitability for the position. Remember, they're not looking for an employee to train up into the position; they will expect you to have the skills, experience and expertise to be up and running from day one.

The client may offer you the contract at the interview. Alternatively, after the interview, the agent will normally phone to find out how it went. That is an opportunity for you to discuss how the interview went and also, if you decided that the contract does not suit you, to tell the agent. Agents can sometimes be very useful in these circumstances, by giving you the client's feedback. Listen carefully, as this feedback could well help you refine your CV and improve your interview technique.

### 3.2.6 Dealing with contracts and IR35 issues

Great news – you have been offered your first contract! There may be some attempts at haggling over the rates by your agent but you will be offered a contract at an agreed rate for a particular starting date. The contract from the agent arrives in your inbox. It looks fine, as most contracts are fairly standard, and so you prepare to sign it. But wait! What about IR35?

As we have explained, IR35 is the tax legislation that means HMRC can tax some contractors as though they are employees of their clients. This could reduce your take-home pay by as much as 25%. So it is essential to be clear on the IR35 implications before you sign any contract. There are many factors that can lead to a contractor being found 'within IR35' by HMRC, and we explain these in detail in chapter 8. The wording in a contractor's contract with their agency and end user client can be one of these factors.

So, at this stage it is worth using some of the funds you have set aside for professional fees to ask a solicitor or specialist IR35 consultancy to review the contract and working conditions. This can cost up to around £200, and frequently much less, but if the review throws up any issues, it could end up saving you tens of thousands.

You can start by assessing your IR35 status by using the free IR35 test, hosted on ContractorCalculator.co.uk.

 contractorcalculator.co.uk/IR35_Test.aspx

Before finally signing the contract with a new client or agency, you also need to check that your potential paymaster actually has the cash to pay you. Credit checking your agency or client is a major departure from what you've been used to as an employee, when you just assumed the money will come into the bank at the end of the month. But you really should credit check any new client or agency before signing the contract. Using a credit checking service is generally inexpensive, and compared with what you could lose financially if a client or agent goes bust, it is a worthwhile investment.

If the credit report you receive is negative, this does not mean you should automatically turn down the contract. The reason to check before signing is because you might at least be able to negotiate different payment terms. For example, you might insist on weekly invoicing with payment required in seven days, rather than monthly invoicing with payment required in 30 days. With the new terms in place, if the client defaults once, you have an early warning system to mitigate any losses.

### 3.2.7 Getting payment structures into place

Once you've landed a contract, how do you bill for it? A lot depends on what choice you've made for the legal organisation of your company – whether you have opted for your own limited company or decided to work through an umbrella company. Chapter 6 discusses these options and how to set up your preferred trading entity in more detail.

But you should understand at this point that you will have great difficulty working as a self-employed person in your own right, because clients don't want the risk. Although there are service providers that can act as an intermediary between self-employed sole traders and the agency or client, most will want to deal with your own limited company or with your 'umbrella company', which is a limited company that treats you as an employee – legally grouping many contractors under its 'umbrella'. Contractors can generally make the most money by working through a limited company. This involves picking up some basic legal knowledge and undertaking some administrative steps, but it's nothing too daunting and there are step-by-step guides later in this book.

You will also need to open a company bank account if you are trading through your own limited company. This is a fairly straightforward process and is explained in chapter 6. If you are working through an umbrella company, you would use its bank account to be paid, and they will then pay you directly into your personal bank account. However, if you have a poor credit history or County Court Judgements on record, getting a business bank account could be very difficult. Added to this, no client or agency will pay into a personal bank account – they want a business bank account.

### 3.2.8 Starting your first contract

You are almost at the end of the transition phase from being a permanent employee to becoming a contractor. All that remains is for you to undertake your first contract and, of course, get paid. Starting a contract is not the same as starting a new permanent job. You are not joining the client company as a member of the 'extended corporate family'; you are there to do a very specific series of tasks for which you expect to be handsomely rewarded in cash. There are no company socials, no benefits and you shouldn't even use the subsidised staff canteen – these might seem petty points, but as we'll explain later in this book, IR35 makes them important to be aware of.

However, starting your first contract is the start of something new and exciting and you will become part of the wider contracting community. Remember that when working for your client, you are not only the operations person expected to deliver on the contract, you are also the account manager for your client, so the relationship is very different from that between a manager and an employee.

### 3.2.9 Getting paid

When you are contracting, you will need to complete timesheets and raise invoices so that you can get paid. Most agencies will provide standard timesheets that you complete on a daily basis, entering the number of hours that you have worked that day. You would normally sign and submit the timesheet for countersignature by the client at the end of each week. Increasingly this happens electronically – you complete the form on-screen and the project manager clicks a button to authorise payment.

If you are running your own limited company, you need to prepare your own invoices and submit them to the agency or direct to the client, if there is no agency. Invoices are required to have specific information about the work, the client and your company, which is explained in chapter 6. If you're contracting through an umbrella company, you'll usually be asked to upload or email timesheets, so that its finance team can prepare an invoice.

Payment times vary and most agencies have strict deadlines, so be sure to submit any paperwork in good time, particularly if cash is tight in the first few months of your first contract. If you are working through an agent, or some umbrella companies, you should not have to wait for the client to pay the agency before you get paid. If your agency does this, then something is not right, and you should take a look at chapter 10 for a solution.

As a new contractor you'll undoubtedly enjoy regularly checking out your bank account balance and looking through your statements; it's a real pleasure seeing just how much more you are now earning. Enjoy it!

# Contracting lessons from this chapter

- Crunch the numbers, consider your market and check whether now is the right time to make the leap.

- If the numbers don't add up, maybe now is not the right time to move into contracting and you need more savings to ensure a smooth transition.

- Searching for a contract, compared with finding a permanent position, is a very different process.

- Do your market research, go online and visit the job boards that cover your industry.

- Speak to as many people as you can. They are the best source of knowledge. Take expert advice from qualified people and qualify the advice you receive.

- Clients generally use agencies because they want to distance the client company from the contractor.

- Avoid working for your current employer on your first contract. There are too many issues.

- Establish contract rates for your skills, so you have a starting point for negotiations with a client or agency.

- Create a high impact targeted contractor CV.

- Plan a daily schedule for your sales process, then monitor and refine.

- Preparation for the interview is hugely important.

- Hand in your notice and manage your departure with your soon to be ex-employer.

- When organising payment structures, bear in mind the timings of payments.

- Be sure to submit any paperwork in good time, particularly in the first few months of your first contract.

# 4

# Marketing yourself – your curriculum vitae (CV)

# 4.1 Introduction to CV writing

Your curriculum vitae, or CV, has one purpose: to get an agent or client interested in speaking to you on the telephone with a view to lining up an interview for a new contract. It is the key marketing document you will use to be shortlisted for a possible contract and start increasing your income. Think of it as a sales brochure – about you.

The crucial decision about whether or not you are shortlisted for an interview is made entirely on the basis of these pages, to which the reader at the agency or client will devote perhaps 20 seconds for the first make-or-break reading. So you need to approach developing your CV as as you would an "elevator pitch".

As a result, to ensure a successful career as a contractor, your CV deserves a lot of thought. That's because it is possible to be really good at what you do, and really experienced at it, but still to be passed over time and again because your CV wasn't eye catching enough and did not do the job of getting you noticed.

Even if you are more comfortable writing computer code or engineering specifications, it is worth your investment in time to write a good CV to ensure a successful contracting career. It is possible to pay a professional CV writer to write a CV for you, but you need to ensure they have a track record in writing high impact CVs that got their clients work, and that they are not just a typing service. You should expect to pay more than £100 for a good CV.

Many people find writing about themselves really tough, particularly understanding what is going to get that agent or client to pick up the phone. So this chapter will guide you through all the key steps to do just that. The following sections detail what makes a CV that will get you an interview; a CV that will put you in front of the decision makers who can then make their own judgments about your skills and expertise.

Remember the key steps in the process are:

Step 1: Get noticed by an agent using your CV

Step 2: Get an interview using your CV (and possibly also a quick phone conversation)

Step 3: Get the contract offer by performing well at interview.

Alongside producing your high impact contracting CV, you should also update your profiles on relevant social networking sites like LinkedIn. Updating your profile on the online professional networks and forums most used for your area of expertise, and becoming active on these, can be a good way to connect with potential future employers and colleagues. Your professional, constructive approach on these sites, and the way you interact with others and demonstrate your expertise, can be a good way to reassure potential clients that you will be a good 'fit' in their organisation. Section 4.7 considers LinkedIn and alternative CV formats in greater detail.

## 4.2 How CVs are used

To fully appreciate how CVs are used by agencies and clients, you need to understand the CV filtering process. For example there might be 200 CVs in the agent's or client's inbox or waiting in a file folder. These CVs need to be filtered down to around ten, which the agent or client will then go over in detail. The process generally works like this:

**Step 1 – The five-second look at each of the first 200 CVs**
Straight into the Recycling Bin goes:

- Anything longer than four pages – this is too long and the agent or client can't be bothered to read it

- Any CV without a profile or list of skills on the front page, there's no time to search for them

- Any CV that is a big essay with sentences, not broken into bite-sized chunks and without bullet points. These CVs are just too much hassle to read.

So, this might leave the client or agent with around 100 CVs for the next stage.

**Step 2 — The ten-second scan of the front page of the next 100 CVs**
Agents or clients put CVs straight into the bin if:

- The profile and skills on front page do not match the contract's requirement.

Clients or agents are then left with probably around 40 CVs for some more serious consideration.

**Step 3 — The 'potentials' pile of 40 CVs for more consideration**
In a nutshell, at this crucial stage, only these types of CVs stay in:

- Those where the profile and skills on front page exactly match the contract's requirements.

At the risk of stating the obvious, a simple principle to adopt is not to apply for any contract where the skills and experience listed on your CV do not specifically match the client's or agent's requirements. This principle does sound obvious, but many contractors are tempted to scatter their vague CVs out to the four winds, "just in case" one gets them an interview. It won't!

## Been there, done that!

## Always read the question (the job advert)

**DAVE SAYS:** ContractorCalculator advertised for an online sales executive and received over 50 CVs. About half of them had profiles from people who said they were marketing executives looking for marketing roles. They all went straight into the bin. Some of those CVs might have been from people that had good sales experience, but we had plenty of other more targeted CVs to wade through.

This approach can also be counterproductive, because you are wasting clients' and agents' time – you need to be targeting your CV to a client's specific requirements. You are also wasting your time, which could be more profitably spent producing that one CV on which you have highlighted your specific expertise that makes you right for the contract. Highly focused surgical strikes are much more likely to hit the target than carpet bombing.

> *Golden rule:* When it comes to job applications, highly focused surgical strikes are much more likely to hit the target than carpet bombing.

Although you should never include falsehoods on a CV, you can and should emphasise those elements of your skills and experience that suit the particular contract you are applying for. Your experience is like a box of chocolates to a client – there are lots of goodies but you need to present the ones the client wants rather than leaving them to have a rummage around to see if there is anything that takes their fancy.

### Step 4 — The 'strong possibilities' pile of the last 10 CVs

There are now 10 CVs left and the agent or client will now feel brave enough to look beyond the first page to find some or all of the non-technical qualities they will be looking for, that:

- You have recent experience using the skills you claim to have on the front of your CV

- You have staying power and a good contracting record, eg past contracts that have been renewed. Lots of small contracts and no renewals can raise warning flags for potential clients

- Your experience was gained with credible firms – preferably blue chip

- You have a good academic background, although in many sectors this is a bonus and not mandatory for many roles, if you have the right experience.

If you meet the criteria at this point you will probably be called by the agent for a reality check to ensure you can speak and sound vaguely like the person described on the CV you sent in. The agent will be looking for around four to six potential candidates who sound like they know what they are talking about.

Try and sound interested; if you don't or indicate you have a number of promising opportunities at this stage the agent probably won't bother with you. It's a numbers game to the agent, whose job is to put bums on seats. So if you don't appear likely to accept an offer, the agent will prioritise other contractors who might. Some agents could also be trying out the contract at less than market rate in the hope of making some extra margin. An experienced contractor with multiple offers is unlikely to fall for that ploy and sell themselves short. So if you are interested in the assignment but do have lots of other opportunities, there's no need to tell the agent this level of detail and risk being struck from the list.

The interview stage then filters out a range of undesirable personality types and those who have made what look to be overinflated claims on their CV. Make sure you are not one of them! A key point to remember is that, in the eyes of the agent or potential client, it really doesn't matter how many letters you have after your name, they don't make you God's gift to British industry. Far from it, in fact – the agent or client has boxes to tick, so target your application accordingly.

# Been there, done that!

## Bad CVs generally mean no interview

**DAVE SAYS:** One of my team recommended someone and they sent their CV over. It was terrible, with ten pages of life history and, under normal circumstances, it would have been binned. But because he was highly recommended, I took the time to go through all those pages and interviewed him anyway. It turned out he was great and I hired him. So, whilst your track record and reputation is incredibly important, so too is your CV and it is doubly important that you get this across to the reader.

## 4.3 CVs, sales and marketing

A CV, alongside a LinkedIn profile and other relevant social networking profiles, is the contractor's primary sales and marketing tool, and without a carefully crafted CV a contractor simply won't win any work. You will fail the tests of how a CV is used and be forced to consider returning to full time permanent employment with its lower pay and lack of flexibility.

Contractors provide a service, in the same way any knowledge-based business does, such as a management consultancy or professional practice. Management consultants have glossy brochures, fancy direct mail campaigns and flash websites to wow clients into hiring them.

A CV is no different. It is your brochure, website, door-to-door flyers, advertising campaign, etc all rolled into one. It tells prospective clients who want to part with their cash for services like yours what features and benefits they will receive from choosing you over and above all the other service providers.

CVs, although a contractor's key marketing and sales tool, are only one component of the contractor's arsenal. The interview is also a vital stage of the sales and marketing process and interview techniques are a fundamental skill for contractors to master; they are covered in more detail in chapter 5. Your LinkedIn profile and other social media profiles and activity play a role in supporting your contract search and must be consistent with the contents of your CV.

Mastering the CV creation process is important for contractors who want to win that next contract, or the best contracts. The important items to include are:

- Your profile
- Your relevant skills
- Your relevant achievements
- Previous relevant clients with skills employed and achievements.

Even with impressive skill sets and decades of relevant experience, if you don't understand how to market and sell yourself, you will not win the best contracts.

Having a winning CV is one of the keys to what makes a successful contractor. And having a first rate profile is what makes a winning CV, because for most agents it's the only thing they read. Or not, if your profile is poor.

## 4.4 Writing a high impact CV

To create the best impression possible – so that the client or agent thinks, 'Wow, this person is perfect!' – you need to understand how to structure your CV for maximum impact. Treat your CV as a work in progress of which you have more than one version. Using it effectively is a learning curve and, after writing your first collection of high impact targeted CVs for your first tranche of contracts, you will then know better how to target your CVs for subsequent contracts, which should be much more lucrative.

As detailed in the previous section, during the filtering process you only have a few seconds of the agent's or client's time to make an impact – or it's the recycle bin. If a contractor's CV does not scream at the reader 'I'm perfect for the job', then the CV has failed. A high-impact targeted CV communicates on the front page that the candidate, you, is perfect for the position that needs to be filled.

### 4.4.1 Front page

You only have one sheet of A4 to make that few-seconds' impact. If you start listing all the studies you completed 20 years ago, and the fact that you love squash and have a clean driving licence, your impact will be minimal and your CV will be one of the first rejected.

As an example, here is a list of unhelpful and unfocused information that wastes space on the front page, and wastes the time of the client or agent:

- A list of schools you attended with examinations, grades, addresses. Who cares! It's better to demonstrate that you have the list of skills they are after

- A list of hobbies. Who cares! Tell them what you have achieved by applying the skills you have

- Your work history. Who cares! Tell them what benefits your clients have gained from your work. Why should they hire you?

So now that you've removed the worthless information, just what should be on the front page of your CV? Well, first of all, why are you the right person for this job? You need to show that you:

- Have the skills they are looking for
- That you have successfully applied those skills for other clients
- That you have provided business value to those clients while using those skills.

There are essentially four sections to the front page of a high-impact CV:

- Your name, address and contact details – three lines
- A profile of you – four lines
- Your list of skills or expertise – about ten bullet points
- Your list of achievements – about five bullet points.

## Been there, done that!

## Life stories must go

**DAVE SAYS:** When I was hiring contractors at a major investment bank I had loads of CVs sent via agents. Being in a major hurry, anyone who presented an essay on their life story was put straight in the bin. I simply hadn't the time to sort through sweetie jars, so others who presented themselves much better were the ones invited to interview.

Here is an example:

---

**Joe Bloggs**
Tel: 01234 5677889  Mobile: 07123 456789
Email: joebloggs@pleasespamme.com
10 Bloggs House, London  E12 4LP

**PROFILE**

Highly proficient SENIOR ANALYST PROGRAMMER with 10 years experience building financial risk applications for major blue chip clients using OO, C++, Oracle, UML, ADO. Full life cycle knowledge, including RUP, SSADM, and PRINCE methodologies. Now seeking next rewarding opportunity to make a successful impact in a customer focused team.

**EXPERTISE**

- C++ (8 years)

- Oracle (version xyx, 9 years)

- OO, Rational Rose, UML, OCL

- Design Patterns, Design By Contract

- SSADM, RAD, DSDM, XP, SCRUM

- Meets tight and demanding deadlines under pressure

(and so on – you need about ten bullet points here).

**ACHIEVEMENTS**

- Successfully re-engineered existing risk analysis application, cutting down the run time from 30 minutes to 10 seconds. This enabled fund managers to risk analyse figures in real time, resulting in the company being more competitive in the marketplace, increasing revenues by 50%

- Trained and mentored junior developers in OO techniques, resulting in significant productivity rate increases and less time to market. Increase in speed of development enabled IT to become 50% more responsive to clients' demands for change and enhancements

- Automated manual reconciliation of system data with market data, resulting in task being completed with 100% accuracy in one minute, as opposed to three hours.

---

*Box 4.1 Sample first page*

The emphasis in these introductory sections should be on your 'features and benefits' and their value to the client; that is to say, how has the client saved money, or become more efficient resulting in cost savings and, as the example in box 4.1 illustrates, it is possible to very clearly define how the contractor can add real value to a client's operation.

Your features and benefits and their value means:

- I have these skills
- Someone has paid me for them
- They generated tangible, positive results.

**Profile**

The profile is a very short (four-line maximum) summary that states three main points:

- What you are – your job title
- Your experience and what you have done.
- What you are now looking for.

It is placed at the top of the front page of your CV below your name.

For example:

> Experienced **DEVELOPMENT TEAM LEADER** with 10 years experience training and leading development teams to build Object Orientated Internet/Intranet applications using C#.NET, ASP.NET, SQL SERVER. Now seeking next challenging and rewarding position in a customer focused organisation.

**Motivation for a well targeted profile**

When the agent or client reads your profile the ideal reaction you want is: 'Wow! This person looks perfect. I'll carry on reading the rest of the CV and probably invite them for interview.'

A poorly targeted profile, on the other hand, might invoke responses of, 'Oh, this person is one of those, and we don't need one of those', or, 'This person is a generalist, and we're looking for a specialist.' Your profile should be adapted to match each application you make to optimise your chances of being selected for interview.

**Your title**

Use **BOLD UPPER CASE LETTERS** for your title. It will have more visual priority over the rest of the front page and ensure it gets read. Use the exact same words for your title as you find in the application. If the requirement is for a 'Software Engineer', then you are a '**SOFTWARE ENGINEER**'. If the requirement is for a 'Senior Developer' then you are now a '**SENIOR DEVELOPER**'.

You do not have to use the same title that you had at your last permanent role. You are now your own boss, so you now call the shots on your title, as long as you are being accurate.

With regard to the IT market, since it is not a profession, such as accounting or law, anyone can call themselves what they like without any formal qualifications. This results in many differences in what people expect certain job titles to mean. Provided you are confident you can do the job, you can be as flexible as you like with your job title. You can also rename previous positions you've had in other companies (permanent or contract) to adapt to the position you are now applying for. You will want your job titles to look like you are progressing through your career.

One word of warning: never try and trade up your skills. For example, 'Senior developer now looking for a team leader position'. It will never work in the contract world. They will simply hire a team leader. Trading up works in the permanent market, because they get you cheaper than contractors in return for training you and offering you career growth. The agency and client are looking for the 'finished article' – that is what contracting is about.

In your 'now seeking…' sentence you simply need to state exactly what they want to hear, rather than what you want or aspire to. For example, there is little point in saying, 'Looking to transfer my expertise to the banking sector'. This would be something you want, not what you can offer. The client is unlikely to have a requirement to pay contract rates to cross train someone for their position!

Contractors are hired because they have the skills the client wants and can hit the ground running. Contractors are never hired to be trained by the client, and neither does the client want the impression that the candidate wants to work for them to learn new skills and add them to their CV.

It is all about the client, and what you can do for them, not about what the client can do for you and your contracting career. This is totally different from job seeking in the permanent sector, where there is a two way exchange. In contracting it is all one way; you are paid big money for what you can do for the client, not what the client can do for you.

## Expertise

This section of a CV needs about 10 bullet points that prove that you are the most qualified and effective person for the contract. A classic approach that will gain the notice of the agent or client is to highlight in bold the words that match the advertisement. It is also important to ensure that you show a broad range of skills, rather than devoting too many lines of the CV to one area. You can put multiple skills from the same area on one line.

Make sure you remember to add personal qualities, like 'Meets tight and demanding deadlines under pressure'. A hugely qualified specialist is of no value to a client if they cannot demonstrate they can perform.

## Been there, done that!

### Up-to-date skills open doors

**DAVE SAYS:** When I passed the Microsoft Certified Solution Developer exam the certification was very new at the time, and I was one of the first 500 in the UK to get it. It came with a logo which I put in the top right hand corner of the front page of my CV. So many agents and interviewers commented on it. The cost of the training provided me with a badge that truly opened doors.

## Achievements

Achievements are about measurable benefits you provided to your clients that justified why you were awarded the contract in the first place. They are things you did that saved time, made things easier, saved money, made more money, and so on. One of the common mistakes when writing a CV is to write the achievements as a set of skills that you have acquired and then to focus on how you benefited from them, rather than on the benefits you generated for the client.

You really have to dig deep and think about what business benefits you added by applying your skills, and how those projects added value to the client's business, be it in terms of time saving or profitability. Something tangible is important. To develop the right content for your CV based on your past projects, think about organisations' objectives and how you have helped your clients (or former employers) achieve them.

Remember, all clients or organisations generally want to achieve some or all of the following, to:

- Make more profits
- Sell more products or services
- Become more efficient
- Get more customers
- Beat the competition
- Improve customer satisfaction
- Enter new markets
- Improve quality.

So bear these in mind and then use the following set formula for writing down your achievements:

- Which set of skills you used
- Who it helped
- A quantifiable measure of how it helped.

Here's a list of classic items that are not achievements:

- "I trained somebody"
- "I built something"
- "I learned X, Y, and Z".

These are not achievements. They are a list of 'stuff that you did'. They do not explain what benefits you created for the client who paid you money and what value you brought to that client.

Another example of an achievement that is starting to get there, but not quite is:

- Developed a spreadsheet that helped save ten staff some time and make money.

That is not quite specific enough. A better example of presenting the above might be:

- Developed and implemented a bespoke spreadsheet application for the client's traders, which reduced the time to calculate financial forecasts from three hours to fifteen seconds. This not only saved time, but enabled the traders to become more responsive to market change, and resulted in a measurable increase in profit of 12% over two months.

Keep a list of around ten achievements in a separate document and then just pick out the four or five most relevant to the position you are applying for.

### Achievements – so what!?

The 'so what!?' test is probably the most important test you need to pass in order to secure that contract. CVs are full of statements that fail the 'so what!?' test, so analyse your achievement in the context of the contract you are applying for. Are you: a) Impressed, b) Mildly impressed, or c) Thinking, 'so what!?

Example 1 – So what!?
Achievement: "Mentored other team members" Response: So what!? You trained some staff, and then what? The client spent money for you to train staff and what benefit did it achieve for them?

Example 2 – So what!?
Achievement: "Made document retrieval faster" Response: So what!?
How much faster? How much did you spend, and how much did you save? What was the measurable benefit to the business?

Example 3 – Slightly better
Achievement: "Mentored team members, which improved their skills"
Response: Better than before, but this does not hugely excite. So, you used your training skills to train some people, which resulted in them getting improved skills, and then what? How did they apply those new skills and what was the result?

Example 4 – Right on the nail
Achievement: "Used expert knowledge of project management to deliver application ahead of schedule and under budget. This resulted in obtaining a first mover advantage over competitors and subsequent capture of 70% of market share."
Response: Very impressed. Can you come and do this for me? Please.

The lesson from the 'so what!?' test is to recognise what achievements have created benefits for the client. When listing achievements, ask 'so what?' for each one – would these stand out from a CV and catch the attention of an agent or potential client?

## 4.4.2 Second page

The second page of the CV is about providing reassurance. The primary task has been achieved – the agent or client has actually turned the page. At this stage they are looking to see that:

- You've worked for the right organisations, preferably in the same industry

- Contracts you've worked on have been renewed – you have staying power

- You've successfully applied the skills mentioned on the front page.

The second page of the CV is all about reinforcing the impression you have given of yourself on the front page as being perfect for the contract.

### Work experience
The second page is also where you list your work experience. No need for essays; the best approach is to use short bullet points. This section explains the things you did and what skills you used. You should also add some examples of added value. Box 4.2 illustrates an example of a contract experience.

*Box 4.2 Work experience example*

Some key factors also include explicitly listing the number of months the contract lasted and the number of renewals. This tells the reader that you are reliable and that people value your work. It also means the reader does not have to struggle with working out contract lengths themselves. They can scan down the page and see you have lots of long contracts and renewals, which is another tick in their box. Keep the information brief yet informative – no one wants to read essays. Highlight the key information in bold text so it stands out when scanned quickly.

**Education, training and hobbies**
Page two is also where you list your education, training, and hobbies. Keep this information compact. Some agents and clients like to see you have the right academic background for the contract; others like the 'Married, 2 children' information because agents and clients think it implies stability. However, it is not necessary to list every GCSE, with grades, and your interest in Carniolan beekeeping. The focus should be on the practical and tangible. If you have 10 years commercial experience, your education is somewhat irrelevant.

## Been there, done that!

### Hobbies can get you in the door

**DAVE SAYS:** One batch of CVs I looked through contained an average CV but the guy had 'rocket science' in his list of hobbies, and he had appeared on Tomorrow's World to talk about it. That's one of the reasons we interviewed him. Interesting chap, but we didn't hire him in the end.

I chatted to an agent once who told me the project manager was really into cooking. I have a sweet tooth and was taught how to cook great desserts by my mother, so I put 'pastry chef' in my hobbies – something normally left out! Five minutes into the interview, I was asked, "So, what's your favourite dessert?" The subsequent conversation helped build rapport and I was offered the contract.

## 4.5 Targeting CVs – you can have more than one

The next step after creating the generic content for your high impact CV is to tailor that content so that it perfectly matches the role that you are applying for.

Say you have worked in circuses for several years, and you regularly perform on the trapeze, alternating your act with a lion-taming show. If the advert for the contract says they are looking for a trapeze artist, then you edit the CV to make it look as though you are the best trapeze artist in the entire country. If the client is looking for a lion tamer, then the same rules apply.

So you effectively have two CVs that focus separately on your most relevant experience for that role. Only if the advertisement is for someone with general circus skills should you give equal weight to both areas of expertise.

Contractors need to emphasise the strengths and experience gained from previous positions and demonstrate they have key transferable skills that can be applied in the new position. So, if you are going for a trapeze artist position for which you have three years experience, but have done five solid years of lion taming, it would be best to play down the lion taming experience and focus more on your trapeze experience. This is often referred to as putting your best foot forward.

The best way to show the targeting approach is to demonstrate how a CV can be developed to match the needs of a particular contract's role.

Overall, the CV in Box 4.3 has many virtues and does not suffer from

---

**Mr John Smith**
99 High Street, Anywhere Town, Sussex AB1 9XY
T: +44 (0) 1323 44444   M: +44 (0) 7321 321321   E: john@johncedricsmithonline.com

**PROFILE**
I am a versatile and energetic problem solver and manager. I have experience in facilities management, project management, staff management, system design and software development. With fifteen years experience in Information Technology I am looking to take my expertise into an organisation requiring a manager focusing on end user requirements.

**EXPERTISE**

| | | |
|---|---|---|
| Microsoft Office | Microsoft Windows | UNIX implementation and administration |
| Systems Analysis | Systems Design | Network Design & Implementation |
| Business Analysis | Macro Programming | InfoBASIC |
| Staff Management | Change management | Perl  Account Management |
| Studying for Security+ | Report Writing for technicians and end users | |

**ABC SOFTWARE COMPANY**
1994 – Present
ABC Software Company provides software and facilities management services to Lloyd's insurance brokers and commodity traders. During my eight years with the company I have had significant exposure to both the facilities and software sides of both client areas.

Director of Facilities Management
Grew department to generate half the company's annual revenue.
Expanded department to service twelve clients over twenty sites.
Grew department from one to eleven staff.
Provided technical consultative services to clients at board level.
Translated client requirements into technical specifications.
Provided lateral thinking solutions for all company clients.
Provided account management for client sites.
Managed budgets and growth in line with company expectations.
Provided day to day technical assistance to staff.
Associate Director
Created the facilities management department.
Provided account management for a variety of company clients.
Specialist project work relating to software systems integration.
Analyst/Programmer
Systems design for insurance and commodity trading packages.
Software development for insurance and commodity trading packages.

---

**XYZ COMPUTERS LTD**
1989 – 1994

XYZ Computers Ltd provides subscription and advertising management software to the magazine publishing industry. During my time at the company I had a customer based role, spending much time on site making bespoke changes to software systems. The systems programming role developed as the company undertook a project to convert the bureau system from a legacy mainframe platform to an open UNIX base.

Systems Programmer
    UNIX systems programmer on an application conversion project.
    Created job and print managing systems familiar to VMS operators.
    Automated the conversion of legacy JCL script to UNIX shell script.
    Created a JCL script generator for UNIX.
Programmer
    Specified and coded changes to the standard subscription packages.
    Specified and coded bespoke modules as defined by clients.
    Liaised with clients at board level regarding change requirements.

**INTERNATIONAL COMMUNICATIONS ASSOCIATION (ICA)**
1987 – 1989

ICA provided communications services to journalists prior to the prevalence of the internet. Specialising in transmission of news stories to and from disparate systems, a great deal of integration and analysis work was required. Specialist work included a pilot project to transmit press releases from the United States Information Agency to major news outlets in Israel via the United States Embassy in Tel Aviv.
    Communications Consultant
    Designed and coded bespoke messaging software.
    Liaised with news providers to integrate with their systems.
    Managed communications systems to ensure prompt delivery of news

**EDUCATION**
BSc (Hons) Upper Second, Open University; Computing Subjects & Change Management 1996
3 GCE A Levels, Trinity School; Physics, Maths, Electronics 1986
Currently studying for the CompTIA Security+ Qualification

**PERSONAL**

| | | |
|---|---|---|
| Date of birth : 21 August 1969 | Nationality : | British |
| Marital status : Divorced | Driving licence : | Full, Clean |
| Dependents : One | Languages : | English, German |

**REFERENCES**
Professional and personal references are available on demand.

*Box 4.3 What could be improved on this CV?*

some of the common mistakes made by contractors when writing their CV. However, it can be enhanced to provide significantly more impact.

Let us take look at each section in turn to see how each could be improved.

Here is the original profile:

> I am a versatile and energetic problem solver and manager. I have experience in facilities management, project management, staff management, system design and software development. With fifteen years experience in Information Technology I am looking to take my expertise into an organisation requiring a manager focusing on end user requirements.

This profile does not quite leap out at the reader. It is not targeted to a specific opportunity and describes a range of skills that can be offered and invites the reader to select one or more of these skills. However, it is very rare that an agency or client places an advert for an all-in-one 'Facilities Manager, Project Manager, Staff Manager, System Designer, Software Developer', so the objective is to target what the client or agency wants to hear in relation to the specific contract they are advertising.

Take the hypothetical case of a vacancy for a project manager. In the advertised vacancy it will probably define experience required and industry sector. The CV has to communicate this information in just a few seconds, because that is how long it will take to find its way into the bin if high impact communication is not successfully achieved.

So, a revised profile could be the following:

> Versatile and very successful **PROJECT MANAGER** with a wealth of technical and commercial skills acquired across a wide range of demanding roles, with over 10 years experience in the insurance and commodities sector. Now seeking next challenging and rewarding opportunity to demonstrate substantial abilities and make an effective contribution in a successful, end user focused team.

The use of the pronoun 'I' has been dropped and then the information in the brief has been targeted with the particular position in mind, using words and phrases that matched the contract description. The contract seeker's main skill that is relevant to the role is emphasised with bold upper case letters and words that match those given in the advertisement.

Now, let's look at the next area on this all-important front page.

| | | |
|---|---|---|
| Microsoft Office | Microsoft Windows | UNIX implementation and administration |
| Systems Analysis | Systems Design | Network Design & Implementation |
| Business Analysis | Macro Programming | Studying for Security+ |
| Staff Management | Change management | Perl Account Management |
| InfoBASIC | Report Writing for technicians and end users | |

*Box 4.4 Original expertise to compare and contrast.*

As written, this expertise section reads more like a list of courses and training that have been attended and does not effectively describe all the skills that will match the job title of 'Project Manager' in the profile. Note that courses and training would be better placed in a section on the second page. The expertise should describe a list of skills you have that are directly relevant to the contract for which you are applying. It should also have a combination of skills, both technical and personal.

- Powerful **project planning** and implementation skills – delivery focused.
- Skilled with MS Office, Windows and UNIX implementation and administration.
- **Full project life cycle** – configuration management and change management.
- Track record of academic achievement and career development – fluent in German.
- Effective communication and negotiation techniques – skilled in **account management**.
- Systems design and software development skills for insurance and commodity trading.
- Reliably **meets demanding deadlines** and targets working under pressure.

*Box 4.5 Updated expertise to compare and contrast*

...and so on. Using around 10 bullet points would be ideal here. Notice that we have used bullet points for more readability. And the items that are most relevant we have put in bold to make them stand out during the kind of five- to ten-second scan a client or agent might make.

If, for example, we were looking to target a systems designer role rather than a project manager one, we would amend the profile and expertise list to suit. The golden rule is always telling the client or agent what they want to hear, without being untruthful, and not going into unnecessary detail about your life story and work history.

The next section to add to the high impact front page in this sample CV highlights your achievements. This is completely missing from the original CV and is probably the most important section of the front page. It shows you have used your skills and expertise to deliver some value to those whom you have worked for. It also shows you think commercially, not just in terms of tasks to be completed.

There are some clues in the work history and we can use some of these to develop a couple of achievements, like this:

---

**ACHIEVEMENTS**

- Played lead role in successful initiative to rapidly expand client base to twelve clients across twenty sites and generate half of company's annual revenues.
- Used extensive technical skills and experience to develop bespoke software packages that gained the company a competitive edge in the insurance and commodities markets.

---

On page two of the original CV, the career history section also requires some work. The original section says:

```
XYZ COMPUTERS LTD
1989 – 1994

XYZ Computers Ltd provides subscription and advertising management
software to the magazine publishing industry. During my time at the
company I had a customer based role, spending much time on site making
bespoke changes to software systems. The systems programming role
developed as the company undertook a project to convert the bureau system
from a legacy mainframe platform to an open UNIX base.

Systems Programmer
        UNIX systems programmer on an application conversion project.
        Created job and print managing systems familiar to VMS operators.
        Automated the conversion of legacy JCL script to UNIX shell script.
        Created a JCL script generator for UNIX.
Programmer
        Specified and coded changes to the standard subscription packages.
        Specified and coded bespoke modules as defined by clients.

Liaised with clients at board level regarding change requirements.
```

Although appearing quite effective, some potential improvements
could include removing the use of 'I', as with the rest of the CV and
using more bullet points.

The education section of the original CV is well written. It lists
higher education qualifications and 'A' levels without giving detailed
information about schools and colleges and years attended.
However, if contractors have gone to schools with a high personal
branding value, eg public schools like Eton and Harrow, or state
schools like Hockerill Anglo-European College or Colchester Royal
Grammar School, then there may be occasions when it is worth
including this information.

Training and development can be an important section and the
original CV does not have one. It would be the place to list all the
courses and training relevant to the contract position being
advertised.

The interests/personal section is fine, although it might be worth
swapping 'divorced' to single and working on the formatting to
improve readability.

John Smith's CV has been totally transformed to reflect a different skill set.

---

**PROFILE**
High calibre **BUSINESS ANALYST** with 7 years experience in business and systems analysis. Heavy emphasis on business process modelling using OO techniques, UML, and case tools. Full life cycle experience. Now seeking next rewarding and challenging opportunity in a successful customer focused team.

**EXPERTISE**
- Powerful **project planning** and implementation skills – delivery focused.
- Skilled with MS Office, Windows and UNIX implementation and administration.
- **Full project life cycle** – configuration management and change management.
- Track record of academic achievement and career development – fluent in German.
- Effective communication and negotiation techniques – skilled in **account management**.
- Systems design and software development skills for insurance and commodity trading.
- Reliably **meets demanding deadlines** and targets working under pressure.

**ACHIEVEMENTS**
- Played lead role in successful initiative to rapidly expand client base to twelve clients across twenty sites and generate half of company's annual revenues.
- Used extensive technical skills and experience to develop bespoke software packages that gained the company a competitive edge in the insurance and commodities markets.

And so on.....

---

*Box 4.6 John Smith's front page*

## CONTRACTING MINDSET TIPS:

### Think in terms of the value you can offer your client

Contractors get hired by because of the value they can add to their clients' organisation. Contractors who focus on communicating how they can add value through productivity and profits, and not just on their specific expertise, will win better contracts.

### Are you interested in the model of blowtorch your plumber uses?

You're online looking for an emergency plumber to fix your leaking pipe, which is already causing your new laminate flooring to peel up and threatening to short your electrics. You find one based just around the corner, but his ad is full of the cutting edge equipment and gadgets he uses.

After calling another plumber, you spend ages on the phone as she explains how it took her years working at night school to qualify to repair boilers. She goes on to explain that as an ex-RAF technician, she's also qualified to fix the hydraulics on fighter jets.

When you're looking for a plumber to fix a specific problem in a short time-frame, are you most interested in the one with the best tools or the most experience? Or are you more likely to favour the plumber who quickly demonstrates that, in addition to being suitably qualified to fix your leaky pipe, they've fixed many just like it before, can deal with it now and will make sure that the pipes around it are sound too.

### Clients hire contractors to add value

Clients, and to a lesser extent recruitment agencies, are looking for relevant evidence from past assignments that you can apply your skills and experience *to add value* to their project.

Filling the pages of your CV with lists of technical programming languages you can use, the equipment you are rated on or even the latest IT or technology buzzwords that sound good, but don't say what you've done with them, is likely to get your CV binned on the first scan-through.

And when you are at your interview, which for contractors is really a sales meeting, don't ramble on about how you have just taught yourself the latest technology in your spare time and what cool things it can do, unless the job ad or client asks for it.

### Demonstrate how you can measurably add value

Value means different things to different organisations. Find out what your potential client values and what they are seeking to achieve from the project you are pitching for. If they are a high tech, innovative company, they may value the latest Eurocodes or web languages on your CV. But most won't – that's why you need to find out first.

Always include measurable outcomes of your projects in your CV and explain them subsequently during the interview. Spell out how you applied the technical skills and experience you have and achieved X outcome over Y timescale, which resulted in Z greater productivity/higher sales/bigger profits.

Tailor the message to the client. One client may be seeking a safe pair of hands with years of experience in the programming language used in their legacy system. Another might want your experience of agile development to help stretch its own developers. But whatever the case, they will want to see what value you can add to their organisation.

**Clients hire contractors based on the proven and quantifiable value their skills and experience can bring to their organisation.**

# 4.6 Common mistakes

Getting to the interview stages involves impressing a potential employer with your CV. But who gets the job offer? The fact is that the contractor who gets the job offer is not always the best contractor available for the job. They are the best person available at knowing how to be offered a job.

To reiterate the key point about the contract search process, to get a job offer you need to get an interview, and to get the interview you need a good CV. Generally the people with the best written and most focused, tailormade CVs will get interviewed. And very often the best available people fall at the first hurdle, with their CVs being put straight into the bin or onto the 'rejects' pile, because they don't make it clear to the reader that they are perfect for the contract on offer.

To avoid being the best contractor that cannot win any work, here are some things to avoid when compiling your CV:

**Far too long:** If a CV is more than three pages long then everything on the third page and beyond is unlikely to be read. If the agent filtering the CVs has 200 to read, contractors have a short window to impress. So keep your CV to a maximum of three pages, preferably two.

**Detail:** Avoid too much detail which overlaps with the purpose of the other CV sections. The number of years and a list of your primary skills are sufficient.

Remember, the purposes of the sections are:

**Profile:** What your primary skills are and what you are looking for.

**Expertise:** List of your skills, which closely matches the client's requirements

**Achievements:** Backs up the expertise list, showing how you create value.

**Career history:** Shows that you've 'been there and done that'.

**Too many sentences:** Often sentences on a CV contain too many words and the reader misses the key points. So it's better to write well spaced bullet points where the most relevant information is highlighted in bold.

For example, which of the following is quicker to read? This:

On this project we made use of the .NET Framework and utilised all the main namespaces. We used an intercepting filter pattern which we hooked into ASP.NET to implement user level functional security for the 5000 users. Model View Controller was used to connect the pages to the middle tier, which was written in C#.

Or this:

- ASP.NET, C#, **.NET Framework**.

- 5,000 users. **Functional security**.

- **Design Patterns:** Intercepting Filter, Model View Controller.

**Avoid irrelevant information:** You may have some aspects of your career that you are quite rightly very proud of but, unfortunately, have nothing to do with the client requirements. Leave them off the CV or mention them in a way that highlights how they might be relevant.

For example: If you are a SENIOR GAMES PROGRAMMER applying for a position in a bank, it would be sensible to change your title to 'SENIOR DEVELOPER'.

Another example: If you have worked for software houses, but are applying to work in an organisation that might have something against the 'software house type mentality', then it would be sensible to leave out 'X years experience working in software houses'. However, if the client was a software house, then of course you would leave it in and highlight it.

The same applies to mentioning skills that have become redundant. You might have been the most highly regarded coal miner in the country, but if no one wants coal miners anymore, don't mention it.

**No profile:** If your CV does not have a profile that says precisely what you are and what you're good at, then the client or agent is going to have to guess by reading your CV. And because they do not have time to read the whole thing, your CV will probably go into the Recycle Bin. Make sure you have a profile on your CV, and ensure it is tailored to the position. Here is an example for a senior lion tamer position for a global circus:

Enthusiastic **LION TAMER** with 10 years experience gained with leading global circuses. Extensive experience teaching and mentoring junior tamers, developing the skills of cubs and adult lions, and attracting audiences with daring new tricks. Now seeking rewarding and challenging position with major circus.

The key element of this profile is the professional title that appears in bold so it stands out. This is what you asked for, and this is what I am!

**No expertise section:** Without a summary of your skills the reader needs to read the whole CV and pick out the skills themselves. This is a real headache and will guarantee your CV is put either in the Recycle Bin or at the bottom of the pile. If an agent or client has 200 CVs to read for one contract, they only need to find ten good candidates from their initial scan of CVs. Make sure yours gets chosen by showing clearly you have the specific skills and expertise required for that particular contract.

**No achievements section:** This key section, which demonstrates to the client that you are commercially focused, rather than someone who just 'does stuff' regardless of the outcome, is the section often missed out on contractors' CVs. So having a good achievements section is likely to put you above the rest who do not. Achievements state the measurable benefits you provided to your clients that justified your existence. They are things you did that saved time, saved money, made more money, won more business and so on.

**Not targeted to the role:** Each time you send your CV out it should be targeted directly to the position you are going for. You may be the best soil nailing geotechnical engineer in Europe, but if that is not what the client wants, then do not call yourself one of those. Find out as much as you can about the role before you send your CV. If the client wants an experienced oil and gas engineer, make sure your profile includes the phrase, 'EXPERIENCED OIL AND GAS ENGINEER'.

**Education details on the front page:** Don't waste the valuable 'real estate' on the front page by cluttering it up with details of your education. For example, if you have 10 years relevant experience, that is what to highlight on page one. If you have only been working for a couple of years, then it might be worth mentioning education in the expertise and achievement section, but still put the main details in a section on the second page.

**Too much detail about your education:** If you have 10 years experience, then no one cares that you achieved a B in religious studies 14 years ago. List your A levels, GCSEs, NVQs, etc as a one line summary, but keep your degree on a separate line. For example:

2:1 in lion taming from Circus University, Nutsville.

2 A levels, 9 GCSEs

One exception is if you are a graduate looking for a position and you have little or no experience. If you have studied courses that are relevant to the role and can show some transferable skills then it is worth going into detail. For example, if you were applying for a lion taming role which involved helping train others and feeding the animals, then it would be worth going into more detail:

> 2:1 in lion taming from Circus University, Nutsville
> Tamed eight lions over course of three years
> Taught and mentored lion taming for last two years
> Studied the diets, health and mating habits of lions.

Once again the key elements of the role have been highlighted in bold.

**Too much use of 'I':** Too much use of the word 'I' can appear self indulgent and does not give the appearance of a professional approach. Remove it entirely from your CV, and instead use action words like 'designed', 'improved', 'completed', 'created' and 'initiated'.

**In summary:** Writing a CV well involves getting inside the head of the people who are going to read it. The front page should convince the reader in no uncertain terms that you are the best person for the role.

## 4.7 Alternative CV formats, LinkedIn and social networks

Your contractor CV remains the primary sales and marketing tool to secure you an interview at which you can win your contract. However, alternative CV formats are emerging, which contractors in some sectors, or who wish to differentiate themselves, can use to really stand out. For example, social networking sites such as LinkedIn have created simple applications that enable you to create PDF CVs based on your online profile. And for the more adventurous contractor – and those in related creative fields – online tools are proliferating that can create infographic CVs, video-based CVs and personal branded adverts.

### Using LinkedIn and other professional online networks to help win contracts

According to LinkedIn, contractors who have completed their online profile are 40 times more likely to receive opportunities. A LinkedIn profile is relatively quick and easy to produce, and requires similar basic information to your contractor CV. However, it is very important that your online profile matches your CV. So, if you are applying for a contract with a CV that shows you to be an expert in skill Z, make sure your online profile doesn't relegate skill Z to sixth place under skills A, B, C, X and Y. You may be a specialist in all six skills, but you should temporarily promote area Z to top billing above A.

LinkedIn profiles also allow other LinkedIn users to recommend you. Asking all your clients to provide a LinkedIn recommendation can build up a powerful sales and marketing tool that allows you to reassure agencies and prospective clients of your expertise and professionalism. LinkedIn allows you to choose which of these recommendations to display. So, using the skills example above, if you are applying for a contract requiring skill Z, you can temporarily 'switch off' all the other irrelevant recommendations. And there's nothing to stop you directing agencies and clients to your LinkedIn recommendations, or even cutting and pasting them into an email or other relevant supporting document.

You should also join relevant LinkedIn groups and play an active part in them. If you build up an online reputation for your expertise, professionalism and peer support, you might well find new contract opportunities coming to you, rather than having to seek them out. The same goes for updating your profile and being active on other social networking sites, as well as on specialist professional networks and forums most used by others with your expertise. Becoming active on these can be a good way to connect with potential future employers and colleagues. Your professional, constructive approach on these sites, and the way you interact with others and demonstrate your expertise, can be a good way to reassure potential clients that you will be a good 'fit' in their organisation.

For clients and agents, LinkedIn is becoming increasingly useful. When faced with hundreds of separate, emailed or uploaded applications, a recruiter can only apply limited filtering. But with a similar number of LinkedIn applications, a recruiter can use online filtering to, for example, filter out any contractor who doesn't have at least five recommendations.

### 'Advertising' and personal brand building on social networking sites

Facebook is widely used by contractors and recruiters. It is not the only social networking site, but at the time of writing was on target to achieve one billion users worldwide, so may have the greatest reach. Google+ is a fast-growing alternative that not only integrates well with Google's other services, but also offers useful functionality, like circles, that can be very attractive to professional contractors.

You can literally advertise yourself on Facebook and other social networks, to help create and manage your personal brand over time. Recruiters increasingly use Facebook and Google+ to find candidates. And clients are increasingly using it to seek out contractors, because it can be much cheaper and far more targeted than using a traditional recruitment agency.

So creating and maintaining Facebook and Google+ pages can be valuable. But there is a health warning with using social media sites: personal and business pages must be kept strictly separate and you should think carefully before making public any personal information that may portray you in a negative light. Monday morning Facebook or Google+ posts complaining of a hangover won't look good to a potential client.

### 'Alternative' CV formats – videos and infographics

Using social and professional networking sites adds further functionality and another dimension to traditional CV formats. But some contractors and other jobseekers have really started to push the boundaries, aided by a suite of online tools and paid-for service providers.

Video CVs allow you to record a video CV describing your skills, experience and past assignments. Some paid-for services will host the video and issue a link recruiters and clients can use. Or you could upload your own video CV to YouTube and also embed the video in your LinkedIn and other social media profiles. Video CVs have yet to take off in mainstream contracting, and you should only attempt one if you are very confident in front of the camera, and can create a tight script and professional presentation for maximum impact.

Infographic CVs present your skills, experience, career information and other data in a graphical format. These can be a powerful marketing tool, particularly in creative and new media sectors, and stand out from mainstream text-based CVs. However, as with video CVs, infographic CVs have yet to enter the mainstream contracting sectors.

The majority of UK-based contracts with mainstream recruitment agencies still require a standard, high impact CV as we have described in this chapter. But if you are seeking to differentiate yourself, it could pay dividends to have an additional CV in another format that could be sent to agencies and clients likely to be receptive to a different approach.

What has not and will not change with CVs is the need for each one to be carefully targeted to highlight the value you can add to the client's project, and the specific skills/expertise you have for that project. So, as with applications for contracts using traditional CV formats, you should do your due diligence on any assignment beforehand and determine what content and format would be most suitable for each application.

# Contracting lessons from this chapter

- Your CV has one purpose: to attract interest and secure an interview.

- A CV is your brochure, website, door-to-door flyers, advertising campaign, etc all rolled into one. It's your "elevator pitch".

- It is possible to be really good at what you do, but passed over time and again because your CV wasn't targeted enough.

- Structure and target your CV for high-impact, demonstrating on the front page that you are perfect for the position.

- Highlight in bold the words and phrases that match the advertisement.

- The client does not want to hire you and teach you new skills. Your CV must demonstrate you already have them.

- Make sure your list of achievements are things you've done for the client, and not for you! They must pass the "So what?" test.

- The second page of the CV reinforces the impression you have given on the front page as being perfect for the contract.

- Use multiple copies of your CV based on different roles you are applying for. Carefully tailor each CV for each application.

- A contractors who secures an interview is not always the best contractor available for the contract. They are the best person at knowing how to get an interview.

- Avoid being the best contractor that cannot win any work.

# 5

# Finding and securing a contract

# 5.1 Overview

There is no better way to start contracting than to win that first contract. If your skills are what they should be and, most importantly, you get the preparation and approach right, this won't be a difficult thing to do. Of course, there are some crucial administrative matters that need to be taken care of – like making sure you are paid! – but we'll deal with those later. First, let's sort out what you need to know to win that first contract. Because there's no better confirmation of having made the right career choice.

Finding and securing a contract is a process with a series of steps that result in paid work. However, you should remember that searching for a contract is different to looking for permanent employment; very different. Not understanding the game and how it is played will mean fewer contracts, and that could lead to long periods when you are not working and not getting paid, which defeats the object of contracting. The key is getting just the right balance between time off and times when you want to be contracting and minimising downtime.

It could also mean working for a daily or hourly rate that is lower than the market rate for the job. Doing that is likely to mean that your recruitment agent will be charging the market rate to the client, and thereby getting a higher share of what you earn than they should. In other words, they'll be pocketing 'your' money! Playing a good game will ensure that you spend little time in-between contracts, and that you are always earning the market rate or higher.

Contractors can in theory deal direct with clients or go via recruitment agencies. The fact is that, as highlighted in the last chapter, most clients prefer to deal through an agency and, as a result, most contracts in most sectors are only available through agencies.

That is not to say a first time contractor cannot find a contract direct with a client; it is certainly possible. But in practice it means much more legwork to try and source a direct contract. Unless you already have an active network of contacts, you will almost certainly never get a direct contract. It will be time consuming to try and source one, and the client will probably put you through an agency anyway, to maintain the arms-length relationship that ensures you cannot later claim employment rights.

But given the volume of contracts available through agencies versus those available direct, the likelihood is that your first contract will be via an agency.

---

## Been there, done that!

### Supply and demand

**DAVE SAYS**: In the late 90s demand was so high that you could pick and choose where you worked, since there weren't enough contractors to go around. I'd got it into my head that I didn't want to wear a suit anymore, so turned down any interviews for firms that didn't allow a casual dress code! Yes, this sounds ridiculous, but I wasn't the only one!

---

## 5.2 Using job boards

The first internet job boards were invented as early as 1994, when the internet was in its infancy and little known outside of academic and specialist IT circles. Now job boards dominate the recruitment sector, providing candidates and recruiters alike with a medium that significantly reduces the time, admin and costs associated with the recruitment process.

Job boards have been of particular benefit to contractors who, unlike permanent job seekers, can be looking for numerous assignments during the course of a year. In addition, as many contractors work in highly specialised areas, equally specialised recruitment sites have been created to bring together contractors and end-user clients, via agencies.

Job boards are a vital tool in the contract search, linking you, the contract seeker, with the recruitment agency or client. With the exception of those contracts won through networking or by word of mouth, which are frequently not advertised at all, virtually every contract is advertised on the internet somewhere.

Although the terms 'job board' and 'CV database' tend to be used interchangeably, they refer to two different parts of the online recruitment process, albeit ones that tend to work in tandem:

- A job board is an online service that contains advertisements for vacant positions and all kinds of work opportunities, including contracts, and is used by recruiters to publicise their need for workers, employees and contractors

- A CV database is an online service that contains the CVs of candidates and contractors seeking work, and which recruiters search to find matches with their vacant positions.

Behind nearly every successful job board is a high quality CV database, and both online services come in all shapes and sizes – from the appropriately named Monster website to highly specialised sites where candidates number in the hundreds or thousands.

Most CV databases allow you to register and upload your CV directly via the website. However, there are some specialist CV databases that only include vetted CVs, so you have to go through a selection process before your CV gets posted. Registration is usually quick and simple, requiring you to input some basic personal details and then upload your CV in a Microsoft Word or similar file.

Part of the registration process also usually allows you to add 'tags' to your CV. These can highlight your areas of specialism, and/or indicate your preferences for the type of contracts you prefer to work on, the geographical areas you cover, etc. Tags and preferences ensure your CV is correctly indexed for the database search engine, and will reduce the chance of time-wasting enquiries from agents looking to fill positions that you have no interest in.

There are hundreds of job boards that focus on virtually every sector in which a company needs to recruit someone to fulfil a need. Most of the major job boards are also subdivided into specialist areas. The largest and most used job boards in the UK are:

- cv-library.co.uk

- monster.co.uk

- jobserve.com

- jobsite.co.uk

- totaljobs.com

In addition to these major job boards, there are various specialist sites generally dedicated to particular sectors, such as IT or engineering, and some drill down even further, focusing specifically on, for example web development or oilfield engineering. Plus there are many others covering other sectors like marketing, finance and medicine, among others.

The first stage of the process is to register with those job boards likely to provide the right sort of contracts. The right job boards should be identified during your market research stage (chapters 2 and 3) when making the transition between permanent employment and contracting.

## Been there, done that!

### Making yourself a target

**DAVE SAYS:** Posting your CV on job boards is a great way to get your name out in the market. Many recruitment agents will start sourcing for their positions by mining those CV databases before they put adverts out.

The only problem is that for first timers it can attract a whole bunch of telephone traffic from agencies who will want to fill the position you are vacating at your current firm. This can result in a lot of wasted telephone calls from agents asking, 'So who was your boss at XYZ'.

If you suspect they are phishing for leads then ask them about the role they are looking to fill. If they are vague and then come back to asking about your old boss then you can be sure they are indeed phishing. Just tell them that if they secure you an interview you'll be happy to give that information out.

The same thing happens when you move from contract to contract. As soon as you put your 'hello I'm looking' flag up agents will call you to find out why you are leaving and what your boss's name is.

Work the job boards hard, particularly by using tools like key word searches and automated alerts. Clients and agencies do not always get the copy and information 100% right in their contract posts, so keep any searches wide enough to capture contracts where the job descriptions and skills required might have 'gone astray'. It is better to spend time deleting contracts not relevant than missing out on contracts that would be perfect for you.

With most contracts being advertised by recruitment agencies, agencies are naturally huge users of job boards and frequently post contract opportunities across many sites, including those named above. Check that you are not looking at the same contract opportunity if you see something interesting on two or more job boards. Job boards present an important route into the recruitment agencies, and give you opportunities to send in highly targeted CVs (see chapter 4) in direct response to contract opportunities.

Agencies are increasingly turning to social networks, like LinkedIn, to advertise contracts and to look for contractors to fill them. Make sure your LinkedIn and other relevant profiles are up-to-date and consistent with your CV. Using social media to secure contracts is covered in section 5.11.

## 5.3 Working with agencies

Most successful contractors have worked with recruitment agencies during their career. Many will never contract direct for a client and always work through agencies. Agencies, or agents, are a vital element of the contracting process, performing a variety of tasks, some of which are not obvious to the contractor but are nonetheless hugely important to the entire sector. However, working with agencies is not always a smooth ride.

### 5.3.1 The agent is not working for you

Agencies do not work for contractors and do not always provide a top quality service. They may take your CV and then you won't hear anything from them again, despite the fact that they promised you work right away. An agency could forget to renew your contract on time. They may try to change the conditions of your contract when you renew, or even in the middle of the contract, so that they earn more money.

The key to all this is to remember that the agent is not working on your behalf. It is the clients who ultimately pay agencies' bills, so the clients' needs will always come before yours. When you start out contracting you will be approached by agents who will assure you that they have only your best interests at heart. They will spend a long time on the telephone asking all about you, and taking all sorts of professional detail to, they say, find just the right slot for you.

But in fact the agent generally has little interest in you personally. Agencies earn commission on your fees from the client company. This is expressed in the form of a 'margin' – in other words, the agency takes a percentage of the total fee that the client pays for your services. The agency has a separate contract with the end-client that regulates all the agency business. This contract does not particularly concern you (although it can be important later should tax issues arise which are covered in chapter 8, when we talk about IR35).

Ultimately, the agent is there to fill a slot for the client and collect your fees for you. The agent earns more money as more slots are filled. In other words, the agent is similar to a salesman working on commission – do not expect more from them than that. They have their own needs and priorities, just like everybody else. However, don't forget that the agency is effectively your commission-only sales force, and so you really should respect them for the essential role they perform in this regard.

## Been there, done that!

### Negotiation woes

**DAVE SAYS:** My initial negotiation was rubbish. In fact you can't even call it negotiation! I asked the agent how much I could charge, and he told me. Then he got me an interview, I was offered a role at the rate he had told me, and I gratefully accepted the deal!

It turned out I was lucky, since the client had fixed margins with the agent, so very fortunately I didn't get a bad deal, but this is certainly not the norm.

Once you fit the slot and start work on a contract, you have made a sale for the agent, and that is what the agent primarily cares about. If you can renew your contract, then the agent will pay attention to you while you negotiate the renewal. Or, if you have the skills to fill another slot on the agent's books, you are of interest for as long as that lasts. After that, all that you mean to the agent is a pile of paperwork.

Remember that you are free to search for other contracts with other agencies, or even direct with other clients, at any time, even during a current contract. You are a business to business service provider and, as such, are free to market your services to potential new customers, just like any other normal business would. In fact, not only can you use other agencies, you must. This is because, although many recruiters tell contractors they are actively searching for new contracts on their contractors' behalf, in reality the agency business model doesn't work that way. You should be searching for that next contract all the time.

### 5.3.2 Treat your agent fairly

But that doesn't mean you should avoid agents, because if you use them right they are likely to be the key to you having a long, happy and profitable contracting career. So it's worth putting in the effort early on to understand where the agent is coming from; that way you will save yourself a lot of time, stress and bother. Provide the agent with the details needed to fill the slot; be polite to the agent while you are both negotiating an agreement; and always be fair and reasonable with the agent.

But do not expect the agent to do more than the business requires: the agent won't help you with your problems, and, in general, will be on the side of the client rather than the contractor. And in business terms that's probably as it should be, because, after all, it is the client who is paying their bills.

Keep an eye on the agent. Make sure you are paid on time. Make sure your renewal goes through as agreed. Read the contracts you receive from an agent carefully, and have them reviewed if they appear to wildly contradict the contract law outlined in chapter 7.

### 5.3.3 Finally, the agent calls

If you've followed the CV guidance in chapter 4 and your CV has found its way to the top of the pile, the agent will give you a call and ask you about arranging an interview with the client. You may be about to make a deal. So what do you, the contractor, charge for your services? Chapter 3 details how to go about setting a rate. But if you're not certain about what to charge, at this stage, just tell the agent that you charge the 'market rate' and wait for an offer.

The agent may offer you a low rate, which will allow for a nice healthy margin for them, but you can negotiate this up a bit. After all, the agent is finding you work, and deserves to be fairly rewarded for that service. Of course, if your particular skill set is in high demand, push for as much as you think you have a right to. Experience in doing these negotiations will soon help you to get the range right.

In the world of permanent employment, a prospective employer (or agent) will ask you what you were earning in your last job. Unfortunately you have no option here but to state the facts, because eventually they will see your tax form P60 from your last employer, which states it clearly. Prospective employees who tell fibs about what they were earning before have been known to have a job offer removed, or to be fired once the client finds out they were not telling the truth.

It isn't like this in the contracting world. Whilst you could of course lie if you wanted to in order to bump your rate up, you are better off just being vague and saying things like, "I was paid market rate for that job, and was happy with the rate." If the agent keeps pestering you about it, just side step it again and say that for this role you would charge £XYZ per day. Think of it this way – would you ask your builder what they charged their last client for changing a boiler? Would you ask a car salesman how much profit they made on their last sale?

When you give agents numbers of previous salaries or rates they tend to respond with, "Oh, this client won't be able to pay that", simply because they are trying to earn a generous margin. If you are charging market rate, then stand your ground and they may well give in.

When you are first negotiating with the agent over money, try to be vague and non-committal, because the agent wants to hear: a) that you are perfect for the role; and b) that you are inexperienced enough to let them get away with enjoying a higher margin by passing on less to you of what the client is prepared to pay. Always try to give a range, if possible, because that eases negotiations if you need to increase your fee, particularly if you are enquiring by email rather than via an online application process that only allows a single rate figure.

## Been there, done that!

### We all get a bad deal first time

**DAVE SAYS:** Don't worry if the agent gets the better of you in your first contract negotiations. It happens to all of us and you'll learn in time to get better at securing yourself a good deal. If I had a penny for every contractor who hadn't got the best deal on their first contract...

So, during conversations, sound really keen about the position, give the impression that you will fit in perfectly, but be vague on rate. You want to have them say a figure first. So, you will say 'market rate' and they will keep asking you what that is.

You then throw it back to them and ask them what they think they can get you in the door for. They may come in low and you can say that it sounds about right for the role, but you could suggest this figure as part of a range, eg £400 to £500 per day. Then when you get the offer you can simply open negotiations at the top end and stick to your range. If you ask for more, you really need to qualify the request by saying something like, "I've been offered more elsewhere and if you match it I'll take this one."

After an interview you might receive a call like, 'They like you, but can only afford XYZ'. This is probably just the agent trying to increase their margin, and they might be playing two contractors off against each other. You'll need to stand your ground here, and balance your negotiation with any other offer you might have. You can help your negotiations by trying to establish the strength of your position at the interview stage by asking at the end:

- Do you have any reservations about hiring me?
- Do you have other candidates to see?
- Have you seen anyone else, and were they any good?
- Are you happy with the rate I am quoting you?

Many managers won't work out you are trying to find out how keen they are in order to establish your bargaining position and will be open and honest about things. So the key is to be vague with the agent and ensure you win yourself an interview, because once you have the offer you have considerably more bargaining power. Agents aren't keen on contractors doing this, in the same way contractors aren't keen on the agents getting the better end of a deal, but it is all par for the course. It is simply business and, as a contractor, you are in business for yourself, so you should not feel guilty about it.

The most important thing to remember about negotiation is that everyone needs to feel they are getting a good deal. If one party feels hard done by then the long term arrangement won't be satisfactory to all.

## Been there, done that!

## Stuffed... for a year

**DAVE SAYS:** On one contract I had to interview and hire other contractors and was given a list of agencies to call. Agents quoted the final rate to me for this one chap at £45 an hour – pretty much the same the rest of us were being charged at.

When he turned up on site we found out he was getting paid only £30 an hour, meaning the agency was taking a huge margin. This was his own fault for poor negotiation, but nonetheless a really bad deal for him. The firm tried to sort it out, but the agency wouldn't budge, and he was stuck on that rate for a year.

I learnt from this, and in the future when I hired contractors I told them what they should be charging, much to the annoyance of the agents. Having upset contractors on your team is much worse than having an upset agent whose wages you pay!

### 5.3.4 Conduct of Employment Agencies and Employment Business Regulations

Contractors starting their first contract, or starting a new contract with a new agency, will find one of the first questions the agency asks is whether they want to opt out of the 'Conduct Regulations'. That is the commonly used phrase for The Conduct of Employment Agencies and Employment Businesses Regulations 2003. These were introduced by the Department for Business, Innovation and Skills (BIS) to provide workers and hirers with minimum standards they could expect from private sector recruitment agencies and employment businesses.

The regulations are designed to apply to workers who are controlled by the client. That means that not only do the vast majority of contractors simply not require the protection the regulations bring, but also as skilled professionals in business in their own right they are not controlled by their clients and so technically the regulations do not apply.

In recognition of the fact that some high earners working through their own limited companies might want to choose whether to be 'protected', when the regulations came into force in 2004 an opt-out provision was introduced. So, even though highly skilled contractors not controlled by their clients are not technically covered by the regulations, most agencies still request that their contractors formally opt out.

Agencies should offer and receive a signed opt-out before the contractor is introduced to the client. If they do not, the opt-out could be invalid, leaving the agency in breach of the regulations, and also preventing the agency from putting restrictions on the contractor that have been requested by the client.

Contractors should also expect to see a clause in the opt-out from the agency to clarify that the regulations don't apply and that the client does not control the contractor. If a contractor is considered to be controlled by the client and does not opt out, then the agency is required to work through a series of steps. These include creating paperwork about the client's requirements and contractor's suitability for the role, possibly checking the contractor's qualifications and completing a Criminal Records Bureau (CRB) check for certain roles.

Contractors do suffer some disadvantages from opting out. For example, the agency is required to pay workers who are covered by the regulations even if they have not been paid; contractors who have opted out lose this protection. Plus, the agency must agree terms with the contractor before introducing them to the client; this significantly reduces contractor flexibility in what is supposed to be a flexible, highly skilled labour resource.

In addition, if a contractor has opted out, then the agency can use restrictive covenants that can potentially restrict the contractor from using a competing agency or going to a competitor of the client. There are other regulations relating to temporary-to-permanent fees, which can negatively impact on the client if they want to take the contractor on as an employee or a direct contractor.

However, although employment status is determined on a case-by-case basis, a limited company contractor accepting on paper that they are controlled by the client and wish to be covered by the regulations is sending a pretty clear message to HMRC about their employment status. Control by the client is a key factor in determining the employment status of a contractor, and can be part of a package of evidence that puts a contractor inside IR35 (see chapter 8).

But, as highlighted earlier, genuine contractors are not controlled by their client, and so technically the regulations do not apply anyway.

## 5.4 Basic sales – the contract search process

As a contractor, you are in business for yourself. Whether working through a limited company or an umbrella company, or contracting directly with a client or through an agent, the responsibility to generate new business (ie keep finding new contracts) lies with you.

This is why developing sales and marketing skills is so important for every contractor. The CV, covered in chapter 4, is the contractor's marketing literature, customised according to the target market and matching the product, ie the contractor, with the market, ie the contract.

Sales is the process of keeping a constant stream of contract leads coming through. The larger the sales hopper, the more potential contracts you can apply for, and the more chance there is of winning a contract. Let that hopper run dry and no more contracts will appear. So the contract search process is no different from how marketing and sales professionals sell products and services throughout industry and commerce. A simplified summary is:

- Lead generation – the contracting equivalent would be finding contracts using job boards and agencies

- Sales proposal – a contractor sending a tailored CV that effectively lays out a solution to the client's project issues and needs

- Closing the deal – this is when a contractor, after interview, has convinced the client that they are the right person for the role, negotiated a good fee and won the contract.

Finding your first contract might appear to be administrative hell, but it gets to be far easier, quicker and, at times, even enjoyable. However it is vital to keep on top of the 'sales' process. Chapter 3 listed a series of daily activities that will drive the contract search process, and these should be followed to ensure success:

- Chase agencies you have sent applications or CVs to by telephone and email

- Keep searching job boards and other sources of contracts

- Maintain a steady stream of applications

- Network, by maintaining social and more formal links with contacts in your industry.

You decrease your chances of securing a contract considerably if all you do is send off emails to agents and wait for the phone to ring. Making contract applications is not like tennis, where you wait for the agent to hit the ball back. You need to keep hitting plenty of balls over the net until they notice you. And you also need to chase the agent to ensure they pick your ball up!

If you are only one of a few who are applying for the position then they might phone you. If they have plenty of applications then your email might not even be read. Other seasoned contractors will be phoning the agents shortly after sending them emails to ensure they get their CV to the top of the pile for review. If you don't also do this you are one step behind the competition. So you need to chase them by phone.

Most good agents are goal-driven and work hard, so they can be difficult to get hold of. Even if you leave a message requesting that they call you back they are unlikely to do so. Whilst this might appear rude, it isn't intentionally done to upset contractors. It is just the way the industry works. Agents would rather spend more time chasing new business than speaking to every contractor who applies for a position. Therefore, if they don't call back then ring them again.

Making lots of telephone calls to chase business can be time consuming. It is therefore important to make optimum use of your time, and that means filtering out time-wasting activities. It is advisable to keep notes of when you have tried to speak to agents about positions so that you develop a good sense of when to cut your losses and move on to the next position. Check out chapter 11 for more tips on how to make the sales process really work in your favour.

## 5.5 Contracting direct

Contracting direct with the client can have advantages as, for example, there is no middleman such as an agency to take a cut of your contract fee. This could work for the client, because you might be slightly cheaper, and it might work for you because you might earn slightly more than if contracting through an agency. Contracting direct with the client, and having no agency in the loop, also means that the Agency Workers Regulations (AWR) can't apply. If contracting direct, you are not an agency worker and there is no temporary work agency involved, which is a requirement for AWR to apply (see chapter 9).

However, the chances of a new contractor securing an immediate contract direct with a client are slim. But contracts can come from anywhere, and there might be opportunities to apply direct, particularly in some sectors and for those with certain skill sets – like highly specialised contractors with a small number of potential clients. A major difference between contracting direct and contracting through an agent is that the contractor is entirely responsible for arranging their own contract between the client and the contractor's limited company.

### Getting started

The first place to start is winning a contract. The process is similar to that described already, but obviously involves considering contracts that are being advertised by end-user clients rather than agencies. Start with market research and work through the job boards and other sources of trade information. For example, if you spot an article in a trade magazine that a major mechanical and electrical engineering firm has started a major job and is already complaining of skills shortages, this may be a good lead. But beware of inefficient use of your time.

It is also worth considering creating the infrastructure to start contracting sooner rather than later. This could mean incorporating a limited company and opening a company bank account or investigating an umbrella company before a contract has been found. As contracts can start within a week (or even sooner!) of the client agreeing the deal, a contractor might have to move fast finding experts to create and check contracts made direct with the client, advising on IR35 status and so on.

### Pitfalls of going direct

When contracting direct chasing payment can be a pain, particularly if you contract with a large organisation that thinks it is fine to pay in 60 days, or more. When you contract via an agent they typically pay you before they are paid, by 'factoring out' their invoices. You could do this yourself if you contract direct, but it does mean time and money spent on chasing payment when you could be doing something more productive and profitable.

Just because you go direct doesn't automatically mean you will earn more. The client has spent more time and resources finding you rather than outsourcing it to an agent. So they will be looking to earn that back. Also, bear in mind the extra time you might spend trying to find a contract, whilst not getting paid.

The cost of your own sales, in downtime when you are not earning, is unlikely to be more than the extra money you might be paid by going direct. So going direct is certainly not the road to significantly increased riches. Even if you find your own contracts through networking, many firms will still insist you bill via their agency, which will take a cut, as this insulates them from legal issues and helps their administration.

## 5.6 Interviews

The agent has made the call and you have made it to the interview stage with the end user client. Or you may have found a contract direct. So you now need to ensure you maximise your chances of being offered the position by effectively preparing for and conducting the interview.

Without effective preparation, it is almost guaranteed that you will not be offered the contract. The prospective client, frequently accompanied by a colleague from the human resources department, will instantly spot lack of preparation and think, "Will this person's slack approach to preparation affect any work they might do for us? Yes, probably."

Preparation does not have to be difficult or overly time consuming and, in fact, can often prove interesting and even enjoyable on a professional level. Do it right and it will easily become part of the natural cycle of your interviews for new contracts.

### 5.6.1 The Basics – Where, when and with whom?

Ensure you know the interview location and leave plenty of time to account for delays in travel. Arriving at an interview late means you already start the interview from behind the rest of the candidates. It gives the impression that you can't organise yourself and plan. Better to be an hour early than a minute late. You can always grab a coffee and go through your notes. It also reduces the panic that could set in if you arrive in a hurry and aren't relaxed.

If you are driving then ensure in advance that you will be able to park, that the car has petrol in it, and that you have change in your pocket for parking meters. On the morning before you set off check the road traffic reports. Take an umbrella in case it rains. You don't want to turn up soaked from head to toe. And make sure you look the part. In many cases this will mean a nice suit or smart trousers/skirt and jacket, with a plain shirt and tie – traditional business wear, in other words.

If you're being interviewed for a consumer brand that appears to be relaxed and laid-back, don't make the mistake of thinking that they have a relaxed approach to their work, too – they will almost certainly want to see that you have a professional attitude and that this is reflected in how you dress for an interview. Don't carry your documents in a plastic bag; neatly folded in an envelope is fine, whilst even better would be to have a smart briefcase or a corporate-looking handbag or folder.

Make sure you know the name of the person or people you are meeting and their job title(s). If the name(s) appears difficult to pronounce then ensure you check first with your agent or the client's HR manager who arranged the interview, so that you get it right. If the person you are meeting has a name that doesn't instantly make their gender obvious, find out from the agent whether they are male or female. This avoids you making mistakes, like assuming they are the secretary to the person you are meeting when in actual fact they are the person you are meeting.

Keep details on you in case you have trouble finding the place and need to make a phone call to confirm them. Also, if you are late then you can phone in advance to warn them. If you are working through an agent, you can always question them about any special dress codes or instructions.

### 5.6.2 Motivation – What the client will be looking for

It is important to try and examine and understand the needs and motivations of the client, so that you can work out why they might need you as a contractor to solve a problem for them. This understanding should help drive the rest of the interview preparation.

An event has occurred which has necessitated the need of the client to hire a contractor. They advertise and filter candidates down to those they wish to interview. These are some of the things they will be looking for in an interview:

- Is this person skilled for the position? Can they achieve what we need them to?

- Do I feel they have a good grasp of their subject matter?

- Do they follow the industry and keep up with the latest advancements?

- Can this person work on their own and use their initiative?

- Is this a nice person to get on with or do I think they are arrogant with a self inflated ego and delusions of grandeur?

- Do I like them?

- Will they fit into our corporate culture?

- Is this person going to make me look stupid, or support me and help me to look good?

- Are they presentable?

- Do they suffer from personal hygiene problems?

- Can they communicate with other human beings?

- Do they perhaps know a little bit more than other candidates, which could help give the company an edge?

- Do they understand my problems and what would be required of them?

- Do they give an indication of laziness or are they prepared to get stuck in?

- Do I feel they are trying to solve my problems or just trying to win a contract?

- Are they a positive person who will motivate those around them or a merchant of doom that will bring everyone down?

- Are they a good listener?

- Are they more focused on telling me how great they are than on trying to understand how they can fulfil the needs of the contract?

- Are they commercially aware? Will they bring that awareness to the contract, helping us achieve our commercial goals by creatively using their skills, rather than just sticking rigidly to the specifications and doing what they're told to and no more?

- Do they know anything about our company? Or the challenges and opportunities facing our sector?

Knowing these are the kind of questions the interviewer will be looking to answer, use them to drive the preparation.

### Step 1: Find out why they need you
They will need you for perhaps one of the following common reasons:

- The client is spending too much money and feel that by spending more money on you, you will make things more efficient

- Someone else has left the job and they need to be replaced

- They need you to do a bespoke piece of work due to legislation they need to adhere to, or because they don't have the skills in-house

- They need you to train some of their staff with the niche skills you offer.

Press your agent to find out what the real reason is. In addition, use other contacts to find out. You might know someone else who works there. If you cannot find this out then it will be the first thing you will need to ascertain at the start of the interview. Without knowing the answer to this basic question, it is pretty much impossible to tailor your responses to meet their requirements.

**Step 2: Learn about the company**
This is to ensure you tick the interviewing client's box for 'at least they did their homework and found out a bit about the company'. At the start of the interview you will most certainly be asked 'Do you know much about the company?'. You will not look convincing if you say no. You need something prepared.

An answer that will normally suffice would be something along the generalised form of 'Yes, I researched your company last week. [tells them you made an effort]. I understand you have 20,000 thousand employees over 40 countries. It was interesting to read recently in the news about XYZ. This might make an impact on the share price, which looks to be holding up well. Do you own shares in the company? [Notice how it finishes on a question to keep the flow of conversation going].

In addition, if you know you are going there to interview for a contract that is to solve a specific problem for them, find out about it. Go to their website if they have one, or trawl the internet to find out what you can. This type of information is very useful background:

- How many employees

- When the company was formed and who started it

- The company mission statement and unique selling proposition (USP)

- Offices locations, both national and international

- Expansion rate of the company

- Annual turnover

- Current share price, and how it has done over time

- Recent press statements.

## Step 3: Write down the skills required for the contract

Make a short list of what you think the requirements are. Use the motivation of what they are looking for in an interview to drive this part. An example of an IT contractor's list might be something like this:

- OO Development – at least 5 years experience – I comfortably qualify

- Replace an existing team member – so some maintenance involved. Wonder why they are leaving?

- Good communication skills – so I will be speaking to end users

- Small project so should have done deployments, maintenance, testing and so on over the whole life cycle

- Can work on my own – so probably need to be commercially aware. Cost versus benefits and so on.

Notice that this example has mainly focused on the technical skills. Keep in mind all the other non-technical ones though, as these will be needed to drive the motivation behind your list of questions.

## Step 4: Your list of questions

This is a key element of the process. There is nothing wrong with physically getting out your list of questions when you are at the interview and using them. It shows you have prepared and made an effort. It is better to commit them to memory as they will then not look as wooden when asked. Even if you do remember the whole lot, still get out your piece of paper at the end to show them that you did do some preparation.

Your list of questions should follow these guidelines:

- The questions you ask must promote discussion about topics where you can demonstrate you have all the skills required for the job

- Your questions must address all of the aspects the interviewer is looking for

- Your questions should also demonstrate that you know just that little bit more than is required. A bit like 'bonus features' for them if they take you on. But take care not to over-do it, as you don't want them to think your core skills lie elsewhere.

### Step 5: The day of the interview
Before you leave the house, do a quick search on the internet to find latest share prices, and any mention of the company in the news. Having fresh up to date information on the company will give you extra points when they ask the inevitable first question.

### Step 6: Waiting in reception
Get your notes out. Brush up on the company facts. Try and commit your questions to memory. If you see one, grab a copy of any magazine published by the company and try and read something about recent press statements and company news – the sort of topics that can generate good, relevant conversation during the interview.

## Been there, done that!

### Research pays

**DAVE SAYS**: I remember once attending an interview with a client that provides breakdown and recovery services to drivers. I was waiting outside the guy's office and picked up an internal magazine that talked about a new laptop they had purpose-made for their drivers, because existing ones couldn't cope with the wet. When I mentioned this in my response to 'what do you know about us' the guy was seriously impressed and said that was news that had only just come out. I was offered the position.

Another good trick is to take a look around the walls of the offices and see if you can spot any award certificates, like ISO 9001, Investors in People and so on. They can be useful in your opening conversation or for answering the first question.

## Step 7: Your opening conversation

You meet, shake hands and then you are led to the room where the interview is taking place. Chances are you are probably met by the person who is interviewing you. It is a good idea to have an opening conversation prepared for the walk between reception and the room. It removes the awkward silence and gets you off to a good start. Some examples might include:

"So, how long have you been working for XYZ Ltd?"

"I noticed you had an award for XYZ. You must be proud of that."

You will tend to find the interviewer will ask the inevitable 'Did you have any trouble getting here? or 'Did you find us OK?' Always answer 'No problem.' Then continue: 'So, tell me, how long have you been working for XYZ Ltd?', or another one of your prepared questions. Don't start going into how you got here, which route you took and so on. It is boring and they really don't care. Switch it round and get them talking about themselves and the company. Take an interest from the start.

## Been there, done that!

### Consultancy interviews

**DAVE SAYS:** It's very rare, but sometimes you'll attend an interview only to discover you are quizzed far too much about finding the solution to a specific problem. You'll get the feeling that there isn't actually a job on offer, but you are just providing free consultancy. This is extremely rare, but it happens.

The key to making an interview a success is demonstrating that you understand the needs of the client, that you have the ability to help them, and that you can provide just that little bit more. Doing your homework in preparation for what is essentially a sales pitch makes all the difference.

## CONTRACTING MINDSET TIPS:

### Contractor interviews are sales meetings – you're a product

Contractors are a human product offering a specific package of skills and experience, designed to be a 'plug-in-and-play' solution to a client's requirements. Therefore, contractors must view their interviews with clients as product sales meetings. During such meetings, contractors must first identify the client's needs, then 'pitch' their own particular 'features' and 'benefits' that will meet those needs and help them secure a 'sale'.

### Do you get frustrated when salespeople can't sell?

When you walk into your local electrical superstore looking for your next flatscreen TV, does your salesperson just stand there listening to a stream of your questions, hoping that one of them might hit on something that gives them a chance to explain one of the TV's unique features?

Or does your salesperson bombard you with facts about the history of flatscreen development, 'TVs I have known and loved' and every detailed specification about each TV in the store?

Then, when you have finally decided which TV you want and that you want to buy it from this store right now, wouldn't you find it strange if the salesperson kept on telling you about other TVs and didn't ask you right off, "How would you like to pay and when would you like delivery?"

### Clients need to be sold to using a professional sales approach

When a client wants to hire a contractor, they have a very specific problem that needs a particular skill or set of skills to solve it. They will have to sit through numerous unfocused interviews with contractors, when what they really want is to receive a purposeful, decisive and reassuring sales pitch from a 'product' solutions supplier who demonstrates they can expertly deal with the issue.

Sitting back and offering a client a double-layer chocolate box of skills and experience in the hope they'll find the flavour they like is a high risk, hit-and-miss strategy. Equally, treating the client to an hour's interrogation will yield zero results.

And, if you don't identify exactly what solution your client is seeking from a contractor, then how can you tailor your interview sales pitch to demonstrate that your skills and experience form the ideal solution?

### Treat your interview like a professional sales pitch and your expertise like a product

Any contractor can, and should, invest in learning professional sales skills, so that they are able to offer themselves as the very best 'product' without their clients even knowing they are being sold to. Selling is a process: you ask questions, define the client's needs, explain your features and benefits to the client and then, very importantly, actually ask for their business.

There is nothing underhand about sales, because there is a major difference between a salesperson and a 'con artist'. A con artist will try and cheat the customer. A professional sales person will use their skill to establish the client's requirements and match a product or service to their needs, before asking for a sale to close the deal.

Use the interview like a sales pitch, don't forget to identify the benefits your skills will bring to the client and identify client reservations now, so you can deal with them – client concerns may be groundless. Then you must ask for the business.

**Use your interview as an opportunity to uncover your client's needs and then pitch your skills as the perfect 'product' solution.**

### 5.6.3 After the interview

After your interview the agent will normally phone you to see how it went. They will naturally want to know if they are close to finalising a deal themselves. The agent will also try to gauge both the strength of the client's interest in you and the strength of your interest in the position.

If you weren't interested in the position, then tell the agent outright to avoid wasting their time, but make sure you tell them why. It will normally be because the position was not as originally described to you, which will be useful feedback for the agent. It helps to maintain a good relationship with the agent who may call you again for a more relevant role.

If you are very interested in the position, then try not to sound overly keen, as it could result in the agent thinking that they can increase their margin by lowering your rate, knowing that you are likely to accept.

It is not uncommon for an agent to later offer you the position with the story "…the client liked you, and wants to hire you but they can only pay XYZ." Try not to be caught out with this common technique, by sticking to your guns over the rate.

### 5.6.4 Where can an interview go wrong?

Other than failing to treat the interview like a sales meeting, which is the number one common mistake, there are some other common mistakes that can also guarantee the client won't be calling you or your agent to offer you the contract:

**Wrongly focused on what the contract does for you rather than how you can help the client:** Never discuss why the role would be good for you and what you would get out of it. The client does not care. They are solely interested in whether they can trust you to do the job on time and to budget. Clients pay you top money to help them solve their problems, not yours.

**Failure to address their problems:** You fail to understand the problems they want solved and summarise how your relevant experience will be of benefit to them in solving their problems. It is down to you to convince them you can meet their needs, not for them to establish this from general stuff you say.

**Not being absolutely honest (in other words, telling lies):** Sometimes candidates pretend they know something rather than admitting that they don't. You will be caught out and no one hires a 'blagger' as they are far too risky. The client wants to know that at the end of the day they can trust you to either get something done, or put your hand up and ask for help.

## Been there, done that!

### Bow out early

**DAVE SAYS:** Some projects that clients want you to do are truly awful and you won't be interested, and neither will many other contractors.

I once attended an interview for an internet start-up that wanted me to 'look after' their current system, which was riddled with software defects, and apply patches to it whilst another team built the replacement. Hardly attractive, so I cut the interview short and wished them the best of luck finding someone.

If you attend an interview and the project has been over-sold to you, then feel free to say so and stop the interview in a polite way. There's no point you all wasting any more time.

In my contracting career I attended three interviews like this. They all had the same thing in common – they wanted contractors to come in and maintain their legacy system. Contractors don't really do this – they live on the cutting edge.

**Inability to listen/failure to answer the question:** Sometimes candidates, particularly technical types, can 'go off on one' and get carried away by drilling down into some detailed technical area when it is not required and/or doesn't answer the question they've been asked.

**Interrupting too much:** This is interpreted as, and is, just plain rude. Wait for the other person to finish speaking. Make notes whilst they are speaking if you are worried you will forget your points by the time they have finished. Be aware that your eagerness may be mistaken for bad manners.

**Talking too much:** Some people simply too talk much – don't be one of them. Ensure the conversation is evenly balanced. If they speak for 90% of the time you won't get your points across and will fail to impress them. If you speak 90% of the time, they will think you talk too much and are a poor listener.

**Lack of preparation:** Lack of preparation means you know nothing about the company and don't have a list of relevant questions to ask that will get everything across that will help you sell yourself. Make sure you at least know the basics about the company and never assume you already have that knowledge – chances are you'll simply end up looking foolish when you discover, for example, that the CEO you're referring to was forced out by shareholders two months ago! You should also create a set of open questions that provoke conversations about topics that you know a lot about.

## Been there, done that!

### Red card for lying

**DAVE SAYS:** Working for one client, we built some bespoke technology that we gave a fancy name to. When chatting to a candidate I said we were using XYZ, to which he replied, "Yep, I know it". There is no way he could have done – red card!

**Poor timing:** Too much focus on one issue means you fail to shine in other areas, and you can reach the end of the interview without having properly sold yourself.

**Poorly targeted answers:** Align your responses to be appropriate for the interviewer. If they are non-technical then don't bore them with deep technical information they know nothing about. They won't be impressed. Use familiar buzzwords and describe the benefits in terms of how your skills will make sure you meet deadlines and how your approach to the project will help improve their business.

**Lack of commercial awareness:** If you fail to show you understand business and the concept of cost versus benefit, then the interviewers will be worried that you will spend too much time building something they don't want. Do demonstrate your commercial acumen.

**Discussion of money:** It is just the wrong place to do this and makes you look like a novice. Do this with the agent or, if contracting direct, with the client's HR people after you've successfully completed the interview. Never discuss money with your prospective project manager or other people that might be interviewing you. That said, there is nothing wrong by finishing with, 'Are you comfortable with the rate I've quoted?'. This is useful to know as sometimes the agent may try and negotiate you down on a rate by saying the client cannot afford you.

**Know it all:** Don't give the impression you know everything. No one likes an ego – they wreck teams, cause mayhem and ultimately don't complete the contract as it should be, preferring to complete it in the way they 'know' is best.

## Been there, done that!

## Reference blues

**DAVE SAYS:** Agents often used to ring up and say 'We have this great role at a City bank, for excellent money, are you interested?'. Of course you are. Then they say something like, "Great, I've got your CV but I need two references before I put you forward."

I fell for this one twice, until I realised those roles never existed in the first place. They were just phishing for leads. You NEVER have to provide references to secure an interview when you are contracting. The only time it will ever happen is when the client has offered you the role.

The agent will want to cover their back by getting some evidence that they have in fact sourced someone who is suitable, otherwise the client could sue them if you make a colossal error. Once you've had the offer then it's fine, of course, to give out references. Doing this your ex-boss won't be pestered anywhere near as much and there's more chance they'll give you a better reference!

**Lack of interest:** Lack of knowledge about the company, the sector and the project will show you are not that bothered. Do some homework about the company.

**Boring:** No one likes working with someone who is dull. Use your sense of humour, within reason, and relax and be yourself.

## 5.7 Negotiation

Assuming the interview was a success, you are now in a good position to negotiate the rate you want with your soon-to-be agent. You have either had a go-ahead from the client, or a lot of encouragement. That means you now tell the agency you want a rate that is at the top end of the range you previously discussed, or maybe a little bit more if you have been offered more elsewhere.

The agency is so close to signing a deal that they will almost certainly accommodate a slightly reduced margin if it means closing the deal, getting a reasonable margin and being able to move on to the next deal. If you decide to walk away now, the agent risks annoying the client, losing money and possibly losing out to another agency. What happens if the agency refuses or says they want to think about it? The course of action is to play the game and just let them dither. They will usually come back to you soon enough. Again though, the important thing here is that everyone is happy with the deal that gets struck.

But you do need to consider whether or not you want to lose the deal altogether. For each deal you refuse you are likely to spend a certain amount of time out of work, unless you have a few on the table at once. You earn nothing when you're not working, so you need to decide if the extra money is worth it for you to say 'no'.

When the agency calls back, agree to the deal if you want to, and then ask the agency to send on the contract as soon as possible – you will want to review this before going any further. Chapter 7 will help you to know what to consider at this point.

If you are contracting direct with the client, negotiating fair and market-based contract rates that are based on equivalent permanent employee salaries and tax calculations is a red herring, as the two costs are not directly comparable. However, you may find that clients use the cost of what they see as equivalent employees as part of their negotiating position. But the comparison is invalid, as contractors are business-to-business service providers supplying their specialist skills to clients on projects with a defined duration and outcome. Permanent employees have a totally different and long-term relationship with their employer; they enjoy a range of benefits that are both financial, such as pension schemes, and intangible, such as employment rights, which contractors do not.

Bear in mind that negotiating a higher rate when your contract is up for renewal makes no financial sense for the agent. The returns to the agency on negotiating a higher rate are generally minimal. After all, they receive a percentage commission of your fees – generally between 4% and 20% – and if they negotiate an extra £25 per day, for them that's between an extra £22 and £110 a month (£25 x 22 days x 4%/20%). Contrast that with the £352 to £1,760 per month an agent landing a new contractor at £400 per day can expect to receive (£400 x 22 days x 4%/20%).

Clearly, the most sensible commercial course of action is for agents to maximise the number of new contract positions they fill, and try to avoid having to spend too much time renegotiating rates for contract renewals. It's important to remember that as a starting point when trying to increase the rate you get at contract renewal time – there's very little incentive for an agent to push this.

But losing one of their 'bums on a seat' is potentially a different story altogether for the agent, and this is where negotiation is similar to playing poker. In theory, the player holding the worst hand should 'lose', but the sign of an expert contractor is one who still comes out on top, even with a terrible hand. A contractor with less-developed negotiating skills may hold all the aces, but can still lose the game. So, unless you can impress upon your agent that you are indeed holding a hand worthy of note to justify a rate increase, then you should expect to receive the brush-off.

## 5.8 Contract offer

The agent will be keen to have you sign the contract immediately to finalise the deal and secure their revenue stream. However, before signing, it is important you have your contract checked by a qualified lawyer, and preferably a specialist in contractor affairs and IR35.

This is to ensure the terms are fair, and most importantly to establish your IR35 position, which was introduced in chapter 3 and is covered in more detail in chapter 8. Failure to invest a little time and money at this stage could potentially cost you huge sums in the future, as has been found out by contractors investigated by HMRC who have been found not to have got the paperwork right from the start.

## Been there, done that!

### Have it checked

**DAVE SAYS:** I started contracting before IR35 even existed, and in those days contractors rarely got their contracts checked by lawyers. Provided there were no crazy clauses about working silly hours for nothing, we tended just to sign them. The contracting landscape is very different now, though, and a legal review is essential if you plan on staying outside IR35.

If you've never used a lawyer before, don't baulk at the process or the cost – it is not difficult and neither is it too expensive. Remember, you should be earning a lot more as a contractor and using a lawyer should be seen as buying you peace of mind and ultimately saving you money. Contractor reviews may seem expensive, but litigation because you have failed to invest in a review can make the cost pale into insignificance! The contract will require the name of the company who the agency will be doing business with – either your own limited company or an umbrella company, both of which are dealt with in future chapters.

After negotiating and agreeing the contract it is simply a case of liaising with the agent to sign it. Most will be keen for this to happen as soon as possible to close the deal, although some will send them via post for your signature and return.

## 5.8.1 Obtaining security clearance

Contractors offered contracts in many government and public sector departments will find they are asked if they have security clearance, or will be required to obtain it, before they can start work. Those routinely requiring contractors with security clearance include:

- Central Government

- Ministry of Defence

- Home Office

- Foreign & Commonwealth Office

- Ministry of Justice

- Office of National Statistics.

In addition, security clearance is likely to be required if working on certain projects for a client that is linked with, or has been retained by, one of the above.

Entry level security clearance is known as the 'BPSS', or Baseline Personnel Security Standard. Although this is not technically a security clearance, it is in effect a Police National Computer (PNC) check to make sure the contractor candidate has no unspent convictions.

The first actual security clearance is the Counter-Terrorist Check, which is commonly required by the police, legal agencies and government agencies hiring contractors. Next up is the 'SC', which stands for Security Clearance and is the most frequently used. It is transferable between government departments, valid for five years for contractors, and ten years for permanent employees.

Some roles require even more stringent checks, so after the SC comes the DV, or Developed Vetting. This is much more specialised and job related. A contractor would go to a specific contract role within a specific organisation and the developed vetting would be tailored specifically to that contract. Because the level of checking increases substantially the higher you move up the security levels, so the time taken to achieve clearance increases, from a typical 14-day wait for BPSS to up to six months for Developed Vetting.

You can apply online for the BPSS clearance and are sent the certificate direct. CTC and SC checks can take up to four to six weeks and involve in-depth background checks conducted by the Defence Vetting Agency, the main government agency that carries out national security vetting. DV is very in-depth and requires personal interviews, as contractors with this level of clearance are likely to have substantial, potentially unsupervised, access to top-secret material.

Cabinet Office guidance confirms that security clearance is not required by a contractor before they apply for a contract. Nor should it be a condition of a contract unless the duration of the contract is likely to be less than the time taken for the clearance to come through, unless there is an urgent operational requirement.

## 5.9 Starting the contract

Starting a contract is not the same as starting a new job when in permanent employment. The client is expecting the contractor to hit the ground running, with no gentle introduction to colleagues, lunches on the first day, silver business card holders or staff induction programmes. Work starts immediately.

As with the interview, do your preparation before you arrive on the first day. Chances are, the location of the interview will be the client's site and the person who conducted the interview will be the project manager. But don't assume this – check beforehand. The client's site, which should always be referred to as such, is not your permanent place of work. If you're working through your own limited company which has a home office, that is your principal place of work.

Why is this important? Because as a contractor you can enjoy travel and subsistence allowances, which will reduce the amount of tax you pay. The client's site is not your place of work so you can claim travel to and from this location, plus subsistence costs like lunches when working on site (but not in the staff canteen! – see chapter 8 to find out why).

Know what time and date you are due to start the contract. As most contracts start very quickly, this is an easier mistake to make than you would imagine, and if a major project is being launched the day you are supposed to start, with project team briefings arranged for many contractors and client employees, arriving a day late will not be popular, and is technically a breach of contract (remember, you are no longer a permanent employee, but a company/contractor providing a service).

Get to know your colleagues and your way around quickly, and get used to doing this. Establishing and maintaining good working relationships is essential not just for the current contract, but also as a source of future contracts. If you are both good at what you do and great to work with people will remember you.

## Been there, done that!

### Keep it brief

**DAVE SAYS:** Once you are on site, in most cases there are other contractors like you and everyone eventually gets around to the 'how much are you charging?' conversation. That's when you'll be able to gauge if you think you got a good deal or not from the agent. That's why, on your first contract, it's important not to commit for a year; give yourself a chance to learn the ropes by starting your contracting career with shorter contracts.

## 5.10 Getting paid

One of the main drivers for becoming a contractor is of course to earn more money. This requires you having a payment mechanism in place so that the agency, or the client if you are contracting direct, can actually pay you. Depending on the nature of the contract and whether it is inside or outside IR35, you will need to decide on a trading option (covered in chapter 6) and then deal with the admin associated with this option. Most contractors either work through their own limited company or an umbrella company, and there will be different payment methods for each.

You need to find out from the agent how their payment mechanism works. Most contractors are paid weekly or monthly and the process is generally:

- The contractor works their hours during the week, completes a weekly timesheet and submits this for sign-off by the client's representative, usually the project manager

- The copy of the signed-off timesheet is sent to the agent or umbrella company by the contractor

- The agent or umbrella company does the sums – typically hourly rate times hours worked – and invoices the client accordingly (in the agent's case the hourly rate will be higher to allow for their margin)

- The contractor working for an agent through their own limited company directly invoices the agent for their fees; contractors working through an umbrella company are paid their PAYE 'salary' by their umbrella company 'employer'.

The above process has been simplified and there are complications regarding Value Added Tax (VAT), travel and subsistence costs and other issues, all of which are covered in later chapters in more detail. It is important for contractors to keep on top of their paperwork. It is worth the effort as the financial rewards can be considerable.

## 5.11 Using social media and social media marketing to win contracts

Contractors may not only use social media to help them win contracts, but can also develop social media marketing campaigns to ensure the best and most lucrative contracts come their way.

As with any marketing channel, social media requires you to have clear objectives as to what you want your social media presence to achieve. And with so many social networks, it is important to focus on those that are most relevant and targeted, and will offer the greatest return on your investment in time, and potentially cash.

Well managed social media marketing can open up new markets and inspire trust, loyalty and repeat business from clients and recruiters. But getting a social media campaign wrong can lead to an online 'train crash', potentially damaging your personal branding and reputation, thereby reducing your chances of winning contracts.

### 5.11.1 What are 'social media' and 'social media marketing'?

Social media, or social networking sites, are simply online communities where users can interact with each other socially to share views, experiences and knowledge in an informal and often fun way. The word 'social' is often a misnomer as businesses, particularly consumer-oriented brands, engage with their customers through what is essentially another marketing channel. Similarly, organisations are using social media to communicate with clients, investors, suppliers and employees. Some of the currently most widely used social media sites include:

- **Facebook**, which is mainly used by individuals to socialise and spread information, although companies and other organisations use it as a marketing and advertising tool

- **Google+** is similar to Facebook and growing rapidly. It not only has similar functionality to Facebook, but also integrates with other Google products and services. Popular features include 'Circles', which allow users to easily organise and network with different groups of their contacts

- **LinkedIn** is the professional network for individuals, businesses and organisations. Because this is the first place many recruiters and clients look to research your professional background, LinkedIn is a potentially powerful social media marketing tool for you

- **Twitter** enables contractors to send tweets (short messages or 'micro blogs'), either by 'broadcasting' them to a global audience or to specific Twitter users. By regularly tweeting and about key business related topics, and by 'conversing' with peers, you can demonstrate your knowledge of a specific subject and enhance your personal brand as an expert in that area. This can be further strengthened by engaging in discussions using hashtags

- **YouTube** is used to upload and share video and multimedia content. A video can be found on virtually any and every topic imaginable. Businesses use YouTube for product and service videos, training and education and news, among other uses. Contractors can use videos to demonstrate their expertise, to engage with prospective clients and recruiters, and to share information with peers. Videos from YouTube, and similar sites, can also be embedded into your website

- **Blogs and forums** are not, strictly speaking, part of social media, but by running your own blog, posting regularly to a highly regarded specialist forum, or commenting on the posts made by others, users can achieve the same marketing objectives as, for example, speaking regularly at seminars and events.

The above list is by no means exhaustive and new social media platforms and networks appear regularly. There are an increasing number of niche social media evolving, which focus on specific topics, technical areas, markets and sectors. In addition, other social networks allow people to share things more easily and to offer information in different ways – Pinterest is a good example.

## 5.11.2 Choosing the right social media platform

Contractors don't need to have a Facebook page, Google+ page, Twitter following, LinkedIn profile, YouTube channel, blog and strong presence on relevant forums all in one go. As with 'traditional' marketing channels that you may use to build and publicise your personal brand, such as writing white papers, networking, seminars, joining committees, advertising, etc doing one or more things well will give a greater return than doing everything adequately, or badly.

So, for example, if there are existing LinkedIn groups that focus on specific technical competencies that you want to highlight as part of your skill set, then creating and maintaining a strong LinkedIn profile and engaging with those groups might be part of an effective social media marketing strategy.

Equally, you may be operating in a fast-paced environment where new advances occur daily and the community working in this sector is highly tech-savvy. An effective method of demonstrating a grasp of cutting-edge techniques is through regularly tweeting or commenting on the latest developments as they occur. In this context, building a strong Twitter following, and investing time in regular tweets, can remind potential clients that you are not only out there, but on top of your game.

Or it may be that you simply want a 'shop window', but do not have the tools or time to create a dedicated business website; so you could choose to set up business Facebook, Google+ and LinkedIn pages that can act as an online brochure for your skills and services.

If you really want to restrict your social media marketing activity, you should probably focus on LinkedIn and Twitter, as evidence at the time of writing suggests that these two networks are used by more recruiters than Facebook.

### 5.11.3 How social media marketing can help win contracts

If used correctly, social media marketing is another highly focused sales and marketing tool, but unlike a brochure or advertisement it can't just be left. Regularly maintaining your social media presence, even when working on a current assignment, demonstrates that a contractor is still active and still an expert in their field.

By blogging about technical topics, or tweeting useful links, you can demonstrate that you are not only technically proficient, but also that you may be a 'guru' or 'thought-leader' – that could give you an edge when up against another similarly qualified contractor for a plum contract.

And, increasingly, online multi-media CVs, social media profiles and other non-traditional non-CV-based résumés are becoming the preferred option for tech-savvy clients and recruiters looking for contractors who can differentiate themselves. For example, at the time of writing more contractors are adding QR ('quick response') codes to their CVs and business cards, which link to YouTube videos demonstrating their expertise.

### 5.11.4 Avoiding a personal brand 'train crash'

The messaging used in social media should be consistent with what you use in your CV. That way, when a client or agency decides to research your background after receiving a CV by email, they won't find obvious gaps in your experience, or worrying inconsistencies that could lead to larger questions.

Even if the inconsistency is a mistake, and not due to some underlying and more sinister issue, it may not present the professional persona that you may wish to convey. And you should keep your online social life totally separate from your professional profile online, just as you would in the office and at home.

Social media offers powerful tools to help contractors win new business. Building and maintaining a social media presence online need not be a hugely time consuming and expensive task, and can pay dividends when it leads to winning new contracts. It can also be fun!

# Contracting lessons from this chapter

- Make yourself known by uploading your CV to the online databases, and using social media.

- Understand what agencies are, and are not, so you can work with them effectively. Remember that although agencies do not work for you, they do need you.

- Identify your preferred formal sales process, and systematically chase those contracts using that process.

- Contracting direct with the client has its advantages, but also its pitfalls, not least of which is the chance of not being paid on time.

- Your interview is a sales meeting to discuss the product – you. So always prepare thoroughly.

- Learn the basics of negotiation to maximise your earnings, and remember you are not negotiating an employment package.

- Make sure you have any legal paperwork reviewed by a specialist. A relatively small expense up front could save you a huge expense at a later date.

# 6

# How to set up and run your business

# 6.1 Introduction

Now you have got you first contract, you will need to create the correct trading vehicle and supporting administration to ensure that you can get paid and are working within the law.

The UK has a variety of ways a contractor can do business, and section 6.2 covers these. However, in practice, most contractors will be either working through their own limited company or through an umbrella company.

A limited company carries a certain burden of administration, duties and responsibilities; they are after all separate legal entities in their own right and the contractor is responsible for ensuring that they are run in accordance with UK law.

However, the major advantage of a limited company is that a contractor can take home a higher proportion of their income through entirely legal tax efficient procedures and, should they desire, be able to make significant provision for retirement or semi-retirement.

Umbrella companies remove most of the administrative burden and much of the responsibility. They allow you to introduce some expenses-related tax efficiencies and you can channel your income into a pension. However, the opportunity to earn and save is lower compared to a limited company.

There is a threshold at which the costs of running a limited company are higher than the tax benefits. This is approximately £25 per hour, although the exact amount will depend on your personal circumstances. If you are paid less than this amount, an umbrella company may be the best option.

It is also important to understand that the nature of the contract with the client may dictate the most tax efficient way to trade. If the contractor is outside the IR35 tax legislation (covered in chapter 8), then it is generally much more effective to work through a limited company. If the contractor is caught by IR35, which means the taxman will treat them as an employee regardless of how they trade, it may be more advantageous for some contractors to use umbrella companies – if they're being taxed as employees, why should they have the burden of a limited company without the financial benefits? Let someone else take the strain.

The final and most important factor that dictates trading options for contractors – and limits most to either limited or umbrella companies – is that clients and agents tend to insist on them.

Most simply will not work with sole traders, although that insistence may change over time following the creation of a new kind of intermediary service provider. But for now, they will insist on having the additional layer of the limited company or umbrella company between them and the contractor. That way, there can be little or no doubt in the taxman's mind that the contractor is not a permanent employee of the client.

## 6.2 Your trading options

### 6.2.1 Limited company

For many contractors, including those new to contracting, a limited company is the ideal solution to maximise all those benefits that led them into contracting in the first place: more net income, flexibility, a better lifestyle, provision for their future, ring-fenced personal and business assets – the list goes on. However, there is an administrative burden of running a limited company that other trading options do not have, or have less of.

A limited company is a separate legal trading entity from the contractor. This means that the company can enter into agreements that are separate from the contractor, like bank loans or lease hire agreements and, most importantly, contracts.

Incorporation of a limited company is a quick and cost-effective process (see section 6.3.1), which usually results in the contractor becoming a director and shareholder of the company. Some contractors have spouses, family members or business colleagues as co-directors and/or shareholders.

Once the limited company is formed and a bank account is opened, the contractor can issue invoices for contracts and start trading. It's as quick and easy as that. However, if you have a poor credit record and County Court Judgements (CCJs) then you may find it very difficult to open a business bank account, which would rule out a limited company as your trading option.

The major difference between a permanent employee being paid a salary once a month, with National Insurance Contributions (NICs) and Pay As You Earn (PAYE) income tax deducted at source, and limited scope to claim for expenses and a contractor being paid through their own limited company can be summed up in one word: dividends.

Shareholders in a limited company receive some or all of their income via dividends instead of salary. Dividends do attract income tax for higher and additional rate taxpayers, but this is calculated some time after the dividends have been paid. And, importantly, dividends do not attract NICs.

Also, because a contractor's legitimate expenses are deductible from their limited company, this can add considerably to their net earnings, mainly by reducing the overall amount on which they have to pay tax. Not only that, but as most contractors will have gross billings in a year that exceed the value added tax (VAT) threshold, they can also save significant sums on purchases, by being able to reclaim the VAT. Further savings are possible for those companies able to enrol on the VAT flat rate scheme (FRS).

On balance, the limited company route is one of the best and lowest risk trading vehicles for maximising earnings. And although the administration can be a nuisance, even this can be considerably reduced by using accountants and other service providers, whose charges are generally a relatively small percentage of the additional income being earned by the contractor.

## 6.2.2 Umbrella company

An umbrella company is, in simple terms, a way for the contractor to "outsource" their payroll to the umbrella company, so that they effectively become a PAYE employee. Umbrella companies are also sometimes referred to as umbrella solution providers and employment management companies.

If caught within IR35, and therefore not able to benefit from limited company status, rather than having the cost and bother of setting up a limited company, a contractor can simply work via an umbrella company, or 'brolly'. The advantage of working via an umbrella company versus, say, an agency's payroll or via a fixed-term employment contract direct with the client, is that contractors can claim expenses and offset them against their tax liabilities.

The umbrella company itself is a perfectly legitimate limited company, with the usual associated shareholders, directors, articles of association and so on. Using this solution, the contractor would not be a director nor have the responsibilities associated with running a limited company. The umbrella company provider would take care of all accountancy and taxation matters, and also deal with most of the administration matters.

It is the umbrella company that enters into the contract with the agency or client, and not the contractor. The contractor is employed by the umbrella company and simply completes a timesheet and forwards it to the umbrella company, which then invoices the agent or client. Following payment by the agent to the umbrella company, a payment is made by the umbrella company to the contractor net of income tax and National Insurance Contributions (NICs), just as if they were a permanent employee. Unlike regular employees, though, the contractor also pays the umbrella company its agreed fee and charges.

Umbrella companies usually have a management team responsible for matters relating to the company and accounts and so on, and a client services team who liaise with contractors on a day to day basis. In this context, the contractor is the client and pays a fee to the umbrella company for the umbrella's services, usually a fixed fee per month.

A PAYE Umbrella treats all your income as salary. This means you pay the employer's NICs, employees NICs and PAYE on all your income. Umbrella company contractors also benefit from tax relief on travel and subsistence expenses and pension contributions. In addition, they can make VAT 'savings' if the umbrella allows the purchase of capital equipment, such as computers.

### 6.2.3 Partnerships and LLPs

Contractors will almost certainly find that there is no particular advantage in choosing a partnership or Limited Liability Partnership (LLP) instead of a limited company as the main vehicle for their businesses.

LLPs were originally created for professionals like accountants and lawyers who wanted to group their companies into large associations of partners. The big accounting firms still use this form of business so that they can share profits, but keep expenses and problems separate.

The advantage of LLPs is that the partners can split all income between them as dividends. You can also do this in a limited company, but the recordkeeping obligations for LLPs are far less complex.

Similar to a partnership, a LLP consists of two or more persons who agree to share a business. They are obliged to register their partnership with Companies House, just like a limited company. The partnership then becomes a company that can do almost everything a limited company can do: own property, sign contracts, incur debts and so on. Liability is limited to the money that the partners invested in the business and any personal guarantees they have given to raise finance.

The difference between a LLP and a limited company is that the LLP cannot issue shares, or hold share capital, nor does it have company directors. The rules that govern how shareholders interact with company assets don't apply to LLPs.

There are a number of disadvantages that LLPs suffer. Because those in the LLP enjoy limited liability, the protection of those dealing with an LLP requires that the LLP maintain accounting records, and that it prepares and delivers audited annual accounts to Companies House. The exemptions available to limited companies, for example with respect to the delivery of abbreviated accounts and exemption from audit, also apply to LLPs.

What is different here for LLPs is that they cannot keep anything secret; all financial information must be disclosed, whereas a limited company runs its finances according to its own requirements. This is not a problem for a major accounting firm, but could be one for a small business.

Then there is a certain amount of legal uncertainty related to running a LLP. The LLP is a relatively new structure in British law, and both HMRC and the courts may not react predictably to it. So unless you have a very good reason for wanting to form a LLP, it's probably best avoided.

### 6.2.4 Sole Trader

Sole traders are probably the oldest trading option known to humankind, where someone has a skill or product to sell – be they stone tools or financial services – and they conduct a transaction directly with the buyer. There is no intermediary, such as a limited company or umbrella company.

Trading as a sole trader can be highly tax efficient, particularly for a tradesperson working from home, as a significant amount of costs can be put through the sole trader's business, reducing their overall income tax and NICs. There is also the greatly reduced regulatory and administrative burden. Tax paperwork for sole traders is much simpler and there is virtually no regulatory burden outside of tax legislation.

To many contractors, the option of trading as a sole trader must be very attractive. But, until relatively recently, the major barrier to contractors wanting to work on contracts as sole traders has been a reluctance on the part of agencies and clients to sign contracts with sole traders. Because there has traditionally been no intermediary, such as a limited company, umbrella company or partnership, the risks of the contractor being considered by HMRC to be an employee with full employment rights is too great for any client.

The other major reason why agencies and clients have been unwilling to contract directly with sole traders is because if the contractor does not pay their full tax and NICs, the agency or client is liable to HMRC for these costs under debt transfer legislation.

With contracting service providers being an enterprising and creative bunch, it was only a matter of time before someone came up with a solution to the sole trader conundrum. And they have in the form of a new kind of intermediary. These new intermediaries – which have yet to gain an industry label – contract directly with the agency or client and supply the contractor's service on a subcontract basis.

The existence of the intermediary transfers the employment rights and debt transfer risk from the client and agency to the intermediary. Only a few service providers of this type are trading at the time of writing in early 2012, and so far contracting has yet to see widespread acceptance of the trading model by agencies and clients.

A potential renaissance of the sole trader trading model for contractors seems some way off.

## 6.2.5 Managed Service Companies

Service providers offering a Managed Service Company (MSC) used to provide contractors with a composite company solution to manage their invoicing and accounting. This typically meant that twenty contractors became non-director shareholders and the company was managed by the organisation running the scheme, usually called the scheme provider, which managed all the administration, invoicing, accountancy and so on.

The contractors were then paid a low salary plus dividends, in addition to claiming various expenses allowable under the corporate structure. This method of payment used to provide many financial benefits, since it avoided large amounts of National Insurance and income tax that would otherwise be payable if the contractor was paid entirely by salary.

But contractors are generally well advised to avoid any company which offers to manage their limited company for them, or which suggests putting them into a limited company it shares with others. Why?

Well, MSCs were once a widely-used trading option for contractors, but have been regulated out of existence by legislation introduced in 2007. The MSC legislation requires contractors using a service provider that meets the legislation's definition of an MSC to treat all income, including dividends, as employment income and therefore subject to income tax and NICs.

If you are concerned that your service provider, or a service provider you are considering, might be classified as an MSC, you should apply the following tests:

- The service provider controls, or attempts to control, the provision of the contractor's services to their client

- The service provider controls the contractor limited company's finances and bank accounts

- The service provider negotiates contracts with end-user clients and agencies without including the contractor in the dialogue

- The service provider insists on becoming a company officer, such as a director or company secretary of the contractor's limited company

- The service provider is clearly lax in its attitude to regulation, such as allowing expenses that HMRC rules say should not be allowed

- There are financial ties between the service provider and the agency or recruitment business that provides work for the contractor

- The service provider undertakes any services that influence the control of the contractor's limited company.

If the service provider fails any of the above tests, it may well be in breach of the MSC rules and you would be well advised to steer well clear. If you're still tempted, take specialist professional advice before proceeding.

## 6.2.6 Using an offshore trading solution

An alternative trading option for contractors with more adventurous risk profiles and who are seeking to substantially reduce their tax liabilities is an offshore tax solution. Providers of these take advantage of complex tax legislation and double taxation treaties, and so are typically based in jurisdictions outside of the UK, such as the Isle of Man, Channel Islands and parts of the Caribbean.

Service providers often advertise substantial increases in net income, up to 90% of contract value in some cases. However, contractor offshore solutions should be treated with caution and are not appropriate for all contractors. Many solutions only offer genuine benefits to very high earners and the offshore route does not fit the risk profile of some contractors, even the higher earners who could benefit most.

Prior to December 2009, the most common offshore trading solution was the employee benefit trust (EBT). The way contractor EBTs worked was to pay contractors a small salary and loan the remainder of the contract value, less fees, to the contractor. Because the cash is in theory a loan and not income, the contractor paid no tax on it. But anti-avoidance legislation that came into force in December 2009 resulted in EBTs losing their tax advantages, so contractors should be wary of any schemes still promoting their services.

Solutions still currently available include devalued currency loans and pension schemes. Devalued currency loans are complex loan-based arrangements that rely on currency devaluation to reduce the paper value of the loan over time to virtually zero. This leaves the contractor with few or no liabilities, despite having 'borrowed' to the value of the contract.

S615 pension schemes are popular with some contractors working overseas. These schemes allow a pension pot to be created over time, and this eventually converts into a tax-free lump sum for the contractor.

If you are considering an offshore trading solution, to ensure that you are taking the right decision that fits not only your commercial and financial profiles, but also and most importantly your risk profile, you should:

- Make sure you understand the entire arrangement and commercial steps in the process

- Check that the scheme is fully disclosed to the UK authorities

- Examine claims about HMRC approval or tax counsel's opinion to ensure your circumstances match the details that have been approved or given an opinion on

- Seek advice from an independent third party – a qualified accountant or tax expert

- Make sure you fully understand and are comfortable with the risks you are taking on.

New offshore solutions are being developed by creative service providers all the time but, as with EBTs, HM Treasury is constantly developing ways to combat what it perceives as barely legal avoidance. If your personal appetite for financial risk is cautious, offshore trading solutions are probably best avoided.

## 6.3 Setting up and running a limited company

Creating and running a limited company may seem like a daunting task for new contractors, but as long as the process is understood, you are organised and you use the right professional advice at the right time, it does not have to be onerous or costly. In fact, setting up your limited company can be remarkably quick, inexpensive and easy.

### 6.3.1 Choosing an accountant

Whilst some contractors attempt to manage their accounting and tax affairs themselves, this is not the most efficient way of doing things and can result in all sorts of time-consuming and costly problems if mistakes are made.

So, when answering the question, 'do I need an accountant?' the answer is almost certainly 'yes'. And not just any old accountant from your local high street. Ideally, you should select a specialist contractor accountant with a strong track record of dealing with clients from the contracting sector.

Increasingly, contractor accountancy service providers are providing a 'true' online service. Online contractor accountants provide an interactive online portal that enables you to upload expenses and timesheets, issue invoices and manage your tax and VAT affairs entirely online and usually in real-time, with phone support when needed.

If you are seeking a more personalised service with a hotline to your personal accountant, who you should ensure is the tax partner, then you will find that you will have to pay the appropriate fee. With accountancy, like many professional services, you simply cannot get something for nothing.

For a comprehensive and specialist service, you should expect to be paying £60-£150 per month, at the time of writing. Bear in mind that as a contractor you are running a business, so you may be able to negotiate a better deal, and should ensure you are getting exactly what you need.

Check carefully what is included in the price – some providers adopt a budget airline model and offer cheaper options, charging extra for completing personal tax returns and other paperwork. It's important to know what other services might be charged as 'extras'; what to you might seem like a quick conversation for a bit of friendly advice, might be charged to you by your accountant as professional consultancy services.

If you feel you are not getting the service you should from your accountant, then it is not a problem to change, as long as you stick to any agreed contract terms. There will be a certain amount of disruption, but it will fairly quickly settle back into a routine again.

As with many service providers, those that come with a personal recommendation from a friend or colleague generally work out well; similarly, asking others for advice will help you find out which accountants to avoid.

When choosing your contractor accountant, ensure the accountant can convincingly answer the following questions:

- What is IR35 and how might it affect me?

- Would I be affected by the settlements legislation Section 624 (formerly known as Section 660) 'family' or 'husband and wife' tax?

- Can you advice me on how to ensure I don't fall foul of the Managed Service Company (MSC) legislation?

- What are the most tax efficient routes to extracting earnings and profits from my contracting business?

- Can you explain how limited company expenses work for contractors?

- Can you tell me how much experience you have advising contractors?

You can download a free and comprehensive checklist, *Contractor Accountant Pricing – Costs to Consider checklist*, from contractorcalculator.co.uk. This has been specifically designed to help you select a contractor accountant best suited to your requirements.

## 6.3.2 Registering a company

The limited company is an organisation that is called a 'moral person' in law: this means that it has its own identity and does business under its own name. It makes or loses money, can acquire debt and pay taxes all by itself, just like a physical person.

Understanding this is important, because it explains why the legal formation of a limited company works the way it does. Just as a baby is registered in the birth rolls when it is born, a company is registered in the official list of companies when you start it. This list is kept by Companies House.

Choose a name for your company, decide where it is based, and decide who's going to be part of it. Try choosing a general name that does not have your name, which may have IR35 implications, and allows some latitude if you branch out in the future.

Let's look at a typical example: "World's Greatest Contractors Ltd." which is being set up by the imaginary contractors John and Joan Dunn. John and Joan will both work for the company, and so they issue £100 worth of ordinary shares that they divide between them, with each owning 50%.

In this division of ordinary shares, dividends paid out will have to be proportional to the shareholding division, but only for ordinary shares. In other words, in the example, each gets 50% of dividend income, but this would not be the case if a preferential share division is used.

They could also include any other shareholders in the company that they might choose to have, so long as the total amount of shares is divided proportionately to the capital (the total number of shares).

John and Joan are also not obliged to issue ordinary shares: there are many different types of shares, for example preference shares, which are linked to specific rules related to the company's operations. If you seek a structure of this kind, you should probably take advice from a professional, as it has tax implications and could significantly affect your earnings if you get it wrong.

Once you've made all the decisions above, you have a choice of options for filing the company:

- Online at Companies House, or via Business Link's website and, for a fee of less than £20 + VAT at the time of writing, set up your company. The online forms will guide you through the setup process. Companies House will check to confirm that the name you've chosen is not in use, and it will ask you to appoint a company director and a company secretary, should your business require one.

- Use a company formation agent, who will go through a very similar process but may be in a position to recommend alternative structures you may not have thought of. Online formation agents advertise incorporation for as little as £4.99, but beware of other chargeable services that might be bundled as a condition of this offer. Fees can vary between £4.99 and well in excess of £100+ for an online service, and VAT will be added

- Use an accountant, who will quite often bundle incorporation into a range of services, such as recommending different share types for tax purposes and supplying standard documents, with correspondingly higher fees. Many contractor accountants will include incorporation as part of their fixed fee package for new contractor clients.

In our example, Joan takes the company directorship and John becomes the company secretary, although one person could take on both roles. Being a director has certain legal responsibilities, which are important and covered in section 6.3.13.

If you chose to file at Companies House yourself, you will also need to file articles of association. This is a document that tells everyone why you've set up the company and how you plan to run it. This document can have significant legal importance in tax disputes and any legal proceedings.

Fortunately, a useful by product of the Companies Act 2006 was Companies House's creation of new model articles of association. All businesses incorporated after 1 October 2009 will have the new model articles applied by default. The new model articles also mean a memorandum of association is no longer required and companies can be incorporated by a single person.

When incorporating online, the service provider will require you to input some quite detailed information and it is useful to have this to hand before you start the process. Online formation agents vary in their exact requirements, but be prepared to provide:

- A company name
- The type of private company: limited by shares or limited by guarantee (limited by shares is generally the best option of contractors)
- Share capital: 1,000 ordinary shares valued at £1 per share is a common choice

- Details of directors and the company secretary, if you have one

- Shareholder details and the number of shares allocated to each.

When inputting online details of company officers, ie the directors, there is no opportunity to create a paper trail or capture signatures. As a result, online formation agents would normally request additional information for each director, so have at least three of the following to hand before you start:

- Passport and National Insurance numbers

- Town of birth

- Eye colour

- Mother's maiden name

- Father's first name.

The online registration will also usually ask for things like the last three digits of the telephone number or the first three letters of the town where the company officer was born, which is why it's useful to have this information handy before you begin!

Contractors incorporating a new limited company must also complete a Statement of Capital. This includes information about the types of shares issued and their status. A Statement of Capital requires the following information:

- The total number of shares created for the company

- The 'aggregate nominal value' of the company's shares, which will typically be £1

- If there are different classes of shares, a breakdown of each of the share types and the 'aggregate nominal value' of the shares in each class

- For all shares, the amount of shares that are 'paid up' and those that are 'unpaid'

- Share currency.

It can take Companies House as little as three hours for an online incorporation to be processed. So you should be wary of online service providers that charge a premium for 'same-day' and 'fast track' applications, as many of these simply rely on the regular speed of the efficient Companies House service.

Once the incorporation has been processed and completed, you will be emailed the certificate of incorporation. This includes the all-important company number, which is essential for setting up bank accounts and registering with HMRC and recruitment agencies, and is also useful when setting up accounts with suppliers.

The new limited company is now ready to start trading.

### 6.3.3 Getting a business bank account

Your contractor limited company is a separate legal entity from you. As such, it requires its own bank account to accept payments from agencies and clients, and to pay for business expenses. The types of activity going through your account will be:

- Receiving money from clients or agents for your work
- Paying your own salary
- Paying dividends
- Paying monthly NICs and PAYE taxes, plus annual Corporation Tax
- Claiming for personal expenses incurred
- Direct debits for items like smartphones and internet connections
- Paying for other business expenses, such as accountant's fees
- Payments to the company credit card
- VAT payments (if you are registered).

UK money laundering regulations mean that in almost every instance before your account can be opened you will be required to present documents confirming your identity and address. This can usually be done either in person at a branch, by mail or by submitting scanned documents online. That means opening an account is rarely an instant process, no matter what banks might claim in their marketing materials, and so you should plan ahead.

Contractors with a poor credit history may find it very difficult to open a business bank account; some high street banks will even refuse an application from contractors who do not have a perfect or near-perfect credit rating. But if this affects you, shop around: there are banks willing to welcome business customers who don't have perfect credit scores.

During the application process, whether it's by telephone, online or in person at a branch, banks will ask you to provide a wealth of business and personal information, typically including:

- Your contact details

- Your contracting business name

- Your business address, which is most likely to be your home address or possibly your accountant's address

- Nature of the business – most banks will class contracting as 'business services' or 'business consultancy'

- Your business's legal status, usually a limited company for contractors

- Business start date, which would usually be the date when you started incurring start-up expenses

- Anticipated turnover – a calculation or estimate of the first year's contract fees will normally suffice

- Any funding requirements, although most contracting businesses do not require loans or overdrafts

- Incorporation details and a copy of the contractor limited company's incorporation certificate.

Some banks say they need to see a business plan, but in practice contractors are unlikely to be expected to provide one. Increasingly, banks say that pre-application interviews are no longer necessary to open an account, but when contacting a bank it is advisable to have the above information to hand, as some or all of it is likely to be requested.

Factors to consider when choosing a business banking package for a contracting business include:

- Choose a well-known high street or online brand. If

considering a lesser known or niche bank, contractors should check with other business owners who use the bank and be sure the specific benefits of using this provider outweigh any risks

- The type and amount of account charges, such as account fees, cheque fees, card charges, bank transfer fees and so on

- Does the business account offer features such as company credit and debit cards, in addition to business cheque books?

- Start-up packages that include periods of free business banking; many banks offer new customers free banking for 12, 18 or 24 months, while others offer free banking 'for life' for members of some business/professional associations

- The availability of telephone and online banking; these are crucial factors for contractors based at client sites without convenient local bank branches

- Interest on deposit accounts, particularly important for contractors who run an ongoing cash surplus. Many banks also offer additional long-term deposit options and corporate investments, such as bonds

- Issues specific to you – for example, if you're likely to contract abroad and be paid by an overseas client or agent, compare what charges might be applied to accepting such payments

- Because business banks offer essentially the same service, the deciding factor may come down to the deal that a bank is providing, such as cash back, a high rate of interest on deposits over a certain amount and free banking offers.

As with all financial services, it is always best to shop around, negotiate and examine the small print before you take the plunge.

Once the account is opened, organised recordkeeping is important. Business bank account statements are essential tools used by your accountants to complete accounts and tax returns, and by HMRC inspectors when conducting an investigation. Failure to keep accurate records, which then results in incorrect company accounts and tax returns could, in the very worst cases, land you in jail for fraud and tax evasion.

Many business bank accounts still send monthly bank statements in hard copy to your business address, although some only provide online statements, in which case you should get into the habit of downloading them regularly. And when you move money around by using cheques and paying-in books, there are physical records for an accountant, or HMRC, to check and match against your bookkeeping records. When moving money around electronically, and if the account only uses online statements and billing, you should also ensure online transfers have notes in the accounting records that relate to each payment, thus providing a clear 'audit trail'.

If you are concerned about the safety of cash held on deposit in your UK business bank account, some reassurance may be provided by knowing that it is covered by the same protections under the Financial Services Compensation Scheme (FSCS) that protects cash bank deposits held by individuals.

If your bank went bust, your limited company would receive compensation of up to £85,000 from the FSCS, because contractor limited companies qualify as 'small businesses' under FCSC rules. However, this means that when your contracting career really takes off, and you are holding potentially larger sums on deposit in your business account, you might want to consider opening a second account with a different bank. That's because the rules say that the company will benefit from the £85,000 compensation coverage only once under each bank's 'compensation licence'.

So, if you have £120,000 on deposit, you could place £85,000 in one business bank account and the balance in an account with a different bank that has a separate compensation licence. This would ensure that, in the event of one or both banks failing, your money should be safe. This may also enable you to take advantage of higher interest rates on savings accounts and bonds not available from your normal business bank.

Note that, because your company is a separate legal entity from you and has its own money, you can't use surplus cash to offset your mortgage without incurring substantial tax charges. Self-employed sole traders often use this method to reduce mortgage interest, but as an employee of your own limited company, you can't do so without paying tax.

### 6.3.4 Getting insurance

New contractors need to consider two broad areas of insurance for contracting through their limited company:

- Company insurances – professional indemnity and 'business insurance'
- Income protection insurances.

Income protection insurances are covered in chapter 12, so in this section the focus will be on company insurances, of which there are generally two types that contractors must have in place when they start contracting: Professional Indemnity (PI) insurance and 'Business insurance'.

**Professional indemnity (PI) insurance**
When working as a full time permanent employee, should you make an error delivering your employer's services to a client, you are not personally liable for the implications of that error, and the costs that might be incurred if the client chose to sue your employer for damages. Your employer's company, or the legal entity that entered into the contract, is liable, as might be the directors of that business, if the error was severe and harmful. Of course, the error might cost you your job, but not millions of pounds.

However, when working as a contractor through your own limited company, your company is liable, and as you are a director and shareholder in the company, the client may come after you for damages.

Professional indemnity insurance is designed for when a client decides to take action over an error or perceived error. It provides defence fees and possibly a payout to the client if professional negligence is proved.

You may consider this a small risk, and that it is therefore not necessary to have PI insurance. But the bottom line is that pretty much all agents and clients will require that, as part of your contract, you hold a current professional indemnity cover up to a certain value. So PI insurance is not only a safety net from writ-happy clients, but also an essential sales tool you must have to be a contractor.

PI insurance is readily available for contractors at reasonable prices from a wide range of insurance brokers. It is worth shopping around and also asking colleagues and contacts, especially if they have had cause to use their insurance. Also check with any professional or business bodies you belong to, as they might have negotiated good deals on behalf of their membership. You can find out more about PI, and even organise a policy online to secure instant cover, by visiting contractorcalculator.co.uk.

Policy prices vary according to a number of factors, including:

- The level of cover you require

- The annual turnover, or forecast turnover, of your limited company

- The number of employees in your company

- Your track record and level of expertise

- The types of projects you work on and clients you work for.

### 'Business insurance'

'Business insurance' is a catch-all term used to describe a basket of other essential or recommended insurances for contractors who are working on client contracts through their own limited company. They can include:

- Public liability, to protect your company against claims by a third party – agents and clients will insist you have this up to a minimum level

- Employers' liability, which is a legal requirement if your business has any employees, including you and co-directors, such as a spouse or business partner

- Portable equipment/business equipment, as domestic contents insurance will not pay out for damage and loss of business assets, such as computers and other equipment you have bought for your company

- Legal expenses, to cover legal actions or investigation by HMRC

- Business interruption, which would compensate for loss of earnings in the case of a fire or flood preventing you from working

- Buildings, if you have your own dedicated business premises.

There are a wide range of options available to suit the needs of most contractors and the cost of each policy will depend on the nature and level required.

## 6.3.5 Running the company – the administration

When contracting through your own limited company, there are always ongoing administration tasks to complete; but these should not be onerous, as long as you keep on top of them. Many contractors employ their spouse or partner to manage this side of the business, which also enables them to be paid a salary.

But ultimately you are in charge. Any accountants or other professional advisers you might hire will only be as good as the information you provide them with. The GIGO principle applies – garbage in, garbage out. So provide accurate and timely records to your accountant and they will more than justify their fees. And the same is true of legal advisers when checking contracts.

### IR35 issues

IR35 is a fundamental issue that you will need to get to grips with at the very start of your contracting career, during the course of your contracts if things change, and every time you accept a contract. The effort you put into understanding IR35 and its implications, for example by reading chapter 8, will more than repay itself both in terms of cash – taking home as much of your gross earnings as you legally can – and in terms of peace of mind – knowing the tax inspector won't be knocking on your door.

You may need to seek specialist legal advice for the various contracts you undertake in order to ensure that the way you are being paid is valid and will stand up to scrutiny on an IR35 inspection. Such advice is not at all expensive in terms of the extra earnings you will enjoy by being legally outside IR35, and the cost is certainly tiny for the peace of mind it will buy.

### Client and contract files

Create and maintain a file for each client and each separate contract, even if you are contracting through an agency. You can keep the bulk of your client and contract files electronically, but you should retain original signed hardcopies of contracts, renewals and other key documents, such as confirmations of arrangements signed by your client for IR35 purposes.

In each client/contract file include:

- Original signed and dated contracts

- Any correspondence between you and the agent and you and the client, including, if appropriate, dated notes of telephone conversations – any hardcopies can be scanned

- Copies of invoices (for the sake of convenience)

- Copies of timesheets.

If you are investigated by HMRC and are represented by your accountant or an IR35 specialist, they will want all this information as soon as possible. Creating and maintaining these files from the start saves you time, and quite possibly large sums of money at a later stage. But don't worry, if you follow the advice in this book you are unlikely to get investigated by HMRC; and even if you are, you will have all the information at your disposal to prove that you are contracting and getting paid legally.

### Invoicing Your Client/Agent

You will need to invoice your agent, or the client's accounts department, each week or month. To do so, your invoice must be accompanied by a timesheet that has been approved by your client.

You will need to ensure it is forwarded to them within their prescribed deadline to avoid delays in payment. Keep copies on file, make sure you get paid on time, and have a system in place to chase for payments as soon as they become overdue.

Each invoice you raise must include your company's details. The following should be included:

- Company name
- Company address
- Company telephone number and email address.
- Company number
- Company VAT registration number (if relevant).

Each of your invoices must have a unique invoice number and be sequential. Although called a number, it can include letters. A common method is to prefix invoices with letters that indicate the client.

For example, if you provided services for IBM and the BBC, for IBM you could use IBM001 and IBM002, and so on. For the BBC you could use BBC001 and BBC002. Using three placements for the numbers will ensure they also sort in order and HMRC requires numbers to be sequential for each client.

Dates are also extremely important, especially when it comes to chasing payments. You should include the following dates:

- Today's date: the date the invoice was raised
- Due date: the date by which payment should be made. Normally 30 days after the invoice date.

The client details should include the name and address of the agency, or client if contracting directly.

In the fees part of the invoice, include:

- A description of the services provided
- The net amount due
- The VAT amount, if you are VAT registered
- The gross/total amount due.

For example:

20 Days @ £500 per day

Amount: £10,000

VAT: £2,000 at current rate of 20%

Total: £12,000

You will have agreed the payment terms with the agent or client at the time you negotiated the contract. It is very important to include the payment terms on the invoice, as these will support your case in the event of any dispute. Also specify how you would like to receive the money. For example:

Payment should be made within 30 days by cheque or money transfer. Cheques should be made payable to 'My Company Ltd'. Money transfers should be sent to:

The Contractors Bank
Sort Code: 01-01-01
Account Number: 012345678
Reference: Use invoice number

Most agencies and clients do not pay via cheque and choose money transfer. Cheques can be inconvenient if you can't get to a branch during opening hours because, for instance, the client's site is a production platform in the North Sea; they also have a habit of 'getting lost in the post', which is a very convenient excuse for clients who want to hold on to their money (your money!) for a few more days. If you wish only to be paid by money transfer, then use the following:

Payment should be made within 30 days by money transfer only to the following account:

The Contractors Bank
Sort Code: 01-01-01
Account Number: 012345678
Reference: Use invoice number

Example invoices and templates can be downloaded from contractorcalculator.co.uk.

Your agency or client will specify how they would like to receive the invoice. Some clients will request a paper copy, others prefer an electronic invoice. If you are permitted to submit your invoice via email then it is useful to convert the invoice into PDF format so that it cannot be altered.

If contracting directly with your client, follow the client's instructions about invoice format to the letter. Finance departments in large organisations have specialist clerks who inspect invoices looking for errors because this gives the client a reason to reject the invoice and delay payment even further. For the sake of an extra five minutes it takes to adjust your invoice template, don't give 'accounts payable' the excuse.

Most agencies and clients require a timesheet to be signed and a copy included with the invoice. Ensure you take a scan or copy of the timesheet for your own records before sending it in.

## Record keeping

HMRC has become very hot on record keeping standards. So much so, that it runs an annual Business Record Checks (BRC) programme to inspect the records of tens of thousands of small businesses, including contractor limited companies. Poor record keeping could result in a fine of up to £3,000, and increases the risk of subsequent VAT, employer compliance and other investigations. As a minimum, do the following:

- Invoices: as explained above, record all invoices in a numbered list as they are issued to clients or agencies and keep copies. The copies can be hardcopies or in electronic form, such as PDFs

- Purchases: list and keep the supplier invoices for larger items such as computers and office equipment, but also record items such as accountancy fees, memberships, books and subscriptions. Electronic versions can be kept instead of hardcopies, but they must be legible

- Expenses: these include day-to-day expenses such as subsistence and travel. Keep all expenses receipts, either the originals or scans, and complete expenses forms regularly. If running a car or claiming mileage, keep a detailed mileage log

- Petty cash: Few contractors run a petty cash book, but if the company has petty cash, run and routinely update a cashbook (your accountant can tell you how).

If you are using a contractor accountant's online system, you will find most of these processes are handled automatically. And if you do keep scans of receipts and other records, you should maintain a regular backup, preferably off-site, because HMRC treats data loss resulting from a lack of backing up very unsympathetically.

Nobody wants a garage full of mouldering business records, and both HMRC and Companies House are moving towards electronic delivery models. But you do need to retain some original documents. So, when it comes to hardcopies, the rule of thumb is that anything requiring a signature or that might need to be used in court should be kept. And for your own sanity, keep things in well labelled files and boxes, so you can actually find them when they're needed.

Specifically you should retain original hardcopies of:

- Share certificates, stock transfer forms, board minutes, shareholders' resolutions and company accounts

- Signed official agreements or documents generated by the company, such as contracts and agreements

- Signed corporation tax returns and personal self-assessment forms

- Bank statements and interest certificates. Annual summary interest certificates and bank statements are acceptable.

Although in theory original bank statements should be kept, in practice so many businesses have switched to online banking that as long as your 'original' statements can be retrieved from your bank's online banking system, you should be in the clear. Check with your bank, though, how far back they keep your statements available online. It might still be worth keeping printed copies, as some banks charge for access to old statements.

You should retain all your business records for at least seven years. This is because different taxes require taxpayers to keep records for longer or shorter periods. If you retain everything for seven years, and this can mostly be done electronically, it will cover all eventualities.

### Payroll Matters

As company director you normally take a salary from the company, whether or not you are working under IR35. You will need to arrange for payslips to be prepared and ensure that the necessary taxes are paid at the right time.

Most accountants include a full payroll service as part of their package to contractors, and most online contractor accountancy services process payroll automatically. This will avoid the need for you to be involved in the detailed calculations. Alternatively, there are companies that specialise just in payroll. If you do want to do it yourself, which is unlikely to be an efficient use of your time, HMRC runs free workshops to help small businesses.

If you use your accountant or a payroll company, they will send you a payslip once a month and you will have to send a cheque to HMRC, or pay online when you are told to if you owe any income tax or NICs. Following the end of the tax year, it will be necessary to file an employer's annual return (form P35), together with forms P14, P60 and P11D if you have taken any expenses or benefits in kind from the company during the year.

There is nothing stopping you doing this yourself, if you wish to. But your accountant would normally deal with these so that your involvement is simply providing all the necessary information and approving the documents before they are submitted to HMRC.

**Dividend Planning**
If you are working outside the scope of IR35, then the bulk of your income from the company will be taken by way of dividends, reducing your tax liabilities. It is vital that the necessary documents (board minutes and dividend counterfoils) are prepared at the time you take each dividend, but these are short documents that take very little time to prepare. Dividend 'vouchers' are prepared automatically by some online contractor accountancy services.

Real problems can arise if the necessary procedures are not followed. In addition, you will need to ensure that your dividend drawings are not in excess of the company's profits after corporation tax – this could leave you with unexpected tax bills. If you are unsure of your profit position, then it is generally prudent to check with your accountant how much you can withdraw as dividends before acting. Most online contractor accountancy services will tell you how much you can take in dividends on a daily basis or in real time, assuming you've updated your invoices and expenses.

Finally, ensure you always leave sufficient cash in your account to cover operating expenses, such as accountancy and insurance fees, plus contingency funds for the unexpected.

## Accounts

The company will need to submit accounts to the Inspector of Taxes and Companies House once each year. Penalties arise for late filing, so it is important that you ensure that the documents are prepared in due time. Your accountant will normally prepare these for you, which you then approve for forwarding.

You need to supply your accountant with all the information and records so they can prepare the accounts on your behalf. Supply these as soon as you can, because it will avoid your accountant having to rush your work because it is being done at the same time as all the other people who have left it until the last minute.

Finally, make sure you do check your accounts before approving them – accountants can make mistakes and, in the eyes of HMRC, any errors are yours, not your accountants.

## Company secretarial matters

Each year Companies House requires you to complete a company return, which includes updating your statement of capital. You will need to complete and forward the annual return to Companies House, together with their annual fee. Or you can file the annual return online, which is very quick and costs less.

Various other forms will have to be submitted to Companies House if the circumstances of the directors or company change, even for such seemingly unconnected matters like you moving home.

Most accountants will take on the administration of company secretarial duties for an additional fee, although you are still required to check and sign all documents yourself, and you remain ultimately liable for them being accurate and returned on time.

## Changes of address

If you move home, this means your company's trading and registered addresses may change, unless you use your accountant's location. There is an extensive list of stakeholders you must inform of any address change:

- Companies House should be informed of both the company's change of trading address, and registered address if applicable, and the changes in directors' particulars, ie your address and that of your spouse or partner if they are a director or company secretary. You can download the required forms from the Companies House website, or update the records online

- HMRC is next on the list and may need to be told via four separate communications for corporation tax, PAYE, VAT and personal income tax, which are generally dealt with at separate tax offices

- In addition to their accountants, contractors should inform other professional advisers and service providers, which could include solicitors, other specialist legal advisers or consultants, independent financial advisers, plus pension companies, insurers and insurance broker as well as relevant professional bodies

- You should write to all current and past agency and direct clients – your customers – ensuring that they are all aware of the change of address. This may require multiple communications to the same organisation, to ensure all relevant contacts are informed.

Your suppliers should also be informed of your address change. If the move is significant, it may mean dealing with a new supplier representative. Suppliers include:

- Business landline, broadband and mobile service suppliers, plus website hosting suppliers, if not the ISP

- Domain name registers for any URLs you own

- IT, computer and software suppliers, particularly for warranties and software licences

- Office stationery and consumables suppliers, especially if the contractor has an account

- Magazine subscriptions and other purchases regularly delivered to the original address

- Delivery addresses in online shopping accounts, with which the contractor regularly buys, for example, business textbooks and stationery.

You may already have your own list of suppliers, and if you use an online accountancy services most suppliers' details will already be captured. But if not, a good tip is to go through the last year's business expenses to see what suppliers have been paid for goods and services.

In addition to all the address changes, you might also need to make some changes within your business, and update the address details on:

- Company websites (this is a legal requirement if the registered address has changed)

- Stationery (this is also a legal requirement if the registered address has been changed)

- On invoices (again a legal requirement if the registered address has been changed)

- Business cards and promotional items.

Because there may still be some contacts who have not been informed or haven't updated their databases, you should also contact Royal Mail and arrange for mail to be re-directed to the new address. If your landline number has changed, it is possible for most telephony suppliers to re-direct calls or leave an automated answerphone message, but this depends on your communications supplier and service agreement.

### Personal tax return

As a company director it will usually be necessary for you to file a personal self-assessment tax return. Your accountant can prepare this for you, but as this is a personal return, if you charge this to your limited company you will incur a benefit in kind income tax charge.

### VAT Return

Assuming you are VAT registered, which you almost certainly will be, you will need to complete your online VAT return every quarter, or each year if you operate annual VAT accounting (but you will be required to make interim payments on account), and transfer the balance of VAT left over after purchases. Some online contractor accountancy services enable you to file your VAT return automatically using invoicing and expenses records you have inputted during the VAT period. Your accountant could do your

VAT return for you for an additional fee, but it's a very simple task to do yourself.

### 6.3.6 Value Added Tax – VAT

Value Added Tax (VAT) is levied on most business transactions and on many goods and some services. Some services, such as insurance, and some types of education, training and loans are deemed to be 'exempt'. However, in nearly all cases, services offered by contractors will attract VAT, both because of the nature of the service – for example, IT and engineering services are not exempt – and because most contractors' companies have a turnover that means registration is compulsory.

It is compulsory to register for VAT if your turnover reaches the VAT registration threshold limit, which tends to change on an annual basis, but usually means if you forecast your contracting gross income that you bill through your company to be above around £73,000 (the compulsory VAT registration threshold at the time of writing), you will have to register anyway. Companies over the limit which fail to register can be fined.

 hmrc.gov.uk/vat/index.htm

Businesses with turnovers of less than the limit can also register if they wish. Many do so for cost efficiency reasons, or because they feel a VAT registration makes their company appear more established.

To make the most of your cash-flow and reduce start-up costs, it's a good idea to apply for VAT registration when you are forming your company. It might not be compulsory at that stage, but most contractors want to apply for "voluntary registration" in order to recover input VAT on start-up expenses, like computer costs, professional fees and other business-related costs on which VAT is charged. There are two types of VAT:

**Output VAT:** This is added to your company invoices. You charge the agent or client £1,000 plus VAT at 20% (the current rate) so your total invoice is for £1,200. Output VAT = £200

**Input VAT:** This is paid on purchases the company makes. If you pay your accountant £500 they will charge you VAT at 20%, so their total invoice will be £600. Input VAT = £100

Every quarter the difference between the amount of input VAT collected and output VAT paid is then paid to HMRC as part of the quarterly VAT return.

As VAT is generally paid to HMRC on a quarterly basis, your company gains a cash-flow advantage and you can even earn interest on this money. Another advantage of registering is to avoid anybody dealing with your company knowing, without checking with Companies House, that your turnover is below £73k per annum.

Although most contractors would agree that VAT registration is an overall benefit to their company, there are disadvantages, the most obvious of which is that you will need to prepare VAT returns and ensure that your accounting records provide the required information for disclosure on the VAT returns. This means keeping accurate, detailed records and VAT receipts and invoices for all transactions in the return. But you should be doing that in any case, and if you use an online contractor accountant, you'll be updating your records in real time.

There are some unusual cases where it is best to delay VAT registration for as long as possible. If, for example, your client was not VAT registered themselves, as in the case of a financial services company, they would not thank you for adding 'unnecessary' VAT to your invoices, as they could not recover that money themselves.

One final downside is that, as a VAT registered trader, you will also be subject to periodic VAT inspections, usually once every six years. But it's not difficult to do everything right, and so these inspections should not be a concern to you.

Contractors have the choice of three schemes through which they can operate their VAT returns to HMRC:

**Cash Accounting:** To qualify for this scheme, your company's estimated annual turnover must be less than £1.35 million per year (at the time of writing). You only account for VAT actually received from your clients and paid to your suppliers for goods and services. This scheme is the most appropriate for most contractors.

**Flat Rate VAT Scheme:** You pay a fixed rate of VAT based on your company's revenue and depending on the sector you work in. You cannot claim VAT back, except on specific large purchases, but this might work better for your business depending on how much you spend on VAT-rated goods and services. Many contractors use the FRS because, with few business purchases, it is possible to make a modest surplus. Seeking advice from an accountant would be valuable to determine if the flat rate scheme is appropriate for you, particularly as there are specific rules relating to the purchase and sale of assets under the scheme that can get quite complicated.

**Annual Accounting:** You make a single annual return and payment is normally made in nine equal instalments, with a tenth balancing payment to settle the liability and balance the books. The maximum turnover limit for this scheme is £1.35 million per year (at the time of writing). Few contractors actually use this scheme in practice and it is probably better to ensure that your books/VAT accounting is fully up to date on a quarterly basis, rather than be faced with an entire year to account for as the annual return deadline approaches. Investing time in understanding how to make VAT work for you is well worth it.

### Filing a late VAT return

The first time you submit your VAT return late, or make a late payment, you will usually receive a warning letter with no penalty. So, one mistake is allowed. However, subsequent late payments without good reason incur a surcharge on the VAT owed, which increases as the number of late filings and payments increase. And all the time you are waving a flag to HMRC saying, 'please come and investigate me'. Don't mess with the 'Vat-man': file your VAT payments in good time, and ensure payments are always up-to-date.

### Charging VAT to overseas, non-UK clients

Under most circumstances, you don't have to charge VAT to your clients based outside of the UK, even if the work is completed in the UK. The general rule for business-to-business customers is that the place of supply is where the customer is based, so if your client is based, for example, in the USA, the service is considered as having been supplied in the USA and therefore no VAT should be charged to the American customer.

For the purposes of VAT, the UK includes the British Isles, Northern Ireland, the 12 nautical mile territorial limit surrounding the coast, and the Isle of Man, but not the Channel Islands, which are outside of both the UK and European Union (EU).

Sales to overseas consumers will attract VAT, which intuitively you'd think excludes your contracting clients. However, under HMRC rules, a 'consumer' is not only a private individual, but also a charity, government department or other organisation that has no business activities, so if you have clients in the public sector in EU member states, you must add VAT to your invoices.

There are also certain types of services where VAT must be charged to clients based outside the UK and, even when VAT is not charged, contractors supplying services to clients in EU member states must now report these transactions to HMRC. If your VAT accounting starts to get complicated, then it is well worth taking advice from your accountant, because their fees are likely to be a fraction of what it might cost you in time and, if you make a mistake, in money.

### De-registering for VAT

HMRC's rule says that you need only deregister for VAT when you have ceased trading or have stopped making VAT-able supplies. This could happen when, for example, you've decided to close your business because you are retiring, or perhaps you've invested your company's surplus cash into property and it turns into a business that lets residential property.

If you wish to cancel your VAT registration, you can download a VAT 7 form from HMRC's website. This asks you to explain why you want to de-register and when. The process is straightforward and inspectors rarely query why a business de-registers. The vast majority of requests to cancel VAT registration are generally accepted by HMRC without question, but there are some catches.

The biggest catch is that, when deregistering, you must pay the VAT-able value, or the market value, on any business capital assets, such as computers and office equipment.

However, for most contractors this is just a formality because if the VAT due is less than £1,000, then you have nothing to pay. So for most contractors who have bought items such as laptops, tablets and office equipment with low market resale values, there are likely to be no costs for de-registering. However, this is definitely an area where an accountant's professional expertise is vital, as mistakes can be costly in terms of penalties.

## VAT inspections

If your limited company is selected for a VAT inspection, it's most likely because you've simply been chosen by chance as part of HMRC's ongoing compliance activity. However, there can often be a reason that a contractor's limited company shows up on HMRC's radar and is targeted. This could be because the contractor has filed a late VAT return, or has unusual fluctuations in the amount of VAT they have paid or reclaimed. Advice on HMRC's website clearly states that businesses that have previously submitted late or incorrect VAT forms and payments will be inspected more often.

But if you have only claimed VAT on eligible business costs and have maintained comprehensive and accurate records, then you should have nothing to be concerned about, as most VAT inspections are routine. In fact, it has been known for HMRC VAT inspectors to identify a business that has been overpaying and under-claiming its VAT, and is therefore due a rebate!

HMRC inspectors are normally pretty good at giving contractors plenty of time to organise the logistics of a VAT inspection, especially as they appreciate most contractors' limited companies are run from home, and contractors tend to be out onsite with clients. You'd normally get a phone call, and sometimes a letter saying an inspector would like to review the company's VAT records. Check immediately with your accountant and insurer if you have investigation insurance, to confirm the best route forward. This will normally require that you have all your financial records available for review by the inspector, including:

- All VAT records and returns
- Annual accounts
- Sales invoices to clients/agencies
- Purchase invoices and receipts for expenses and business costs
- Bank statements

- VAT certificate

- Any supporting documents, such as contracts and relevant correspondence.

If most of your records are stored electronically, this is not a problem, as the inspector will be happy to view your records on screen. The inspector may need to be guided through how a contractor's records are structured and, of course, full cooperation is strongly advised. HMRC inspectors then have to spend a lot of time trawling through hard copy records and online accounts.

Ideally, during the VAT inspection, you should have your accountant or similar professional adviser present at any initial meeting with an HMRC VAT inspector. Different inspectors vary in their style and some can be 'challenging' in the way they question you. It may need a professional adviser to step in and qualify some responses.

According to HMRC's own guidance on the topic, an inspector's role is to ensure VAT is being collected and claimed correctly and compliantly, and to check a contractor limited company's VAT processes follow best practice. At the end of the inspection, the inspector will always run through what they've done during the inspection, identify any concerns they might have and assess whether there have been any under or overpayments. All this will be confirmed in writing, and you will have the opportunity to appeal any decision if you, or your accountant, have any concerns.

### 6.3.7 Expenses

Efficient recording and processing of expenses can significantly reduce a contractor's tax bill, and thus boost their net income. In addition, understanding what is allowable and making full use of those allowances can significantly reduce a contractor's personal outgoings. So time invested in understanding the rules surrounding expenses is likely to be time well spent.

Every legitimate business expense is deductible against your final tax bill. This means that allowable expenses become part of the overhead of your company. The higher the overhead, the less profit the business makes and the lower will be your company's corporation tax bill.

This may sound back to front – after all, surely you want to have as much profit as possible to maximise your net income? Well, yes, but it's a balancing act: by understanding and applying the full range of allowances available to you and your business you can shift costs around from your personal net income (you buy a sandwich for lunch when working at a client's site) to the company's gross income (the company buys your lunch when you're working at a client's site).

According to HMRC, expenses are deductible if incurred wholly, necessarily and exclusively in the performance of duties. Technically speaking, this means if you buy a laptop or tablet that is exclusively for your work, it can be deducted. And technically speaking, if it is used as a family computer evenings and weekends, it is in theory not deductible. Or only that proportion that is used for work may be deductible. You work it out!

HMRC's rules on eligible business expenses and allowable expenses for the employees of limited companies (and that means you if you are trading via your own limited company) are complex, confusing, and often counter-intuitive. They are designed to minimise allowable expenses, thus maximising corporation tax take, and so you need to be sure only to claim what's allowable in the rules.

The rest of this section explains how you should claim and account for expenses in your limited company. Precisely what expenses you can claim is tackled in section 6.6.

**How to claim expenses**
When running your own company and paying out of your own pocket for contracting expenses, especially cash expenses, it really pays to have a simple system to ensure that not only are you are keeping statutory accounting records for tax and VAT purposes, but that you are also claiming everything you are entitled to. If you use an online contractor accountancy service, it will have an established expenses recording and payment process, which will maintain your up-to-date expenses records.

Many contractors are used to the expenses systems that big companies have for their employees. Usually, the company has a standard expenses form on the company intranet that employees fill in each month, and then the next month the money they have paid out on behalf of the company is paid back to them alongside their salary.

When you are contracting through your own limited company and you don't use an online accountancy service, then you must always keep a clear record of any expenses you wish to claim. These records do not need to be complex, as long as they keep to the rules laid down by HMRC. And the good thing about having a system in place is that it can act as a reminder to you to claim everything that is allowable by the taxman.

It is very important to get receipts for every business related purchase. Where it might not be possible to provide a receipt – say, for example, your train ticket gets swallowed by the ticket barrier – the expense can still be claimed, but careful note must be made of exact amounts, times and reasons for travel. This is because it might be necessary to prove to the HMRC at a later date that you were on that train, or had bought that snack from a street vendor.

If you are planning on claiming VAT on expenses, then you must get a VAT receipt for each specific expense for any costs that are VAT rated. Most suppliers, such as petrol stations or sandwich shops, will provide a receipt that includes the necessary information. If using your local stationers to buy printer ink and you get an old fashioned till receipt without the details make sure you ask for a separate VAT receipt if VAT is charged – for example, train tickets do not have VAT added, but motoring expenses do.

You can claim expenses from your own limited company at any time. It could be daily, weekly, monthly, quarterly or even annually. Many contractors claim expenses quarterly, as this matches the cycle of their company's VAT returns.

Cash flow may also determine when you claim expenses. If client invoices, billed monthly, are outstanding and there is not enough cash in the business to pay you, then there is little point making a claim at that time. However, the paperwork could be uploaded to your online accountancy portal and the expenses accrued, or delayed, until there is enough cash in the company bank account.

Although the requirements of online accountancy portals and expenses forms can vary, there is always some key information required:

- Date of the expense

- Nature of the expense

- Amount of expense.

If you don't have an online form or template from your accountant, a basic expenses form can be created in Excel, and look something like this:

| Date | Details | Amount (£) |
|------|---------|------------|
| 1st May 2012 | Train fare to client X at client's site in Basingstoke | £22.80 |
| 23rd May 2012 | Mono printer cartridge | £27.49 |
| 10th June 2012 | Stationery – 100 x stamps | £48.00 |
| Total | | £98.29 |

- The first column contains the date on the receipt, or the date of the expense if there is no receipt

- The second column contains a sentence about the nature of the expense; "Trip to client X's site in Basingstoke"

- The third column contains the amount of the expense.

Your expenses forms may have to have a fourth column for VAT. If you use an online accountancy service, you'll most likely be provided with online training on how to use the expenses module. Or you need to check with your accountants about how best to manage your VAT claims, at least initially until you get into the swing of things. Obviously this only applies if you are VAT-registered, which you almost certainly will be.

At the time of writing the standard VAT rate is 20%. So to calculate the VAT of most VAT-rated goods and services, divide the price you paid by 120, and then multiply that figure by 20 to give the VAT. Fortunately, most receipts provide this calculation for you, or you can request a VAT receipt for most purchases, such as fuel. Not all goods and services are VAT rated, so make sure you only claim what you can.

If using a hardcopy system, total the amounts, print the expenses form, attach the receipts and at the end of the expenses period, transfer exactly that amount of money from your company's business bank account to your personal account, or write yourself a business cheque. Then make sure you file the paperwork somewhere safe or send it to your accountant for record keeping. An online accountancy portal will pretty much do everything for you automatically, except actually transferring the cash, once you've uploaded the expenses details.

### 6.3.8 Taxation

If you are typical of most contractors outside IR35 working through your own limited company, you will at some point during the year have to be aware of, manage, calculate and pay the following taxes:

- Value Added Tax (VAT)
- Corporation tax
- Income tax
- National Insurance Contributions (NICs)
- Capital Gains Tax (CGT).

VAT has been listed first because, if you process your VAT quarterly, you are managing it yourself on an ongoing basis and it is purely through your limited company. The other taxes tend to be calculated by your accountant, or sometimes HMRC, on your behalf. Some of these taxes will be paid through your limited company and some you will pay personally.

**Taxes paid through your limited company**

**Corporation Tax:** All limited companies are subject to Corporation Tax at varying rates, usually between 20% and 25% (at the time of writing). These rates tend to be changed on a generally annual basis, with announcements typically made in the Chancellor's Budget. Probably the majority of contracting companies will pay at the lowest rate, which at the time of writing is applied to companies with profits of up to £300,000.

If your contract is not caught by IR35, then you will most likely take the traditional route of a low salary combined with high dividends. Since dividends can only be paid from company profits, you will need to pay corporation tax at the prevailing rate on your net company profit.

Your accountant will prepare and submit a company tax return on your behalf, based on the financial records you have provided and after you have checked and signed the return. Corporation Tax is payable nine months after your company year end.

**Employer's National Insurance Contributions (NICs):** This is a company cost based on the amount of your gross salary at the rate of 13.8% (at the time of writing). If your contract is not caught by IR35, then the best advice would be to take a lower salary, potentially avoiding employer's NICs altogether. No NICs are chargeable on company dividends. Employer's National Insurance is paid monthly. However, if you do take a salary that is high enough to qualify for NIC payments, you are more likely to receive a full state pension on retirement.

**VAT:** VAT is covered in detail in section 6.3.6.

### Taxes you pay personally

**Income tax:** If you are working in an IR35-caught contract, your entire income from the company will be treated as employment income and subject to Pay As You Earn (PAYE) income tax and will be deducted at source; this is also the case if you are working through an umbrella company. If your contract is not caught by IR35, then only a very small amount of your income tax liability, if any, will be deducted through PAYE, assuming you are taking a low salary and high dividends.

On IR35 exempt contracts, you will receive dividends, on which there will be tax credits covering your basic rate tax liability. If your taxable income is less than the higher rate threshold, then you will not have any further income tax liability. Any income in excess of the higher rate tax threshold, or even the additional rate for very high earning contractors, means you will pay more tax on it. Income tax is paid monthly through PAYE and calculated annually if you take the low salary-high dividend approach.

**Employee's National Insurance Contributions (NICs):** If your contract is caught by IR35, then you will have to pay employee's NICs on your salary (not dividends), at varying rates.

If your contract is not caught by IR35, then you will pay very little, if any, employee's NICs, since the bulk of your income will be taken through dividends, which do not attract NICs of any kind. Employee's NICs are paid monthly.

**Capital Gains Tax:** You may be subject to Capital Gains Tax when you close your company and make a capital distribution to yourself as shareholder. Exemptions and reliefs are available through which it may be possible to reduce your tax bill.

Of course if you do have other assets and incomes, such as property, shares and other financial assets, there are various other taxes, payments, duties and methods by which HMRC will tax you. This scenario definitely requires specialist accounting and financial expertise from your accountant.

### 6.3.9 Salaries

Tax efficiency, and therefore higher earnings, is one of the common reasons contractors choose to start a career in contracting. Despite various tax and related legislation over the past couple of decades, you can still trade perfectly within the law in a highly tax efficient manner.

In your previous role as a permanent employee, you would have been used to being paid your annual gross salary on a monthly basis net of income tax, deducted by your employer via Pay As You Earn (PAYE) and NICs. You'll probably have been vaguely aware of something called your 'personal allowance', which sets out what you can earn each year before you pay tax. Chances are, you'd have been very aware of the higher rate tax threshold, because the salary you earned in excess of that threshold attracted 40% income tax. You may even have been subject to a 50/45% tax rate.

But because you've probably only ever earned employment income, you may not be aware that different types of income are treated differently in tax terms. This underpins the tax efficiency of the contractor model because, if you are outside IR35, you can choose how much employment income you pay yourself and how much of your company's profit you distribute to the shareholders – you and possibly your spouse or partner – as dividends.

If your contract is outside IR35 (see chapter 8), then the best strategy to adopt to maximise net earnings is the low salary-high dividend approach. This takes advantage of the tax-free personal allowances and the different treatment of dividends when compared to employment income. You do not start paying income tax on a salary until you have reached the basic rate, which creeps up most years and is currently £8,105. That means you can pay yourself, and potentially your spouse or partner, £675 per month each without attracting income tax and with minimal employee NICs.

If you then take most of the remaining profits after salaries, costs and corporation tax as a dividend, you do not pay any NICs on this sum, and you also do not pay any income tax until your total earnings – minimum salary plus dividends and any other income such as from investments and rental properties – reach the higher rate tax threshold. Then you pay income tax according to the prevailing lower and upper rates.

What this means is that you, or your company, typically pay 20-25% of your fee income into the Exchequer, mainly as corporation tax, compared to the 35-40% tax you pay from employment income.

Dividends and dividend strategies are covered in section 6.3.10.

## CONTRACTING MINDSET TIPS:

### Contractors are not paid the same as employees

As a limited company contractor you manage your own tax affairs and, unlike employees, pay corporation tax, income tax and National Insurance Contributions (NICs) yourself. That means you can't directly compare contractor day rates with employee salaries.

### Do you know how much it costs to employ someone?

Say you had your own business and decided to hire an employee on a salary of £50,000 a year. Do you know how much it would actually cost your company to employ this person, taking into account employer costs like NICs, paid holidays and other benefits, such as pensions?

If you're a permanent employee earning a gross salary of £52,000 a year, or £1,000 a week, do you know how you would calculate what contracting day rate you need to secure the equivalent net take-home pay?

As a limited company contractor, if you invoiced your client for the same amount of money in fees as your gross annual salary as a permanent employee, would you expect to pay a greater or lesser amount of tax?

### Contractors factor tax, holidays and other 'employment costs' into day rates

When you become a contractor and work through your own limited company, your company becomes your employer. So you become responsible for both your company and personal tax affairs, which means you have to be your own finance and payroll department.

What this means practically is that a gross employee salary of £1,000 per week is certainly not the same as a contracting day rate of £200 per day. That's because out of that £200 your contractor limited company would have to pay corporation tax, income tax, NICs, an allowance for time off for holiday and possible sickness, money towards a pension and all the expenses of running your company.

By working through your own limited company, you are able to pay yourself tax efficiently, with a low salary and high dividends. The effect is that you pay less tax than an employee, which is your reward for taking the risk of being in business, rather than being employed.

### Contractors are not employees and get paid differently

To work out your day rate, start by working backwards from your desired net income – for many contractors, this is probably close to or more than what they were paid after taxes when they were employed. Then add in taxes, allowances for time off, pensions and expenses, and you will reach your desired day rate. You can use one of the interactive online financial calculators on contractorcalculator.co.uk to calculate your desired income and day rate.

After taking advice from your accountant or contracting advisor, you can minimise employment costs by paying yourself a small salary and the balance in dividends. In that way, you reduce employer's NICs and may claim all the expenses you are entitled to, so you can offset them against your company's corporation tax. You can also invest in a pension, paid directly from your company, to further reduce your corporation tax liability and to provide for your retirement.

Don't forget to factor in direct and indirect taxes, costs of employment, holidays, bank holidays, sickness, pensions and operating expenses when comparing a permanent employee gross salary with contracting fees.

**Contractors pay for their own tax, benefits and time off, so you can't directly compare employee salaries and contracting rates.**

## Paying a salary to a spouse or civil partner

Spouses and partners working in a contractor limited company fulfil a vital role that frees up the fee earner to maximise their income. But if you involve your spouse or partner in your contracting business, they must actually be doing something for the business, and being paid according to their role and hours. They should not be being paid simply as a means of generating costs within the business or using a spouse's tax allowances.

If your contract is inside IR35 you can still pay a salary to your spouse and it will form part of the 5% overheads allowance when calculating your deemed payment (see chapter 8 for an explanation), so the amount you can pay your spouse or partner will be limited. But assuming your contract is outside IR35, the full salary is a legitimate business expense and wholly deductible against your limited company's corporation tax.

In addition to actually undertaking work for the business, and having proof of that if the business or contractor becomes the subject of a tax investigation, your spouse should only be paid what they are worth for the job they do and hours they work. This is a tough call; what value do you put on someone who is a receptionist, personal assistant, bookkeeper, post room manager, accounts department and company secretary all rolled into one? Paying your spouse £100 per hour would be hard to justify to HMRC: the key question you should ask when deciding to pay your spouse or partner a salary is what the reasonable market rate is. In other worlds, what would you pay someone who wasn't your spouse to do the same job?

## 6.3.10 Dividends

Alongside minimum or low salaries, dividends, their payment and management underpin the tax efficiency of the limited company contractor model. You've probably come across the concept of dividends being paid out by large quoted companies on financial markets, and chances are you, or friends and family, have owned shares that paid their owners a few pence per share in dividends. The principle is exactly the same for contractor limited companies. The business's profits are distributed to its owners, the shareholders, pro rata according to the number of shares they own.

Only profits can be distributed as a dividend. A very simple 'back of a napkin' profit and dividend calculation is as follows: add together expenses, salary, and corporation tax at 20%, include a reasonable margin for error, forthcoming bills and emergencies, then take the total away from your fee income. What remains can be paid to the shareholders of your company as a dividend. Some online contractor accountancy services perform this calculation in real time as you input your fees and expenses, so you know pretty much exactly what your profit, and potential dividend, might be at any one time.

Dividends have two important distinguishing features from employment income. Firstly, dividends don't attract National Insurance Contributions (NICs) like employment income does. And secondly, dividends up to the higher rate tax threshold are considered to be 'franked'; that is to say the taxman considers that the basic tax liability has already been covered by the corporation tax already paid by the company, so dividends less than the higher rate tax threshold receive what is in effect a tax credit. That ultimately means you get more cash in your pocket from a dividend when compared to employment income.

The dividend tax credit, which is designed so profits are not taxed twice through corporation tax and income tax, is 10% of the 'gross dividend'. What you actually receive from the company is the 'net dividend'.

### Calculating dividend tax credits and income tax on dividends

Because the calculations are complex and get more so the higher a contractor's earnings, if you want to calculate your tax credits, you can use the ContractorCalculator Dividend Tax Calculator (it's on contractorcalculator.co.uk), or ask your accountant. But to show how the final tax figures are arrived at, here are some examples.

The dividend tax rates (at the time of writing) are as follows:

| Tax band | Tax rate | From | To | Gross rate (Tax rate – 10% credit) | Equivalent net rate |
|---|---|---|---|---|---|
| Basic rate | 10% | 0 | £35,000 | 0% | 0.00% |
| Higher rate | 32.5% | £35,001 | £150,000 | 22.5% | 25.00% |
| Additional rate | 42.5% | £150,001 | - | 32.5% | 36.11% |

The gross rate of tax is what is applied to your income from dividends. The dividend tax up to £35,000, the higher rate tax threshold, is 10%. But there is a tax credit of 10% and the taxman assumes this has already been paid through corporation tax, so in fact there is no tax to pay for basic rate taxpayers. The "equivalent net rate" is the equivalent percentage applied to the net dividend, and is equal to the gross rate multiplied by 10/9.

If your gross salary plus dividends take you above the higher rate, then if you decided to pay a net dividend of £60,000 plus a basic tax-free salary of £8,000, you would pay an additional £7,101 in income tax.

How did these figures arise? To keep things simple, let's say your company made a profit of £75,000, on which £15,000 in corporation tax at 20% is payable. That leaves a profit of £60,000, which you decide to take as a dividend.

In order that the taxable income can be used to calculate the income tax liability, the first step is to gross up the dividend to allow for the dividend tax credit, by multiplying £60,000 by 10/9, to give £66,667. Then add the basic tax-free salary of £8,000 to total £74,667. Take away the tax-free allowance of £8,105 (correct at the time of writing) and that results in a taxable income of £66,562.

Plug £66,562 into the dividend tax table:

| Taxation rate | Percent | From | To | Gross rate | Tax (£) |
|---|---|---|---|---|---|
| Basic rate | 10% | 0 | £35,000 | 0% | 0 |
| Higher rate | 32.5% | £35,001 | £150,000 | 22.5% | £7,101 |
| Additional rate | 42.5% | £150,001 | - | 32.5% | 0 |

So, the first £35,000 is tax free. The difference of £35,000 and £66,562 is £31,562, which attracts a gross rate of 22.5% income tax; 22.5% of £31,562 is £7,101.

So, based on the £60,000 dividend and £8,000 salary, there would be an income tax bill of £7,101.

Fortunately, you don't have to worry about doing this calculation yourself. You can simply visit the Dividend Tax Calculator on contractorcalculator.co.uk:

 contractorcalculator.co.uk/Dividend_Tax_Calculator.aspx

This calculator can be particularly useful when you are estimating your future tax liabilities, in addition to what you might already owe. As a general rule, for those earning under £150,000 it's a good idea to save 25% of all your net dividends for tax – and wait for the pleasant surprise at the end of the tax year when you don't need all of it.

### Dividend administration – minutes and vouchers
Before you get too excited about the concept of this pot of company money that you can draw on when you fancy, you should be aware that there are some tough rules imposed by HMRC on how you administer and pay out dividends. But as long as you adopt some basic best practice and stay organised, staying within HMRC's rules is not difficult.

Many small business owners, including limited company contractors who have been trading for many years, traditionally declare a final dividend for the entire financial year when their company accounts are completed, which may be many months after the actual year end. However, if you've been paying yourself throughout the year as dividends but without backing up the payments with the right formal paperwork, you could come seriously unstuck if a tax inspector investigates.

When paying yourself, and other shareholders, a dividend you must:

- Follow Companies Act requirements by preparing a board minute and dividend vouchers each time a dividend is paid

- Ensure there are sufficient profits in the company to cover the dividend. For most contractors, paying a dividend without enough profit is illegal and the company, which is a separate legal entity, can and should ask for the money back.

Never be tempted to backdate board minutes and dividend vouchers, as the documents will be legally void and can constitute a criminal offence. HMRC won't be impressed and, in extreme cases, has been known to prosecute offenders under criminal law.

If you have kept your income and expenses up-to-date, most online contractor accountancy services will tell you exactly how much dividend you can pay and even automatically create a board minute and dividend voucher.

 Contractorcalculator.co.uk/declaring_dividends_paperwork.aspx

### Contractor dividends – now or in future?

Assuming your limited company is forecast to make a profit, the end of a financial year is always a key time to make decisions about dividends. You have a number of choices, which can be affected if you have a spouse who is also a shareholder in the business.

In essence, you need to decide whether you:

- Should raise an additional dividend at year-end because you and your spouse have not earned enough to fall into the higher rate tax band

- Should defer a dividend payment because you have already earned enough in the year to fall into the higher rate tax band, but might not earn so much in the following tax year.

Any decision about dividends should be taken by considering what the company's profit position at the end of the financial year is likely to be. Dividends can be taken at any time during the year, but by year end the numbers must add up such that all dividends taken were distributed from profits. And of course all dividend paperwork must be completed for any declared dividends.

If you use an online contractor accountancy service, all of this information should be at your fingertips. Alternatively, you may wish to work with your accountant to produce some up-to-date and detailed management accounts you can use to assist decision making.

### Splitting dividends and sharing contracting dividend income with a spouse

To exploit unused personal tax allowances, contractors running their own limited company and whose contracts are outside IR35 have by long tradition maximised net income by splitting the shareholdings in their contractor limited company with a spouse or partner.

This is often entirely justified. But HMRC got wise to this being used as a tax avoidance strategy and, to combat what was perceived by the taxman as 'systemic tax avoidance by contracting couples', it dusted-off the little known Section 660 settlements legislation, which in its original form dates back to the 1920s. The settlements legislation was subsequently updated first in 1988, when it became the more familiar Section 660. It was changed again in 2005, when it was updated and rewritten into its current form, and is now known as Section 624 of the Income Tax (Trading and Other Income) Act (ITTOIA) 2005.

Also known as the 'Husband and Wife Tax' or 'Family Business Tax', when HMRC first tried to apply Section 624, it caused uproar. This was because it threatened the incomes of all family businesses, not just contractors'. Decades later, it even resulted in a tax case making the national news by way of the infamous Arctic Systems case. This confirmed that, under certain circumstances, giving shares to a spouse or civil partner and splitting dividend income is exempt from Section 624. Splitting dividends is actually quite straightforward and simply requires that the contractor's spouse or partner owns a percentage of the shares in the contractor limited company.

Despite the exemption for spouses and civil partners, it is well worth considering a belt and braces approach to demonstrate that any share transfer to your spouse is a commercial transaction. The shares can be part of your spouse's remuneration for working on the business alongside you, the main fee-earning contractor. Although this is not essential and your spouse or civil partner enjoys complete exemption for the transfer of ordinary shares, a record of time spent and tasks completed, such as company secretarial duties and administration tasks, would be good evidence that they have a role in your business.

When splitting dividends, you should consider the following:

1. **Make sure shares given to a spouse are ordinary shares:** preference shares or other classes of shares will not qualify for the spouse's exemption

2. **Make sure the gift is an "outright gift":** any dividends paid to the spouse should be their income to spend as they wish and not just a mechanism for routing money back to the main shareholder

3. **Avoid dividend waivers:** these are viewed by HMRC as only diverting income to the spouse and the exemption clarified in the Arctic Systems case does not apply

4. **Ensure all share transfers and dividends are backed up by paperwork:** use signed stock transfer forms and produce board minutes and vouchers for dividends

5. **Record the spouse's contribution to the business:** Document evidence that the spouse works in the business, so that this can be supplied to HMRC if required.

### Transferring shares within a limited company

There is nothing in the law that says a contractor cannot transfer shares to any person they wish to, including their children, mother-in-law, or even their mate down the pub, and many have in the past. But problems will arise if the shares are transferred to anyone who is not actively working in the business, spouses and civil partners excluded, and Section 624 rules will almost certainly apply.

In an ideal world, you should only transfer shares as a last resort, and consider alternatives that could still achieve your objectives but use alternative routes. If you want to jointly own your new contracting limited company with a partner, family member or friend who is not the main fee earner, but who nevertheless plays a vital role in the running of the business and is a director, you should register all the shares on incorporation in their name, and then transfer an agreed proportion to yourself. This can reduce the chances of the transfer of ownership being viewed as a 'settlement' under Section 624, which in the eyes of HMRC is a tax avoidance ploy and will instantly attract their attention

If you decide that you want to transfer shares you currently own in your contractor limited company to a partner, family member or friend, then you need to complete and sign a stock transfer form. This should be sent to the company secretary, who may be your accountant or possibly your spouse/partner, who should then update the company's records accordingly. Companies House should also be informed when the next annual return is completed, when you should also update your statement of capital. Some online contractor accountancy services have a company secretarial module that you may need to update.

Share transfers, which are also often referred to as stock transfers, from zero pounds to less than £1,000 are exempt from stamp duty. The term 'consideration' is often used to refer to the value of the shares being transferred, and this is where further complications often arise. If the value of the shares is calculated to be in excess of £1,000, then the stock transfer form must be sent to HMRC's Birmingham Stamp Office with a cheque for the duty, which is calculated at 0.5% of the consideration value.

So, for example, if your 50% shareholding was valued at £5,000 then the 'responsible person' within your business, which may be you or your company secretary, should send the signed and dated stock transfer form with a cheque for the 'stamping' fee – £25 at the time of writing.

Valuation of shares in a contractor limited company is extremely difficult and, if absolutely necessary should only be undertaken with advice from your accountant. The consideration must be a fair market value of the shares, which can be interpreted in a huge number of ways. The recommendation to use an accountant is no ploy to up accountancy fees, but because HMRC will have a keen interest in how the fair market value was calculated. The taxman may ask very awkward questions if you cannot substantiate the valuation to their satisfaction, and you could end up paying more in duty, tax and penalties.

## Illegal dividends

HMRC uses the term ultra vires dividends to describe dividends it considers illegal, with ultra vires literally meaning 'beyond the powers'. In plain English, it means that company directors declaring a dividend when there are insufficient profits don't actually have the authority to make that decision.

If you follow the advice in this book on dividend administration, it is highly unlikely that you will ever be in the position of declaring an illegal dividend. However, if you fail to justify dividend declaration decisions and don't complete the correct paperwork, you could have your dividends declared illegal by HMRC. Should that happen, HMRC can force you to pay income tax and National Insurance Contributions (NICs) on income it then reclassifies as salary.

But there are times when contractors can unwittingly 'overpay' themselves a dividend. This typically happens when income that was genuinely expected to be made is not forthcoming, perhaps because a client cancels a project.

So the most effective way to deal with an 'overpaid dividend' is to treat it as a loan to the director: If you've paid yourself, for example, a dividend of £10,000 and the profit in the period was only £9,000, you should treat the remaining £1,000 as a loan from the company. As long as the loan amount is less than £5,000 and the loan is repaid within nine months of the end of the tax year in question, you won't fall foul of what's known as S455 (formerly S419) corporation tax and a charge for benefit in kind (BIK) on the interest. Directors' loans are covered in greater detail in section 6.3.15.

And if you've overpaid yourself a dividend, don't backdate documents, such as board minutes, dividend vouchers and calculations, as that makes them legally void and is a criminal act.

### Contractor dividend waivers – best avoided

Another issue to be aware of is dividend waivers. Many contractor limited companies are husband-and-wife teams, and it is common for them to split shareholdings 50:50, which means the tax allowances of both spouses can be fully utilised.

In the past, some shareholders have waived their rights to a dividend to enable other shareholders to benefit from a greater share of dividend income than their shareholding entitled them to. However, since a landmark ruling, the Buck v HMRC case, if you tried to use a dividend waiver in this way, HMRC would almost certainly insist the resulting payment to a spouse or other shareholder was a 'settlement', and tax you accordingly.

---

## Been there, done that!

### Divi-what?

**DAVE SAYS:** The whole net dividend/gross dividend thing can sound confusing, and frankly still confuses me sometimes. But there is a simple way of looking at it:

Just save 25% of any net dividends paid from the company to you out of the profits after corporation tax. This is assuming you don't earn more than £150,000. And if you do, you might want to consider additional tax planning avenues.

At the end of the year you will have an extra tax bill to pay on those dividends, but it can't be more than what you have saved, and is likely to be less, because you've not used up your whole basic rate tax allowance.

So, after your accountant works out your dividend tax liability you'll discover you have money left over that you weren't expecting

---

### 6.3.11 Personal taxation and Self Assessment

As a director of your own limited company, you will be required to complete a Self-Assessment personal tax return to "self assess" the amount of income tax and capital gains tax you must pay each year. This is in addition to your responsibilities for completing any corporation tax paperwork.

The tax year in the UK runs from 6th April to the 5th April the following year. The final deadline for filing your tax return online with HMRC is 31st January following the end of the tax year. The deadline for paper returns is 31st October. These dates are correct at the time of writing, but you should always check in case there have been changes.

If you fail to file your tax return by HMRC's deadlines you will be fined £100, and the penalties escalate rapidly after 3, 6 and 12 months. In practice, though, your accountant will complete the return and calculations of tax due and file your personal tax return on your behalf, after you have checked and signed it. Easy!

Working outside IR35 through your own limited company, you will only be paying income tax on your small salary as you go along, and if your earnings are below the higher rate threshold and you have no other sources of income, it is unlikely that you pay any (or much) income tax at all. This can take a bit of getting used to and if you do earn above the higher rate threshold, it is essential to get into the discipline of putting aside a proportion of your net income to allow for your tax liabilities. The nice thing is you will be earning interest on the amount, rather than it already being in the government's coffers.

In addition, after your first year, if you have paid higher and additional rate tax, HMRC will start asking for 'payments on account'. They now know what you should expect to be earning so have some basis for calculating what to ask you for. You can ask your accountant to negotiate the figure if, for example, you know your income may drop because, say, you plan to have a month's holiday between contracts, and HMRC rarely disputes a lower estimate. If you do end up owing more tax and should have paid additional sums on account, then you will be charged interest on the difference.

However, regularly stashing away money is a good habit. It means you are more likely to have a pleasant surprise when the tax bill becomes due, because you have 'over-provisioned' for tax. If your earnings fall into the higher tax bracket, then saving 25% of your dividend should be more than sufficient, although as with all tax planning you should run this by your accountant. If you are an additional rate taxpayer, you should agree a tax mitigation plan with your accountant or tax advisor, as there are more creative tax reduction strategies that can be applied for very high earners.

## 6.3.12 HMRC investigations

If you do things right, and contract by the rules, there is no reason to fear an HMRC investigation. Nevertheless, if you or your limited company learn that an investigation is underway, it is prudent to take professional advice before talking to or corresponding with HMRC.

The reason is not to hide anything, but because the UK's taxation authorities have an extremely broad investigative remit, with tremendous powers – in many cases, unlike other areas of UK law, you can be found guilty until you can prove your innocence. That is why care should be taken when disclosing information to a tax inspector, because even seemingly innocent statements you make informally or 'off the record' can be used against you in a court of law. Take care.

HMRC has IT systems that work very effectively – probably because they were largely built by IT contractors – which means that all the information they gather on you, and others doing similar work to you, is captured and cross referenced in a series of sophisticated databases.

The tax authorities have the luxury of being able to look back through up to seven years of your records, which means that they can come after you for what they perceive to be unpaid tax from many years ago. This can add up to quite a sum, especially when interest and penalties are added.

HMRC investigations can become costly, time consuming and very stressful for you, even if you know you are entirely innocent. But there are ways you can minimise the risk of an investigation. And the best defence against an investigation is to prevent one happening in the first place.

There is a wide range of insurance policies specially designed to provide contractors with expert assistance in the event that they come under investigation. Most investigation insurance will cover the costs of the defence, even if it goes to court, but check carefully what your policy covers.

HMRC looks for particular features of companies when targeting them for inspections, and some of the more common clues they look for are covered below.

**IR35:** Factors leading to an IR35/payroll inspection include:

- Ticking the box on your employer's annual return (form P35) that some or all of your income may fall within IR35

- Paying a small salary/large dividend

- Having a company name which is obviously that of a contractor's company. If you look and sound like an employee, this may lead to questions about your IR35 status.

If you claim you are outside IR35 you will be asked to justify your reasons. You should ensure that you have a very good justification and strong argument for your decision. Chapter 8 covers IR35 extensively.

**Changes in share structure:** Factors that could trigger an investigation are:

- Major changes in a company's shareholding structures, including dividend waivers

- Any shareholders who are non productive or aren't working in the business

- Any shareholders who are not resident in the UK.

HMRC may well ask you for a commercial justification of the arrangements above.

**Non-allowable expenses:** HMRC is aware that many contractors may not know that certain expenses are not allowable. Examples include business entertaining, business clothing and private use of company assets. Expenses have been covered in sections 6.3.7 and 6.6 – take heed, don't take advantage and if in doubt don't claim it as a company expense.

**Travel expenses:** If you submit high claims for travel you are likely to be asked by HMRC to provide both justification and documentary evidence. Claims without receipts for travel and subsistence should be avoided wherever possible.

**Use of home as office:** Any claims you make for expenses for "use of home as office" should be fully justifiable. HMRC is aware that contractors have previously made claims without any real justification.

**Company car expenses:** Company cars in a one-person contractor company are becoming highly unusual, as it is rarely a cost-effective option. If you do have a company car, you should fully account for the benefit-in-kind tax arising and also the Class 1A National Insurance.

HMRC cross checks the accounts of companies with cars to P11D forms and any under-declaration or non compliance is likely to be picked up and investigated.

**P11D compliance:** This is a key expenses form that has to be submitted at the end of the tax year by every contractor who is a director of their limited company and has expenses reimbursed by that company.

You should ensure that a form P11D is completed, making full disclosure of any benefits in kind and expenses reimbursed. HMRC do cross check expenses claimed in one-person companies to the director's form P11D, particularly if expense claims are high.

Closing down or making a limited company dormant does not completely absolve a limited company contractor from their responsibilities for contracts they worked on whilst the company was trading. And it does not prevent HMRC from investigating your tax affairs. In fact, if HMRC suspect foul play, closing down your company may actually prompt a compliance review; and HMRC has a window of 12 months to investigate the business if they suspect there is tax still to pay.

## 6.3.13 Directors' roles and responsibilities

As a director of a limited company, it is your responsibility to manage the company in accordance with the Articles of Association and company law. UK company law had a significant upgrade with the introduction of the Companies Act 2006. These changes were rolled out over three years, and as a company director you should familiarise yourself with the legislation, which is summarised on the Companies House website.

 companieshouse.gov.uk

You should also ensure that your professional advisers are working to up-to-date provisions, as it is you and any other directors who are responsible if things go wrong, not your advisers. This sounds quite scary, but if you are organised, thorough and use professional help like accountants when necessary, nothing need go wrong.

### Statutory documents

Your main personal responsibility is to ensure that statutory documents are delivered to the Registrar of Companies as and when required by the Companies Act. In particular, you are required to file:

- Accounts
- Annual returns and statement of capital
- Notice of change of directors and secretary, or in their particulars (for example a change of address)
- Notice of change of the company Registered Office.

Failure to file these documents correctly and on time could ultimately result in prosecution, a criminal conviction and a significant fine for each offence. But again, it's easy to do it right, particularly if you employ professional help, like an accountant.

### Company accounts

As a director of a Private Limited Company, you will normally have a maximum of nine months from the accounting reference date in which to deliver your company's accounts to the Registrar of Companies. If you file the accounts late, then the minimum fine is £150, which rises up to a maximum of £1,500 if the accounts are more than six months late. However your accountant should have all this under control as long as you provide them with the information they need in good time.

Before approving your accounts, read through them carefully and check the following:

- **Directors' report**: Check the dates match your company's accounting reference dates (also known as its ARD) and that the company activities and directors' details are correct. This page needs to be signed by a director.

- **Profit and loss account**: This is a summary of the income less the expenditure to show the profit during the previous financial year. HMRC uses this profit to calculate the Corporation Tax to be paid. You should check that the sales invoiced, or turnover, is in line with what you have billed clients for the year, and that the costs, including salaries, are accurate.

- **Balance sheet and statement of directors' responsibilities**: The balance sheet shows the company's assets and liabilities and is simply a snapshot of the company's position at the accounting reference date. For most contractors, the assets will usually consist of items like computer and office equipment, the cash in the bank and anything owed to the company, such as unpaid invoices.

- **Liabilities**: These include amounts due for VAT, PAYE, and possibly funds owed to directors. Unless you've made some huge purchases or are owed a lot of money as a director, most of these amounts should be small. If any of the totals look high, it might be worth checking with the accountant.

- **Balance sheet**: The balance sheet and statement of directors' responsibilities should normally be signed by a director.

- **Notes to the financial statements**: Most of these notes are to do with technical accounting issues. However it is a worthwhile exercise to familiarise yourself with the notes so you are aware of how the company is being managed financially.

These might sound quite complicated, but in practice they are fairly straightforward, as the accountant has already done the complicated part by preparing the accounts. If you are using an online accountancy service, you will have seen these figures evolve during the financial year, so should already have a good idea of what your accounts should say.

Companies House will be sent abbreviated accounts, which will include the directors' report and an abbreviated balance sheet. You will have to sign these before they are submitted. HMRC will be sent the full accounts, including detailed profit and loss details and a Company Tax Return (see below).

### Corporation tax

In addition to filing the annual accounts with Companies House, you must also file them with HMRC, together with a corporation tax return (form CT600) and a corporation tax computation. The corporation tax must be paid within 9 months and tax return forms and computations must be filed within 12 months of the company's year-end. A failure to do so will result in a penalty, set at £100 at the time of writing, which increases after 3 months. In addition, interest may be charged on overdue tax. Again, your accountant will manage this for you, and simply tell you how much and how to pay.

### Payroll, PAYE, NICs and IR35

As a company director, it is your responsibility to fully comply with all payroll regulations, including IR35 issues. This includes filing of the employers annual return (form P35), forms P60, P14, P11D, P11D (b) and an IR35 calculation where appropriate. You are required to make PAYE and National Insurance payments in due time throughout the year by the due dates. In addition, if VAT registered, you will have a duty to complete VAT returns on time (see section 6.3.6 for more information about VAT).

**P35 Employer annual return:** You must complete a P35 employer annual return and submit this to HMRC electronically by 19 May (but always check the deadline in case it changes), or you will suffer an automatic penalty. The P35 asks for detailed information about income tax and NICs for directors and employees of your limited company, and your P35 will include information about you and your spouse or partner if they have a role in the business.

HMRC does provide detailed guidance on how to complete the

P35, but contractors should take particular care when completing question six (although of course the actual question number may change in future). That question is specifically designed to target contractors to find out their IR35 status. It changed extensively over the first ten years since first appearing on the P35, so you should consult your accountant before deciding on a response. Typically, there have been two parts to question six: the first asks contractors to confirm if they are a service company; the second asks if they have operated the 'Intermediaries Legislation', ie whether they have been working inside IR35.

**P11D:** You are required to complete a P11D primarily to provide HMRC with details of your non-cash income arising from employment, such as benefits and expenses. HMRC uses its copy of your P11D to cross-reference against tax returns. Employers complete the P11D, which for most limited company contractors means their accountant will prepare the form based on the year's financial records, and then ask the contractor to check and sign it.

Expenses you charge to your company credit card and which are paid directly by your company would not appear on the P11D, nor would any payments for expenses made direct by the limited company, say by paying a hotel invoice with a company cheque.

The penalties for completing an incorrect P11D are steep and each incorrect P11D costs employers, your limited company, £3,000 at the time of writing. Problems most commonly occur either because a contractor is trying to put a dubious expense through as a business cost, or because they have forgotten to include a genuine expense.

### Directors' obligations under the Data Protection Act
You may have obligations under the Data Protection Act 1998 (DPA) and be required to register with the Information Commissioners Office. This applies to all companies that electronically store and/or process certain personal information. Fortunately, the vast majority of contractors only have to register as Data Controllers when their contractor limited company processes non-exempt personal data about individuals.

You might also have to register if your activities are on the mandatory registration list, which includes sectors such as consulting, accountancy, marketing and journalism. Failure to comply with the act is a criminal offence that can result in steep fines from the Information Commissioner. These could arise, for example, as a result of failing to register or losing/inadvertently publishing records containing personal information about an individual.

## Other directors' responsibilities

Technically, contractor directors are responsible for a number of other areas covered by the Companies Act and other legislation, and these include:

- Acting in good faith and in a way most likely to promote the success of the business

- Exercising a degree of skill and care in the running of the company

- Ensuring the company is compliant with employment law

- Completing risk assessments and a health and safety policy

- Being responsible for the actions of company employees

- Abiding by data protection legislation.

You, alongside the vast majority of contractors, will automatically abide by these requirements by being good business managers of your own contracting business, and because you do not employ anyone apart from yourself. However, it is important to be aware of these additional responsibilities.

## Professional assistance

Your accountants' responsibilities depend on the agreement you have with them, and they are of course ethically bound to carry out all duties and responsibilities for which they are instructed and paid, but most have a standard service that will incorporate all the above.

It is, however, your personal responsibility to ensure that the accounts and other statutory documents are done as required by law and by the due dates. You also have to supply a lot of the information to your accountants like all the financial records so they can complete the paperwork for you.

If necessary, you may need to chase them – don't just assume that they are getting on with the job. But if they're not, it's probably worth looking for another accountant.

### 6.3.14 Managing surplus cash and tax efficiently extracting company profits

If you've grown a cash surplus in your contractor business, there are a range of strategies you can apply to make this money work harder, particularly when corporate deposit interest rates are low or inflation is eating away at cash deposits. These range from investing company cash in a pension, property or tangible assets such as gold or art, to closing the company and benefitting from the lower taxes capital distribution enjoys.

Whatever strategies you eventually adopt, this is definitely an area in which you will benefit from expert advice – both from your accountant, who will be able to minimise your tax liabilities, and from an independent financial adviser (IFA), who will maximise your potential investment returns. In both cases, the costs in professional fees should be more than covered by the tax saved and the return on investment. You should also ensure that you choose a specialist contractor accountant and an IFA with a strong track record managing clients in the contracting sector. Personal finance for contractors is covered in chapter 13.

But before taking the decision to pay dividends, declare bonuses or make significant investments with your company's money, you should first confirm that you have any tax liabilities covered and ensure you have sufficient financial reserves in the event that you can't find work for an extended period.

#### Companies can invest in assets, just as individuals can, but there are pitfalls

You can choose to invest your limited company's surplus cash in the same types of assets and investments as an individual can, with the exception of specific personal investments, such as Individual Savings Accounts (ISAs). These include assets such as shares, bonds and real estate property. You could even buy precious metals such as gold, or art, antiques, wine or vintage vehicles – anything that has the potential to grow in value.

Investing your company's money in gold, for example, can offer an alternative to 'traditional' options and could provide significant returns that, although not guaranteed, could certainly be greater than those offered by low interest on cash deposits. If your company owns an asset that has appreciated in value, such as a precious metal, but the asset is not sold during the financial year, the company's accounts will reflect that increase in value, but there is no corporation tax charge until the company sells the asset and the profit is realised.

However, there's a catch. HMRC's rules mean that when a company's income from non-property investments exceeds a certain level, the company becomes a Close Investment Company (CIC) and a higher rate of corporation tax kicks in – 25% at the time of writing. And the capital gains tax treatment of company investments is highly complex, so this is definitely an area where you should seek expert advice.

### Extracting cash tax efficiently using entrepreneur's relief and Section 1030A

If you have built up a significant cash surplus in your limited company and are considering taking a break from contracting, perhaps to work on a fixed term or permanent employment contract or take a year out to travel or study, the most tax efficient method of extracting your cash might be to close your company.

That's because it is possible to extract cash from a company being closed as capital, rather than income. Because the cash is treated as capital being returned to the shareholders, ie the original investors in the business, it attracts the lower rates of capital gains tax, rather than income tax.

As its name suggests, Entrepreneur's Relief (ER) is designed to allow entrepreneurs who start and grow a company to exit from the business tax efficiently. Companies that qualify pay a special capital gains tax rate of only 10%. Unfortunately, most contractor businesses that have run up a large cash pile are excluded from ER on the grounds that they have more than 20% of their assets as non-trading assets, or income from the company's investments is greater than the income from trading, meaning the company becomes a Close Investment Company (CIC).

An alternative solution is for you to apply to Companies House to have your limited company struck off the register (see section 6.3.17) and apply what's known as a Section 1030A distribution. This was formerly known as Extra Statutory Concession C16, or ESC C16 for short. If adopting this approach, then you are required to distribute all the assets, including any cash left in the company's bank account, to the shareholders and ensure the limited company is struck off from the register at Companies House.

This might sound painful, but what it actually means is you will pay tax at the capital gains tax rate of 18%, rather than income tax potentially at the higher or additional rates. It is quite a technical accounting exercise, so it is likely to be best to ask your accountant to manage the process on your behalf. To qualify, you must;

- Have applied to Companies House to strike off the company

- Have commenced striking off under section 1000 of the Companies Act 2006, or the contractor must have the intention of applying for striking off

- Have secured, or intend to secure, any outstanding fees owed to the company by clients

- Have paid, or intend to pay, any company debts and liabilities

- Have £25,000 or less in funds to be distributed – this limit is per company and not per shareholder.

The £25,000 is a 'cliff edge' limit. That means if you exceed the limit even by only a single pound, none of the funds held in the company can be distributed as capital. When the cash reserves to distribute start reaching sums in excess of £50,000 you might be financially better off using a liquidator, which will result in all the funds being treated as capital, regardless of the £25,000 limit. The liquidator's typical fees of £2,500 – £4,000 may be considerably less than the resulting income tax savings.

## 6.3.15 Directors' loan accounts and borrowing money

If you are a director and shareholder of your own limited company, you can have a director's loan account with the company. This does not mean your business becomes your private piggy bank.

In practice, if you've personally paid the company's bills, perhaps in its early weeks of life, then the directors' loan account is in credit. Your director's loan account, also known as a director's current account, can also be in credit if you don't draw any or all of your salary and dividend entitlement, which means your company owes you money. And when you take your money back from the loan account, it is classed by HMRC as a loan repayment and does not attract tax or National Insurance Contributions (NICs) liabilities.

However, when you take out more cash from the company than has been earned, or has been put in by you in the past, then the director's loan account goes into debit. Technically, an overdrawn loan account is illegal under the Companies Act, although there are no fines payable for breaking this aspect of company law.

This is because in practice this part of the Companies Act was created to protect shareholders from maverick directors taking money out of the business, and the chances of prosecution are rare for a 'close' company; that's one where the sole director is also the only or majority shareholder, as is the case with most contractors' limited companies.

However, there can be tax penalties. The maximum you can borrow from your company using a director's loan before incurring any tax liabilities is £5,000 at the time of writing. If the debit balance of the loan, or current account, is in excess of this amount, then you may be liable for tax and NICs.

### S455 (formerly S419) corporation tax and benefit in kind (BIK) charges

When you take your directors' loan account debit balance to more than £5,000, then it is classed as a benefit in kind and has to be reported on your P11D (see section 6.3.13 for an explanation of P11D). You can avoid this if your company charges interest on its director's loan, which should be the official HMRC rate, available from the HMRC website, or higher. You should remember that interest will increase the amount you owe the company, and your company's taxable profits will also increase as a result.

If you don't repay the loan by the end of the company's financial year in which you first took out the loan, then the loan account will be liable for an S455 (formerly known as S419) tax charge of 25% on the balance. This means your limited company will have to pay 25% of the outstanding director's loan amount as extra corporation tax. If you subsequently repay the entire loan after their company has paid the additional 25% corporation tax, the 25% corporation tax can be reclaimed.

However, if you repay the loan within nine months of the company's financial year end, so before their company has to pay the 25% surcharge, the company won't have to pay the tax bill at all. However, it should be noted that in that case you should not then withdraw the full amount again immediately, as HMRC will smell a rat and may well decide you're taking the money as salary rather than a loan.

HMRC dislikes overdrawn loan accounts and, depending on the pattern of payments to the contractor, may decide that the monies paid are not a loan but are a salary. This may happen if the contractor is regularly taking cash out of the business without corresponding dividends being declared, or if there are insufficient profits to declare a dividend. If HMRC investigates and spots this pattern in your company, then the taxman may insist that you pay income tax and NICs on the amount the company has paid you.

Bear in mind that overdrawn loan accounts are easy for HMRC to identify, as they have to be noted in the corporation tax return. So the best advice is to not let your director's loan account overlap into the next financial year, otherwise the tax implications can be complex and costly.

### 6.3.16 Making the company dormant

You might decide to take a break from contracting, or perhaps use an umbrella company during a series of contracts that might be inside IR35. One option would be closing down your limited company, but if you believe you will need the company in the future, then it might be better to make your company dormant. There are only really four scenarios when you might want to make your company dormant, rather than simply close it:

- To protect a brand by registering a limited company with that name

- Incorporating a company at the start of a contracting career that fails to get off the ground in the first 12 months

- A gap between contracts in excess of 12 months, or longer, as you've been unable to find work, or unable to work through illness, but intend to resume trading as a contractor

- If you are planning to remove the company from the Companies Register, but have not yet done so.

To make your limited company dormant, you must:

**Prepare final trading accounts:** Even if you cease trading halfway through your normal financial year, you must still use your usual accounting reference date. Companies House expects accounts made up to the usual financial year end, regardless of the date that the company actually ceased trading within the year.

**Pay final Corporation Tax:** Final trading accounts must be filed with HMRC's corporation tax inspector, as must your final corporation tax return (form CT600) with computation included. Once you have agreed and settled the final corporation tax assessment, you can then advise the corporation tax inspector that the company is now dormant.

**Close payroll:** You should close your company's payroll scheme by notifying the relevant HMRC Inspector of Taxes who deals with your PAYE that trading has now ceased and there are no employees. The Inspector of Taxes will then issue a final form P35 for the current tax year ending on the following 5 April. This form should be completed without delay and filed together with any associated P14s and P11Ds.

**Close bank accounts:** All interest-bearing bank accounts should be closed and it may be worth closing any non interest-bearing current accounts so you can avoid bank correspondence and statements being issued.

**Terminate accountant/professional services and other suppliers:** Advise your company accountant and let any other professional acting for your company know that any ongoing services and agreements are to be terminated while the company is dormant. You may also need to alert business suppliers, such as broadband and smartphone suppliers, that your company will cease trading and ask for a final account to be supplied.

When you are working through your new umbrella company, or during a period of permanent employment, to maintain the company's dormant status there are still some tasks to complete:

**Companies House:** Even though your company is dormant, an annual return must be filed at Companies House together with the fee. You need to complete an abbreviated balance sheet and submit these accounts nine months after your financial year end.

**Registered Address:** Your company will need to maintain a registered office address, which can be either your home address or your accountant's office address.

**Notice of change of directors and secretary or in their particulars:** Even when your company is dormant, you still have a responsibility to advise Companies House if there are any changes in the company director's or secretary's circumstances by filing the appropriate change of director/secretary paperwork, which can be filed online or downloaded from the Companies House website.

**Cease Trading:** It is vitally important to ensure that your company does not undertake even a single trading transaction, including receipt of bank interest or revenue generating transaction, during this period. Any such transactions occurring would require full trading accounts to be filed and the corporation tax return made to HMRC.

### 6.3.17 Closing down the company

You may have decided to close your company because you are thinking about returning to permanent work from contracting, or perhaps moving from a limited company to an umbrella solution on a permanent basis, and therefore do not want or need to keep the company dormant.

Because it is costly and time consuming to open and close companies frequently, if you think you will be only be dipping into the contract market occasionally between periods of permanent employment, then an umbrella company is likely to be a better solution for you than your own limited company, even if you think you will be contracting outside IR35.

If you are absolutely sure you want to close (or 'strike off') your limited company, then the following process applies. Many of these tasks must be completed promptly to avoid complications leading to further delays and costs:

**Inform all the company's stakeholders:** Many limited companies with long and complex trading histories that have creditors and perhaps numerous shareholders and directors have to inform a long list of people/organisations previously associated with the company.

In practice, assuming you are the sole director and shareholder with no creditors or employees, you simply need to inform:

- HMRC (for corporation tax, payroll and VAT purposes)
- The company's business insurer
- The company's banker
- Accountants and other professional advisers
- Suppliers, such as smartphone and broadband providers.

Technically, if there is a co-director and additional shareholders, they must be informed in writing and be sent a copy of the DS01 application for striking off. Co-directors will also be required to sign the striking off request.

**Prepare final accounts:** You should prepare your final trading accounts covering the period from the last annual accounts to the final date of trading. These must be submitted to HMRC, together with the corporation tax computation and Company Tax Return (form CT600). You should advise HMRC that these are the final trading accounts and that the company will shortly be dissolved.

HMRC will issue its final assessment and the final balance of corporation tax should be paid immediately, otherwise you run the risk of the Inspector of Taxes objecting to your company's striking off.

**Close down the corporation tax scheme:** Once you have settled your final corporation tax liability, you need to ask HMRC to close down the corporation tax scheme they have for the company.

**Close payroll:** Your Inspector of Taxes who deals with payroll should be advised that the company has ceased trading and will shortly be dissolved. They will issue you with a final employers annual return (form P35), which you should complete immediately. You will then need to pay the final balance of PAYE income tax and NICs and then ask HMRC to close down your payroll scheme.

**VAT registration:** HMRC should be advised by you that the company has ceased trading and should be deregistered for VAT. They will issue a standard questionnaire that you need to complete and return. When HMRC receives your questionnaire it will issue a final VAT return. You should complete the return in the usual way and account for the final disposal of any fixed assets or trading stock, if appropriate (you might need to ask an accountant to help you with this.)

**Application to Companies House:** After your company has ceased trading for three months, you should complete and send Companies House form 652a together with your cheque for the current dissolution fee, which you'll find on the Companies House website. Companies House will then advertise your company in the London Gazette and, following a period of up to nine months, your company will be dissolved, when it officially ceases to exist.

You must ensure that on the date of dissolution there is no money in the company bank account or other assets held in the company's name, since bank accounts may be frozen and the sums transferred to the Treasury Solicitor acting for the Crown.

**Final dividend:** Finally, you need to calculate a final dividend, or capital distribution, for distribution to the shareholders. Shareholders are the lowest in the food chain for any final payments from the company, as final payments of corporation tax, VAT, PAYE and so on take precedence. You must pay your final dividend prior to the date of dissolution by Companies House.

It might be possible for you to distribute the funds in your company as capital, which attracts a lower rate of tax, via Entrepreneur's Relief or Section 1030A. Section 6.3.14 explains these schemes in greater detail.

Contractors who show a pattern of starting up contractor limited companies and then winding them up, only to start another, will almost certainly attract HMRC's attention as running a series of 'phoenix jobs'. HMRC has access to impressive databases of company and individual tax records. It uses powerful data mining techniques to target companies and individuals for investigation.

You won't have past tax liabilities from wound up limited companies being attached to any new businesses that you start, but you may find that HMRC targets you personally for investigation and possible transfer of outstanding tax balances to you personally.

If your company is experiencing financial difficulties or is insolvent when you want to close it down, you must talk to an accountant or insolvency practitioner, as this process is more complex.

### 6.3.18 Activity diary – regular tasks

To help you stay organised when you start running your limited company, it is sensible to put together a diary of those regular tasks you need to complete. Some tasks will vary according to the date of your financial year; others are set according to the tax year.

Variable diary dates:

- Annual return (end of financial year on date of incorporation)
- Corporation tax self assessment return to HMRC (12 months after year end)
- Company accounts (9 months after year end)
- Changes in company and director particulars (as needed)
- VAT returns (quarterly).

Fixed diary dates (although always check, in case there's an extraordinary reason for them being changed):

- 6 April        Official start of the tax year
- 19 May        Form P35 to HMRC
- 31 May        Issue P60 to employees
- 6 July        Forms P11D sent to HMRC
- 31 July        Income tax, second payment on account
- 31 October    Personal tax return (paper)
- 31 January    Personal tax return (electronic)
- 31 January    Income tax, first payment on account.

If you use an online accountancy service, and you have kept your income and expenses information completely up-to-date, then it is likely that most of the above will be handled automatically. All the forms, accounts and tax returns will be generated automatically and all you will need to do it check them before they are submitted.

However, if using a traditional accountant, it is advisable to check with your accountant any lead times they need for the preparation of the above documents because, in some cases, it could be weeks or months ahead.

## 6.3.19 Changing accountants

You may reach a stage when your business is growing more complex than your original accountant is accustomed to handling. Or you may have had problems with the accountant's work, for example, they may have given you bad advice that led to problems with the taxman, or papers might have been filed late, leading you to be hit with penalties. Or you may wish to move all of your accounting online, but your current accountant does not offer a full online service and has no plans to do so.

Whatever drives you to it, there might come a time when you decide to change your accountant. Whatever your reason may be, there is a procedure that allows you to change accountants seamlessly. The professional accounting bodies, such as the Institute of Chartered Accountants, have set up a process that helps avoid disagreements and limits difficulties as much as possible.

There are two basic scenarios: either you and your accountant agree to part company, or you don't.

When you agree, your accountant may be sorry to see you go, but is obliged to allow you to change. In this case, ask your new accountant to contact the old one, and the necessary exchange of information and paperwork will take place. The professional accountancy bodies oblige members to provide documents without charge; nor should there be any charge for copies being made which the old accountant must keep.

When you disagree, your accountant still has to advise the new accountant about your affairs, but there are three areas in which problems may arise: non-payment, money-laundering, and matters about which the accountant would be responsible for reporting you to tax authorities. These are discussed below.

## Been there, done that!

### Accountants — service is the key

**DAVE SAYS:** After three years of using the same accountant, I found that the service levels were dropping. I didn't speak to the same person every time I phoned up for help, and different people gave conflicting answers. I wanted a more personal service, so changed to another accountant who was recommended by a friend. I pay twice as much but I prefer the more personal service.

You and your accountant may not agree on fees owed. In this case, you should contact the accountant's professional body, which will arrange a fee arbitration. This is undoubtedly the fastest and fairest way for you to come to an agreement. Your original accountant may have the right to refuse to transfer information to the new accountant if fees are not paid, so the best way forward is arbitration.

Your original accountant may have other reasons for refusing to transfer your accounts to the new one. These would all involve unethical or illegal behaviour on your part. If your original accountant believes that you have committed fraud, for instance, you will have to permit the new accountant to discuss this with the original one. Should you believe this to be unfair, you will need to challenge the original accountant directly. You cannot ignore the allegation and move to a new accountant.

The same goes for accounting irregularities. If there are issues about your financial reporting, you have to settle them with the old accountant before moving on to the new one. But hopefully you've been running your business properly, and your change to a new accountant should be simple and a positive move forward for your business.

## 6.4 Trading through an umbrella company

Umbrella companies are designed to remove nearly all of the administration and company management associated with a limited company, which is why they are such a popular choice for contractors.

The main advantages for using an umbrella company are:

- It means you avoid the hassle of running a limited company

- There is no need to be involved with running a spreadsheet, keeping the books, completing VAT returns, payroll matters, company accounts, taxation, director's responsibilities and so on

- For short-term contractors, a main advantage is not having the costly process of forming a company and then arranging for it to be dissolved.

Naturally, there is a charge for such relative ease and convenience and, for those whose contracts are outside IR35, the real cost of using an umbrella company is in a considerably lower net income than they could otherwise earn by contracting through a limited company.

However, one of the principal features of life as a contractor is its flexibility, and different times or contracts may require different trading solutions. Switching between the two, or even sometimes running them concurrently, is certainly possible and sometimes advisable.

Another important point to remember is that compliant umbrella companies will offer you a full employment contract, together with all the employment rights and benefits that come with it. Umbrella companies that do not operate on this basis are falling down on a very basic compliance requirement; so consider what other areas of compliance they may also be avoiding.

### 6.4.1 Choosing an umbrella scheme

Contractors seeking an umbrella company solution have well over 200 suppliers with a UK presence to choose from, and that number is growing. However, you may find the advertised fees do not necessarily include everything you thought you were buying. Unexpected costs are a typical contractor complaint.

And there are companies purportedly selling umbrella solutions that may not be umbrellas at all, masking any number of different structures and tax solutions that may fall well short of fulfilling your actual requirements.

You can download the free Contractor Umbrella Pricing – Costs to Consider checklist from contractorcalculator.co.uk, so you can be sure you have asked a potential umbrella employer all the right questions. You can either send the checklist out and ask umbrella companies to fill in the boxes, or use it to jog your memory when talking to a provider or researching online.

 contractorcalculator.co.uk/Docs/ContractorCalculator_
Contractor_Umbrella_Costs_to_Consider_Checklist.pdf

When selecting an umbrella company consider:

**Types of scheme:** You can choose from three broad umbrella company scheme types:

- The most common 'traditional' PAYE umbrella solutions providers, which offer an employment solution

- A Swedish Derogation umbrella solution, created in response to the Agency Workers Directive (see chapter 9). This solution is distinguished from the traditional model because it offers contractors employment between assignments and helps them find new contracts

- Offshore umbrellas, which are typically not umbrella companies at all but offer a variety of tax avoidance strategies (see section 6.2.6).

Offshore schemes are promoted on the basis that their payment methods give them an advantage over the standard UK-based umbrella company schemes. It is important to ensure that you are fully comfortable with the system being offered, and that it is appropriate to your own circumstances. You must also personally check very carefully the legality of any arrangement being offered, and take appropriate independent professional advice.

Bear in mind that legislation was introduced in the 2004 Budget making it a legal requirement for 'tax avoidance' schemes to be registered with HMRC. Suffice to say, some of these schemes present an even greater risk than others.

The traditional umbrella solutions providers can be further subdivided into three further groupings which tend to be differentiated by price and service levels:

- Basic payroll umbrellas that do little more than invoice the client and pay the contractor net of income tax, National Insurance Contributions (NICs) and their fees

- Full service umbrellas that provide the basic service plus expenses and often other benefits, such as pension schemes and insurances

- 'Premium' umbrellas that place an emphasis on high levels of personal service. These tend to focus on higher earning contractors who simply don't want to run a limited company despite the significant additional take-home pay that would result.

**Speed of processing transactions and payments:** The most common complaint by contractors about their umbrella companies is that the speed of processing payments and quality of service is less than they had expected. So, before signing up with an umbrella company, it is advisable to check the following with potential providers:

- How quickly they will send an invoice to the agent following receipt of your timesheet

- How quickly they will they pay you when they receive the agency's money for your work

- Do they have any service guarantees and/or money-back promises for service failures?

**Monies held back:** Some umbrella company providers make a point of holding back a proportion of your money. It is still your money, but it is there to cover holiday and sick pay, to cover periods between contracts, and even to cover bad debts arising from non-payment by your agency or client.

Other umbrella companies do not make any deductions whatsoever and simply pay out the full weekly/monthly amount of your agency payment. It is important to clarify in advance exactly when you will be paid and whether any monies will be retained for whatever reason.

**Agency recommended umbrellas, preferred supplier lists (PSLs) and timesheet levies:** Most agencies will recommend an umbrella company. These are in theory judged on the quality of service the umbrella company offers both the agency and the contractor. The agency is looking for umbrella companies that offer hassle free options – hassle-free for the agency, primarily!

Some agencies have fixed policies for recommendations, whilst others have "commercial arrangements" with umbrellas' preferred supplier lists, or PSLs. The choice of suppliers is not necessarily based on the quality of service provided to the contractor. It is always a good idea to ask the agency why they recommend a particular umbrella company.

This is because agency-supplier relationships are increasingly based on what are known as 'timesheet levies'. Umbrella companies that refuse to pay a fee to the agency for each contractor timesheet submitted, a timesheet levy, are unlikely to make it onto the PSL. As businesses umbrella companies have to make their margins, so the costs of timesheet levies are invariably passed onto contractors. Agencies using this practice, which includes some of the biggest recruiters in the UK and globally, get both their margin from the client and the levy from umbrellas.

**Expenses allowed:** Some umbrella companies market their 'dispensation' arrangement with HMRC for paying expenses without receipts. However, compliant umbrella companies will still insist contractors can only justify legitimate expenses by retaining receipts in case they are investigated by HMRC.

HMRC takes a close interest in umbrella companies that have dispensations, particularly where expenses are paid without any justification or supporting vouchers – so beware! Only ever claim legitimate expenses and always keep records and receipts; even if your umbrella company doesn't want to see them, the taxman might.

**Fees charged:** The marketing of fees by different umbrella companies varies considerably. At the time of writing, you should expect to pay between £25 and £30 per week for a high quality service, and as low as £10 per week for a basic payroll service. Check whether or not that includes VAT, and see whether you can negotiate the fees down. Some umbrella companies charge on a percentage basis, but will often be prepared to negotiate, particularly with contractors on higher rates.

**Experience and qualifications:** Anybody can set themselves up as an umbrella company, without any experience or qualifications, so it is important to know exactly who you are trusting to handle your hard-earned money. Most of the quality umbrella schemes are run by qualified accountants, who will be able to offer personal and professional guarantees.

### 6.4.2 Joining an umbrella scheme

When joining an umbrella company for your first contract, or moving from a limited company arrangement, there is usually a process to work through. Having said that, you can usually be up and running with an umbrella within 24 hours, subject to some due diligence checks they will make.

#### Step 1: Inform your agent or client
You need to advise your agency or direct client of the name of the umbrella company you are using, so that they can prepare their contract with the umbrella company's name as "contractor".

#### Step 2: Contract preparation and signing
The contract will usually be sent directly to the umbrella company by the agent. The umbrella company will arrange for it to be signed by their director and forwarded onto you for checking/countersignature as required.

#### Step 3: Personal and bank details
The umbrella company will also have a standard application form for you to advise them of your name, address and bank details for transfers to your account.

#### Step 4: Tax details – P45
You will need to send the umbrella company your form P45 from your last employer.

If you do not have a form P45 they will issue you a form P46, which will enable them to obtain a tax code to operate on your salary. You may find you are on an emergency tax code for a short period of time while your tax paperwork catches up with you.

### Step 5: Umbrella contract

Some umbrella companies will ask you to sign their own standard contract between yourself as an individual employee and themselves. This contract will specify the terms and conditions of the umbrella company service under which you agree to work and be paid. All compliant umbrella companies should offer you a full contract of employment. If one does not, you are well advised to consider an alternative service provider that does.

Some contractors move from umbrella to umbrella in the hope of 'resetting' their expenses allowances or to escape a difficult contract. A reputable umbrella company will conduct due diligence on new contractors who join, so if you are attempting to escape problems you will almost certainly get found out.

## 6.4.3 Expenses and dispensations

A small minority of umbrella companies aggressively market their ability to maximise contractors' net pay, usually through ramping-up expenses claims that qualify for tax relief, such as travel and subsistence.

Most promote their dispensation from HMRC. A dispensation is not a 'get out of jail free' card for contractors to claim whatever expenses they like without proof. A dispensation is granted by HMRC to employers that can prove sufficient internal or external audit and oversight that they don't have to submit a separate P11D for each employee.

Some contractors automatically claim for the entire dispensation amount to maximise their tax relief and thus their net pay, even if they have not spent the money or cannot provide receipts. They have sometimes been encouraged to do so by their own umbrella companies, as part of their marketing and contractor retention strategies.

It is a terrible idea for any contractor to falsely claim for expenses they have not incurred. Even if your umbrella company has a dispensation and encourages you to use it, HMRC can and does investigate specific individual contractors and ask them to validate their expenses. And it is not difficult for HMRC to locate the miscreants, because umbrella companies marketing their dispensation splash their elevated claims across the internet.

The few extra quid you might 'earn' by falsifying your expenses will never compensate for the hassle in time, money and stress it will cause you if/when the taxman catches up with you. You might even end up with a criminal conviction, which could prevent you from winning future contracts.

### 6.4.4 Employment rights and benefits

Contractors have traditionally resisted all attempts to turn them into employees, and whilst contractors working through an umbrella company have no employment rights with their client, they should have rights with their umbrella.

Any umbrella company that genuinely employs its contractors will provide the full range of employment rights – everything a regular permanent employee would expect to receive. Different umbrella companies will vary in how they fulfil their obligations to provide employment rights for their contractors, but the statutory benefits offered by umbrella companies that genuinely employ their contractors include:

- Statutory sick pay
- Holiday pay
- Maternity and paternity benefits
- Minimum wage/guaranteed minimum hours
- Redundancy payments.

Without efficient and experienced finance, payroll and human resources teams in place, as you would find with a regular large employer, the umbrella company would be unlikely to be able to fulfil its obligation to its contractor employees. This 'regular employer' infrastructure brings added benefits; for example, contractors who require a mortgage reference have a recognised employer to provide a reference, and an HR department that can process the reference request.

Umbrella companies with good HR support also operate employee grievance and disciplinary procedures, should there be issues with a contractor's performance when working for the client.

**Maternity pay**
Any contractor working through an umbrella company should be fully employed by that umbrella company. Assuming the pregnant contractor meets the qualification criteria, she can claim a range of statutory benefits. The rules regarding maternity benefits and eligibility criteria can be quite complex. So a fully compliant umbrella company should have policies and procedures in place to guide their pregnant contractor clients through their entitlements.

Maternity benefits for pregnant contractors include time off for antenatal care, maternity leave, maternity pay and a raft of measures designed to protect pregnant contractors' workplace rights, benefits and any contractual conditions. If a contractor does not qualify for their umbrella company's benefits, they may still qualify for state maternity benefit, which they claim directly from the government.

### 6.4.5 Changing umbrella company

You can opt to change your umbrella company at any time, but to minimise the disruption it is best to do so between contracts. It may be that you are not happy with the level of fees or service from your current supplier, or you may switch to take advantage of a new contract.

You will have a contract of employment with your umbrella company and this will usually contain a notice period. Your first step is to write to your umbrella company giving formal notice. Reputable umbrella companies will not have exit fees or a need to hold back money. You should expect to receive a P45 fairly soon after you have left, unless there are outstanding invoices from your contract with the old umbrella company.

Contractors who hop from contract to contract and regularly change umbrella company will experience a time lag as their tax paperwork catches up; this is normal and the contractor's tax situation will 'net out' over time. It can take up to 12 weeks with a new umbrella company before your paperwork is in order and during that time you may be on an emergency tax code, paying more tax than you should. But don't worry – eventually this will correct itself.

However, if you've not saved a sufficient level of fees for a 'rainy day', cash flow issues could arise.

When you start with a new umbrella, the umbrella is required to conduct a range of identity and due diligence checks. These include confirming your identity to conform with money laundering regulations, and also checking your tax and expenses history.

Contractors have been known to change umbrellas because they think they can 'reset' their expenses allowances, but this is not possible with a fully compliant umbrella company. In addition to the P45, which provides a snapshot of your tax and National Insurance Contributions (NICs) status, you will also be asked to supply your expenses history.

If you want to avoid the attention of HMRC, stay within the rules and inform your new umbrella company of your contracting history. You should also note that expenses incurred when working for previous umbrella companies are not allowable with your new umbrella, as they have technically been incurred with a former employer.

When you change umbrella company, you must also renew your contract with the agency or end-user client. Most agencies will issue a fresh contract with the new umbrella company without complaint.

It can be an end client that proves difficult and often does not understand why they should issue a new contract. So you should ensure you manage your clients' expectations when you are changing umbrella and clearly explain the situation to them.

The new contract with the agency or end-user client should be signed by a company officer of the umbrella company, as this is the legal entity entering into the deal. But some agencies require all parties to sign. In cases where, for example, intellectual property is an issue, the agency will want the contractor to sign as well as the umbrella company.

Contractors who are sometimes in the middle of one contract are offered another contract by a different agency or end-user client, perhaps with higher rates of pay, and are tempted to make the switch, changing umbrella company at the same time.

But you should think carefully about doing this, as the consequences could be severe if it is a breach of contract between the contractor and the umbrella, or the end-user client. You may find the agency or client pursues the umbrella, which in turn may seek to obtain redress from you.

# 6.5 Moving between trading vehicles

There could be very good business or personal reasons why you might want to move from one trading vehicle to another, and such reasons may outweigh the work required to make the transition. As long as the change is made with a good lead time and in an organised fashion, any disruption will be minimised.

### 6.5.1 Moving from a limited company to an umbrella

There are many potential reasons why you might want to move your contracting business from your own limited company to an umbrella company, and it is generally not an issue as long as you follow the correct process.

**The 'hassle factor':** Although most contractors find it easy to get into the habit of keeping up to date with their limited company obligations – especially if they use professional help – some might come to the decision that it's not for them. For example, they might simply get fed up with:

- The responsibility of being a director of their own limited company
- The discipline of regularly updating a spreadsheet or online accounting system
- Responding to communications from accountants, HMRC, Companies House and so on
- Invoicing the agent every week
- Arranging insurances
- Running a company bank account
- Arranging for all documents and returns to be filed in good time to avoid late filing penalties.

By switching to an umbrella, some of these tasks disappear and others are completed by the umbrella company's operations team. But remember, you will still have to claim expenses, complete timesheets and send these to your umbrella company as a matter of routine. And you'll still have to keep proper records of your client, agency, contracting and tax affairs – there's no getting away from admin!

**Existing legal, accounting or taxation problems:** Your existing limited company may be encountering legal, accounting or taxation problems and you may not wish to place a new contract within that company. But don't feel that changing to an umbrella company will make those problems go away; in fact, it's unlikely to and could even make things worse, if only because you might be seen to be 'cutting and running'.

A reputable umbrella company will conduct its own due diligence on your background, so any skeletons will come to light, and you may have to make provisions for them with your new umbrella company.

**IR35 issues:** Some contractors go through periods when all their contracts are inside IR35. If this is happening beyond a financial year for your limited company, and is not likely to change in the foreseeable future, it might be time to cut your losses and make the switch. And if things do change, as long as you made your limited company dormant and did not dissolve it, then you can easily and inexpensively return to limited company status.

**Self containment:** An umbrella company may be ideal for short term situations or to keep the income and expenses of a particular contract 'self contained', outside of your usual limited company arrangement.

**Overseas contracts:** You may wish to accept a contract outside the UK, which could involve offshore arrangements that can be placed through a specialist offshore umbrella company.

**Personal issues:** There may be personal reasons why a new contract is kept outside the existing limited company, for example:

- Matrimonial or separation/divorce issues
- Agency contractual commitments
- Differing profit sharing arrangements between contracts. For example, where the existing limited company is

owned by more than one shareholder but a new short term contract is to be entirely for the benefit of one contractor only.

Whatever the reason, there is generally a trading solution to be found by most contractors to suit their current conditions.

**Practicalities:** If you want to change from your own limited company to an umbrella company, you will need to consider the formal process of closing down the company or, alternatively, arranging to keep it on a dormant company basis.

## 6.5.2 Moving from an umbrella to a limited company

As circumstances may point you towards contracting through an umbrella company from your limited company, so the reverse is true. You may have started contracting through an umbrella company and now want to continue your contracting career through your own limited company.

The potential reasons why you would wish to move from an umbrella company arrangement to that of having your own limited company could include the following:

- When you started life as a contractor, you were not sure if it would be a long term prospect, so decided to go for an umbrella company as a short term option. You have now decided that you like being a contractor, and having your own limited company seems a more appropriate solution for the future

- You wish to have a degree of control over your company affairs, to enable you to be more directly involved in expanding and developing your own limited company

- You are unhappy with the service of your existing umbrella company and feel you may avoid some of the problems if you take control yourself

- You are sensitive to umbrella company costs (they are usually more expensive than running your own limited company, since they do more work and take more responsibility). This is analogous to the difference between owning and renting a car.

**Practicalities:** Moving from an umbrella company to a limited company should be fairly painless, as long as you follow some simple steps.

Firstly, you will need to examine the existing contractual arrangements you have committed to with your existing umbrella company and your agency.

It will be difficult to transfer an existing running contract from an umbrella company to a new limited company, unless you have the co-operation of the umbrella company and the client and/or agency concerned. Difficult, but not impossible. Often it is the client who is the most awkward, as they have to sign a new contract which may involve a long-winded process with their HR or procurement teams. Some umbrella companies have a tie-in period with penalties or additional costs if you leave early – make sure you check your contract first.

There may be a 'closing down' process or dissolution procedure for leaving an umbrella company which is effectively giving notice as you would to any employer. You should ensure that the umbrella company pays you fully for all amounts owed and any retentions for holiday pay or contingencies, which they may have held back during the period of the contract.

Section 6.3 details all the stages of setting up and running your own limited company.

## 6.6 Employee expenses

Alongside factors such as choice, freedom and flexibility, expenses are one of the fundamental factors that differentiate contracting from employment and leave contractors better off financially than if they were permanent employees. Yet, ironically, to get the best out of HMRC's expenses rules, contractors must have a thorough understanding of how expenses rules work for employees.

That's because, as an employee of your own limited company, your expenses are subject to employee rules and not expenses rules as they relate to self-employment and sole traders, which are very different. This understanding is also a crucial differentiator between specialist contractor accountants and high street accountants: the former typically have a better understanding of applying employee expenses rules than the latter.

The golden rule is that you can only claim expenses that are 'wholly, exclusively and necessarily' incurred for the purposes of your business. On most occasions, you won't find this to be an issue. But what happens if a visit to a client's site is required to a European city that might be renowned for its culture or cuisine, and you fancy staying on an extra day or two and take in the sights, thus incurring 'dual purpose' expenses?

Fortunately, HMRC will allow a contractor's expenses when there is obviously a business purpose motivating the expense, as long as there is no other obvious purpose. This is a key point to understand because, if there is another purpose, HMRC will dispute the expense. You should therefore always be aware of this 'duality of purpose' trap. So, if you incur an expense that right from the start is partly for business and partly for personal reasons then, regardless of the nature of the expense, you should recognise that it will not be allowed by HMRC.

Expenses can be claimed for the six years prior to the claim being made by the contractor. So if you did not include expenses in your accounts and tax documentation in the past, they can be brought forward and claimed in the next appropriate accounting period.

## CONTRACTING MINDSET TIPS:
### Contractors can claim expenses formerly paid by themselves

Once you start contracting, you can claim business expenses in a way that permanent employees can't, even if you are employed by an umbrella company. Many expenses you pay out of your own pocket as an employee come directly out of your fees when you contract and can help reduce your tax bill.

### How would you like to offset travel, computers and even household bills against tax?

Wouldn't you think it was great if your employer offered to subsidise your travel, home office equipment and a proportion of your household bills?

Ask yourself how much you spend on books, online courses and training workshops to improve your work and business skills. Don't you think it would save you a fortune if you were able to buy all these items at a massive discount?

Work out how much gross income you have to earn as an employee to pay for a £1,200 laptop after you've paid tax in your salary. Then work out how much you save if your employer deducted the cost from your salary before and excluded the VAT; how would it impact on your net income after tax?

### Employees pay for everything net of taxes; contractors pay for many things pre-tax

As an employee, all your home office needs and household bills are paid out of your personal income after you've paid your taxes. Any travel and subsistence expenses are reimbursed by your employer at cost. So, on an employee salary of £50,000 a year, you'd need to earn £2,069 before tax to buy a £1,200 laptop (including VAT at 20%)

When you buy a book about management to improve your business skills, or the latest how-to software manual, you pay the cover price. And you probably do the same if you're a professional required to go on courses to maintain your professional membership. As an employee you bear these costs from your net income.

Because VAT is charged on nearly everything we buy, as a permanent employee we rarely think about the fact that the retail price of nearly everything includes a sales tax. When we are employed, we routinely pay a 20% premium on everything we buy, including office equipment, computers and software.

### Contractors claim business expenses before tax, and use expenses to reduce tax

As a contractor, your place of work is your home office. That means that when you start work at your client's location, you're working in a temporary workplace. HMRC has rules about temporary workplaces that allow you to claim back some of the costs of travel, meals and hotels when working away from home.

You claim expenses, which can also include the cost of office equipment, furniture, computers, books, training courses and many other business expenses, out of your gross fees before tax. That means not only do you need to earn less to pay for these items, but as a cost to your business they are offset against your profits and reduce your tax bill.

If your contracting business has fees that are greater than the VAT threshold, then you can register for VAT and claim back the VAT you pay out on business expenses. That means a laptop retailing at £1,200 costs your business only £1,000 ex-VAT. Plus, that's £1,000 paid out of pre-tax earnings, in other words £1,000 off your business profits, potentially saving you £200 in corporation tax. That laptop, and any other expenses for that matter, is suddenly costing you a lot less than it would if you were an employee.

**Contractors can claim business expenses before tax and VAT that, as employees, they would pay for out of personal net earnings.**

### 6.6.1 Pre-incorporation, formation and pre-trading expenses

When starting out in contracting, or if you are changing trading vehicle from an umbrella company to a limited company, you will find that you will almost certainly incur up-front costs setting up the business.

Many of these pre-incorporation, formation and pre-trading expenses are likely to be paid out of your own pocket, because your company has no clients yet and therefore no cash; it may not even have a bank account. But this is not a problem, as the taxman reasonably says that these expenses can still be claimed, as long as they are legitimate. They should ideally be claimed all in one go and as soon as the company has the cash to pay you for them.

Your formation expenses are the costs you incurred to register your company. You will probably have a bill for at least one of the following:

- Registering the company with Companies House
- Using a an online or offline formation agent
- Using an accountant.

This bill, which could be between anything from about five to many hundreds of pounds, is an allowable expense.

Any valid expenses you can claim whilst contracting that are incurred in anticipation of your trading, or pre-trading expenses, can be claimed as if they have been incurred on the first day of trading. These might include:

- Professional fees to accountants and lawyers, perhaps for accountancy advice or preparing contracts or terms and conditions
- Marketing costs, such as domain purchasing, website hosting and design, design and printing of business cards and stationery, and maybe some advertising
- Travel and subsistence whilst setting up the business and travelling expenses for interviews

- Costs, such as relevant reference books (like this one), subscriptions, membership of trade or professional organisations directly related to the contractor's business

- Equipment, such as a laptop, tablet and smartphones, software, office furniture, office stationery and consumables, plus other admin-type costs

- Home office running costs, such as fixed line telephone and fax, broadband access and a proportion of utility bills in line with HMRC's guidance

- Insurances, such as public and employee liability, professional indemnity insurance and business asset contents insurances (home policies typically won't cover assets owned by a contractor limited company)

- Eligible training, which could mean refreshers on the latest tax laws for an interim accountant – or gaining certification on advanced software

- Reasonable entertainment can also be a start-up cost for many contractor limited companies, but entertainment costs are not tax deductible, although they can be recorded as costs to the business.

You must keep all receipts and invoices for company expenses right from the start. This includes keeping meticulous records of travel and mileage, especially as many of the receipts and invoices will not be in the name of your limited company.

Keeping a paper trail is essential, as your accountant, and later a tax inspector, may challenge any suspect costs. HMRC will examine the first months of company activity and costs very carefully if they investigate the business early on in its life. All business records must legally be retained for six years, and seven years is recommended to allow for all HMRC requirements, as that is how far back the taxman can investigate.

It is also possible to claim the VAT on past expenditure on products and services, once you have registered your company for VAT, but only if a valid VAT receipt has been obtained for each expense.

On the day the company starts trading, usually when you issue your first invoice in expectation of your first payment, you can present your limited company with an expenses form detailing all the above costs. It is unlikely that the full amount can be reclaimed in one go, but you can transfer the amount in tranches as long as you make a careful note of what each payment from your company account into your personal account is for.

## 6.6.2 Ongoing expenses you can claim

After formation and for as long as you are contracting through your own limited company, you will incur ongoing expenses. These should be claimed on an ongoing basis, weekly, monthly or as appropriate. Most contractors process expenses at least every three months in the same cycle as completing their VAT return.

These expenses are incurred as part of the ongoing operations of the business and should be claimed on a regular basis.

- Travel expenses, such as rail, bus, taxi and air fares

- Motor expenses (mileage claims, if the car is personally owned)

- Accommodation and subsistence

- Certain books, magazines, subscriptions and courses – where directly related to business and your contract work.

These above expenses are likely to be paid for out of your own pocket and reclaimed using an expenses form. Wherever possible separate your personal and business spending; therefore, it is best to pay for these expenses using a company credit card or cheque when possible.

Other expenses that are paid for directly by the company include:

- Your gross salary

- Your spouse's or partner's salary, which must be actually paid to that person for a real job, and should be at a realistic level for the actual duties performed

- Salaries for other employees or, more likely, payments to other contractors you hire as substitutes or to handle specialist areas of a contract you are working on

- Bank charges and interest charges on your company bank account

- Pension scheme – where paid by the company to a scheme approved by HMRC

- Business insurances – professional indemnity, business contents and other business-related insurances

- Corporation tax, employer's NICs and VAT, if your company is VAT registered

- Professional fees, such as for accountants and solicitors

- Marketing expenses, including advertising, company flyers and updating your website

- Office expenses and stationery

- Communication costs, such as mobile and fixed telephony and broadband

- IT hardware and software costs, including hardware, software licenses and peripherals.

There are specific and often complex rules associated with each of the above classes of business expenses, and these are covered in subsequent sections.

### 6.6.3 Travel and subsistence costs

If your expenses have been 'necessarily incurred in the performance of duties', then you can claim subsistence costs, such as food and beverages, plus travel and accommodation expenses when working at a temporary workplace (see section 6.6.4 for the definition of a temporary workplace). You must be working away from your normal place of work at a temporary workplace to be able to claim for the travelling expenses to get there, as well as for the subsistence and accommodation costs whilst working there.

HMRC publishes what it calls 'scale rates', which are its allowances employees can claim for subsistence. You should always keep receipts for all your expenses because HMRC is likely to be suspicious of contractors working through their own contractor limited company who always use its scale rates. Contractors who try to claim scale rates without receipts may find that, on inspection,

HMRC will consider their expenses to be an 'allowance', and thus deemed as pay, or employment income. Therefore, the 'expenses' would attract back payments of PAYE, National Insurance Contributions (NICs) and interest, not to mention penalties.

HMRC has strict rules about the circumstances under which contractors can claim travel expenses, depending on the type and location of the contract and the time spent working at each client site. You can claim the full range of travel expenses incurred travelling to and from a client's site, which may involve:

- Train, coach or bus journeys, at the ticket price
- Car journeys, including mileage at 45p per business mile up to 10,000 miles and 25p per mile thereafter when using a private vehicle (correct at the time of writing)
- Taxi fares
- Air fares, at the ticket price.

As with all expenses, you should keep accurate records of your business travel expenses, including all receipts and vehicle mileage logs.

### 6.6.4 Temporary workplace rules and the 24-month rule

For most contractors their permanent place of work is their home office. Daily travel to a client's site is considered legitimate business travel as long as the contractor satisfies the criteria laid down by HMRC.

The first test is called the 24-month rule. You can claim tax relief on your travel expenses up to the point when you *know* that your contract at the client's site is likely to exceed 24 months. The period starts from the day that you start working at the new site. Say you start off on a 12-month contract, have a six-month renewal and then have another six-month renewal, to take the total contract length to 24 months, you have to stop claiming expenses after 18 months when you know the total contract length at that site will be more than 24 months.

The second test is the 40% rule, which will affect you if you might be spending time at a number of client sites during the course of a working month. Basically, if you are spending three days at one site and two days at another, you can continue to claim travel expenses up to the point that you know you'll be spending 40% or more of your time at a particular client site. As soon as you know that, then you cannot claim tax relief on travel expenses to and from that particular site, although if you have individual trips to different locations you can still claim for these.

This also applies if a contractor takes a break for a month or more – the time period that would otherwise be used to calculate the 24 month rule is not 'reset'; the contractor should use the 40% rule instead.

If you have been working for one client in a building with other tenants, and win a contract with one of the other tenants, which is genuinely a completely separate company in different offices in the building, then the 24-month rule is reset and you can claim travel expenses.

### 6.6.5 Accommodation costs

Hotel and other accommodation costs incurred when staying away from home to work on a specific contract can also be claimed. And it's not just hotels and bed and breakfast accommodation which qualifies. You can claim expenses for staying with friends and family and even some of the expense of buying a property near to your client.

#### Claiming costs for staying with friends and family

HMRC allows contractors to claim a contribution towards the cost of working away from home when they choose to stay with a friend or relative, rather than in a hotel or other lodging. HMRC accepts that you may wish to show gratitude to the friend or relative by treating them to a meal, and whilst HMRC is quite clear that they would not expect a meal for two to be a legitimate expense, a contribution would be accepted towards the cost of your meal only.

The friend or relative can also benefit if their guest, the contractor, pays them rent whenever they stay for business reasons. The rent charge again would vary, but is likely to be more than the rates recommended by HMRC, but less than the cost of a hotel room in the same area, which, in some locations can be hundreds of pounds a night. You can claim the rent as an expense, but beware of paying your friend or relative too much rent otherwise it may increase their tax bills as a result!

## Buying a property close to the client

If your contract is located beyond reasonable commuting distance and, perhaps due to the contract's length, you choose to buy a property close to your client, you can claim all the non-capital costs of running and financing this second property as a legitimate business expense. Because you only use the property five days a week, it is business accommodation and the entire amount is allowable, not just a proportion.

However, only revenue and finance costs can be claimed through your company, not capital costs. This means that mortgage interest payments can be claimed in full, but payments towards the capital cost of the property, or the cost of alterations or extensions cannot. Revenue expenditure includes utilities like heat, light and water, plus communication costs, such as business broadband and a phone line, as well as council tax, which are all allowable.

## Combining business trips with holidays

Contractors taking genuine business trips can legitimately tag a holiday onto their trip and still claim expenses. You could even fit in some client entertainment or take your family on a holiday, as long as the original trip is essential for the performance of your work duties and you also keep to HMRC's normal rules regarding business expenses.

If there is a genuine reason for your spouse or partner to accompany you on a business trip, for example if your spouse performs legitimate business duties that are needed on the trip, then it might also be possible to claim their travel, accommodation and subsistence expenses in full. On the family front, if you were taking the car on a business trip to, for example, Edinburgh and the hotel did not charge extra for a family room, then you could take both spouse and children on the trip and still claim 100% of the travel and accommodation expenses.

### 6.6.6 Company cars

Contractors trading through their own limited company have the option of running a company car. But the calculation to work out whether it's more tax efficient to personally own a car versus running it through the company is not only complex, but also different for every contractor. And the government changes company car legislation almost every year, so the tax efficient model you bought last year might end up costing you a whole lot more this year because of changes in the Chancellor's next Budget.

Although when you use your personal car for business trips you can claim 45p per business mile up to 10,000 miles, and 25p per mile thereafter, this rarely covers the costs of running a car. Conversely, if your limited company provides a car for both business and private use, you will pay income tax at your highest rate on the benefit provided. As a result, every contractor's case has to be judged on its own merits and there is no simple curve over which it becomes cost effective to choose one option over the other.

Company car tax charges are mainly based on vehicle emissions, and new models with ultra-low emissions are constantly being launched, which mean that some contractors could find it more tax-efficient to buy a new car through their limited company. However, for most contractors, it generally works out cheaper to run a private vehicle rather than a company car. Your accountant is likely to have a spreadsheet-based model into which they will plug all your relevant personal and vehicle details to help determine your options.

### 6.6.7 Mobile phones and smartphones

HMRC's rules for contractors claiming the cost of a mobile phone or smartphone or similar mobile device from their contracting business are not straightforward and can catch contractors unawares. You should always start a mobile phone and smartphone contract in the name of your business. Simply asking the mobile operator to add the company name and address to the monthly invoice is not enough; the actual contract must be with the contracting business and not you personally. This is an important subtlety that catches out many contractors.

If the contract is directly between your limited company and the mobile operator, then the full cost is an allowable expense paid directly by the business. That's because HMRC expenses rules state that the company can provide contractors with one mobile phone or smartphone for business purposes that is exempt from tax as a benefit in kind (BIK).

Incorrect expenses claims for the business use of a personal mobile phone or smartphone are one of the most common contractor expenses accounting mistakes, and claims largely arise because the rules can seem counterintuitive. If you have a personal mobile phone or smartphone costing £30 a month with an inclusive calls allowance, and you work out from your itemised bill that you have used half the call allowance for business purposes, logic would suggest that you could claim half the monthly line rental as a business expense.

But that's not the case. HMRC's expenses rules always consider the 'marginal cost', or additional costs, of what an employee incurs in the performance of their duties. In this example, you paid £30 per month before making business calls, but there was no marginal cost of the business calls, so you cannot claim any element of the line rental as an expense. And what's even worse, if you have claimed £15 a month for 50% of the line rental in this scenario, this payment should be taxed as salary and attract income tax, as well as employee's and employer's NICs.

Note that tablets are treated as computers, just like a laptop or desktop PC. Even if your tablet is not much larger than your smartphone and has mobile broadband functionality via a mobile operator, it does not qualify for the exemption that allows you unlimited personal use of your mobile phone and smartphone with no benefit in kind tax charge.

### 6.6.8 Company benefits such as healthcare and gyms

You can pay for healthcare insurance, medical expenses and gym memberships directly via your contractor limited company. However, you will pay tax in exchange for most of these benefits. The only exceptions are for medical check-ups, health screening and overseas medical costs, which are usually legitimate business expenses that can be claimed by contractors, without them having to pay a benefit in kind tax charge.

Sports facilities provided by employers can be tax free, but only if the facilities:

- Are provided for use by all the employer's employees

- Are not open to the general public, and

- Are used 'wholly or mainly by persons whose right or opportunity to use them is employment-related'.

As a result of the above, your local gym or health club is unlikely to qualify. A gym at your home won't qualify because facilities provided on domestic premises, ie premises 'used wholly or mainly as a private dwelling', are specifically excluded. When you charge gym membership back to your company as an expense, it is treated as salary and you must pay income tax, as well as both employee's and employer's NICs on the full amount. If your limited company is invoiced directly by the gym or health club, then you incur a tax charge as a benefit in kind.

### 6.6.9 Calculating the costs for running a home office

Contractors trading through a limited company are typically employed by their own business, so in order to claim more home office expenses than HMRC's minimum rate, they should create a rental licence. As a limited company contractor, you differ from contractors working as sole traders and partnerships, because you are an employee. And as such, HMRC rules say you can only claim £3 per week for the use of your home as an office. However you can charge rent to your limited company at commercial rates that are substantially more than HMRC's employees' rates.

To do this, you need to put a commercial rental licence in place between you and your limited company. This rent can reduce your limited company's corporation tax liability, but need not increase your income tax charge if properly calculated. You calculate the costs of your home office using exactly the same guidance used by sole traders and partnerships (see below). Any profit could be liable to income tax, but the objective is to set a level of rent that covers your home office expenses and minimises the potential income tax liability.

HMRC's rules for the self-employed will allow you to claim a proportion of your household costs as a deductible expense if the right criteria are met. These criteria include:

- If an area of the home is used exclusively for business purposes and is in use during specific hours of the day. The room used must look like an office, so have for example, a workstation, desk, chair and filing cabinets. Using a laptop or tablet at the kitchen table won't qualify

- A reasonable claim relating to the business. The time spent should be realistic, for example from nine in the morning until five thirty in the evening. Also, the area used should not be a disproportionately large area of the domestic living space.

If you meet these criteria, then the types of household expenses that can be claimed include:

- Utilities, such as gas, electricity and water and waste, or fuel oil depending on your heating system

- Insurance – if there is no separate business policy, a proportion of the household policy can be allowed

- Council tax – a proportion of the total bill can be claimed

- Mortgage interest – A proportion of the mortgage interest is allowable, but capital repayments are excluded

- Rent – A proportion of the rent of a home is allowable if a part of the property qualifies as being used for business purposes

- Repairs and maintenance – A proportion of the total cost of general repairs and maintenance can be claimed; this would include roof repairs, for example, but not decorating a room that is not used for business purposes.

So how does it work? Well, you basically calculate the proportion of the house space used and the time spent using that area of the house as an office, then apply that multiple to the household expenses. That provides you with an indication of the rent you can charge your limited company under the terms of your rental license.

## Been there, done that!

## Expenses claims...and cons

**DAVE SAYS:** Some contractors really push the boat out when claiming expenses, going as far as claiming things that aren't proper business expenses. This is not only illegal, but a really bad idea.

The trick with your expenses is just to play the game and don't break the rules. Don't raise any red flags. If you try to be "creative" with your accounts you'll get investigated by HMRC, and the time, effort, stress and money you'll incur due to an investigation isn't worth the few extra pennies you might make by cheating.

Similarly, as a contractor, one of your biggest selling points will be the reputation you build up with clients, agencies and other contractors. Screw this up by being caught fiddling your expenses, and you could well be screwing up your future contracting career.

Just stick to the rules.

# Contracting lessons from this chapter

- Most contractors either work through their own limited company or through an umbrella company, and many switch between the two.

- The major advantage of trading via a limited company is its tax efficiency.

- If you are paid less than around £25 per hour, or are caught by IR35, then an umbrella company may be the best option for you.

- Being a sole trader is rarely an option, because agencies/clients won't hire sole traders, fearing they may become liable for employment rights or unpaid taxes.

- Offshore solutions only suit certain contractors with a strong appetite for risk. You should conduct due diligence before using aggressive tax planning schemes.

- The limited company learning curve can be steep, but once it is up and running, the admin burden is quite low.

- As a limited company contractor, make sure you attend to IR35 issues – always.

- Claim all legitimate business expenses to which you are entitled to minimise your tax liabilities.

- Ensure you have all your business records in order, and never claim for any expense that is not legitimate – it's just not worth it.

- Using online contractor accountancy systems can save you considerable time and automate much of the routine administration.

- Make sure you use a specialist contractor accountant, not a high street accountant. Specialists will understand IR35, limited company expenses and tax planning from the point of view of the contracting model.

# 7

# Contracts and contract law

# 7.1 Introduction to law for contractors

A contractor, by definition, is reviewing and signing contracts on an ongoing basis, unlike a permanent employee who may only sign one employment contract that will last several years. That is why contractors need just enough contract law knowledge to ensure that they're aware of the point when they need to seek professional help. That's the point of this chapter.

In fact, it is hugely important for contractors to understand that, at times, there is absolutely no substitute for professional legal advice. Legal experts are expensive, but such is the law of market forces that if their services were not of such high value (although generally modest compared to the much more costly alternative of you getting it wrong) they wouldn't be able to charge so much.

To put a contractor's legal expenses into context, at the time of writing a simple contract review by a specialist solicitor might cost up to £200; if the legal representative is then asked to negotiate changes with the agency, the cost could rise to about £1,000. That might sound expensive, but these sums pale into insignificance when seen in the context of that same contractor being found to be within IR35.

In one case that a contractor lost at the High Court, being found to be within IR35 ended up with him facing a bill for back taxes and penalties of almost £100,000. Suddenly that £200 contract review doesn't seem quite so expensive, does it?

If you use an agency, then generally they will give you a contract to sign. If you go direct then you will need to prepare contracts for the client to sign. The best way to use your own contracts with a client is to use templates supplied by an industry organisation and get them checked by a solicitor.

## 7.1.1 How much law do you need?

To launch and maintain a successful contracting career, you only need enough law to be able to do two things:

- Understand and know how to use the law to protect yourself and negotiate your way through business life

- Know when you have reached the limit of your legal knowledge and that you should consult a legal expert.

As mentioned in the introduction to this chapter, there are some key areas where a small investment in legal advice will be more than worth it in the long run. These include:

- Checking final contracts, particularly with new agents and clients
- Evaluating IR35 status from contracts.

The old adage 'a little knowledge is a dangerous thing' is very true of the law, but there are some lessons that can be learned as they crop up again and again; so contractors with some basic legal knowledge will be in a better position to enjoy a successful contracting career.

However, the law changes on an ongoing basis and it is important to regularly check with a solicitor, whose duty it is to keep abreast of changes in the law. You should also keep yourself informed by following the contracting media, so that you have a good idea of when to ask your solicitor and/or accountant if a recent change in taxation, company or contract law might affect you.

## 7.1.2 Understanding the law

To be convincing when you are negotiating legal matters, it is essential that you understand some of the concepts behind UK Common Law. Law in the UK, as in most Anglo-Saxon countries, is based on interpretation. Jokes abound about lawyers 'splitting hairs' but in fact the legal rights and wrongs of an argument are only rarely black and white, especially in business law.

It is easy, if you only have a little understanding and knowledge of the law to assume that 'the law says that x is allowed, and my contract says x, therefore I'm right.' The real situation is more complicated. Each statement and clause in a contract is interpreted in terms of the legal concepts behind it. And this is also why it is important to get your solicitor to check your contract and not your accountant. Your accountant is not an expert in contract law, in the same way that your solicitor would not be qualified to give you tax advice.

Another common misconception is that people imagine that the law is a long list of do's and don'ts. The law is more of a philosophy, a group of related ideas which judges interpret. Judges are guided and in some cases directed in their interpretation by case law. Case law is simply a written decision made by a judge on a similar issue in the past.

Judges judge arguments:

- You argue that 'x is allowed since there is a law that says it's allowed', and your contract says x, so you are allowed to do x.

- Your opponent will argue that either 'your contract doesn't really say x,' or 'the law that says x is allowed doesn't mean the kind of x in your contract,' or 'the law says that x is only allowed in different circumstances from the one in your contract.'

The judges will rule on which argument has the greatest merits according to the written legislation, or the rules, and the interpretation, or the case law.

Whilst the notion of a list of do's and don'ts and 'can dos' and 'can't dos' might seem attractive and certainly simplify matters, in practice the system of common law allows interpretation by judges which is a good thing. Life and society are complex and no one set of absolute rules can apply in every context. One day you might be thankful that, although the law says 'x', in your case, it might not.

It is worth noting that in some circumstances the Laws of Scotland are different from the Laws of England and Wales. However the broad principles remain the same. Some contractors working in the engineering and construction sector will already be aware of this.

## 7.1.3 Know your rights and protect yourself

As a contractor, a person who signs contracts with clients and agents, you need to understand how to read the contracts you are signing and to spot areas of concern that you may choose to fix yourself, or you may choose to seek the assistance of a legal expert. It is important to remember that sometimes what contracts don't include can be just as important as what they do include. This is a good example where knowing enough about the law can enable you to push for any missing items to be included.

Contracts can also include dangerous or objectionable material that you need to have removed. This can happen sometimes through ignorance on the agent or client's part and sometimes through design, so having a basic understanding of how contracts are structured can be a valuable tool at this time. Contracts are not the only area of the law where contractors may have to protect themselves, and this is where knowing enough about how the law works and how to use the law can be of immense value.

### 7.1.4 How the law works, or how to use the law

In the UK, the principal organisations for interpreting and enforcing the law are the courts and the judiciary. However, before you plan on taking someone to court, bear in mind that the civil courts in the UK can be very slow. Complex cases that involve attempting to recover large sums of money from debtors can take years and cost significant sums in costs.

For smaller sums under £5,000, there is a fast track service through the County Courts, often known as the 'small claims court' but still a part of the County Court system. There is even an online service available through HM Courts Service, MoneyClaim Online, which means you can file a claim against, for example a debtor who owes you money, and assuming it is uncontested and a low enough sum you never have to leave your office.

However, a fundamental principle of civil law practice requires parties to make reasonable attempts to resolve a dispute before resorting to legal action. As a result, courts like to see evidence of non-legal attempts to resolve an issue. So if someone owes you money, it's best you talk to them first and ask for it nicely before getting tough and resorting to the law.

It is therefore advisable to see if you can use your knowledge of the law to convince the other party to settle before resorting to the courts. It is surprising how effective this approach can be, because eventually, if the other party is really wrong, they could pay damages and costs. And if they know they are really wrong, and you call their bluff, they know they are going to lose and have to pay you anyway.

It is also possible to put indirect pressure on the source of your problems. For example, if an agency is requesting what in your view are unreasonable contractual changes and you are prepared to walk away rather than sign, it is worth talking to the client, who under some circumstances can be your best ally. In this situation, if you informed the client that you are unlikely to be completing the contract because the agency has breached the terms of your contract or is planning to, the client is not going to be happy. They are expecting you to complete the work.

The client can read your contract and see what the agency is doing. The client also expects the agency to respect the law, and can pressure the agency with non-payment or worse if the agency doesn't get in line. You could not put that sort of pressure on the agency.

## 7.2 Contracts

Contract law is, alongside IR35, the greatest area of the law that a contractor needs to understand; because, by the very nature of contracting, contractors are frequently negotiating and signing contracts!

Knowing when to ask for expert help is just as valid in contract law as it is in IR35. Most agencies and clients use standard contracts and you need to know at least enough to identify when these contain unwelcome clauses that will require you to seek professional advice.

### 7.2.1 What is a contract?

A contract is a legally binding engagement between your limited company and the agency or the end-user client if contracting direct. If inside IR35 and contracting through an umbrella company, the contract would be between the umbrella company and the agent or end user client but essentially the content is the same.

Under UK law, there are three essential elements to all contracts, and these would normally form part of a written contract:

- An agreement between the parties to the contract – usually the contractor and agency, or the contractor and client

- A consideration, which confirms the agency or client will pay the contractor

- An intention to form legal relations by all parties, whereby it is clear from correspondence that the contractor and the agency or client were planning to agree on a contract.

If one of these key elements of contract law is missing, if the dispute ended in court, a judge would rule that there was no contract between a contractor and the client or agency.

Naturally, being subject to the principles of common law, volumes of contract law and case law have been created. However, specific areas tend to come up again and again in contracting.

A contract is an agreement to do something in exchange for a consideration, usually in the context of contracting it is a payment. When you accept an offer, you agree to a contract.

If you receive an offer, and make a counteroffer, the other party may accept and a binding contract is the result. Usually the acceptance of an offer is indicated by the signature of a contract, which is described as a fully-executed, or 'live', contract when both parties sign. Both parties must enter into the contract freely, before it is binding.

This is important for contractors, because what you agree to do has to be carefully described in the contract. You should not agree to perform vague or general work, you must agree to perform a specific task or series of tasks for a specific fee, which is the consideration.

Having a contract relating to specific projects is also essential if a contract is to remain outside of IR35.

Once the contract has been executed, if you are asked to do more things than are listed in the contract, you have a perfect legal right to refuse. Of course you could re-negotiate the contract or even have an additional contract specifying a separate consideration for the additional work.

In general, avoid anything in contracts that you don't understand, or find odd. Never allow yourself to be told that it's 'normal,' or 'standard;' if you don't like it, have it taken out or renegotiate it.

## Been there, done that!

### Yes, it's binding

**DAVE SAYS:** Many contractors have emailed ContractorCalculator describing clauses in their contracts that they deem to be unfair; and then go on to ask: 'Are they really binding?'

Often, the queries are about things like asking whether they can give notice even though their contract says they can't. One contractor recently asked whether he would be in breach of contract if he decided to jump ship early.

Although we always have these queries checked by our relevant legal specialists, up to now the answer in each and every case has been a resounding, "YES, it is binding."

So make sure you carefully read through your contracts before you sign them, and get them reviewed by a lawyer.

## Been there, done that!

### Get it right, first time

**DAVE SAYS:** A deal's a deal, so make sure you're happy before agreeing to it.

Let's say you want more money. It's not unknown for an agent to suggest you start on the rate being offered and that it will be reviewed after three months. Take it from me, this "review" will never happen. It's just a sales tactic to get you started on the rate and to keep you on it. And there's nothing you can do about it except exercise your termination clause, if your contract has one.

If you sign a deal for X pounds a day for Y months, that's the deal. It isn't going to change. That's how business works.

## CONTRACTING MINDSET TIPS:
### Deliver what you promise or expect to pay the price
Employees have employment contracts and multi-levelled disciplinary procedures before they get fired. Contractors have a legally binding contract for services, so if they don't deliver, the client or agency can withhold payment and sue for damages.

### Would you pay someone if they walked out leaving the job unfinished?
You've hired a designer to make over your bedroom for a fixed price. Halfway through the job, she walks out. Do you pay her pro rata, or less because you need to find someone else to finish the work?

Let's say you have a house sitter, being paid a day rate for looking after your home and feeding the pets while you are on a two-week holiday. He only turns-up for the first week. Should you pay just for the first week, or sue him because the goldfish died?

The gardener hurts her back and takes a month off, but sends her brother to mow your lawn instead. It's never looked so tidy. Do you care who does the work as long as the weeding gets done? And will you still be happy to pay?

### Employment contracts are not binding business-to-business agreements
If you resigned from your employment half-way through completing a project for one of your employer's clients, it's your employer's problem to find a replacement to finish the job, not yours.

Say you didn't get round to finishing a project for one of your employer's customers and it cost the customer money. The customer wouldn't sue you for damages; it would sue your employer.

When you're employed, your employment contract is an agreement between you personally and your employer. So, for example, you can't decide you fancy a couple of months off and instead send someone else in to do the work in your place.

### Contracts are binding agreements entered into willingly
As a contractor, things are different. If you have willingly entered into a fixed contract, whereby you must provide your client with specific deliverables, and you then fail to deliver, then you are in breach of contract. As such, your client can withhold payment for you failing to complete the entire project, and could even sue you.

Contractors on a day rate who unilaterally end the contract early should be paid for work already satisfactorily completed. However, the client could sue the contractor's limited company for the cost of hiring another contractor to complete the job.

Assuming your contract allows it, if you find for whatever reason that you can't complete the contract yourself, then you can send a substitute in your place. That's because the contract with the client is one of service with your company, and not one of employment with you.

**Contractors enter into binding legal agreements when they take on a contract: failure to deliver will have financial consequences.**

## 7.2.2 The difference between contract work and employment

Contractors are not employees. Previous chapters have laboured the point and highlight the differences. It becomes of huge importance in the contract between the contractor and the agent or end-user client that there is not even the slightest indication that you could be an employee.

However, HMRC can apply the tests of employment (see chapter 8) to a contractor to determine whether they are judged to be a disguised employee for tax purposes and if it is concluded that you are inside IR35, your net pay drops by a significant amount, up to 25%. Even if you think you are a contractor, if HMRC rules you are a disguised employee, then you have to pay tax like an employee. And you still won't get any employment rights.

The key tests of employment are generally recognised as:

- Control
- Substitution
- Mutuality of obligation (MOO).

Each of these is described in detail in chapter 8. They are particularly important to limited company contractors, and will be applied by HMRC each time a contractor's employment status is in question. There are many other factors that may also be considered, but case law has led to control, substitution and MOO being regarded as key.

A famous employment status case known as the MacKenna's Ready Mixed Concrete ruling, or more formally as "the judgment of MacKenna J. in *Ready Mixed Concrete (South East) Ltd v Minister of Pensions and National Insurance* [1968]", says that a contract of service exists when there is mutuality, control and "the other provisions of the contract are consistent with it being a contract of service".

Although in more recent employment status rulings mutuality of obligation has been treated with less weight by tribunal judges, MOO and control are considered to be "the irreducible minimum" in any contract of employment.

You should understand the difference between a contractor and an employee, and you should scrutinise your contracts carefully for anything that makes you appear in any way like an employee. And even then it is a worthwhile investment to have the contract checked by a specialist IR35 legal expert.

## Been there, done that!

### Let's meet now

**DAVE SAYS:** When you get an offer and agree it with an agent they will be keen to meet up with you as soon as possible to get the paperwork done. Because once you've signed you are committed. But it's always best to give yourself enough time to properly consider a contract and have it checked by a lawyer.

Being an employee is a special legal situation. Employees have a specific commitment to the companies they work for, and the companies have to ensure them a certain number of basic rights and privileges. These are detailed in employment legislation and involve items such as holiday pay, sick leave and termination and redundancy rights. An employer cannot simply fire an employee for no good reason. Contractors, of course, have none of these rights nor do they expect them.

One of the most basic employer/employee rights is mutuality of obligation (MOO). Employers have an obligation to provide work for employees and employees have to do that work. Employees have an obligation to present themselves at their place of employment every day, they can't send someone else instead like a substitute, and they are expected to do whatever the employer requires of them, subject to their job description.

Contractors are engaged to complete a specific project for a client, usually a company that employs people. Contractors aren't employees, so they have no obligation to be at their client's site unless their contract requires them to be there, and they only perform tasks related to the specific project that is described in their contract.

If the project is cancelled or if the tasks on the project run out, the client has no obligation to the contractor to provide more work. Contractors in turn have the right of substitution; they have the right to send a suitably qualified replacement to continue and if necessary complete the project.

Contractors have control over the way they complete their tasks. The work an employee does is controlled by the employer.

The employer also assumes all the risk involved with the business, not the employee. Contractors are responsible for the business risk on their projects (but see section 7.3 regarding liability).

Employees do not have expenses directly related to their day-to-day work (in practice of course they do but claim them back, so don't really have expenses). Contractors supply their own equipment at the cost to their business and pay their own expenses.

To make the essential difference between a contractor and employee perfectly clear, consider what happens when you hire a plumber to fix your boiler. You don't employ the plumber, you engage the plumber's services for a specific task for which the plumber bills you.

You don't offer the plumber holiday pay, nor does the plumber expect you to supply equipment, nor for you to guarantee work for a given period – they usually do. The plumber does the job for you and goes on to another one for someone else. If, after you have the plumber fix the boiler, you want the pipes fixed, then you agree another contract.

The difference between an employee and a contractor is that an employee has **a contract of service** with their employer and a contractor working through their own limited company or umbrella company has a **contract for services** with an agency or an end user client. This is defined in more detail in section 7.3.

### 7.2.3 The different between contracting and temping

The term 'temp' means that a worker accepts assignments on the basis that they will not become a permanent employee. The temporary worker is paid by an agency, but their work is not under their own control.

The temp works for one agency, and then perhaps does other work for another. Temping is a very flexible form of work, but one that is changeable and, as its name suggests, is not one to take a worker through their entire career. Temps do have one advantage though: if they work for one agency on a regular basis they are able to claim benefits like holiday pay and sick pay under employment legislation.

The term 'agency worker' is one used by a number of sources, in particular the trade unions. Trade unions like to feel they have a role to protect vulnerable agency workers, often on minimum wage doing low grade jobs.

However the issue is what kind of agency is described? A temporary work agency uses temps; an employment agency may handle a short-term assignment, such as maternity leave cover, interim executives and there are, of course, agencies that place contractors. 'Agency worker' is used to describe people who work through agencies, but temps employed by an agency are a world apart from interim executives and contractors working through an agency.

This difference is very important in legal terms for contractors. A contractor either works for their own limited company, or for an umbrella company which simply keeps the accounts for the contractor.

### 7.2.4 Contract of service vs contract for services

The distinction between the employed and self-employed and businesses has long been characterised by the nature of the contract they have with the organisation requiring the work, or services.

**Contract of service:** A worker with a contract of service is employed. They satisfy all the tests of employment described in section 7.2.2. Their contract is with their employer.

**Contract for services:** A major corporation can have a contract for services with a customer who is also a major corporation. A contractor has a contract for services with their client, if contracting direct, or with their agency. This is an arms length business to business arrangement (including the self-employed) where services are provided by a supplier to a buyer. There is no question of any employment relationship.

Although only differing by a few letters, these two phrases describe fundamentally different contractual relationships and it is vital that any contract between a contractor and an agency or client makes it completely clear that it is a contract of services.

### 7.2.5 Fixed-term contracts

Workers hired by clients under fixed-term employment contracts are not contractors running a business supplying a service, but employees whose employment has an end date or finishes when a specific task or outcome has been achieved. Fixed-term employment contracts may superficially resemble a contractor's contract, in that they are typically for a fixed duration for the purposes of a specific project, but the nature of the relationship between the client and worker is one of employment, and not business-to-business. It is a contract of service.

Under certain circumstances, fixed-term contracts can offer benefits to both clients and contractors, particularly where employee benefits or line management (eg being in a position of authority) are a feature of the role. You may often see two day rates quoted: the higher one referring to limited company contractors and the lower rate to the fixed-term employment contract option.

For a worker to be a fixed-term employee, they must have an employment contract, or 'contract of service', directly with the client, or employer. That contract must be 'fixed term', so it must end on a particular date, when a specific task or outcome has been completed or when a particular event occurs.

Fixed-term employment contracts are very common outside the core contracting disciplines in both the private and public sectors. They are frequently used to bring on board a worker for a fixed period to cover maternity leave and long-term sickness, or perhaps for a single academic year in a school, or when future funding for a role may be uncertain.

## 7.3 The elements of a contract

Agencies and clients like to use their standard contracts, and most contracts will have a broadly similar structure and content. In fact, some parts of a contract with one client may be virtually indistinguishable from a contract supplied by another. After all, most UK companies work within the jurisdiction of the courts of England and Wales and want the contracts to be subject to the laws of England and Wales.

But just because the agency or client prefers to use their standard contract, it does not automatically mean that you have to accept every clause. Negotiation is healthy because it removes potentially unhelpful clauses and demonstrates to all – including an IR35 status inspector – that you are behaving like a proper business, which is of course exactly what you are.

Most contractor contracts are divided into two sections: the standard or permanent section and the schedule. The permanent section includes all the standard clauses that relate to both parties, such as jurisdiction, liabilities, termination and so on.

The schedule defines the precise deliverables for the specific project the contractor will be working on. If the contractor is engaged by the same client through the same agency, the permanent section can generally remain the same and a new schedule is issued to reflect the new project and deliverables.

Either part of the contract can be changed when renegotiating or a completely new contract can be issued. However the division into contract and schedule helps significantly to demonstrate that the contractor is working on a specific project and not just working on whatever the client needs doing. This is essential if the contractor has any chances of remaining outside IR35 if they are investigated by HMRC.

**Schedules and deliverables:** This section is generally found at end of most contractor contracts and corresponds to the basic contract theory of an offer of a consideration (payment) and acceptance with supply of services. The front of the contract has details of the parties, such as the contractor and the agent, plus all the standard clauses.

Most contracts begin by defining the two contracting parties and the consideration/acceptance:

- The contractor – you
- The 'contractee' – the agency in most cases, sometimes the client

- What is the nature of the offer; a certain hourly or daily rate you get paid

- In exchange for what; specific services as part of a specific project, what you have to do.

The time period is generally next: for how long must you provide these services. This should be fairly straightforward. If it gets any more complex then start asking questions.

This section of your contract, the schedule, defines how you should perform your work, and what you can expect from the contractee (the agent/client). It will normally require that the work be done with reasonable skill and care and to the timescale agreed on in the schedule.

The schedule would also include a number of warrants: you are warranting, or confirming, that you have the skills to perform the tasks required to complete the contract. Be careful not to warrant anything you cannot provide. For example, do not warrant that you can speak Russian if you can't; you may be held responsible for damages.

Schedules generally oblige you to provide your own insurance, administration, support, and equipment. If it doesn't, it should state specifically why this is being waived for the purposes of the project. If there is no reason given, start asking questions.

It should also state what the client will provide. The agency has the right to certify this in your contract, but you hold the agency responsible if the client doesn't provide it. Remember you have no contract with the client, and the client has no legal obligation in your regard.

**Payment:** This section of your contract simply lays out how and when you get paid. Billing is most often weekly or monthly (but need not be) and you are usually obliged to submit time sheets to the agency to justify it. The client must sign these time sheets. You have every right to assume, as a result of this clause, that when you submit a signed time sheet, you should be paid.

It is best that the contract states billing dates without equivocation. If billing is linked to your completion of certain milestones, which does happen on occasion, see that these phases are accurately described.

**Right of substitution:** As case law grows around the IR35 tax legislation, the importance not only of having a Right of Substitution clause but, and this might sound odd, the right to exercise it, are becoming increasingly important. Having the right to substitute is a key test of employment status and partially determines whether an arrangement is a contract of service or a contract for services. However it is put, contractors must have a substitution clause in the contract with their agent or end user client.

The elements of correct Right of Substitution are:

- You must have an unfettered right to substitute yourself for someone else

- You should pay for the substitute (not the client), since you are effectively subcontracting the work

- You should pay for the handover period (for example a training period) for the substitute to replace you

- The client must not have the right to refuse a substitute without reason. Bear in mind that if the substitute does not have the necessary skills and cannot fulfil the contractual requirements then the client reserves the right to terminate the contract.

Some clients have not investigated the law in sufficient detail and form worrying, often emotional, conclusions from the right of substitution clause. In chapter 8, we cover handling objections, such as when a client or agency seeks to dispute or remove a substitution clause.

**Mutuality of obligation (MOO):** As explained in section 7.2.2 on the difference between employment and contracting, if mutuality of obligation can be established alongside control, then the relationship is almost certainly one of employment, or a contract of service.

There may not be a clause specifically called mutuality of obligation but the following clause is typically used in contracts to ensure there is no contract of employment (contract of service):

*"The client is not obliged to offer ongoing contracts or work to the company nor is the company obliged to accept such contracts or work if offered"*

As long as you ensure you work on a project basis and do not take any work that needs doing, then this points strongly to a contract for services, putting you outside of IR35.

**Control:** To contribute towards establishing that a contract is outside IR35, the written contract must have no indications that the contractor is under the control of the end-user client. So it must not detail a line manager that the contractor reports to and should not indicate that the contractor's work is regularly checked.

The contract must also be specific about what the contractor can and cannot do. A manager at the end user client has no right under the agreement to insist that the contractor takes any work that is available, only that they work on the project covered by the contract.

## Been there, done that!

### Buying IR35-free contracts

**DAVE SAYS:** Shortly after the IR35 legislation came into force in April 2000, a few firms were trying to sell IR35 contracts to contractors saying that if they used them then they would definitely pass IR35 tests. Whilst that may have been true at the time it wouldn't be now as the courts look at the notional contract (the real relationship between the contractor and the client) and not the one on paper.

The other pointless thing about buying any contract is that unless you are contracting directly with the client then you have no chance of forcing your own contract on the agency. They would have already put contracts in place with the client, and have something ready for you to sign – and most of the time they won't want to spend more time and money on negotiating changes with you.

Except for reasons of health and safety and security, the contract must not specify hours to be worked, such as nine to five. The contractor should be free to take holidays and work at home according to their requirements without asking permission from the client, although it would be professional courtesy and good client management to negotiate time away from the contract and any days working off site.

If a contract is within IR35, then it may include clauses saying the contractor must work under direct supervision and control of the client.

**Termination:** Most contracts include a termination clause for both parties. Contractor contracts are often different. Quite often, the agency retains the right to terminate, but the contractor is not permitted to do so. This is acceptable because one of the services demanded of a contractor is to be available for the full length of the project. It is simply part of what you do. This is not usually an issue and all goes smoothly: you finish the project so the termination clause will never be brought to bear. However, should the agency wish to terminate early, they do have the right to do so.

You, on the other hand, will have limited options when trying to exit a contract that has no notice or termination clause. By leaving the contract early, you run the risk of exposing your business to a claim for damages for breach of contract. So often, the only way to end a contract prematurely is through a negotiated settlement or by offering a substitute to complete the work, if the contract allows it.

The agency must pay you for all time through the termination period: this means that if the agency commits to a two week notice before termination, then they pay you for those two weeks whether you work or not, and assuming no other factors intervene like the quality of your work.

You are however bound by a "duty to mitigate", which means that you need to go looking for more work after you stop working under this contract regardless of the termination period. You can't just sit around and watch the television and expect the agency to pay you for it. Courts won't enforce your payment for the termination period if you cannot demonstrate that you have tried to 'mitigate.'

Always make sure that the termination clause clearly states what notice must be given. Try to avoid clauses allowing that termination be permitted without notice. Ideally, the only way your contract can be terminated without notice is if you are in serious breach of contract, and it must be a pretty major breach for the client not to allow the contractor to remedy the breach. In this instance you would probably be marched off site and not paid any more.

It is also perfectly acceptable for your client to have a different termination period to yours. Where a client is proposing a shorter notice period for termination that applies to them, this usually means they may want to be able to stop the project as soon as possible with minimum risk and the lowest possible project cancellation costs. They might need to do so if, for example, the budget is cut or the project is no longer necessary. But having a clause that says you have to give a longer notice period if you choose to terminate means you are tied in for longer. Therefore, you are less likely to 'jump ship' and leave the client without a contractor to complete the project.

**Restrictive covenants:** Contracts with agencies often include what is legally defined as a 'covenant in restraint of trade'. More commonly known to contractors as 'restrictive covenants', they are a form of protection for the agency and typically have two key components:

- Scope, which covers what the restrictions are, such as not contracting directly with the client or placing a geographical limit where you can contract with a client outside of the agency's sphere of operations
- Duration, covering how long the restriction will remain in force.

Typically, such covenants restrict you from working for the client directly without going through the agency, and they are sometimes extended to client subsidiaries. The duration will depend on the circumstances. For a contract lasting three months, a restrictive covenant remaining in force for twelve months after its finish may well be considered unreasonable. The converse could also be true, so for a contract lasting twelve months, a subsequent three-month ban on direct dealings may not be considered to amount to more than a reasonable level of protection for the agency. Each case depends on the exact wording of the contract and a consideration of your overall situation

Restrictive covenants are enforceable in law, so it is advisable that you don't try to circumvent them. They are a reasonable form of protection for the agencies, which spend money and time getting you your first contract with the client. They have a right recognisable in law to continue to profit from the effort they have made. If covenants had no teeth, every contractor could cut out the agency and work directly for the client after the first contract period and no agencies would be left in business.

An important point to remember is that the restrictive covenant can only be used for its original purpose and in the specific circumstances for which it was drawn up. Some agents might try and tell you that you have to reduce your fee if you want to continue working for a client, or they will exercise their rights under the covenant. That's completely unfair, and you can ignore the threat with complete safety.

If a clause in a contract places a restriction on trade that only favours one of the parties, and if there is some ambiguity in it, then the courts will generally use 'contra proferentem', an approach designed to encourage clarity in contracts. What it means in practice is that the clause will be interpreted in the way least favourable to the interests of the party set to benefit, or which imposed the condition.

The covenant is not a bargaining tool. If the agent wants to continue under the same contract terms, then the covenant has force. If the agency wants to change the terms, by making you take a rate cut for example, then the covenant has no value. The application of covenants in restraint of trade is, however, a very complex and difficult area of contract law. There is relatively little case law to depend on, and the number of challenging exceptions continues to rise: does it apply in public services where there is no competition? Does it apply if the agent does not make a good faith effort to renew the contract?

There are no exact answers to these questions but the rule of thumb should be to assume the covenant has force if the agency respects the terms of the contract and does not attempt to change them. In situations where you believe the covenant should not apply, enlist the help of a professional. If you are facing what appears to be an excessively onerous restrictive covenant, and you have cause to seek a break with the agency, that would be when you may find drawing the clause to the attention of their legal adviser advantageous.

Potentially your best ally in conflicts involving the covenant is the client. Explain to the client what the agency is doing and see if you cannot get the client to negotiate on your side.

## CONTRACTING MINDSET TIPS:
### Clauses preventing you bypassing agencies are enforceable
Your agency has invested considerable time and money in brokering the deal between you and your client. It is therefore perfectly reasonable for agencies to include restrictive covenants in the contract that prevent you from contracting direct with the client. These covenants are enforceable and should not be taken lightly.

### When you broker a deal, you expect to receive your cut, don't you?
Let's say you're running a small building firm and you've just won the contract to build a new leisure centre pool. You've lined up all the subcontractors and built your margin into the price. But in week two the subcontractors up sticks and start working for the client direct, cutting you out. Would you take that lying down, after all the time and money you invested to win the work?

You want to downsize from your large townhouse, asking a local estate agent to make the sale. They run an ad campaign and throw a couple of open house receptions and find you a buyer. You promptly try to cut out the estate agent and deal direct. What action do you think the estate agent would take?

### Restrictive covenants are contractual clauses to protect agencies' investment
Despite the fact that an estimated 80% of all UK contract work is sourced via recruitment agencies, some contractors think that it is perfectly acceptable to circumvent the agent and work for the client direct. This is the case even though it is the agency, in common with the building contractor, which has spent time and money assembling the team of contractors required by the client to complete the project.

Recruitment agencies, just like estate agencies, incur advertising and marketing costs to attract contractors to contract opportunities with clients that they would otherwise be unaware of or unable to sell their services to.

Some sector-specialist agencies also carefully follow their client markets and then spot and exploit brand new markets for their 'roster' of contractors. These contracts might otherwise not even exist, if it were not for such switched on and market savvy agents.

### Clauses stopping you from bypassing agencies are enforceable
Having a contract in place protects agencies from the actions of less than scrupulous contractors who don't appreciate the value that agencies bring to the contracting marketplace.

Like the scheming swimming pool subcontractors, if you decided you'd get a better deal dealing direct with the client following an introduction by the agency, the agency's restrictive covenant is enforceable and would prevent you from doing so. If you went ahead anyway, the covenant is likely to be enforced to ensure that the agency receives the agreed share of your earnings for effectively brokering the deal.

Equally, if the client suggests that you might want to come and work direct for them, this is like a house owner inviting a prospective buyer to deal direct and split the difference of the agency's margin. So beware, because it is likely that the agency will come after you for their share and not the client.

**Contractors who flout contract terms by trying to deal direct with the client should expect enforcement action from the agency.**

**Intellectual property rights (IPR):** Intellectual property can be an issue in contractor contracts. Problems arise as sometimes the contractor brings their own IPR to the table. The most effective approach to this section in the contract is simply to set out what belongs to your company, and what belongs to the client. The agency has no rights in this area. If you are working with client-developed material, clearly you won't obtain any rights to it. But see that it is all clearly stated.

**Liability and indemnity:** You are a business in your own right and you are therefore liable if you cause loss or damage. If you call a plumber to install the dishwasher and they then flood your kitchen, they will have to pay for the damages and clean-up. You will have to indemnify the client or the agency or both if you do something you're not supposed to.

However you are not responsible for third-party liability. You are responsible to the agency through your contract; you are not responsible if the client takes action that brings in the lawyers. It should clearly state in this section in the contract that you are liable for yourself, but not for anything else. If the client sells a product you worked on to another company and they then get sued it is not your fault. It is the client's responsibility to ensure that the product works before selling it.

Many contractor contracts call upon the contractor to 'indemnify' the client or agent if something goes wrong. The one thing that you have to make sure doesn't go wrong is your providing the deliverable on time: should you have doubts about your ability to do that, include them in the contract, or just don't take the job. If you foresee problems, you should get the client to agree in the contract that they may arise, and that you expect to be paid anyway.

Obviously, things do go wrong. However it is unreasonable to expect the contractor to pay for it if the contractor hasn't been dishonest about the services provided. Some agents or clients try to include 'indemnification clauses' in contractor contracts. These clauses oblige the contractor to pay for losses incurred under specific situations. You should try to renegotiate these, as they are very easy to abuse and it is the responsibility of the client to pay for business losses. The client is in a better position to handle these situations than the contractor. What the contractor can and should do is to agree in the contract to cooperate with the client to help make good the loss.

**Governing law:** Most contracts will state the legal system to which appeal may be made if there is a problem. This is only to prevent parties from claiming that they want to go to court in Singapore if the work takes place in the UK. For the most part, you will want UK jurisdiction and indeed the legal system works better here for litigation than in most other countries.

**Confidentiality:** Confidentiality should not prove to be a difficult issue. You will probably be contractually bound to keep all your work confidential. If a non-disclosure agreement is added to the contract that should also pose no great problem. However always check the 'field' of the confidential material and the term.

**Force majeure:** This is a standard clause in nearly all contracts and essential allows for the unexpected and catastrophic events that can't have a separate clause to themselves. If your client's offices are destroyed by a hurricane, you will not be able to enforce your rights.

## 7.3.1 Things to avoid

To ensure that the contract is one for services, not one of employment, there are some clauses that should not be present, as they may point towards employment.

**Holidays:** Contractors are not employees and do not receive paid holidays. Any reference to holidays must be removed. If you want to take a holiday during a contract, then the best option is to informally discuss this with the project manager and if it can be accommodated take the time off. Obviously you won't be able to bill for that time. Ideally take time off between contracts. That is one of the benefits of the contracting lifestyle.

**Ongoing contracts:** If there is reference to ongoing contracts, the inference is that this is ongoing work and not project work and thus implies a mutuality of obligation and thus employment. Make sure there is no mention of ongoing contracts anywhere in your contracts.

**Automatic renewal clauses:** If the contract is automatically renewed, it suggests that there is ongoing work and a mutuality of obligation exists – there will always be work for you if you are always there to complete it and you are not working on projects with a defined completion date. Remove any mention of automatic renewal clauses, however tempting they may seem, from your contract.

## 7.4 Protocol for confirming contractual agreements

You should always have a signed contract before you start working on a project or at the client's site. However, in practice, deadlines and delays sometimes mean that the paperwork has not been signed by the time the contract starts. But by sending or exchanging confirmation emails, you can ensure your interests are protected.

Having no signed contract right at the start is inadvisable, but is not usually a problem unless something goes wrong. And that's when records of conversations and correspondence between contractors and their agents and clients are vital. They are likely to help quickly bring an end to disputes, or to provide you with valuable evidence should the dispute escalate or reach the courts.

Even if a contract has not been formally finalised and signed, evidence such as emails can be used in resolving a dispute or in court to determine what was agreed and whether a contract was, in fact, in place.

### 7.4.1 Verbal contracts

Although in theory verbal contracts are valid under UK contract law, and technically a verbal contract is made when the agent or client makes an offer that you agree, verbal contracts are notoriously difficult to enforce.

If a dispute reaches court, verbal contracts can be determined by a judge, who will look at what has already occurred – things like how much have you been paid and what work you have been doing – and identify standard industry practice.

You should therefore follow up any verbal agreements made during an interview or over the phone in writing. That usually means sending an email, but belt and braces' approach would be to follow-up with recorded delivery letters.

## 7.4.2 Email confirmation of contractual terms

Immediately after discussing contractual terms with an agent or client by phone or face to face, you should follow up with an email detailing:

- The parties to the contract, which would normally be your limited company or umbrella and the agency, or the client if contracting direct

- Rate of pay, hourly or daily, and whether additional payments, such as expenses or disbursements, are to be paid

- How payment will be made – weekly on provision of a timesheet, monthly on invoice, and payment terms

- Start date and duration of the contract, including number of hours in a day if paid on a daily rate

- Specific contractual terms agreed, such as including a substitution clause, termination notice periods and so on.

You should also ensure that the three key elements of a contract apply: that there has been an agreement; that a consideration (the rate) has been discussed and agreed; and that the agency or client clearly intends to hire you for the contract.

In addition, you should carefully check your contracts when they arrive for signature, to be sure they include everything that was discussed and agreed. Once a contract has been signed, it will supersede what was previously agreed.

## 7.4.3 Confirming renewals by email

It is quite common for a contract renewal to be agreed verbally between an agency or client and the contractor. Sometimes this happens just before the contract end date, so the documentation may not arrive until after the contract officially ended.

In this situation, you should also confirm any conversations and verbal agreements with follow-up emails that detail the points in section 7.4.2. Alternatively, if no changes have been requested or made by any of the parties, you could simply confirm that the existing terms will apply to the renewal, then add the new dates.

Most contractors can work on multiple contracts for years and their contract paperwork will always arrive as agreed and without any hitches. But by taking the simple precaution of diligently following up key conversations with emails, you can be sure that any potential disputes will never even arise. And, if they do, you will have the evidence of the emails you have sent, making it easy for a judge to determine the true contractual position.

So the simple lesson is: for anything to do with contract negotiations, get it in writing and put it in writing!

# Contracting lessons from this chapter

- Take time to understand the basics of UK contract law – not because you want to be a lawyer, but so you know when it is time to call one.

- You have a duty to resolve issues by agreement prior to seeking redress through the courts, so be nice and make up if you can.

- Ideally, never start a contract without signed paperwork

- Contracts work both ways, so make sure you are able and prepared to fulfil all the obligations under contracts you have signed.

- When seeking professional advice about contracts, always use a specialist contract lawyer who has contracting sector experience.

- Pay careful attention to IR35, and seek advice from an IR35 specialist if in doubt. To help keep you outside IR35, make sure you sign a contract for services, and not a contract of service.

- Verbal contracts are best avoided, but are as valid as written contracts. So beware of committing to an agreement over the phone or face-to-face, because your client or agency can hold you to it.

- Confirm via email any agreements made verbally, and dispute any contractual issues you don't like formally and in writing.

# 8
# IR35

# 8.1 What is IR35?

IR35 is tax legislation aimed at countering tax avoidance by individuals supplying their services to clients via an intermediary who, if it weren't for the intermediary, such as a limited company or partnership, would be an employee of the client. In the eyes of the Treasury, such individuals are 'disguised employees' who should therefore be taxed as employees. However, although such individuals might be treated as employees for tax purposes, they do not qualify for any of the rights associated with employment from their client 'employers'.

The idea behind IR35 is sound: to stop people who are really employees pretending that they have rights to all the tax breaks that limited companies get, without having to take on the risks that companies run. In other words, it's the Treasury's and HMRC's way of making sure people pay the tax they're supposed to. 'Disguised employees' are not genuine contractors and should really be employed, paying income tax and National Insurance Contributions (NICs) as an employee.

Because the practical application of IR35 is intent on proving that contractors are not really small businesses, but are actually really employees, employment status case law is used as a guide. That's why you will see frequent references to employment law, 'status tests', 'status enquiries' and 'tests of employment' in writings about IR35.

So why should you be worrying about complex tax and employment legislation? Well, for the very good reason that getting caught by IR35 could result in a serious decrease in your net income, to the tune of up to 25%. IR35 is also known as the 'contractor tax' and so, by definition, as long as you are contracting via a limited company you will always be at risk of HMRC conducting an IR35 review to determine whether your contracts are covered by the legislation and you are in fact a 'disguised employee'.

Whether a contract is within IR35 or not is not a black and white decision for you and your accountant, or your agency or client for that matter. An already complex area was in May 2012 further complicated by an added layer of 'business entity tests'. These are not part of the legislation, but the results of the tests are used by HMRC as an initial filter to place you in an IR35 risk category, which could then have a bearing on whether you are investigated by the taxman. When the business entity tests were first published, because of the way the tests were scored, most classic contractors, or indeed anyone using a personal service company, would fall into the medium and high risk categories.

You need to take reasonable care to make a judgement on behalf of your company based on the results of HMRC's 'business entity tests' and the advice from an IR35 and employment law specialist, should you use one. But ultimately it is your responsibility to determine your IR35 status; not your accountant's or IR35 adviser's.

Even having concluded that you are trading outside the scope of IR35, you may still be investigated by HMRC at a later date and the taxman could decide that you had, in fact, been working within IR35 for some or all of your past contracts. This might lead to HMRC deciding that you owe a significant sum in unpaid back taxes, interest and penalties of up to 70% of the unpaid tax.

That is why it is so important for you to understand IR35, how it works and its potential impact on you and your livelihood. But don't worry – it needn't be as scary as this makes it sound, if you take some straightforward, sensible precautions.

IR35 only applies to contractors who operate via limited companies, the majority of whom run their contracts and their companies entirely legitimately. If you work through an umbrella company, you are already technically an employee subject to full PAYE and NICs, so you are not affected. Similarly, as a sole trader you pay income tax and NICs on your profits, so IR35 does not apply. If you have chosen to trade via an offshore solution, you should check with your scheme provider about your employment status and whether IR35 applies.

Whilst all contractors using limited companies need to be concerned by IR35, very few contractors are automatically caught by it. There is an estimated population of around 400,000 contractors operating through limited companies in the UK at any one time. But HMRC's records, revealed by a Freedom of Information (FOI) request by this book's publisher, ContractorCalculator, show that during the first decade that IR35 was in force, between 2,000 and 29,000 contractors self-certified themselves as within IR35 each year.

To put those figures into context, that's roughly between 0.005% and 0.07% of the total limited company contractor population, so the potential risks may seem minimal. However, survey evidence suggests that many contractors choose to simply ignore IR35, and the fact that few contractors self-certify themselves inside IR35 does not remove the significant risk that IR35 represents.

And unofficial statistics demonstrate that thousands of cases never made the official list because the contractors concerned, and their professional advisers, shut down the initial IR35 investigation immediately. This was because they had a watertight case for being outside IR35 based on the strategies described in this chapter. The evidence was sent to HMRC by the contractor's IR35 professional advisers on day one and that meant any further IR35 investigation was doomed to failure from the outset.

With forethought and correct planning, you too can ensure you remain outside IR35 throughout your contracting career and never have to worry. That is the objective of this chapter.

You can use ContractorCalculator's free Online IR35 Status Test to gain an early indication of your IR35 status:

 http://www.contractorcalculator.co.uk/IR35_Test.aspx

### 8.1.1 A brief history of IR35

The name, IR35, stems from the original Inland Revenue (now HMRC) press release announcing the new tax rules. Its more formal name is the 'Intermediaries Legislation', which was first announced in the Pre-Budget speech of 1999 by then Chancellor Gordon Brown, and adopted as part of the Finance Act for April 2000.

The motivation of the Treasury at that time was to tackle what they perceived as tax and NIC avoidance schemes through the use of intermediaries, such as partnerships or limited companies. And there was a serious problem, where lax tax legislation was leading to employees being able to change their status to limited companies or partnerships, thereby considerably increasing their take home pay, almost overnight. They did this by paying considerably less tax, which was not only a problem for HM Treasury, but also put additional burdens on PAYE taxpayers.

But despite their new limited company or partnership status, many of these contractors were really still employees – in the most blatant cases still working for the same boss, doing the same work, at the same desk, in the same way they had done before, and at the same company!

The limited companies used by individuals to offer their services to clients became referred to as personal service companies (PSCs). Although there is no statutory legal definition, typically a PSC is either a limited company with a sole director who owns all of the shares and who provides services via the company, or a contractor sharing ownership of the business with a spouse or civil partner but still delivering the vast majority of the fee-earning services.

Contractors who work through limited companies and take some, most or all of their remuneration in the form of dividends pay far less tax. HMRC's aim is to keep those it sees as employees from 'pretending' to be contractors and thereby reducing considerably the tax they must pay to the taxman.

So the Treasury's view was that a large number of IT consultants, engineers, interim executives, non-executive directors and "one man band companies" were often treated as employees and shareholders of their own companies, with the resulting low tax regime, when in fact they should have been treated as employees of the end client.

If the intermediary, such as the limited company were removed, the Treasury argued, a large number of these workers would be 'disguised employees' who should therefore be included on the client payroll and have income tax and NICs deducted at source each month.

From its inception, the Intermediaries Legislation sent shock waves through the contracting sector. IR35 originally had a noble purpose and was designed to address a very real problem – that a minority of workers were abusing the system to avoid paying tax and NICs, whilst at the same time employers were turning their employees into contractors to save on taxes and costs.

Unfortunately, most now agree that the legislation was poorly thought through and badly drafted in the rush to get it onto the statue books. In addition, the Treasury's use of the then Inland Revenue (now HMRC) as a blunt instrument to enforce the legislation resulted in its virtually indiscriminate application.

As a result, IR35 is often characterised as a 'sledgehammer used to crack a nut', largely because it threatened not only the majority of contractors, but also the livelihoods of other occupations and professions that had used limited companies and partnerships for over a century to legally ply their trade.

There have been attempts to remove IR35 from the statue book. A March 2011 report by the Office of Tax Simplification, a body introduced by the Chancellor to simplify the UK's tax code, recommended that either IR35 be suspended, or its administration be approved. Although he had the opportunity to remove the threat of IR35 for the vast majority of genuine contractors, the Chancellor of the day George Osborne chose the 'better administration' route, and in April 2011 appointed a body called the IR35 Forum to identify how this could be done.

The Forum's membership includes relevant HMRC department heads and technical staff, and a range of tax and accounting profession, recruitment and contracting sector representatives, including PCG. It spent 12 months working on a new framework to 'better administer' IR35 that was released in May 2012 to much criticism not only by advisers, tax professionals and contractor service providers, but also by most of the non-HMRC members of the Forum as well.

It seemed that HMRC was unwilling to accept the advice and input of its fellow IR35 Forum members and created new business entity tests, guidance and an enforcement regime that, far from simplifying IR35, has added an additional layer of complexity (see section 8.3). On its release in May 2012, the intention was to trial the new framework for 12 months and then to review its effectiveness. At the time of writing, that trial is a long way from being completed, so the framework described in this chapter is as it was originally launched.

Despite issuing a new framework and guidance, it is important to understand that the underlying legislation has not changed, so you should still adopt all the IR35 'best practice' detailed in the rest of this chapter in sections 8.4 and 8.5.

There are many critics of the basic IR35 legislation and the additional framework introduced by HMRC in May 2012. Most conclude that IR35 is unworkable. But, unworkable or not, it is law and HMRC has to apply it, and apply it rigorously, to meet its revenue-collection targets.

The UK tax authority has the powers to investigate an individual's or company's tax affairs going back six years. The same is true of IR35, so HMRC can look at past contracts and, if it successfully proves that any of those were inside IR35, you will have to pay back taxes, plus NICs, interest and penalties. This can amount to a great deal of money.

The danger is that nearly any contractor could be considered 'caught' by IR35, and become the subject of an HMRC investigation. That's because the IR35 Intermediaries Legislation is based on the model provided by employment law, and employment law has very extensive and often contradictory case law (see section 7.1 for an explanation of case law).

Whilst investigations up to May 2012 have been relatively rare, and only a few contractors find themselves in the courts each year, you must ensure you take adequate precautions to stay outside IR35. In one past case won by HMRC, the contractor had to pay £99,000 in back taxes, interest and penalties for being caught, because he had not made sure of the fundamentals.

Defending your IR35 status is very much a pre-emptive strategy. HMRC's inspectors are looking for easy targets – don't be one.

You can stay current with new IR35 case law and changes to HMRC's administration of the legislation by visiting ContractorCalculator's dedicated IR35 section:

 Contractorcalculator.co.uk/IR35.aspx

## 8.1.2 The financial impact of IR35

If your contract is caught within the IR35 legislation, then all income for that contract is 'deemed salary'. In other words, income tax and National Insurance Contributions should be deducted as if you were an employee. As a result, a contractor caught by IR35 will typically receive up to 25% less take home pay (the 'cash' left in your pocket after paying all your taxes and National Insurance Contributions) than they would if their contract was outside IR35.

For a contractor on £40 per hour, the difference would be approximately £800 per month or £9,600 per year after taxes – not an insignificant sum! And many contractors can earn considerably more than £40 per hour. As you can see from table 8.1, the financial impact of a contractor being inside IR35 is considerable. But don't fear – not all is lost, because avoiding IR35 is certainly possible if you are a genuine business and are clear about how to demonstrate your non-employee status.

To avoid IR35 requires you to understand not only the legal aspects of the legislation, but also how and when to negotiate with clients and agents to avoid it.

| Rate per hour | Monthly take home pay | Impact on monthly take home pay after taxes |
|---|---|---|
| £20 | £2124 | Decreases 21% (£450) |
| £30 | £3224 | Decreases 23% (£769) |
| £40 | £4055 | Decreases 22% (£911) |
| £50 | £4880 | Decreases 21% (£1070) |
| £75 | £6800 | Decreases 19% (£1352) |
| £100 | £8720 | Decreases 21% (£1851) |
| £125 | £10520 | Decreases 20% (£2157) |

*Table 8.1 Typical reduction to net take home pay*
*for a contractor inside IR35*

## 8.2 HMRC risk-based approach and the business entity tests

In May 2012, HMRC introduced a new risk-based approach to its administration of IR35, based in large part on the work of the IR35 Forum. The objectives of the new risk-based framework are to categorise limited company contractors according to the risk that they might be caught by the legislation. HMRC's intention is to provide certainty for those contractors considered to be at low risk of being caught by IR35 so that they may be able to enjoy three years without fear of an investigation, whilst alerting those at medium and high risk that they may be at risk of an IR35 review, and that the IR35 review might find them inside IR35.

The risk-based approach framework is underpinned by a set of business entity tests and supported by guidance in the form of IR35 example scenarios, an IR35 helpline and HMRC's contract review service. It is HMRC's intention that you should use these tests to determine your risk category so that if, for whatever reason, you end up on its radar and it asks you about your risk profile, you can choose to answer that you are 'high', 'medium' or 'low', and substantiate your answer with evidence.

You are under no obligation to take the tests, nor to reveal your score to HMRC if you do. But HMRC makes it clear that if you take the tests and are in the low risk category, and can prove it, HMRC will undertake to close any IR35 review and not to investigate you for three years.

HMRC's risk-based approach has two components:

- Contractors who contact HMRC's confidential IR35 helpline and use its contract review service

- Contractors targeted as a result of general compliance activity and who will be asked whether they have considered IR35.

If you choose to use HMRC's contract review service (and it is recommended that you don't - see section 8.3.3) and then pass you will be provided with a certificate and unique reference number that will be valid for three years. If contacted by an inspector seeking to conduct an IR35 review within three years, you would supply your certificate and the review would be suspended whilst HMRC reviews your latest circumstances. If these have not changed significantly, the IR35 review will be closed.

However, contractors who do not use the contract review service (which will include the vast majority of contractors), or whose certificate has expired and/or their circumstances have changed, and are then challenged by HMRC as part of its broader compliance activity will have a choice. In this situation, you could take the business entity tests (see section 8.3.1) and share the results with HMRC. If you are in the low risk category, and can prove it, HMRC will close its IR35 review and undertake not to investigate you for three years.

Alternatively, you can choose not to take the tests, which could lead to HMRC opening a full IR35 review of your status. In this scenario, you would have to demonstrate that you are outside of IR35 using broader evidence, and you will most likely need expert IR35 assistance.

You should understand that HMRC's IR35 risk-based approach framework does not represent a change to the underlying IR35 legislation, nor are the business entity tests any kind of 'IR35 test' – they are not. In fact, the 'risk' being evaluated here is not your risk of being inside IR35, it is HMRC's perception of the risk that you might be inside IR35, without having examined your contract or your actual working arrangements.

So, no matter what you might read elsewhere, the IR35 best practice described in sections 8.4 and 8.5 still very much applies. In fact, the business entity tests are entirely voluntary and you are under no obligation to take them and HMRC has no statutory power to make you take them.

But HMRC's own guidance says that it will grant contractors in the low-risk category a three-year moratorium on further IR35 reviews, so taking the tests could work in your favour. Unfortunately, though, the converse is also true if, having taken the tests, you find yourself in the medium- or high-risk category. And, at the time of writing, the scoring used for the tests places most contractors in the medium and high risk categories, even though other factors would place them well outside of IR35 were the legislation to be applied in full.

You can read the full guidance, which includes the IR35 example scenarios, online:

 hmrc.gov.uk/ir35/guidance.pdf

### 8.2.1 Business entity tests

HMRC introduced the business entity tests as part of its risk-based strategy to eliminate those contractors who are clearly running a business and outside IR35 right at the outset, allowing it to focus compliance activities on 'disguised employees'.

You can use HMRC's business entity tests to determine into which of three risk bands – high, medium and low – your contracting business falls. If you find your contracting business falls into the high or medium risk bands, you are more likely to undergo an IR35 review by HMRC.

There are twelve business entity tests which are, according to HMRC's guidance, designed to build up a picture of a contractor's business. The idea is that you work through each test, answering the questions and ensuring you can evidence your answers. The results of each test will provide a certain number of points, and you add your points at the end to provide a final score. You fall into a risk profile that depends on the overall score:

- High Risk = 0 – 9 points
- Medium Risk = 10 – 20 points
- Low Risk = 21 points and above.

HMRC's guidance emphasises that taking the tests is voluntary. However, HMRC also says that taking the tests and providing the results, with evidence, could result in the IR35 review being closed immediately. Conversely, that suggests not taking the tests, or refusing to cooperate, could result in you being subjected to a full blown IR35 review and repeat visits by HMRC inspectors. Bear in mind that you may also be 'required' to take the test multiple times to ensure that changing circumstances don't also change your risk score.

The 12 questions and scores that make up HMRC's business entity tests, HMRC's guidance and the evidence you might be required to produce in order to substantiate your answer, are as follows:

### Test 1: Business premises test – score = 10

Does your business own or rent business premises which are separate both from your home and from the end client's premises?

HMRC says: "For the purposes of this test, it makes no difference which of you owns or rents the business premises – you yourself or your intermediary."

Suitable evidence you might present to HMRC could include:

- Address of your business premises
- Lease or contract for business premises
- Utility bills for business premises
- Home address
- Client's address.

### Test 2: Professional indemnity insurance test – score = 2

Do you need professional indemnity insurance?

Suitable evidence you might present to HMRC could include:

- PII policy document
- PII premium note
- An explanation of why PII is needed.

### Test 3: Efficiency test – score = 10

Has your business had the opportunity in the last 24 months to increase your business income by working more efficiently?

HMRC says: "One way of doing this is finishing a fixed-price contract early. Say you agreed with the end client that the work would take three months and the fee would be £10,000. And say you finished in two months and received the full £10,000 at that point. You would have freed up a month to take on new business. So the answer to this question would be Yes."

Suitable evidence you might present to HMRC could include:

- Clauses in the contract. Here are some examples.

    - The contractor receives a fixed payment on completion

    - The contractor 'crystallises' the profit when making the supply of services to the end client

    - The contractor's business can provide extra workers to complete the job more quickly.

- Copies of:

    - Costings for proposals

    - Tenders submitted

    - Letters from clients accepting offers. These would show the proposal options and related costs that you submitted for clients to approve and accept.

### Test 4: Assistance test – score = 35

Does your business engage any workers who bring in at least 25% of your yearly turnover?

HMRC says:

- "If the contractor's trading vehicle is a company, these workers need to be people other than directors or shareholders of the company.

- If the contractor's trading vehicle is a partnership, these workers need to be people other than partners in the partnership."

Suitable evidence you might present to HMRC could include:

- Accounting records

- Details of tasks carried out

- Names and payment details of workers who carried them out.

### Test 5: Advertising test – score = 2

Has your business spent over £1,200 on advertising in the last 12 months?

HMRC says: "Entertainment does not count as advertising."

Suitable evidence you might present to HMRC could include:

- Copy of advertisement(s) placed
- Copy of invoice(s).

### Test 6: Previous PAYE test – score = minus 15
Has the current end client engaged you:

- on PAYE employment terms
- within the 12 months which ended on the last 31 March
- with no major changes to your working arrangements?

HMRC says: "If you are doing the same work, the answer to this question is Yes. Working at a different location does not count as a major change. If you were working for a company that is connected to the current end client, that counts as working for the current end client. For example, if the two companies are part of the same group."

In terms of evidence, HMRC says: "We will be able to check your employment history on our systems."

### Test 7: Business Plan test – score = 1 if the answer to both parts is 'yes'
This test has two parts:

- Does your business have a business plan with a cash flow forecast which you update regularly?
- Does your business have a business bank account, identified as such by the bank, which is separate from your personal account?

Suitable evidence you might present to HMRC could include:

- Copy of business plan
- Copies of updates
- Statements of business bank account.

### Test 8: Repair At Own Expense test – score = 4

Would your business have to bear the cost of having to put right any mistakes?

Suitable evidence you might present to HMRC could include:

- Clause in contract

- Details of what could go wrong

- Details of how the contractor would put it right

- Details of the cost to a contractor's business of putting mistakes right.

### Test 9: Client Risk test – score = 10

Has your business been unable to recover payment:

- for work done in the last 24 months more than 10% of yearly turnover?

Suitable evidence you might present to HMRC could include:

- Accounting records showing write-offs

- Copies of letters and emails between a contractor's limited company and client

- Copies of letters and emails about legal action for debt recovery.

### Test 10: Billing test – score = 2

Do you invoice for work carried out before being paid and negotiate payment terms?

Suitable evidence you might present to HMRC could include:

- Copies of invoices

- Copies of letters and emails about billing.

### Test 11: Personal Service test – score = 2

Does your business have the right to send a substitute?

Suitable evidence you might present to HMRC could include:

- Clause in contract

- Details of who would supply the substitute
- Details of who would be responsible for the substitute's performance
- Details of who would pay the substitute
- Details of what level of veto the end client has.

**Test 12: Substitution test – score = 20**
Have you hired anyone in the last 24 months to do the work you have taken on?

HMRC says: "You could do this by sending someone to do the work in your place. You could also do this by sub-contracting. But your business has to remain responsible for the work and for paying the person who does the work you have taken on. You can still pass this test if you had to tell your end client the name of the person who would be doing the work you took on."

Suitable evidence you might present to HMRC could include:

- Details of end client
- Details of who was hired
- Details of why the substitute was hired
- Details of who was responsible for finding the substitute
- Details of who was responsible for paying the substitute
- Payment terms
- Audit trail of payment from end client to contractor limited company and from contractor limited company to substitute.

Having taken the test, HMRC's guidance indicates that if you are found to be in the high or medium risk bands you have a correspondingly higher risk of an IR35 review. The guidance goes on to suggest that contractors in these bands should establish their own IR35 status and potentially make provision for making a deemed payment of additional income tax and NICs as if they are inside IR35 (see section 8.7). At this point, if your score is very low, placing you in the high risk category, you might wish to engage the services of an IR35 expert.

And there is no point trying to fiddle the results by, say, hiring an office from your accountant that you never actually use, because if HMRC investigated the real facts would come to light, and such 'dodges' would be disregarded.

If, according to your business entity test results, you are in the low risk band you must keep the evidence to support this status and be prepared to supply it to HMRC on demand in the event of an IR35 review. The good news then is that if you are investigated and the evidence confirms your low risk status, HMRC will close the review and undertake not to investigate you again for three years, assuming your circumstances do not change.

It is the scoring of these tests that drew so much criticism from tax experts, professional advisers and non-members of the IR35 Forum when the framework was first released, because in its current form it puts most typical genuine contractors in the medium and high risk categories. As you worked through the tests above, even if you are new to running a small business, you will have noticed that some of the scores are, to say the least, odd.

For example, if your limited company has a high level of bad debt, HMRC rewards this with 10 points placing you immediately into the medium risk category. Most accountants would recommend that you give up trying to run a business and return to permanent employment if you run a business that loses so much money! Similarly, when they represent such a major financial commitment, why do the advertising and business premises tests score relatively poorly?

On release of its new risk-based approach in May 2012, HMRC confirmed that the framework was to be trialled for 12 months and then reviewed. This is positive news, because if the scoring were to become more realistic and place the vast majority of genuine contractors into the low risk category where they should be, you could enjoy rolling three-year periods when you can be certain of your IR35 status. Use the resources available on ContractorCalculator.co.uk to stay abreast of any changes to the tests and their scores.

## 8.2.2 IR35 example scenarios

Alongside the business entity tests, HMRC's risk-based approach includes updated guidance in the form of six IR35 example scenarios. The idea is that you can use these to help you evaluate your IR35 status. The scenarios are intended to illustrate when and why IR35 will apply to a specific contract, and when and why it will not. You can download the examples by using the web address given in the introduction of section 8.2.

The IR35 example scenarios are also independent of the business entity tests. This is because the scenarios focus on individual contracts, which is how the IR35 legislation actually works, whereas the business entity tests are designed to look at your contracting business as a whole and provide an overall picture of whether you are a business.

The benefit of these scenarios is that they provide insights into what HMRC considers to be important when determining your employment status. That means you can shape your IR35 defence strategy accordingly. The lessons from the examples have been included in the IR35 best practice detailed in sections 8.3 and 8.4.

The scenarios have no bearing on how the underlying IR35 legislation will be applied. But if, having downloaded and read through the examples you recognise factors in the borderline and inside-IR35 scenarios as resembling your own contracts, you should seek professional advice from an IR35 expert.

## 8.2.3 HMRC's contract review service and helpline

HMRC launched a contract review service and IR35 helpline when IR35 was first introduced in 2000, but evidence gleaned through a Freedom of Information Act (FOI) request by this book's publisher, ContractorCalculator, suggests that take-up then – and now – has been low. One of the reasons is that HMRC invariably seeks to contact end-clients to establish the exact nature of the working relationship, which is so important in determining IR35 status. Unsurprisingly, few contractors choose to have an HMRC inspector asking their clients detailed questions about the exact nature of their working relationships.

HMRC has used the risk-based approach, launched in May 2012, as an opportunity to 'relaunch' its contract review service alongside a new IR35 helpline it says is confidential. The idea is that if you have your contract reviewed by HMRC and it is outside IR35, you may be exempt from further investigations and IR35 reviews for three years, assuming your circumstances don't change. By all means, get your contract reviewed – section 8.4.4 provides guidance on how to do this. But don't ask HMRC to do it.

HMRC insists that its confidential IR35 helpline is independent from and does not share information with its compliance teams. However, given that at the same time as launching its new risk-based approach in May 2012 it also launched a major compliance campaign supported by three dedicated teams based in Salford, Croydon and Edinburgh each with a dozen inspectors and a status specialist embedded, is this claim credible?

If, during the course of a helpline call, it became apparent that the contractor concerned was clearly inside IR35, is it realistic to expect the HMRC call handler – said by HMRC to be an IR35 compliance expert – to keep it to themselves? And all organisations promote staff and move them around; so if a helpline IR35 expert is moved to an IR35 compliance team under pressure to scalp more IR35 heads, are they really going to avoid going after anyone they spoke to 'in confidence' on the helpline?

As with the contract review service, don't even think about asking the helpline for a review. There are plenty of expert IR35 advisers out there who can do a better job for a reasonable fee and who prioritise only your interests. And a good starting point if you're concerned about a contract being inside IR35 is to use ContractorCalculator's free online IR35 test.

## 8.3 Factors determining your employment and IR35 status

IR35 has evolved considerably since it first came into force in 2000, although it still suffers from being poorly drafted and decidedly opaque in areas! And, despite the major changes to HMRC's administration of IR35 introduced in May 2012, the underlying IR35 legislation has not been changed.

As chapter 7 outlined, no law contains a definitive list of do's and don'ts, and IR35 is no different. When making a ruling in an IR35 case, a judge will consider all the evidence before them. So to prepare an effective IR35 defence, contractors must effectively maximise the chances that they are working outside IR35 by having as many 'contra-indicators' in place as possible.

That is to say, contractors should stack the odds in their favour to prove that they are outside IR35. This is not about trying to prove that white is black or vice versa – if your contract means that you are effectively an employee then you must pay taxes as an employee. But if your contract places you outside IR35, you must ensure that there is no possible room for misinterpretation by a tax inspector or tax tribunal judge. That's what we'll go on to discuss.

### 8.3.1 IR35 key factors overview

Determining whether one of your contracts is caught by or 'inside' IR35 depends on whether there is sufficient evidence to suggest that you are a 'disguised employee', which can depend on a number of factors. It is not entirely objective whether a contractor's contract is caught, and depends on the terms and conditions in the contract, together with the contractor's actual working arrangements.

It is also important to understand that it is not the 'contractor' being judged on IR35 status, but the specific contract. So, you could have three contracts in a year two of which are outside IR35 and one of which is inside. There is no single reason why a contract fails IR35 and it is normally a combination of reasons. One has to stand back and consider the whole picture to arrive at the decision – that's what a tribunal judge will do if your case gets as far as a tax tribunal. But what you learn from this chapter should prevent that happening.

The key factors in an IR35 decision, some of which will be familiar from chapter 7, are:

- Contract type – has the client hired your company or you personally?

- Control – does the client control you?

- Right of substitution – can you provide a substitute to do the work?

- Mutuality of obligation – are you obliged to accept work offered, and is the client obliged to offer you work?

The three factors – control, substitution or personal service, and mutuality of obligation –are often known as the 'tests of employment' and underpin all UK employment status cases, not just IR35 cases.

Other factors include:

- Financial risk – do you risk your own money and is there opportunity for you to gain financially through sound management?

- Part and parcel – are you a 'fixture' of the client's organisation?

- Being in business on your own account – are you really running a business?

- Provision of equipment – do you use your own equipment to do the job?

If you come under tax investigation and are suspected to be incorrectly paying tax as if outside IR35, all these factors will be examined to decide your true IR35 status – firstly by an HMRC inspector and then, if you choose to fight it, in a tax tribunal.

All these factors are based on case law – previous employment status cases that have been in the courts – which is why it's worth you knowing a little bit about how we've got to where we are now.

### 8.3.2 IR35 case law and the tests of employment

There is no statutory definition in law for 'employment' and 'self-employment'. The definition of who is an employee and who is not depends heavily on case law, or jurisprudence, which is basically a set of principles of law established through precedent by judges over the years, decades and centuries.

HMRC itself makes this clear in leaflet IR56, which deals with employment status:

*"The law for tax and social security legislation does not define 'employment' and 'self-employment'. But, over the years, the Courts have considered this issue and their guidance on whether an individual is an employee or self-employed is known as case law."*

So it is this case law that is used to determine whether a contractor is either employed, inside IR35, or self-employed, outside IR35.

But don't worry. You certainly don't need to learn all the case law surrounding employment status; the subject is vast and best left to experts. It is more productive for you to engage professional lawyers who specialise in employment law and IR35, although you should read on so that you understand the basics. If you decide to fight status disputes with HMRC yourself, your chance of success is significantly reduced. Leave it to the professionals! The costs of professional help can be insured against, but the very best insurance is to not get yourself into bother in the first place!

As described in section 7.2.2, the tests of employment applied to employment status cases and used by tax tribunal judges to determine a contractor's IR35 status arose from a famous employment status case known as the MacKenna's Ready Mixed Concrete ruling. Its full citation is "The judgment of MacKenna J. in Ready Mixed Concrete (South East) Ltd v Minister of Pensions and National Insurance [1968]":

 http://www.hmrc.gov.uk/manuals/esmmanual/esm7030.htm

In this ruling, Judge MacKenna laid down the key tests of employment a worker must pass in order that their status is that of an employee, and that an employment contract, or "contract of service" exists. Of greater interest to contractors is that, in the context of an IR35 case, the converse is true: if a contractor fails the test, then there can be no contract of service and the worker is not a 'disguised employee'.

Judge MacKenna's specific words were:

*"A contract of service exists if these three conditions are fulfilled.*

(i) *The servant agrees that, in consideration of a wage or other remuneration, he will provide his own work and skill in the performance of some service for his master.*

(ii) *He agrees, expressly or impliedly, that in the performance of that service he will be subject to the other's control in a sufficient degree to make that other master.*

*(iii) The other provisions of the contract are consistent with its being a contract of service."*

All three of these conditions must be satisfied for a contract of service to exist.

From these conditions arise the key IR35 status factors of:

- Control

- Substitution

- Mutuality of obligation

- Other factors, such as financial risk, the opportunity to profit and so on.

These factors underpin your ability to demonstrate to an HMRC inspector or a tribunal judge that you are outside IR35. The following factors in sections 8.3.3 to 8.3.11 are the current guidelines based on an analysis of all the existing case law.

Once you have learnt the factors involved it is very useful for you to keep abreast of any IR35 cases that go through the courts to see if any precedents are set. Although the numbers of cases look set to increase as HMRC's compliance activities ramp up, there is only a handful of these each year and the results and analysis are widely reported. You can find out about the latest IR35 case law by visiting ContractorCalculator:

 http://www.contractorcalculator.co.uk/ir35_history.aspx

### 8.3.3 Notional contract – it's not a paper exercise

Unfortunately IR35 can seem to come at contractors from all angles. If a contract is badly written, HMRC will flag this as a reason why the contractor must be inside IR35. If the contract is well written, then HMRC will fall back on what is called the 'notional contract', or the hypothetical contract that is formed by the taxman after examining the true nature of the relationship between the contractor and the client.

Since a landmark employment status case in 2011, the 'Autoclenz ruling', the actual written contract may be completely disregarded by an HMRC status inspector or tribunal judge. This means there is an increasing tendency on the part of HMRC inspectors and judges to look at what actually happens in the workplace and to base much of their decision on testimony that reflects the day-to-day operations on the job. When judging a contractor's IR35 status, an inspector or judge will form a notional contract that expresses the real relationship between the contractor and client.

This means that a contractor may have a written contract with all the right clauses regarding control, right of substitution and mutuality of obligation, but if the client thinks differently – and tells HMRC investigators so – implying that the notional contract is different from the written contract – then the contractor could be in trouble.

On the reverse side, the concept of the notional contract has saved many contractors from falling within IR35. An example would be a contractor whose contract did not explicitly include a substitution clause. However when investigated it was discovered that the contractor had actually used a substitute, and that fact put the contractor outside IR35.

The other defence against a badly worded contract is to seek a written "confirmation of arrangements" from the client, detailed in section 8.4.5.

An added complication is that most contractors have no idea of the exact contractual relationship between their agency and client and have little realistic chance of securing what the agency and client rightly consider to be a confidential document.

HMRC will certainly want to see the agency-client contract, known as the 'upper level contract', while the contract between the contractor and the agency is known as the 'lower level contract'. This is another reason why the notional contract is so important. If the upper level contract between the agency and the client differs from the lower level contract between the contractor and the agency – for example by not including a right of substitution – the notional contract could work to the contractor's advantage.

### 8.3.4 "Contract for services" versus "contract of service"

This key issue has been introduced in chapter 7 and it's a fundamental underlying concept for determining whether a contractor is inside or outside IR35. To recap, a "contract for services" is where the client engages your company to provide services to them. You then decide how and who is going to provide those services. A "contract of service" is where the client engages you as a named individual to provide services to them. This is employment.

As highlighted in chapter 7, ideally your contract must show that your company, not you as a named individual, is providing services, and you therefore need a "contract for services". Your contract should state the terms for the services that your company provides, but should try avoid any mention of personal service, although in practice many clients insist that the contractor is named in any contract. If possible, the contract should reflect that it is not you the client wants: the client wants an action performed; your company decides the rest.

### 8.3.5 Control

The issue of control is a key factor that determines whether or not you are an employee, although HMRC's guidance to its own inspectors says that, although control is an important factor, it may not necessarily be the determining factor.

The factor of control is typically broken down into four sub-factors:

- What work you are told to perform
- When you are told to perform the work
- Where you are told to perform the work, and
- How you should perform the work.

You will often see the phase 'what, when, where and how' used by IR35 experts and in articles about IR35. If you think about your current or most recent contract in the context of these four sub-factors, you'll realise that you may have actually been under quite a degree of control by your client, but this does not necessarily mean you are caught by IR35.

Some contractors don't control what they work on because they have applied to work on a specific project. Nor do many contactors have much control over where or when, because they have to work on the client's site to access its systems and staff. And because accessing its systems and staff can only be done during working hours, they may have little control over when they work.

But you've become a contractor because you are a highly knowledgeable specialist expert in a particular field and that's why you have been hired. So, very few contractors are told how to perform their tasks, which is often a critical factor in IR35 cases. And if you are not controlled, then you may fail the test of employment and be found to be a genuine contractor.

Clauses in the contract showing that you have to regularly report to the client are not going to help you. The more control is mentioned in the contract and the more control the client exercises in the actual relationship, the more HMRC will believe you are an employee. Plus, if you look like an employee, are dealt with like an employee, and act like an employee, then in the eyes of the taxman you are an employee, whether or not you are working through your own limited company.

You should try to make it clear from the contract that most decisions about how the service you deliver is provided are yours to make, assuming they do not affect the final deliverable. Where possible and practical, you should decide what hours you work, choose who else from your company can do the job, select a substitute if needed or appropriate for a specialist part of the job, and provide your own equipment.

The issue of control, because it has much wider implications in employment law, is a particularly large and complex area of employment law; as such, it is one area where the advice of a professional is highly desirable.

## 8.3.6 Substitution

Substitution, the right of substitution, and the act of actually sending a substitute, has consistently been one of the central areas of focus by tribunal judges and a key factor that can place contractors outside IR35. The introduction of HMRC's business entity tests has reinforced this view, by highly scoring the act of providing a substitute. If you can provide a substitute, then your personal service is clearly not required, so you fail the test of employment. Making a genuine substitution is widely believed to be the single 'silver bullet' that will kill off any IR35 challenge by HMRC.

As a small business supplier to your client, if you are genuinely providing a service then another contractor with your skill set able to provide the same service could take your place. In addition, you should have the choice of the substitute, not the client or agency, to ensure that the right of substitution is 'unfettered'.

Unless the work is very much back-end administration, you should ensure the client is aware of the substitution, otherwise it is not a genuine substitution. If the client still thinks they are receiving the services of you only, then if the notional contract or the real situation is examined – as it will be during an HMRC investigation and possibly later in court – then according to the client no substitution has taken place.

A substitute qualifies as genuine when substituting for all or part of the work that the client is expecting to be completed. However, you do not have to hand over all the work to the substitute. It is possible for the substitute to work on a small part of the overall contract, for example some low grade repetitive tasks, and still be seen a genuine substitute, working alongside you, the main contractor. You must also make the arrangements for the substitute, negotiate their contract and rate and pay them directly, otherwise it is not a genuine substitution.

Chapter 7 shows that your contract should have a right of substitution clause and your company should be able to substitute another contractor at your own expense, who can provide the services instead. Case law suggests this is one of the more important tests demonstrating that you are outside IR35.

Remembering the concepts introduced in section 8.3.3, any clause in a contract must be based on the real situation. Can someone else really substitute for you? If you are a famous television personality, a world-renowned expert on a recondite subject, or the last- surviving programmer in a software language that no one uses anymore, the court is likely to rule that you have no possibility of substitution, although this does not necessarily mean you are within IR35.

On the other hand, if you have the right to replace yourself with another contractor who has much the same skills that you do, then you are obviously not providing the services 'yourself', as an employee would. This strongly points away from employment and that you are outside IR35.

In chapter 7 it was stressed how important it is that you retain full control over any substitution. Clauses that require client approval or satisfaction, usually worded: '...the right to substitute another representative of the Company to provide the Services provided that the Client is satisfied that the proposed substitute possesses the necessary skills, expertise and resources to perform the Services' are to be avoided, if possible.

If the client has too much control over the substitution process, the court may claim that the client is simply looking for another employee like you. So ensure you retain the right to find and furnish the substitute yourself in the contract – you must maintain an unfettered right of substitution. Restrictive clauses are not necessary, because if the client is not satisfied with the substitute's services, then your company is responsible no matter what and could be in breach of contract. You should at no time suggest that the client has control over the provision of services that you make.

Therefore, a more relevant phrase in your contract might say something like: '...any costs incurred in providing a substitute will be at the expense of the Company.' That nullifies the risk of sending in a substitute who cannot do the job.

You also have the option of hiring a sub-contractor or helper to work on a specific contract. The distinctions between substitutes and subcontractors/helpers are important in the eyes of a tax tribunal or court, because they demonstrate different aspects of how you might be outside IR35 and not a disguised employee.

A substitute is usually considered a short-term fix to cover for you during periods of holiday, illness or other unexpected absence. An individual with the right skill set replaces you direct on the project for a short period of time, and the client is informed that a substitute is to be supplied by the contractor's limited company.

Helpers or subcontractors generally refers to additional workers that you use to perform tasks to help cope with periods of intense activity, or to lend specialist skills to one particular aspect of the project. Subcontractors who have been engaged on a basis that is intrinsic to the completion of the contract, or where you need additional specialist skills to complete the project, are the most likely to be viewed by HMRC as evidence that you are not a disguised employee. Case law dating back 20 years recognises the importance of being able to provide a substitute and hiring helpers.

### 8.3.7 Mutuality of obligation (MOO)

Mutuality of Obligation (MOO) is one of the key tests of employment status. As outlined in section 7.2.2, mutuality of obligation between an organisation and a worker implies a contract of service and that the worker is employed.

HMRC's definition of MOO says that:

"There must be an irreducible minimum of mutual obligation for there to be a contract of service. That irreducible minimum is

- that the engager [client] must be obliged to pay a wage or other remuneration, and

- that the worker [contractor] must be obliged to provide his or her own work or skill.

However, the irreducible minimum could be present in either a contract of service or a contract for services and therefore, by itself, it will not determine the nature of a contract."

Under normal conditions of employment there is a mutuality of obligation between worker and employer. The employer is obliged to provide paid work for the employee, and the employee is obliged to accept it. There is an expectation of regular employment by the employee until they are made redundant or leave of their own accord.

This situation is typical of most employer-employee relationships, in which the employee is paid by their employer each week or month and, within the bounds of job descriptions, can be asked to undertake tasks across a spectrum of activities that go beyond their core role. This state of affairs continues until the employee decides to take another job, or is made redundant. One worker could have a career within a single organisation that spans many job roles over many decades.

For most contractors this status does not exist, and is one factor towards arguing that the contractor is outside IR35. After an initial contract, the contractor is not obliged to accept another one and is free to go. Neither is the company obliged to offer a new contract or continue paying the contractor.

However, when the contractor regularly works for the same client on new or rolling contracts, HMRC will say this suggests employment. If you are doing whatever work is available and not specific project work, this makes it worse.

In one IR35 judgement, the judges cited a statement by the client manager calling the contractor a 'tail-end Charlie', meaning that the contractor did whatever other members of the team didn't complete. That is powerful evidence of you being treated as an employee, and will therefore act against you in an IR35 case.

You should show that you have the right to refuse further work from the client. You are not obliged to turn up at the client's office every day and just work at what is assigned. You pick and choose your assignments: you accept one, perform it, and then choose whether or not to accept another.

Crucially, mutuality of obligation can exist without a contract. For example, a contractor may be working on a project specified in the contract and the client then asks the contractor to do something outside the scope of the original contract. If the contractor completes the task, this is evidence of mutuality of obligation.

Contractors who operate more as consultants with a multiple client base will be at less risk of IR35, since they regularly accept or refuse work from different companies.

### 8.3.8 Financial risk

Your own financial position will be examined if you are required to contest your IR35 status. Employees are protected from any exposure to financial loss, whatever involvement they may have in a given project. This is not the case for a contractor, who may find a project terminated before completion and who then may not collect the full fee. Exposure of this kind is a key factor in determining IR35 status and it should be clear in any contract that you sign. If you appear to have the same protection as that enjoyed by an employee, HMRC and the judge may consider you one.

You can demonstrate financial risk in many ways. These include:

- Having to invoice for work
- Having to negotiate rates
- Working on a fixed price per project basis
- Being able to profit, for example by finishing a fixed-price contract early
- Making a loss on a project
- Suffering bad debts
- Having to correct mistakes in your own time and at your own cost
- Buying stocks or supplies.

A contract that does not show a price for the work and an approximate date for completion implies there is no financial risk. It would simply state that you will work a set number of hours per week for an hourly rate, which is little different from an employment contract.

### 8.3.9 Part and parcel

Want to use the company canteen when you're working on assignment? Want to share car rides with other employees when you go home? Want to get a security pass to avoid the bother of signing in each time you have to get in to the office you're working at? Well, don't even think about it, because even these small things can help to put you inside IR35.

Unfortunately, when you are working on site under contract, you can easily get mistaken for an employee. It can be hard to distinguish what you are doing from what the permanent employees are doing. You can also find yourself being sucked into the employee workforce: eating at the company cafeteria, being added to internal phone directories and organisation charts and even given business cards to use.

Yet another of HMRC's tests of IR35 is whether you are 'part and parcel' of the client's organisation or not. HMRC will contend that the provision of work by a contractor is the same as that of an employee and that the contractor is part and parcel of the end user client's business. In other words, the taxman will see that contractor as an employee, with all the tax implications that brings with it.

In case law there are no clear determinations of what 'part and parcel' means. In fact, some judges don't consider this test a very useful one in determining employment status. But others do, and HMRC certainly use part and parcel as a test of IR35, so you need to be careful in how you manage the relationship with your client.

To make certain that you avoid the attention of HMRC inspectors, simply avoid looking like an employee and don't accept any of the conveniences that employees take for granted:

- Don't accept a pass that lets you into the building through the employee gate; sign-in every day

- Don't allow yourself to become listed in the company telephone directory

- Don't get your business cards from the company

- Accept no sick pay or holiday pay from the client

- Don't eat at the company canteen

- In so far as possible, see that you're not listed on company materials as part of the organisation.

If you have a management role, make it clear in written form that this is strictly related to the project you have contracted for. In general, it is best to avoid written materials that put you in the light of being an employee in any way; this is just what HMRC will be looking for.

Make sure you document some facts to back up your arguments during the course of your current contract in case of an investigation – which could be six years from now and you may have forgotten the details if you haven't added them to your contract file.

Draw up a list of the differences between the contractor and the client's employees. As you are not an employee, there should be some fairly obvious differences, such as not having set hours, benefits, pension arrangements, access to social clubs, parking, expenses arrangements, use of a subsidised staff canteen and so on.

Try and keep any correspondence with the client that shows clearly you are not under complete control of the client's project manager. Keep this file safe with the relevant financial records from the same period. If HMRC come knocking, you can simply reach out and produce the file. Section 8.4.9 details setting up and maintaining the right records to support your case if you come under HMRC investigation.

### 8.3.10 Provision of equipment

This is a particularly difficult test of IR35. For the vast majority of contracts, contractors will need to use the client's equipment. For IT contractors in particular, using the client's computers and networks is just a basic requirement of IT security; an IT director would be irresponsible to let hundreds of contractors into the organisation using their own equipment and posing a huge range of risks to mission critical operations.

Unfortunately, several conclusions can be drawn if you use a client's equipment:

- You are part and parcel of the client's business
- You are taking no financial risk by investing in your own equipment
- You are being controlled by the client.

However, if HMRC can draw conclusions about your use of the client's equipment there are actions you can take to counter the conclusions.

Section 8.3.9 details how to avoid being labelled part and parcel. Section 8.3.11 details how, by demonstrating you are in business in your own right, which might involve you buying equipment that you simply do not use on the client's networks, you are taking financial risks. To demonstrate that you are not under the control of the client, section 8.4.6 details how to ask a client to confirm this statement in a confirmation of arrangements letter.

## 8.3.11 Being in business on your own account (IBOYOA)

If you are in business on your own account, a condition increasingly known by the acronym 'IBOYOA', then you are clearly not an employee – you are a legitimate businessperson supplying services via a limited company.

There is a range of activities that can demonstrate that you are in business in your own right, rather than a de facto employee. Initially, these activities are likely to take the form of marketing – after all, if you were not in business, why would you market your company?

Simple steps include:

- A company website, business cards and company stationery
- Listings in online directories like yell.com
- Advertising on business websites and in trade publications.

There is of course a cost associated with each of these activities, but compared with what you would lose if found within IR35, the cost is trivial. Not only that, as you've seen in chapter 4 and will learn in Chapter 11, marketing your company and services effectively is a crucial part of being a successful contractor.

When naming your limited company, avoid using your own name, as this implies you are only providing your own services. If you have Jane Smith Ltd on your business card, the implication is that Jane Smith will be completing the work. If the right of substitution is exercised and John Smith turns up, this might, understandably, cause some confusion.

It is also recommended that you do not use a company name that clearly says you are a contractor, such as IT Contractor Solutions

Ltd, as this could also imply that you are the IT contractor, leading to similar confusion.

If however, you call the company ABC Computing, you are simply providing computing services that could be supplied by anyone from your firm, John or Jane Smith or, indeed, another contractor that you might sub-contract some or all of the work to.

Contractors who can show they have invested in business equipment also demonstrate that they are running a business. Business equipment could include:

- Tablets, laptops, software, peripherals and consumables
- Business telephone, web-enabled smartphone, fixed-line broadband
- Office equipment, such as a desk, office chair and a filing cabinet
- Business insurances, including professional indemnity, public liability, employee liability and business contents.

A library of training material, investment in membership of a professional body, training courses and subscriptions to trade magazines all paid for by your limited company can all be indication that you are in business for yourself. Never charge materials like these back to a client, even if they offer, as it could be used as evidence of you being an employee.

Some contractors, particularly in the engineering, financial and construction fields, are required to invest in personal continued professional development (CPD) in order to retain their chartered status, and payment for CPD by the contractor can be used as another indication of being in business.

Having concurrent clients can be a strong indication of being in business for yourself, but as evidence it tends to be treated on a case by case basis. For example if you are earning £75,000 a year doing high end development work for a corporate client, and maybe £5,000 per year producing websites for family and friends, then HMRC would not take this as evidence by itself that you are in business for yourself.

However, if you work two days on one contract for £35,000 per year and three days for £40,000 on another contract for a separate client, then this is strong evidence of genuine concurrent clients.

## 8.4 Ensuring IR35 doesn't affect you

The best IR35 defence begins before an investigation even starts and, ideally, before you even accept a contract. If you invest time in engineering out the risk of IR35, as you would engineer out risk in your work as a contractor, it is likely to save you money, time and considerable stress.

This is true even if you take HMRC's business entity tests and find yourself in the low risk category. HMRC has committed to not investigating contractors in the low risk category for three-years on the condition that their circumstances do not change. But that does not mean you have to stop checking your contract, securing a 'confirmation of arrangements' from your client and performing all the IR35 best practice described in this section. That is because HMRC can still investigate you after three years and may decide that one of your contracts was inside IR35, or even that part of a contract was.

This section is also not about pretending to be in business for yourself if you are not. If your contract and working conditions put you inside IR35, then you must pay tax as an employee; it's as clear-cut as that. But what this section is about is making sure that in your legitimate work as a contractor running a limited company there can be no room for doubt by HMRC or a judge that you are clearly not an employee.

There is a range of pre-emptive strategies you can adopt to prepare for an HMRC challenge. Have all your defence paperwork and other evidence prepared and filed in case you are investigated by HMRC, and the chances are that investigation will never happen. If you've prepared well, the tax inspector is likely to look into your case, quickly conclude that you're acting in full accordance with the law, and move on to easier targets.

The other key fact to consider is that an investigation can go back six years. Can you remember exactly what you were doing on every contract six years ago? Will your client be able to remember? Collecting and keeping some simple records as you go means that you won't have to scramble to prepare a defence when it may be too late.

### 8.4.1 Steps to avoiding IR35

Firstly, under no circumstances sign a contract without being fully aware of the IR35 implications. It does not matter if you are within IR35 or outside, as long as you know and you can plan for it.

Never, ever accept assurances from agencies or clients that you are outside IR35. Agencies are not particularly interested in your IR35 status – they get paid the same regardless. Some might even try and tell you the contract is outside IR35, but review it yourself and get the contract checked out by an expert if there is even the smallest sliver of doubt.

Remember that the agent is not your friend, but a salesperson whose interests are likely in places to conflict with your own. They are certainly not experts in employment law, and even if you are convinced they know what they're talking about and are sincerely giving you correct advice, don't trust it! Otherwise, you could find yourself in court saying something the equivalent of, "Some bloke called Bob told me it was alright." The judge might find it amusing, but it certainly won't help your case.

Once you have secured an interview, or even beforehand if you have sufficient information, start evaluating your IR35 position based on a very realistic evaluation of what you will actually be doing on the contract. Make sure the client describes this clearly and unequivocally in your meeting. Use the questions in your interview to clarify what you will be doing and how you will be working.

Once you are offered the contract and get the contract paperwork you have everything you need to review your decision. Your written contract will need to cover all the key IR35 concepts already discussed, such as project-based work, control, mutuality of obligation, right of substitution, use of own equipment, financial risk and so on.

If possible, you should also try and get a copy of the agency-client contract (the 'upper contract') to check that it mirrors your own, although in practice this is rarely possible.

You can try and evaluate the position yourself, but if you are in any doubt, get professional advice. In fact, even if you are not in any doubt, it is generally advisable to ask an IR35 expert to review your status, and give you an accurate assessment based on your situation. Asking a lawyer to review your contracts not only makes sound IR35 sense, it also makes sound business sense, because there may be commercial factors you would wish to challenge, as outlined in chapter 7.

To avoid any further penalties on top of the extra tax if you are caught by IR35, you will need to show 'reasonable care' has been taken when evaluating your IR35 status. If you have done it yourself this isn't as strong evidence as getting a professional to do it. If you get a specialist to do a review you can mitigate any need to pay penalties if you are caught, because you can show you have taken 'reasonable care'. It will cost you a fee, but this is nothing compared to the extra tax you would pay if you are caught by IR35. This assessment, along with other testimony and materials, can also be useful to you if HMRC comes knocking at your door. At the very least, you can consider it investment in your own peace of mind.

If the agency won't budge on changes to the contract then insist on getting the client to sign a confirmation of arrangements, covered in more detail in section 8.5.6, which clearly states the real relationship you have with them.

Some accountants may ask you to declare your IR35 status for each contract so they can process your tax correctly. You may also be asked to sign a statement saying that the accountant is not liable for a false declaration. You should not be afraid to sign this, as the accountant is in no position to assess whether or not you are 'inside' or not. IR35 is primarily a legal issue, not an accounting one, although you will find some contractor accountants include IR35 contract reviews as part of their service.

Always, on every contract, create a compliance file, containing every piece of useful proof you can get. This can be enormously important in a court case. Keep all the paperwork and/or electronic files from every contract for six years.

While at work, obtain and save as much evidence as you can that shows that you are doing a project and not working as an employee. Also, don't get involved in any activities that might make you appear as part and parcel of the client's company – see section 8.4.9.

### 8.4.2 Getting the contract right

Many contractors, particularly if it is their first, wait until they have signed a contract before they start addressing IR35, significantly increasing their chances of being caught by IR35.

If you sign the contract without getting it reviewed you will eliminate any opportunity to negotiate the contract for IR35 compliance. Whilst you can provisionally check the contract yourself to determine if you are outside IR35, make sure you get any new contract and your working arrangements professionally reviewed before you sign it or agree to it verbally.

If the contract is not genuine (ie you are working as an employee, whatever the contract might say); has been copied and presented as a 'standard contract'; or is a 'do it yourself IR35 contract', HMRC will identify it, and disregard it as not being 'a live contract'. For example, in one case a judge ruled that the substitution clause was 'window dressing'. So beware and take care!

## Been there, done that!

## True flexibility

## Review saved thousands

**DAVE SAYS:** When IR35 came into force in 1999 the market demand was still very high. So in addition to being able to insist on no suit wearing (!), we contractors also had a chance to be very firm in our contract negotiations.

I got a lawyer involved and had some key aspects changed in my contract and, then got it reviewed by HMRC who, after much persuasion by my lawyer, issued me a letter saying I was outside IR35. The whole process cost me £700.

A contractor colleague of mine who did exactly the same job didn't bother with a review, out of laziness more than anything, and found to his cost that his contract didn't pass IR35. His laziness cost him about £50,000 in extra tax.

Although HMRC will consider the notional contract, that is the real relationship between the contractor and the client, it is vital that contractors get their written contracts reviewed by a specialist before they sign it. A poorly worded contract will immediately attract HMRC's attention.

Avoid buying 'IR35 proof' contracts. Passing IR35 is not a paper exercise and the agency is unlikely to accept a new contract replacing theirs. There is no such thing as a standard IR35-free contract. In fact, the most important thing you should know about IR35 compliant contracts is that there really aren't any.

Most agencies and clients use their own forms of standard contracts, so it is difficult to do more than tinker around the edges and to change the contract schedule. But that should not prevent you from seeking a professional contract review and making the attempt to negotiate out any particularly 'unfriendly' clauses.

In the event of an investigation by HMRC – and later on a judge if it goes to court – your case for being outside IR35 will be strengthened if it can been seen that both you and the client have made a special effort to come to a specific agreement for this particular project. You may create a different one for a different project, or you may use a similar one, but the contract should reflect the specific intentions of you both.

In the light of the High Court's ruling in 2008 on Dragonfly Consulting Ltd, if you have a series of contracts with a client renewed over time, but that were not correct from the start, HMRC (and subsequently a judge) can take this to mean later contracts were purely cosmetic or "window dressing", as the judge in that case called it. So it is vitally important to get the contract correct, right from the start.

It is also important to ensure contracts remain valid throughout the course of each contract, particularly if you are working on a project or series of projects that last many years. In the 2011 JLJ Services ruling, the contractor was found to be outside IR35 for the first three years of his contract as he worked on a series of discrete projects. The tribunal judge then found him to be inside IR35 after the first three years because he did not update the contract – it was kept rolling over without reflecting what the contractor was actually doing.

Beware of contracts that are home-made and based on a normal employment contract. These contracts are dangerous and will not only put you inside IR35, but could also contain clauses you don't want, and be missing clauses that you really need. A lawyer who reviews your contract will easily be able to spot this. Large agencies are unlikely to send out contracts like this, but some of the smaller ones might.

The contract should be between the client/agency and your limited company; ideally it should not mention a named individual. If the client does insist on naming you in the contract, as many will, ensure this is only in the schedule, which should describe the work to be done, preferably referencing a project by name, and the skills/services supplied.

In addition to the general points above designed to minimise IR35 risk, you should consider the following specific points that should appear as clauses or within the schedule of the contract:

**Intention of the parties:** Your agreement should specify the intentions of the parties, that you are offering services through a limited company and the client is engaging your company to perform those services.

**Contractor engagements should be fixed term:** As a key test of employment it is very important that your contract is for a fixed term and not renewable. If you have a two-year contract with one client and it is renewable for two years, HMRC is going to ask some questions, particularly if you have few or no other clients.

**Mutuality of Obligation:** You should display clearly in the contract that there is no 'mutuality of obligation' between you and the client – sample text has been provided in chapter 7.

**Setting own hours of work:** Demonstrate in your contract that you are able to set your own hours of work. If you work on the client's premises, make it clear in the contract that at least part of the work may be performed in your own offices.

**Contractors pay their own expenses:** Some clients are prepared to pay certain contractor expenses. This can attract attention as it can be seen as a sign of employment. You should include expenses as part of your rate, or only claim expenses for agreed exceptional items, such as if your Manchester-based project required you to visit the client's Brussels office.

**Contractors don't get to take holidays:** You should not expect clients to pay for holidays, nor should you expect to take a break during a contract. To allow for holidays, fix your contract periods with gaps in them so that there are breaks in between. Paid holidays are a certain indication of employment status and should not be accepted under any circumstances.

**Contractors do not receive sick pay:** The same rules apply to sick pay as those previously explained for holiday payments. This does not mean that you cannot get sick. It means that you should not expect to be paid for the time you cannot work. Ideally, you should arrange for a substitute, if you get sick.

**Contractors supply their own equipment:** This may be difficult for contractors to arrange in practice, but the contract should at least state that you are responsible for the supply of your own equipment. You may well find yourself working with the client's equipment, but at least you have undertaken to supply your own.

**Contractors find their own substitutes:** One of the key tests of employment status is whether you must provide the services yourself, as an employee would, or whether a substitute can provide them. You should plan to find suitably qualified and experienced substitutes and be prepared to provide them if necessary.

**Upper level contracts:** If you are not contracting direct and are working through an agency, which is very likely, you may encounter problems with the agency-client, or upper level contract. There may well be important differences between your contract and the one the agency has with the client.

For example, you may have done your best to show in your contract that you are outside IR35, but there could be elements in the agency-client contract that contradict those in yours. HMRC will try to show that the real contract is reflected by the agency-client contract and not by your contract with the agency.

HMRC will claim that your contract does not mirror the real situation in your day-to-day work, and that the agency-client contract does. There is unfortunately very little contractors can do to protect themselves in this situation.

In almost all of the IR35 cases reviewed by the tax tribunals and courts, the judges take the agency-client contract into consideration and quote it extensively in their final judgement. This may seem unfair, since the agency-client contract often covers a large number of contractors, and not just the one hit by an IR35 case. Unfair or not, though, that's the situation.

The main issue is that the language of the agency-client contract can be directly contradictory to that of your contract with the agency. And if you are facing an IR35 investigation by HMRC, discrepancies between the agency-client and agency-contractor contracts add weight to their conclusions.

### 8.4.3 Termination clauses that avoid IR35 risk

Termination clauses and notice periods vary considerably from contract to contract, but could play a role in keeping you outside IR35. Most are designed to protect the client from the sudden departure of a contractor mid-contract, as well as to provide a safety net for the contractor to find alternative work.

But termination clauses can provide a tax tribunal or court with insights into the level of mutuality of obligation between you and your client and therefore your IR35 status. Wherever possible, termination clauses should only be included to cover the most serious breaches, such as where a contractor makes a serious and costly error or is giving away trade secrets.

From an IR35 perspective, the best kind of termination clause is one that doesn't exist, so that there is no notice period either way. But that may be an unrealistic scenario, particularly as most clients will insist on a termination clause, so that they can quickly shed contractors if a project is cancelled or completed early.

If a project ends naturally ahead of schedule and you stay on because the termination clause says there are four weeks left to run, it is likely the client will be finding you new things to do, and that points strongly towards mutuality of obligation. If there is no notice period it is indicative of self-employment and, when viewed with the rest of the evidence, not having that notice period could tip the decision of a tribunal judge in your favour.

### 8.4.4 Contract reviews for IR35 status

The first key fact to remember about contract reviews is to get the contract reviewed before you sign it. If you have it looked at after you have signed it, and there are IR35 issues, it is too late to renegotiate. The agency will simply say it's too late and there will be nothing you can do about it.

When reviewing a contract for a new assignment you have four options:

- Don't review your contract (a horrifyingly common approach)
- Review the contract yourself
- Get the contract reviewed by an IR35 legal specialist
- Ask HMRC to review your contract for you.

## Been there, done that!

## Ask the taxman?

**DAVE SAYS:** I actually used the Revenue's IR35 review service in 2000, shortly after the rules came into force. I wanted peace of mind and thought that was the best way to get it. It turned out to be both a good idea and a bad one. Bad in that their default reaction was 'you're caught' but good in that after much persuasion by my lawyer I got a letter stating I was outside.

Still, I wouldn't recommend any contractor do the same, particularly now after several years of IR35 legislation. It's the notional contract that is important, so until the contract has been completed a proper judgment can't be made anyway; therefore, why stick your neck out?

If you choose to conduct your own preliminary review that is quite sensible, as it will prepare you for any future legal expert view. However, to rely completely on your own knowledge, no matter how experienced a contractor you are, could backfire, as it has already backfired on others. To their considerable cost.

Choosing not to review your contract leaves you at risk and may cost you a large amount of money in the long run. The contract may be within IR35, you may get investigated and you have no idea about the facts. Remember that HMRC has six years to review your contract themselves.

When you get your contract reviewed by a specialist, make sure:

- You are using a legal specialist and not an accountant, because IR35 is a legal and not an accounting issue. Accountants increasingly offer free IR35 contract reviews as part of their ongoing service. That's fine as long as the accountant outsources the reviews to an IR35 specialist, which many do

- The legal specialist you use is highly experienced in the IR35 arena; your local family solicitor is unlikely to have that experience

- Ex-HMRC inspectors are an excellent source of expert IR35 assistance, but they are not lawyers. You still need the non-IR35 elements of the contract reviewed by a lawyer.

It is very strongly recommended that you do not use HMRC's contract review service. To do so is like waving a flag saying, 'Please come and investigate me!' Plus, if HMRC is asked if there is any doubt about IR35 status, they will almost certainly say, 'There's no doubt – you are inside IR35 and should pay tax and National Insurance Contributions as an employee'.

Even if you have not reviewed contracts in the past, it is a valuable exercise to review them now, so you can accurately plan for any tax implications and structure your payments and tax savings accordingly.

HMRC requires that all taxpayers, contractors and otherwise, demonstrate 'reasonable care' in the management of their tax affairs. Failure to do so could result in a range of sanctions, including fines and even imprisonment in extreme cases. True to form, however, HMRC fails to provide a definition of what reasonable care might entail, but having a contract reviewed by an IR35 expert clearly demonstrates that you are taking a high degree of reasonable care to determine your tax status.

## 8.4.5 Negotiating IR35 compliance with agents and clients

The important thing to remember when trying to negotiate IR35 compliance into a contract with an agent or directly with a client is that IR35 does not matter to them.

The agent gets paid the same whether or not you are inside IR35. And not only do they not care, but it is generally in their interests to get you to sign the contract as quickly as possible, so that they can start taking their cut and then move on to another 'sale'.

Similarly, the client probably won't have any real reason to negotiate with you on your contract – after all, they're not going to pay any less for your services; they're likely to have a million and one other priorities; and some of the things you might be talking about, like substitution, could get them worried about the project being satisfactorily completed.

If there is nothing in it for them why should the agent or client change the standard contract they are comfortable with just to please you?

Agencies have a number of tactics they use in an attempt to grind you down into submission so they don't have to change their standard contract. Often, according to the agent, it is the client who won't change. Sometimes, even if the contractor and client are in agreement, the agency won't change the contract. There are also underlying issues for the agency, such as trying to reduce their liability because if something goes wrong, the client has the relationship with the agency and can sue, leaving the agency to chase the contractor.

A typical example of an agency mitigating this liability is when it attempts to write into its contract with the client a clause saying the contractor is under the client's control. Obviously, as the contractor, you simply must not accept this clause as you are in business in your own right and not controlled by the client.

Negotiating with the agency is often the only way to remove such risky IR35 clauses from the contract, and the discussion must happen before the contract is signed. Afterwards, the agency won't be interested, unless you threaten to leave, but of course you may not have a termination clause so could be in breach of contract.

There are key occasions when you may wish to negotiate with the agent about contract clauses: when you are discussing a new contract or when a contract is being renewed.

How receptive an agent is likely to be to such IR35 contract negotiations depends largely on the market conditions. In a depressed market where there are lots of contractors chasing few contracts, agents will not be interested in holding conversations about contract amendments. If you try, they will move on until they find a contractor who will accept the contract as it stands.

If the market is buoyant, and agents are desperate to fill positions, they will be much more likely to compromise about specific contractual clauses. The same is true at renewal time if the client is keen to renew the contractor. In fact, if the client fears losing your company's services, they may well put pressure on the agent to make the changes you are requesting.

## Been there, done that!

### Market forces can force contractors into IR35

**DAVE SAYS:** During the dot com boom, demand was so high that contractors simply wouldn't consider contracts that were inside IR35. Being outside IR35 became a sales point for agents trying to attract contractors, and was even listed in job adverts.

After the crash, when things were reversed, the power was back in the hands of agents. With people lining up to take positions, agents avoided any contractors who were 'awkward' about things like IR35. Contractors prepared to 'do as they were told' were more likely to be sent for interviews.

Ensure you have had expert help in preparing the negotiation; prepare a list with your legal adviser of what you want removed and what you want included, down to the specific wording. Also make it easy for the agent by preparing clauses in bite-sized chunks that integrate seamlessly with the original contract.

Trying to negotiate your way out of an 'inside IR35' contract at renewal time also depends on the state of the market, and the same principles apply. However there is a different process for making what are likely to be substantial changes, and having a legal expert involved in the process is well worth the investment:

- Get legal help to compile a list of the changes that need to be made

- Speak to the agent first and request the changes for the renewal. After they refuse them (most likely) ask to speak to the person who deals with the legal aspects of the contracts. Trying to negotiate contractual issues with an agent can prove unproductive, as they just want you to sign again and have other more pressing things to attend to

- Get your lawyer to speak to the agency's legal person on your behalf. This is much more effective than trying to do it yourself

- Speak to your client directly if you are not getting results. Tell them you desperately want to renew the contract, but give the impression that you might be forced to consider your renewal position if they cannot get it sorted out. They might then put pressure on the agency to compromise

- You can also use the same 'I'm not sure I want to renew unless you sort out the contract' tactic with the agent. They don't want to appear bad in front of their client by not treating their contractors well. But be careful with this tactic: you don't want to give them a month to find someone else to replace you!

You could spend a tidy sum in legal fees being given the run-around. So try and establish early if the agency is paying lip service and trying to stall you, in the hope that when renewal time comes you'll just sign the contract again.

At some point it could become clear that you are going to be unsuccessful with the changes. There are a few options:

- Grin and bear it. You tried

- Threaten to not take (or renew) the contract. This might make things happen. Beware of burning bridges though

- Ask for a rate rise. It's unlikely to cover the whole gap, but you might get something.

If a month before renewal you feel you are getting nowhere and could get a better contract elsewhere, then it might be worth looking for one. Having a back-up plan is always useful.

Bear in mind that getting individual contracts changed for contractors at a site where the agency has many other contractors is hard. They will have their upper level contract with the client and the lower level contract with you. Changing your contract means either opening up a risk to them if they don't change their contract with the client, or spending money changing it.

Also, as most agencies don't have separate legal departments and lawyers are expensive, agents will try and prevent any changes getting made. Understanding this when you approach them, and making it as simple and inexpensive as possible to make the changes you want, will give you a much higher chance of success.

### 8.4.6 Confirming arrangements with your client

Even if you have a first class contract with all the correct clauses and wording, HMRC and, at a later stage, a judge, will examine the real nature of the relationship between you and your client, and then come to conclusions about the nature of your 'notional contract'.

You might find it shocking that a judge could conclude you are employed, when neither you nor your client had any intention of creating an employment relationship. In other words, your supposedly legally binding contract could be judged to be not worth the paper it is written on. But whatever your views on the fairness or otherwise of this, accept that is the law and you must look after your own interests in light of it.

It is therefore very important that as much evidence as possible is available for each contract demonstrating the true nature of your working relationship. Items such as emails between you and the client over key issues can help.

What has happened in several high profile IR35 cases is that the contractor has believed, and has on paper, that the contract is outside IR35; that they are not controlled by their client; and that they have an unfettered right of substitution. But when the client has been asked about these matters during subsequent investigations, they have directly contradicted this.

In addition, upper level contracts between the agent and the client can contradict lower level contracts between the contractor and the agent. HMRC use these contradictions against contractors, even though contractors cannot possibly have any knowledge of the exact contents of these documents.

One tool that contractors can employ in a number of circumstances is the confirmation of arrangements letter with the client. This is basically a document that outlines the working practices of the contractor, confirms there is no control and that the client is aware that the contractor has an unfettered right of substitution in their contract with the agency, and so on. It is also a key step towards ensuring the client understands that their relationship with you is not one of manager and employee.

Your client sets the specifications and expectations of the work to be completed, but that's where their controlling input should end. From the outset, you should make it clear that you are the skilled professional or knowledge worker whose business has been contracted to complete a specific project. As such, you are not subject to supervision, although it is of course acceptable that the client checks the work has been completed to their satisfaction and within agreed deadlines.

Furthermore, the covering letter, or email, that accompanies the confirmation of arrangements to be signed by your client provides you with an opportunity to manage the client's expectations about the working relationship they are about to embark upon. This is also an early indication to warn the client of the consequences of deviating from the confirmation of arrangements.

The objective is for the client to sign and date the letter, so if you are asked by HMRC in the future the exact nature of the relationship you had with your client on a given contract, you have written evidence to back up your claims.

Although the letter confirming arrangements should remain valid as long as the original contract is in force, if the project manager at the client changes it is important to ensure they understand the situation, as they may well be giving evidence at your hearing if you get investigated.

Where HMRC try and use a contradictory upper level contract against you, you can use the notional contract in your favour in this context by producing the confirmation of arrangements that shows the true nature of the relationship.

You also have a handy summary that you can keep in your compliance file (section 8.4.9) that will still be valid in six years if HMRC decide to go back that far.

Ideally you should draft the covering letter and confirmation of arrangements, perhaps exchanging a few drafts with your immediate project manager who actually knows what you do, and then ask them to sign it. Don't ask someone from the human resources or legal department to sign it – they don't know how you work and will probably come up with lots of reasons why they shouldn't sign it anyway.

Although it is not always possible, particularly with contractors such as offshore engineers or IT contractors requiring access to sensitive secure internal systems, where there is a genuine need to work on-site within prescribed hours, try to include an opening paragraph about hours and location; this should include statements along the following lines:

- Start and end times of the day are at the contractor's discretion, allowing for factors such as professional courtesy and access to systems and key client personnel

- Where possible and where work schedules and the practicalities of the project permit, the contractor shall be able to work at their own premises.

Where you must adhere to time and location constraints, the covering letter should explain why this is required, for example because health and safety or security requirements only allow access to a site at specific times.

And to get around the issue of mutuality of obligation in the covering letter you could include the following: 'I would welcome the opportunity to work on additional projects, but I understand that I am under no obligation to do so, and any I do consider are at my discretion. Any work outside the original contract specifications will require a separate specification, negotiation for the rate or project fee, and a separate contract.'

Each contractor will have individual needs, but the core components of the covering letter should include a preamble covering time and location, a bit on control and substitution, a sentence about mutuality of obligation, and, of course, deal with the part and parcel issue.

To accompany the covering letter, a typical confirmation of arrangements would contain the following:

- The precise nature of the services you provide

- The exact dates of your contract

- Confirmation that a substitute can be supplied, at your expense and your choice

- The financial arrangements, such as daily/hourly rates or a fixed fee

- The location of the contract, including other client sites

- Confirmation you can work from your own office

- If you need to be on site what is the reason

- Confirmation you can't be asked to do something not in your contract

- You work according to your own hours

- Your client does not instruct you on how to perform your tasks

- Confirmation that you are not governed by the same rules as permanent employees, except for obvious exceptions, like health and safety

- Confirmation that you supply your own equipment, and if you have to use the client's equipment why, for example reasons of security or health and safety

- Confirmation you are liable for damage or loss through negligence

- Confirmation you have to rectify defective work at your own expense

- Confirmation you can work for other clients during the course of the contract

- Confirmation you do not receive any form of benefits enjoyed by full time employees, not even use of the company canteen

- Confirmation that you do not take work not specified in the contract

- Confirmation that if you do not work, you do not get paid

- Confirmation that you could supply a substitute, for example in the event that you are unable to work due to illness.

Ideally, when submitting the confirmation of arrangements with the covering letter, you should also supply a list of your preferred substitutes, possibly even including brief CVs and inviting the client to inspect these potential replacements.

This is becoming an increasingly important document in proving that a contractor is outside IR35, so it is important to have a copy on record for each and every contract you undertake.

You can obtain a draft from ContractorCalculator:

http://www.contractorcalculator.co.uk/
contractors_ir35_confirmation_letter.aspx

### 8.4.7 Setting and managing client expectations

Many clients simply do not know what IR35 means, or choose to ignore it. The sooner you are able to set and manage your client's expectations, the better. Speak to your main contact with the client, probably your project manager, and explain to them very briefly about the key issues covered so far in this chapter.

Ideally, you should broach the topic of the confirmation of arrangements as soon as you feel comfortable, which can be daunting, especially the first time you do it. The covering letter will also help to clarify exactly how the relationship will work, and that you are not just another employee but a highly qualified professional brought in to apply your specialist skills to a particular aspect of a project.

Whatever you do, don't allow yourself to become a 'tail-end Charlie' and take on tasks outside your contract to please the client, or to ramp up billable hours. If HMRC or a judge creates a notional contract on that basis you will be inside IR35.

Remember some client managers might simply be inexperienced at hiring and managing contractors, or divorced from what they mean by the human resources department. To them you might be just like an employee who will do any work they choose to send your way. Contractors need to set expectations right from the start, and throughout the project, and also keep evidence (emails etc) that conversations like this have gone on.

This tactic is all about one thing: mitigating the chance that the manager/client says something untrue – sometimes in the mistaken belief they are being helpful to you – if HMRC comes knocking on the door. HMRC has been known to ask questions like, "So, tell me Mr Z, how do you control your contractors?" Your client needs to know right from the start that they don't control you.

Think of your relationship with your client like this: if you ask a builder to build a wall, you tell them where and how high, but you don't tell the builder how to mix the mortar and lay the bricks. Clients should extend the same professional courtesy to you.

Follow these steps to ensure the client knows exactly how the relationship works:

1. Get the confirmation of arrangements signed

2. Make sure you read through this with the manager so they digest everything in it

3. Make minutes about what happened in the meeting when the letter was signed

4. Send a copy to your project manager – and keep a copy of the email in your contract file

5.  If you are asked to do something that is not part of the services you are contracted to do, make it clear verbally that you won't/cannot do that. Then send a further email to your boss – and keep a record of that email and any responses.

### 8.4.8 More on being in business on your own account – working practices

Your working practices are a crucial factor that will determine your IR35 status. If you work and act like an independent professional running a business, the likelihood is that you will be treated like one by your client. So, as well as ensuring you have in place all the requirements of section 8.3.11, such as your own business cards, laptop or tablet, home office and so on it is important to act like you are in business in your own right. Because, actually you are and every day you are on the client's site you are 'client facing'.

This means ensuring that your working practices change so that you run your company and your work like a proper business, and that your professional working practices and standards adhere to the content of the contract document.

## Been there, done that!

### IR35 party planning?

Dave says: At one firm one of the contractors was responsible for organising the Christmas party. Not a good move from an IR35 perspective and certainly something that would strongly point to being caught by IR35, unless of course he had agreed to deliver and charge for social event planning. Perhaps his CV would read: "Software Developer/Party Organiser seeks fun company to deliver software solutions and organise parties for staff."

Avoid becoming 'part and parcel' of the organisation by distinguishing yourself as an independent contractor. And if that means you have to maintain your professional distance from colleagues, wear a smart suit to the office every day when all around you are in casual clothes, then do so – stand out as a professional contractor.

Your working practices will contribute hugely to any construction of a notional contract by HMRC, or a judge. If your working practices fail to adhere to the contract and to your position as an independent, professional contractor, it could be deemed not to be genuine and ignored.

### 8.4.9 Building an IR35 compliance file for each contract

Should HMRC start an investigation, then your comprehensive, well-organised and accurate business records could make the difference between you winning or losing your case. It could also make the difference between a quick and straightforward investigation that HMRC will take no further, and a full investigation that could lead to a judgement against you and a court case.

So it is essential that you keep a record of each separate contract and schedules for each different project going back six years. It's not a difficult task, and well worth it. Remember that HMRC will look for every opportunity to justify its inspection by claiming back-taxes, NICs and penalties, so investigators will want to go through your trading history in detail.

Should HMRC conduct a tax inspection and dispute your status, you will be faced with your local tax inspector, who will look at your evidence, and then eventually with the First Tier tax tribunal if you appeal. If you do go to appeal, you are likely to face a tribunal judge. They will all need convincing, with as much proof as possible, of what actually took place between you and the agency, and between you and the client.

You may have some proof in your letter of engagement. Again this may not be specific enough, but it may help. If you can't get terms into the contract that clearly put you outside IR35, you have to find other means of proof. And even if you have a sound contract, you might need to back it up. So aim to achieve the following:

- Get a signed confirmation of arrangements letter

- Bring some of your own equipment and get some proof that it is used in the project by, for example, sending emails showing that you are using it

- Get your project manager to let you do some of the work at home, and see that the email record shows this is taking place. Or simply get a note saying you can work at home

- The right of substitution is a very important proof of being outside IR35. Send the client or the agent emails about this. If you get a reply, that may prove extremely useful. Any other proof of that kind, like letters or notes from the agent or client could help too

- Keep any proof you can get that you've paid your own expenses. Not just receipts, but also any requests for materials needed from the client, any email asking you to pay expenses and so on.

Fill your IR35 compliance file with evidence of your day to day working practices – this evidence may seem innocuous at the time, but could tip the balance towards a judge finding you outside IR35. For each contract:

- Retain copies of emails where you and your client discuss key elements of a contract

- Maintain a diary of how you, not your client, made fundamental decisions about how you should do the work on the project, note general issues showing lack of client control, your independence and the application of your special skills

- Record important conversations and events where contractual issues have been discussed, and, whenever possible, get the client to sign the notes.

Make an effort to get as much proof as you can. Remember, HMRC may go back six years if it decides to review your status, so you will need to save everything relevant. Make sure that you get proof while the project is taking place, as you'll certainly struggle to obtain it six years later.

## 8.4.10 Insuring yourself against IR35

An investigation can take years and, if it goes as far as a tax tribunal and appeals, can cost tens of thousands of pounds in defence costs. This doesn't include back taxes, NICs and penalties you might have to pay if you lose; in one case a contractor received a tax bill of £99,000. The financial cost will be considerable; the emotional cost to you and your family could be even greater.

In the UK, if HMRC demands a settlement from you of unpaid taxes, penalties and interest, it is your responsibility to challenge the settlement; if you don't, you will be required to pay up. It is therefore down to you to mount a defence; if you do not, you are assumed to be liable and will have to pay any outstanding taxes, NICs and penalties that HMRC demands.

Contractors subject to tax investigations have few protections. HMRC's investigators can delve into every aspect of your life and use any evidence against you. And because the investigations can take so much time and have such potentially dramatic consequences, the stress for the contractor can be incredible.

Fighting inspections and rulings by HMRC is not for the uninitiated. Many cash businesses, even small firms like corner shops, have tax enquiry and investigation insurance that can remove some of the stress associated with the process. If you choose to take out a similar insurance, do it sooner rather than later so you have maximum cover by investing in a good policy before an inspection starts.

In addition to investigation insurance, you may be able to take out a tax liability cover policy too, which, in addition to paying the costs associated with running a defence, would also pay out if you lost the case and owed money to HMRC.

The cost of tax investigation insurance is typically in the low hundreds of pounds each year. What makes it a 'no brainer' for most contractors is that if you don't have insurance and need to pay your own costs for a defence, a judge won't award you costs, even if you win the case.

### 8.4.11 Staying outside IR35 if you go contracting for your former employer

Contractors returning to work for a former employer, or being asked to return immediately on a contract basis after redundancy, face a very real threat of being found inside IR35. By continuing to work for your ex-employer immediately after your contract of employment has been terminated, you have no time to establish yourself in the eyes of the taxman as being in business on your own account. Your client, and former employer, could also be entering a minefield of employment legislation if they hire you, a worker turned contractor who they've just made redundant. Clearly there could be questions put to your employer/client about the legitimacy of their redundancy process.

But it is possible for you to remain outside IR35 when contracting for a former employer; you just have to work that much harder to prove you are not a disguised employee. Not only do you have to avoid falling foul of the standard tests of employment, but you also have to clearly identify and demonstrate how the relationship and working practices have changed since changing status from employee to contractor

You must actively avoid any old roles that place you in an employee's shoes, like being a fire marshal or first aider. You should sign in every morning, use visitor parking spaces and make sure you are no longer part of company organisational charts and telephone directories, unless clearly identified as a contractor. You should even steer clear of organised staff social events, like Christmas parties, although you can still join your former workmates for an informal drink after work.

If you absolutely have to start on the Monday after leaving on the Friday, then the first contract you work on should ideally be a project with clearly defined outcomes, preferably on a fixed-price basis, rather than an hourly or daily rate. Staged payments on achieving significant project milestones should be written into the contract, leaving little doubt that you, the ex-employee, are now taking a significant business risk.

In addition, you must be confident that not only has your former employer understood the legal and tax implications of the new arrangement, but is also prepared to treat you as a business-to-business supplier. You should also be confident that the former employer would be able to accurately explain and defend the new relationship to an HMRC inspector, and potentially to a tribunal judge.

## 8.4.12 How to manage bonus payments to avoid IR35

Don't be discouraged from working on a performance-related basis, as that's precisely how many businesses operate. But if you've negotiated a contract where you receive bonus payments, you might find yourself pitched straight into IR35, as HMRC is likely to see such bonuses as being evidence that you are a disguised employee. But you can legitimately receive 'bonuses' and remain outside IR35 if you pay attention to detail.

Something as simple as the wrong word on a document could tip the balance against you in an IR35 review. The first lesson is never to call a bonus a 'bonus', because that is associated with employment. In fact, that simple word on a contract may be sufficient to spark a full-blown IR35 enquiry. So, if you are offered a bonus during contract negotiations, you should ensure that the contract and surrounding 'paperwork' never refers to the payment as a 'bonus'. The wording should always be amended to say 'incentive' or 'completion' payment.

In addition to correcting the terminology, ensure that the incentive payments are specifically related to a project and will only be paid on completion of milestones, or once the project has been successfully completed and the specifications met.

## 8.4.13 IR35 issues for project managers

If you choose contracts with project management responsibility, by definition you are there to manage projects, which under certain circumstances could give the impression of disguised employment. But with the right documentation in place, and regular updates made as required, you are likely not to be judged as inside IR35, particularly if it is clear you have no line management responsibility.

Clearly identify the services to be performed, project deliverables and any milestones. This should include creating a confirmation of arrangements, so the client also understands the true situation. Just as importantly, any services that lay outside your responsibility should also be clearly documented, for avoidance of doubt during a later investigation.

If you are directly managing suppliers, signing off work others complete and managing supplier performance, then those project deliverables must be understood by all parties at the outset. Write these deliverables into the contract so they are unlikely to put you inside IR35.

Project management comes with a health warning, because getting involved in any kind of human resources processes with the client is a sure-fire way to subsequently become involved with HMRC in IR35 issues. You should refuse to be involved in their client's formal HR procedures, whether they involve recruitment, performance appraisals or grievance and disciplinary processes.

There may also be employment law implications for the client if they let a contractor implement HR processes, as the contractor may not technically be authorised. Also, by implication, if you do perform those duties you are almost certainly caught by IR35. Line management and project management are not the same thing. If you adopt best practice from the outset, you should emerge from an IR35 investigation unscathed.

### 8.4.14 IR35 Issues for contractors working overseas

IR35 can follow you across borders when you go contracting overseas. If you remain liable for tax in the UK, then you are liable for an IR35 re-assessment of whether you were actually an employee of a foreign company or whether you were a genuine contractor. You will only cease to be tax-liable on earned income in the UK after a full year abroad.

When you cease to be liable for taxes in the UK, you can forget about IR35, but you will have to think very carefully about the rules in the country you are now working in, because these can be quite restrictive. The same rules for best contracting practice apply, and an IR35 contract-assessment can be made based on contracts drawn up anywhere in the world.

HMRC will follow the same procedure that it always does if it wishes to prove that you are caught by IR35. The first step is to obtain a copy of the contract between your end client and the agency you worked for to compare it with the one you have with the agency. If the agency-client contract sounds a lot like an employment contract, you will almost certainly experience the start of an IR35 investigation.

In practice, HMRC may not find it easy to obtain contracts drawn up between two foreign companies, that is, the agency abroad and the end client abroad. HMRC has no jurisdiction outside the UK, and foreign tax authorities are rarely cooperative with each other.

But don't count on avoiding the IR35 issue in this way. Should HMRC manage to obtain what it needs, you could be in trouble. It is best to ensure that your contract clearly addresses the IR35 issues, just as if you remained in the UK.

## 8.5 IR35 reviews by HMRC

For most contractors, an HMRC IR35 review is possibly one of the worst things that *could* happen to them in their professional lives. And for many contractors, an HMRC IR35 review *has been* the worst thing that has happened to them.

When you first find out about it, it is likely to come as a tremendous shock. However, if you have taken all the steps recommended in chapters 7 and 8, it can prove a relatively quick and easy process.

If your evidence and defence are already in place – because you've taken care over things like your contract and your working arrangements, plus kept a detailed contract file – there is every chance that the investigators will be satisfied that you have been correctly working outside IR35, and therefore move on to another case. Unfortunately there are many contractors who do not pay enough attention to IR35 issues and are 'low hanging fruit' to an inspector. Make sure you stay at the top of the tree!

Nevertheless, even if you have done absolutely everything as you should, you should still tread very carefully throughout every step of an investigation. Remember, unlike other parts of the UK law, when you are dealing with HMRC you are liable to pay any settlement until you can prove that you shouldn't have to; it is your responsibility to appeal.

The rules of evidence are not as strict as they are in criminal law, so even a light-hearted, off-the-cuff remark while you're offering the tax inspector a cup of tea can take on huge significance if your case goes to court. So take great care.

It helps to have an understanding of what is going to happen so you can prepare yourself.

Don't confuse an 'IR35 review' with a contract review. HMRC calls its status enquiries an 'IR35 review' when investigating a contractor suspected of being inside IR35, and also uses the phrase in its guidance. A contract review is where you pay a lawyer to go through your contract and highlight any elements that are IR35-unfriendly or commercially undesirable.

### 8.5.1 How HMRC might challenge you

An experienced HMRC inspector can glance at the profit and loss account of a large business, like an engineering firm, oil company or bank, and immediately spot unusually high bills in the professional services costs line. That means the firm probably uses a lot of contractors, which will be of immediate interest to the inspector.

HMRC then only has to identify the contractors from their invoices in the firm's accounting records, and for the inspectors it has suddenly become a target rich environment – with contractors firmly in their sights.

The investigation starts when the inspector reviews the contractor's accounts. HMRC has an extremely sophisticated IT set-up (ironically, largely built by contractors!) that allows it to drill down into your accounts and compare you with thousands, possibly even tens/hundreds of thousands, of very similar businesses.

Any discrepancies in your accounts will be quickly and easily spotted – almost like a big red flashing light next to your company name saying, 'look at me, look at me!'.

There are a number of instant giveaways that a contractor might fall within IR35 and merit an inspection:

- No employees, other than directors
- The directors pay themselves a low wage as salary

- The directors, possibly husband and wife, take most of the cash out of the business as dividends

- There are no or few materials charged through the business.

HMRC will view each of these factors as pointing to a personal service company, which will almost certainly result in an inspection. Warning bells should ring the day a contractor receives a letter from the HMRC informing them of an Employer Compliance Review.

This means the early stages of a status inspection has begun and the inspector will be out to prove the contractor falls within IR35 – classic HMRC tactics. HMRC will look into all the points highlighted in the bullet points above, along with your contract with the agency and/or client, and the contract between the agency and the client.

The agency-client contract can cause you a great deal of trouble, and there is nothing you can do about it. While the agency may have agreed to good contract terms with you, the agent may have promised the client all sorts of things in terms that make you sound like a 'disguised' employee. You can always ask for a copy of this contract when you are negotiating with an agency, but most will refuse as it is probably confidential and protected by a Non-Disclosure Agreement.

You can also ask the agency to include a clause in your contract saying that it is faithful to the agency-client contract, but this is of little use in court as HMRC will argue that it may say so, but it really isn't. If the agency agreed to this clause, and subsequently misrepresents the assignment, you may be able to sue them later for the breach (see 8.6.2). But it won't help the IR35 situation and there is, in practice, little you can do involving the agency-client contract to protect yourself.

Most of all, HMRC will try and get your on-site manager to describe what you do. This is the most important aspect of the case, because the courts will base their judgement on what actually happens in the workplace – to the best of their ability. They will ask about how the work is controlled – do you decide or does the client? Is it project-based, or are you just doing whatever the manager asks? Are you supplying your own equipment, or if you must use the on-site equipment, is there a good reason why?

This is where a confirmation of arrangements letter (see section 8.4.6) can be so useful if the client inadvertently says something to HMRC that sounds suspicious, although it could be perfectly innocent.

The worst of all this is that HMRC has the right to go back six years into your records and try to prove you were 'inside' IR35 on any given contract. So you may wind up trying to find people at the client who can remember back that far just to state what you really did.

The review is contract-based, so you may have had 20 contracts that were clearly not caught by the legislation, but HMRC can still come after you for the one that sounds like it was.

You can fight an HMRC judgement in court, but it's going to take a long time and cost you a lot of money, unless you have comprehensive tax investigation insurance. So, it's best to find ways to avoid an HMRC inspection in the first place, or to make sure you can effectively defend your position as being outside IR35 on all the relevant contracts.

### 8.5.2 Steps to mitigate a challenge

The ideal strategy to avoid an investigation and challenge by HMRC is to avoid being noticed in the first place. This is subtly different from ensuring your IR35 defence is in place before you get inspected, although of course you must keep on top of IR35 issues. The object is to do nothing out of the ordinary to attract the attention of HMRC, by truly working as a contractor and not a 'disguised' employee. Basic practices include:

- Take professional advice before you sign any contract from either an agency or a client

- The contract should make it clear from the clauses and conditions that you are an independent contractor and not an employee

- Ensure all tax documents are filed online before they become due and do not have mistakes on them

- Ensure that all tax assessments and demands are paid on time with all payments being sent to the correct office or processing centre

- Make sure all expenses are categorised correctly on your company and personal tax forms – ask your accountant if in doubt

- If there are any significant changes to any expenses on tax forms, include a note in "additional notes", as this can make it clear to HMRC that there is a perfectly good explanation for these changes

- If you have ever been instructed by HMRC to make changes to your records, make sure these are done. If they're not, then you will be listed for another review.

If you are contacted by HMRC about an inspection, do not to speak to HMRC or contact them in any way. You could inadvertently say something, however innocent it might appear to you, which is later used as a central feature of the evidence against you. If you have tax investigation insurance, now is the time to get in touch with your insurer.

Ideally, all contact with HMRC should be through your specialist IR35 lawyer, accountant or approved advisor, again to ensure you don't say something that might harm your case. Personal contact could jeopardise the chances of successfully defending the inspection.

Even a chance remark to what sounds like a friendly enquiry from a tax inspector can become the basis of a strong case against you. This is so important because HMRC will start the investigation before they even arrive at your premises.

HMRC will have already considered the main issues and great care needs to be taken at the initial meeting – that's when you really need your expert adviser present.

Just to give a real-life example: a contractor who runs a business that uses a lot of sub-contractors on various projects had their tax adviser present. The sub-contractors were not employees. However the first question the inspector asked when the meeting began was, 'So, Mr Smith, how exactly do you control your employees?'

Two key IR35 tests were satisfied in that statement; employment status and control. Had the tax lawyer not intervened at that point and halted the meeting, the client would have responded to the inspector's question as he was invited to do. The inspector would have written in the notes of the investigation: 'When we arrived, Mr Smith explained to us how he controlled his employees.' And this simple statement would have become a conclusive piece of evidence throughout the case, alongside the HMRC inspectors' account of the meeting, during which they would have used similar questioning.

Another example is of an IT contractor who had been targeted by HMRC for a Pay As You Earn (PAYE) employer's compliance review, but because the contractor involved their professional advisers from the outset, the case never even progressed to a meeting and was handled completely by correspondence. The contractor in question was clearly 'in business' and ticked all the right boxes, which included:

- The contractor limited company had a website
- Some client projects were performed on a fixed-price basis
- The contractor had a dedicated and well equipped home office
- The company had made a substantial investment in computer equipment required to fulfil client projects.

This evidence was presented in a dossier to the HMRC inspector with a recommendation that there was no status case to answer. The inspector agreed, and the review was halted before it even got started.

The key lesson is, in order to mitigate the impact of a challenge, you need professional advice involved from the outset.

### 8.5.3 Why IR35 cases can take so long to be resolved

One of the commitments made by HMRC when it introduced its risk-based approach framework in May 2012 was to reduce the time it takes for an IR35 review to be completed. That's because IR35 cases have historically taken years to resolve: one case, that of engineering contractor Mark Fitzpatrick's company MBF Design Ltd, took seven years to resolve, and at the end the contractor was totally exonerated. Fitzpatrick's experiences of HMRC's IR35 procedures are far from unique and only time will tell as to whether HMRC was genuine in May 2012 about its intention to speed up the process.

There is no single reason why IR35 cases can take so long and there are usually a number of factors adding to the delays. Typically, this is because cases can be complex and depend on expert interpretation of evidence, which takes time to gather. 'Soft' variables, such as the personalities of the HMRC inspector, the contractor and their agent, plus the speed and efficiency of the client and agent, who both play a significant role in an IR35 case, can easily add weeks and months to the process.

The first stage in an IR35 investigation is information gathering by the HMRC inspector leading the case. An investigator will want to know the details of each of your contracts for every tax year being investigated. That means that if you are under investigation for several tax years, each with multiple contracts, then a considerable amount of information must be gathered from you, your client and your agency. If you and your IR35 adviser choose to deal with the process purely by correspondence, rather than through meetings, a simple exchange of letters to answer a basic question of fact can take months.

Clients involved in the various contracts being investigated can also add delays. Because the inspector will want to understand the exact nature of the real working relationship between you and your client, the client is typically sent a questionnaire with as many as 150 questions to answer. This can extend the investigation timeline in a number of ways. If your client responds promptly, the inspector may have further questions based on the client's responses, and even more questions on those responses. But often your client project manager will pass the inspector's questionnaire to the human resources, or legal or procurement teams in the company, who may choose not to reply at all, or only to reply in very guarded terms that are unhelpful to both sides.

Particularly stubborn or tenacious inspectors, with support from their HMRC managers, have been known to insist on taking cases right through to their conclusion in the courts, even if the evidence is weak, such as in the MBF Design case. Nowadays the scope for 'maverick' inspectors is much reduced, as the tax tribunal system that came into force in April 2011 allows taxpayers to request an independent review, albeit from an 'independent' HMRC inspector. But that fresh pair of eyes may well find in favour of the taxpayer.

## 8.6 If HMRC rules against you – the appeal process

If everything you have tried in creating an IR35 defence, avoiding notice by HMRC and defending yourself during the investigation fails, there is still the appeals process. This allows you to appeal to the First Tier Tribunal (Tax) and the Upper Tribunal (Finance and Tax). The tax tribunals replaced the old General Commissioners and Special Commissioners in April 2009, and a key advantage of the newer system is that it is totally independent of HMRC.

If, having been through an IR35 review, HMRC decides that some or all of your contracts over the last six years are within scope of the IR35 legislation, you will receive formal notification and a settlement. The settlement is HMRC-speak for your tax bill as a result of being found inside IR35. The bill, which has been as high as £99,000 for some contractors in the past, will include back taxes, NICs, penalties and interest. A tough new penalty regime was introduced in April 2009 (see section 8.6.1), and you could receive a penalty that can add as much as 70% of your unpaid tax to the settlement.

The settlement will be accompanied by information about what rights of appeal you have. In almost all cases, contractors will have the right to appeal against the HMRC ruling by applying to the First Tier Tribunal (Tax) to review their case. Under certain circumstances, especially with complex cases or those testing an important point of law, the case can be referred to the Upper Tribunal (Finance and Tax).

Assuming you've been represented by an IR35 expert throughout, your professional advisers should offer you their opinion as to whether you are likely to succeed at appeal and in which tribunal. Should they feel your case has a chance of overturning HMRC's settlement assessment at the tax tribunal, then your next step is to appeal the settlement.

The First Tier tax tribunal will be your first port of call to appeal against HMRC's IR35 decision. Ideally, you should have IR35 tax investigation insurance that will pay for the costs of a professional adviser to assist with the case. However, you can download an application form and complete an appeal yourself without a specialist adviser. But this can be risky and is not recommended.

Depending on the nature and complexity of your appeal, one of four First-tier tribunal categories will be allocated:

- Default paper
- Basic
- Standard
- Complex.

An IR35 appeal will almost certainly be placed into the complex category, as most IR35 cases require expert understanding of the issues. This adds weight to the argument that you really should have expert assistance with your IR35 appeal.

Should you lose at First Tier tribunal you can appeal to the Upper Tribunal (Finance and Tax). Your IR35 adviser may recommend the Upper Tribunal if a point of law is being tested or challenged. Alternatively, if HMRC has lost in the First Tier, it may also apply to have a case heard in the Upper Tribunal. In both cases, the Upper Tribunal is designed to hear appeals where it is thought that the First Tier was 'wrong in law'. This might be where the correct law may not have been applied, where there was not enough evidence, or where the First Tier tribunal did not give adequate reasons for its ruling.

This tribunal is for serious cases that are highly complex and/or are testing major points of law. The Upper Tribunal is what is known as a Superior Court of Record, so its judiciary are both High Court Judges and specialists in finance and tax. Although the rules don't require the contractor to have expert assistance, this is not a tribunal a contractor should expect to survive without very good professional assistance and representation.

Should the case go against you, any back taxes, interest or penalties will need to come out of your own pocket. Unless, of course, you have taken out insurance against this risk.

### 8.6.1 The IR35 penalty regime

If you knew your contract was inside IR35 and choose to conceal it, or if you are subsequently found inside IR35 following an HMRC review, you could be facing steep IR35 penalties. A new penalty regime was introduced by HMRC in April 2009, doing away with the previous negotiated settlement. Prior to April 2009, your tax adviser could negotiate away much of your tax liability and reduce payments; but the new system introduced the concept that taxpayers must exercise 'reasonable care'.

IR35 penalties will be levied when you under-declare your tax liability by not calculating your deemed payment of additional tax and NICs as a result of being inside IR35. These penalties will be still be payable whether you introduced the inaccuracy by being careless, by deliberately not calculating the deemed payment when you knew were inside IR35, or by deliberately under-declaring and concealing the facts.

The penalty is 30% of unpaid tax if HMRC considers you to have been careless. But the IR35 penalties are really steep if HMRC believes your underpayment to be deliberate: 70% of unpaid tax if you knew they were inside IR35 but deliberately did not make the deemed payment calculation; and 100% of unpaid tax if you knew you were inside IR35, deliberately did not calculate the deemed payment and attempted to conceal the underpayment.

### 8.6.2 Grounds for suing your agent if you are found to be inside IR35

So you've been found inside IR35 and want to pass the blame to your agency, claiming you were not told the full story and that the contractual terms implicating you were withheld. Unfortunately, the grounds for taking legal action and seeking financial redress from your agency are few, and you face an uphill struggle from the outset.

Your tax affairs are ultimately your problem, not the agency's or the client's. Unless an agency can be proven to have been dishonest in their dealings with you, then a successful legal challenge is unlikely.

Your IR35 status will depend on three factors:

- The reality of the contractor's working relationship with the client, which includes the 'notional contract';

- The actual contractual terms; and

- Other evidence that suggests you are in business on your own account.

You have some control and influence over all three factors. But as for the agency, it only has 'control' over the contract, to the extent that the agency influences its contents. What that means is that you are in the better position to influence two of the major factors on which your IR35 status will be tested. So, when considering whether to accept a particular contract, you must exercise your business judgement – and accept responsibility for the consequences of your decisions.

Taking responsibility means following through to make sure any IR35-friendly terms of the contract are actually stuck to. For example, if a contract shows the client has no 'control' over your, yet you arrive on site only to find that the client tries to boss you about, thereby exercising control and placing you at greater risk of being found to be inside IR35, it is your choice as to whether you should accept this, or challenge the client.

There are only two sets of circumstances in which you may have grounds to take legal action against an agency if your contract is found inside IR35 and you suffer financially as a result:

- If in the contract, the agency has made an express assurance which has been broken, or which events have subsequently shown to be untrue, and (in either case) if that has a material adverse effect on your IR35 status

- If the agency misrepresented the contract opportunity to you, you took your decision to enter the contract relying on that misrepresentation, and the result had a material adverse effect on your IR35 status.

You have to prove that the agency was at fault and that the agency misled you. In addition, many agency contracts have exclusion clauses that disallow you from taking action where the misrepresentation is innocent or negligent. It is not however generally possible to exclude liability for fraudulent misrepresentations – one which the person who gave it knew at the time to be false.

Where your agent made an untrue statement and they knew it to be untrue when they were making it, this qualifies as fraudulent misrepresentation and, under these circumstances, you may have a case. You would have to show fault on the part of the agent, show that you had actually been misled by the agent and relied on the misrepresentation, and also prove you suffered loss as a direct result of having done so.

To date, there have been no publicised cases where a contractor has been found inside IR35 by HMRC and successfully litigated against an agency. It's an untested area.

If you have any doubt about the contents of a contract under negotiation, you should always seek professional advice – it's a small investment compared to the money that would be lost if HMRC found a contract to be inside IR35.

## 8.7    Contractors caught by IR35

### 8.7.1 Treatment of expenses and the 5% rule

If you are caught by IR35 and use your limited company and your trading option and payment structure, you need to take into account the HMRC 5% expense allowance rule.

Basically if you receive income caught by the rules of IR35, you must carry out a deemed salary calculation each tax year, based on income received from relevant engagements. It's worth checking with your accountant about this calculation, but the basics follow.

HMRC allows an expense allowance equal to 5% of the income received from relevant engagements in calculating the deemed salary. This is intended to cover the following 'administration' costs:

1.   Premises costs, including home as office

2.   Administration and secretarial support

3.   Accountancy and tax advice

4.   Costs of seeking contracts

5. Printing, postage and stationery

6. Employer's and Public Liability Insurance

7. Training costs

8. Computer equipment (if not eligible for capital allowances)

9. Bank and overdraft interest

10. Hire purchase payments.

The 5% deduction is given at a flat rate on gross fees receivable and is not available to employees as an expense which they can draw from the company. It is simply allowed in the deemed calculation of IR35 salary as a fixed and limited claim against the above expenses. In granting the 5% allowance, HMRC does not require proof of expenditure and the full 5% is granted, even if there is no actual expenditure whatsoever.

The 5% allowance is only for 'administration' and is to cover the ten points above. In addition to the 5% for administration costs, a contractor can also claim direct costs such as travel, IT hardware costs, subsistence, direct training, sub-contractors and so on. So basically, legitimate business expenses not covered by the ten points can be claimed on top.

## 8.7.2 How your taxes are calculated – the deemed payment

There are some odd terms used, like 'Net Result' and 'Deemed Payment', but actually the concept is very simple. Basically, the way it works is you run your company as normal, paying yourself a salary, and claiming the expenses that you are allowed to, then see what is left in the pot at the end of the year.

This then has to be considered as paid as salary from an employer. So a calculation is done to work out what the salary would be ("deemed payment"), a figure which employer's National Insurance Contributions (NICs) would then be applied to.

Eg Net Result = Deemed Payment + Employer's NICs

Then the employee's NI and PAYE is applied to the deemed payment, just as taxes are applied to salaries.

In practice, most contractors caught by IR35 take everything they earn as a salary along the way, so there is only a small deemed payment, if any, at the end of the year. Your accountant will be able to help out with all this, and you really don't have to worry about it yourself. But here's a typical example:

Contractor details:

£80K annual revenue, £5K salary, and £5K legitimate expenses.

| Revenue | £80,000 |
|---|---|
| Allowable Expenses (5% of revenue) | £4,000 |
| Salary | £9,000 |
| Legitimate Expenses | £5,000 |
| Net Result | £62,000 |
| Additional Employer's NI due | £7,518 |
| Deemed Payment | £54482 |
| Additional Employee's NI | £4,409 |
| Additional PAYE | £15,097 |

### 8.7.3 When you have a mix of contracts – some caught, some not

During your accounting year you may earn revenue from several contracts, some of which will fall inside the scope of IR35 and others outside. When this occurs it is important to arrange your records to clearly record both types of income and the expenses which relate to 'inside' and 'outside' IR35 contract work.

Receipts and payments for IR35 contract work will need to be identifiable for use in a year end calculation – your accountant will have to do a different set of calculations for each contract. At the end of each tax year an IR35 calculation for 'deemed salary' will be done, which takes into account the IR35 contract income and expenditure relating to those specific contracts.

Any salary you pay yourself during the year can be allocated to your IR35 income, so that any profits, excluding salary payments generated by the non IR35 work, can be either paid out as dividends to shareholders or carried forward for distribution in a future year.

The IR35 status of one contract does not affect the IR35 status of another. Each needs to be judged on its own merits.

### 8.7.4 Why contractors caught by IR35 cannot claim employment rights

If you have been caught by IR35 and are being taxed as if you were an employee, you may be tempted to go for the 'nuclear option' and try to claim employment rights from your client. Many contractors see this as a possible way forward if they have been mistreated by the client and/or their contract has been terminated early.

However, you are unable to do so because of a precedent set by an Employment Appeals Tribunal ruling in 2001. This was the case of O'Murphy v Hewlett Packard, the results of which created case law that effectively bars nearly all contractors from claiming employment rights, even when caught by IR35. O'Murphy v Hewlett Packard remains the main determinant of 'employment rights for contractors' cases today.

The key to understanding the reasons lies in grasping that there are two fundamentally different tests. The tests to establish whether you are caught by IR35, and whether a worker is in fact an employee, and therefore entitled to employment rights, are fundamentally different.

The precedent set by O'Murphy v Hewlett Packard requires that for any claim for employment rights to succeed, you will have to prove:

a) That there is a contract between you and your client, and

b) Having first established that there is such a contract, to go on to prove that the true nature of that contract is one of employment.

The essential elements of forming a contract under the UK's legal code, as described in chapter 7, must be present. These are that you and your client must have agreed

a) All the material terms of the contract

b) The 'consideration' ( which is usually your payment), and

c) That you and your client share the mutual intent to be legally bound.

Where there is doubt that you and your client actually meant to create a contract, then there will generally be no contract. And, if there is no contract, then there can't be a contract of employment, and so you cannot claim employment rights.

The Finance Act 2000, which introduced IR35, has no bearing on fundamental contract law. Further, the notional contract created for the purposes of determining whether a contractor should be taxed as an employee is not relevant to establishing whether a contractor should have employment rights.

The concept of a notional contract is purely a construct of the IR35 legislation and has no bearing or relevance in any other context. So the fact that you may be considered a deemed employee for IR35 tax purposes will have no bearing on whether you have a claim for employment rights against the client.

The fact that there is an intermediary, such as a limited company, between you and your client will generally mean that there is no contract directly between you, the individual worker, and your client, nor any intention that there should be such a contract.

This means that you can be caught by IR35 but not be able to claim employment rights. That's because the tests for the two are totally different, and employment rights are a legal consequence of the employment relationship, rather than an indicator of its existence.

# Contracting lessons from this chapter

- The objective of IR35 is to combat tax avoidance by individuals supplying services via limited companies, when they should really be employed.

- If the IR35 legislation is found to apply to you, it could result in additional tax of up to 25% of your net income.

- Those caught by IR35 do not qualify for any employment rights.

- IR35 status is evaluated by considering employment status case law.

- Get an expert to review your IR35 status for each contract. Don't ask HMRC for an opinion.

- Take active steps before and during your contract to ensure that you are outside IR35.

- Collect evidence in a file to help you defend any future challenge by HMRC.

- It is prudent to take out tax investigation insurance.

- With forethought and correct planning, you can comfortably remain outside IR35.

- You can use ContractorCalculator's free Online IR35 Status Test to evaluate your IR35 Status:
  http://www.contractorcalculator.co.uk/IR35_Test.aspx

# 9
# Agency Workers Regulations

# 9.1 Introduction – AWR risks for contractors, clients and agencies

Having won a contract, adopted a trading vehicle, learned all about contract law and worked your way through the complexities of IR35, you might think that the rest is plain sailing. Unfortunately, there is one more potential hurdle to overcome in the form of the Agency Workers Regulations (AWR).

These regulations provide agency workers with additional rights, similar to those of permanent employees – some kick in from the first day of the assignment, others after 12 weeks (section 9.3.3 has more details). Whilst on the face of it that sounds great for contractors, there are potentially many more negatives than positives for the higher-paid contractors, with sought-after skill sets, who are likely to be reading this book. The fear is that AWR could have a profound and negative long-term impact on the UK's flexible labour market generally, and on contractors and contracting specifically.

The regulations – originally intended to protect vulnerable agency workers and those subjected to exploitation by gangmasters – have attracted much media attention throughout their long gestation and adoption. In the run-up to AWR coming into force on 1 October 2011, much media hype surrounded, on the one hand, the potential damage AWR might do to the UK's economy, and on the other the benefits AWR would bring to vulnerable and exploited agency workers.

At the time of writing, we still don't know what the long-term impact of the legislation is going to be on contracting. In the months following 1 October 2011 and at the time of writing in early 2012, it quickly became clear that some of the very workers supposed to be protected by the regulations were suffering from them. For example, many heavy users of agency workers slashed temporary headcounts and 'encouraged' – or in some cases bullied – workers into unsuitable employment models.

So there is still some uncertainty for contractors because, at the time of writing, the legislation has not been extensively tested through employment tribunals and the courts. There are still many unknowns, which may be already be impacting on the contracting sector. Both limited company and umbrella company contractors face the challenge of communicating to clients that the ongoing provision of their services won't present clients with increased risks and costs.

The better you understand AWR and its implications, the greater the chances you have of convincing clients and agencies that you present them with no AWR compliance risk. In fact, your knowledge of AWR risks and how to overcome them may well provide you with a source of competitive advantage over contractors who have not read this chapter and the regularly updated AWR section on ContractorCalculator.co.uk.

 contractorcalculator.co.uk/agency_workers_regulations.aspx

### 9.1.1 The risks for contractors

Contractors are facing the risk that many clients will be 'spooked' by AWR, or not make the effort to understand the implications of the regulations. As a result, clients could choose to use fewer contractors, or to move operations, and contracts, outside the UK.

The main AWR risks facing contractors include:

- Managing the perception that AWR will result in contractors becoming more expensive, with the resulting reduction in the number of contracts being offered by clients, or even more assignments going overseas to less regulated jurisdictions

- The uncertainty facing limited company contractors working via agencies. Contractors must help other stakeholders such as agencies to gain clarity, to ensure that they have the right contracts in place to be classed as 'business undertakings'

- Clients turning away from using umbrella company contractors, who are automatically in the scope of AWR.

### 9.1.2 The risks for clients

Clients, who are facing a combination of financial and organisational risks from AWR, are also footing the majority of the bill for the regulations.

The main AWR risks clients are managing include:

- Increased cost of hiring contractors who are in the scope of AWR and therefore must receive equal pay after 12 weeks on assignment

- Increased cost of making available shared facilities, such as canteens and crèches for any contractors in AWR's scope

- Increased cost of compliance and administering agency workers and contractors, determining 'equal pay' and funding legal defences

- Reputational risk of not implementing AWR according to its requirements, and of being perceived as a poor employer abusing vulnerable agency workers

- Organisational risk of the morale of permanent employees dropping with agency workers receiving equal access to shared services and equal pay.

### 9.1.3 The risks for agencies

Before AWR came into force, agencies already performed a wide range of services in addition to their core brokerage role between workers and clients. Now clients are pressuring agencies to take on the compliance burden of AWR and absorb some of the potential cost increases by reducing their margins.

The main AWR risks facing agencies include:

- Increased cost of administering agency workers, as the burden of compliance is passed from client to agency

- Reduced margins as clients insist agencies part-fund the hike in costs for agency workers and contractors who are in AWR's scope and who meet the equal pay requirements

- The cost of defending legal action by a client when agencies fail in their compliance duties and a worker has taken the client to a tribunal.

AWR will be with us for some time. It is therefore in the best interests of contractors, clients and agencies that the risks associated with

AWR are understood and mitigated. The greatest threat to your livelihood is that clients put AWR in the 'too hard' basket and either choose to employ workers rather than hire contractors, or send roles offshore to jurisdictions unaffected by AWR, leaving you with fewer contract opportunities.

Of course clients could choose to hire contractors directly, which would remove any risk of AWR. But cutting out the agency not only removes an intermediary which reduces employment rights risks for the client. The client would also lose access to the expertise agencies can offer in many other areas, such as compliance, selection and recruitment.

## 9.2 The history of the Agency Workers Regulations

The Agency Workers Regulations (AWR) were originally intended to promote "more flexible forms of work". The theory was that AWR would facilitate Europe's transition towards a knowledge-based economy; the reality is proving to be very different.

But why did the UK require these new employment laws and how have they evolved into the legislation that came into force on 1 October 2011? Proposals to tighten up Europe-wide legislation covering temporary workers had been debated for some years before the original formal proposal for the Agency Workers Directive (AWD) was published by the Commission of the European Communities in March 2002. Up until that point, treatment of temporary workers across the European Union's member states varied hugely. In some member states, temporary labour markets were dominated by vulnerable low paid and low skilled agency workers, who were frequently abused by hirers and agencies.

At the other end of the scale, markets like the UK, Holland, Denmark, Sweden and Norway included substantial numbers of highly paid and highly skilled knowledge workers, such as contractors and freelancers, who would fiercely deny any suggestion of vulnerability. The AWD was created to provide European Union member states with a common approach to regulating their temporary labour markets. In some countries it would also protect temporary workers from abuses by hirers and agencies.

The original intention for AWD to promote Europe's knowledge economy and flexible working has been considerably watered down.

Now, the main thrust is to ensure that temporary workers receive equal treatment from their hirers, comparable to if they'd been recruited as a permanent employee for the role. Specifically, article 5 of the directive says:

> *The basic working and employment conditions of temporary agency workers shall be, for the duration of their assignment at a user undertaking, at least those that would apply if they had been recruited directly by that undertaking to occupy the same job.*

The idea was to prevent unscrupulous hirers, aided by agencies, from shipping in lots of low-paid temps to take the place of expensive employees, as is common practice in some member states. However, and crucially, the directive did not clarify or change the employment status of agency workers. What took the next five years to resolve was the qualification period, ie the length of time a temp would work on a given assignment before being awarded equal pay and conditions.

And, although in 2004 the then Labour government did a deal, the Warwick Agreement, with unions promising to implement the directive, the UK proceeded to successfully block progress throughout that period. The government argued that the proposed directive was more likely to destroy jobs by making temps a much less attractive option for hirers. A series of events led to the UK losing its ability to block progress on the directive in December 2007. A combination of concessions granted over the working time opt-out provisions and domestic pressure from the UK finally resulted in agreement over the qualification period.

And then what sealed the deal was a back-room agreement between the Trades Union Congress (TUC) and the Confederation of British Industry (CBI), two of the UK's social partners working towards agreement on the directive. They finally agreed on a qualifying period of 12 weeks as the time after which temporary workers gained the same rights as their full-time counterparts. In June 2008 the European Council agreed on a common position over the directive, and in October 2008 the European Parliament approved the directive without amendment. At long last, and after six years of wrangling, the Agency Workers Directive was passed.

Once the final form of the Agency Workers Directive was agreed, with the qualifying period set at 12 weeks and further amendments, such as the Swedish Derogation, negotiated by other member states, progress towards the Agency Workers Regulations was swift. Some might say too swift, and that the schedule did not allow time for proper scrutiny.

The first stage of consultation on the draft directive, plus the CBI/TUC proposals and when the regulations should come into effect all took place very quickly, between May and June 2009. Then, during another short period in October to December 2009, the Department for Business, Innovation and Skills (then the Department for Business, Enterprise and Regulatory Reform), consulted over the draft regulations.

The draft Agency Workers Regulations, as the directive had now become, were laid before Parliament on 21 January 2010, allowing just a few short weeks for consultation and scrutiny. However, despite the haste in which the process had been rushed through up until then, it suddenly slowed down, as the then Business Secretary Lord Mandelson delayed implementation. This was to allow UK businesses to prepare for the new legislation, which finally came into force on 1 October 2011.

## 9.3 Using the law to gain competitive advantage and win contracts

If you can demonstrate a thorough knowledge of the Agency Workers Regulations (AWR) and argue convincingly that it does not apply to you, you are likely to have a competitive advantage when dealing with clients and agencies, who might otherwise have viewed you as a threat. This will certainly be true in the early years of AWR, until case law provides a greater degree of certainty.

Even though AWR came into force on 1 October 2011, contractors are likely to continue to encounter clients and agencies that have little understanding of AWR and its implications. That lack of understanding may lead them automatically to assume that all contractors are agency workers and are therefore a threat to their business.

But with your good understanding of AWR gained from reading this chapter and ongoing updates on ContractorCalculator.co.uk, you will be in a much stronger position to win over such clients and agencies. At least until the regulations are embedded into the UK's business psyche, the best contracts may well go to contractors who can argue most convincingly that AWR does not apply to them.

Understanding the source legislation and its legal interpretation are important steps towards you gaining the confidence to convincingly argue your case.

## 9.3.1 What is legislation and what is guidance?

The best place to find out what the law actually says is to go to the source legislation and associated documents. There are three documents, and a further class of documentation, that you should be aware of:

- The Agency Workers Directive (AWD): the original directive issued by the European Commission and ratified by the European Parliament on 19 November 2008. It is this directive on which all member states' individual legislation must be based

- The Agency Workers Regulations (AWR): the UK legislation that was 'gold plated' by the government and came into force on 1 October 2011

- Guidance from the Department for Business Innovation and Skills (BIS): At the time of writing, its 'final' guidance for agencies and hirers was published in May 2011

- Unofficial guidance and guides: The internet abounds with unofficial guides from a number of sources. Many of these guides are informative and useful; others include numerous inaccuracies and in some cases are downright wrong on crucial aspects of AWR. Approach with caution.

You can access all of these documents online through ContractorCalculator.co.uk. The site will also continue to provide the very latest official and unofficial guidance, as well as ongoing news and updates as case law is made.

### 9.3.2 What the law actually says

The Agency Works Regulations legislation is 36 pages long. The six pages of the original directive became 18 pages of core legislation in five parts, and a further 18 pages of accompanying schedules in two parts. As legislation goes, it's actually relatively short and accessible. The key elements, of which Parts 1 and 2 are the most important for contractors, are:

**PART 1** explains the definitions of agency workers and temporary work agencies. Clause (2)(a) contains the crucial phrase of most interest to limited company contractors, which confirms that an individual is not an agency worker if they are carrying out a "business undertaking"

**PART 2** lays out the rights that agency workers will receive on the first day of each assignment and after 12 weeks. It also explains how the 'qualifying period' of 12 weeks works, how to calculate pay, and many other practical details. Part 2 also contains Regulation 10, also known as the Swedish Derogation, which is one trading solution for umbrella company contractors who wish to remain out of the scope of AWR.

**PART 3** largely covers what action agency workers can take to ensure they are granted the new rights and what to do if those rights are infringed. Part 3 also includes anti-avoidance measures. There is less material of interest here for genuine contractors.

**PART 4** deals with special cases and exemptions, while **PART 5** is a technical note referring to the main schedule 2. **SCHEDULE 1** is a technical note, but **SCHEDULE 2** details how AWR will integrate with existing legislation. This schedule is as long as the core legislation. These sections contain little that is of interest to contractors.

Parts 1 and 2 of AWR are of crucial importance, because they explain who is in AWR's scope and who is outside it. But, in some respects, their real value is that they drive the guidance from BIS, which is what most agencies and clients turn to when considering whether a contractor is an 'AWR risk'.

## 9.4 Who is in AWR's scope and what additional rights do they have

Contractors are affected by the Agency Workers Regulations (AWR), either because they will need to demonstrate to agencies and clients that they are outside of its scope, or because they are in its scope. Those who are in its scope can choose to claim a range of new employment rights on the first day of a new assignment. They will also be able to claim additional rights after working on an assignment for 12 weeks.

Contrary to common belief, if you are a limited company contractor you will not be automatically excluded from AWR's scope – you may have to demonstrate to clients and agencies that yours is a genuine business and that you are therefore not an agency worker. This is why you need to familiarise yourself with some quite complex employment legislation. Limited company contractors have not been explicitly excluded from AWR, to prevent unscrupulous agencies forcing lower skilled and potentially vulnerable workers to incorporate as an AWR avoidance tactic.

If you are trading as an umbrella company contractor, you are automatically considered to be in AWR's scope, unless your service provider offers one of two solutions: either a full employment umbrella solution, with elements of what is known as the Swedish Derogation, or a matched permanent pay (MPP) solution.

According to AWR, there are three parties affected:

- The agency worker, for example a temp or, under certain circumstances, a contractor

- The temporary work agency, for example a recruitment or staffing agency

- The hirer, typically a contractor's end-user client.

The definition of a temporary work agency provided in the regulations, and in the guidance for hirers and agencies supplied by the Department for Business Innovation and Skills (BIS), is very wide. The regulations state that a temporary work agency is "a person in business ... involved in the supply of temporary agency workers".

This means that, for example, your contractor limited company could be viewed as a temporary work agency if it subcontracts work to other contractors (see section 9.6 for more information about this).

The 'hirer', or in contracting terms the 'client', is defined as:

> ... *a person engaged in economic activity, public or private, whether or not operating for profit, to whom individuals are supplied, to work temporarily for and under the supervision and direction of that person.*

This definition potentially applies to all contractor clients, except in the unusual cases where the contractor is genuinely not supervised or directed by the client.

### 9.4.1 Who is in the scope of AWR and qualifies as an agency worker?

The guidance for clients and agencies specifically identifies contractors using umbrella solutions providers as being within the scope of the regulations. It also confirms that contractors trading via limited companies could still be covered by AWR.

In clause 3(1) of the regulations, an agency worker is defined as an individual who:

> a) *is supplied by a temporary work agency to work temporarily for and under the supervision and direction of a hirer; and*

> b) *has a contract with the temporary work agency which is —*

> i. *a contract of employment with the agency, or*

> ii. *any other contract to perform work and services personally for the agency.*

The key term in the definition is 'supervision and direction', because that basically means virtually any contractor irrespective of their trading vehicle could choose to be in AWR's scope if they wanted to be. And that's because very few contractors are not in some form or other under the 'supervision and direction' of their client.

For you to be supervised and directed by your client, the client would merely need to ask you to work on a specific project and periodically check how you are progressing. But note that 'supervision and direction' are not the same as 'control' in the context of IR35. As AWR is understood at the time of writing, a contractor could be quite happily directed and supervised by their client, and claim rights under AWR, but not be controlled by the client and still be trading outside of IR35.

## 9.4.2 Who is out of the scope of AWR, and a genuine contractor?

The regulations state that an individual is not an agency worker if:

a) *the contract the individual has with the temporary work agency has the effect that the status of the agency is that of a client or customer of a profession or business undertaking carried on by the individual; or*

b) *there is a contract, by virtue of which the individual is available to work for the hirer, having the effect that the status of the hirer is that of a client or customer of a profession or business undertaking carried on by the individual.*

If you are a limited company contractor you can demonstrate that you are outside AWR if you are in a profession or business undertaking. Thinking at the time of writing suggests that a contractor's personal service company would qualify as a business undertaking, although there are currently no formal tests that can categorically define whether a contractor's limited company is a 'business undertaking'.

The tests of employment used to define whether a contractor is a disguised employee for the purposes of IR35 are not relevant to a contractor trying to prove their status under AWR. However, it is likely that if you show all the signs of being a disguised employee and not a genuine business, that same evidence would apply when considering AWR status.

## 9.4.3 Rights granted under AWR

Contractors who are in the scope of AWR will qualify for a range of 'day one' rights. A further range of equal rights are granted after 12 weeks.

**From day 1**

If you are in the scope of AWR, then the day one rights you can claim each time you start a new assignment with a client are:

- Access to shared facilities at the client's site – eg canteens, crèches and transport services, such as a staff minibus from the nearest station or car park

- Access to information about client vacancies.

**After 12 weeks**

Once you have been on assignment for 12 weeks, you can claim the same terms and conditions as a full-time permanent employee performing the same role. These include:

- Pay

- Bonuses that are dependent solely on your performance

- Holidays and holiday pay

- Working hours and rest breaks

- Maternity benefits, such as paid time off for ante-natal appointments.

However, equal pay rights exclude company-wide bonuses, expenses, pensions and life assurance, share options, redundancy pay, sick pay and maternity/paternity pay if the client's scheme is more generous than the statutory payments.

At the time of writing, it appears that, technically, most contractors will be able to choose to claim these additional rights under AWR and remain outside IR35, because they are 'supervised and directed', but not controlled, by their clients. However, by claiming rights under AWR you are sending a pretty strong message that you don't consider yourself to be a genuine contractor in business on your own account, and that you are still clinging to the notion that you are 'owed' rights of some description, like an employee. Chances are if you think that, then you'll be exhibiting other employee-like behaviours and may well be judged to be inside IR35.

With a good understanding of AWR, you should be able to demonstrate that your limited company is a business undertaking, and that you won't be responsible for increasing your client's costs by trying to claim employment rights under AWR.

**CONTRACTING MINDSET TIPS:**

**There are no such things as "contractors' rights"**

Contractors have a business-to-business contract of services with their clients or agencies and, as with any other business arrangement between two businesses, the contractor has no rights except under contract law.

Bob's been hired to tile your bathroom, and you agree to pay him £200 a day. But he does not turn up for work one day, so do you still pay him?

Sue's a landscape gardener and starts work on what you anticipate to be a three-month project. But after two months, you run out of money and tell Sue to stop work at the end of the week. Is she entitled to redundancy?

You're unhappy with the quality of the work by Andy, your builder. It's not according to your original specifications, so you terminate the contract. Could he take you to an employment tribunal for unfair dismissal?

**Businesses don't have employment rights**

If you have hired a service provider in business on their own account to complete a job for you, you don't pay them if they don't come into work, if the work is not up to scratch or when you no longer require the services. Bob, Sue and Andy don't get employment rights.

When you are a contractor providing a business-to-business service to your clients, you should not expect to receive any employment rights. You agree a contract that says you will provide your client with a specific set of deliverables in exchange for your fee. That contract, and contract law, are what constitute your rights.

Expecting rights is like waving a flag to tell HMRC that you are a disguised employee, and not a true contractor. So if you have been enjoying the tax benefits of operating through a limited company, you may attract the unwelcome attention of HMRC.

**Contract laws are your rights**

If your client does not pay you, the client is in breach of contract and you can seek redress through the courts using contract law. Similarly, if you fail to deliver what the contract specifies, they, too, can go to law. So get the contract right from the start.

Contractor limited companies are small businesses like any other – even if they only employ a single, highly skilled flexible worker, it does not differentiate them from other small limited companies.

**Contractor mindset tip: Contractors have a purely business relationship with their client or agency and do not qualify for employment rights.**

## 9.5 How the law should be interpreted – formal guidance from BIS

To demonstrate to clients and agencies that you really know your stuff, you can use the *Guidance for agencies and hirers* published in May 2011 by the Department for Business Innovation and Skills (BIS) to help determine whether you are in the scope of the Agency Workers Regulations (AWR).

The guidance is valuable because it offers examples of individuals who are in AWR's scope and includes detail of BIS's interpretation of who is out of its scope. It can be downloaded from the BIS website, and it would be prudent before proceeding with this section to check that new guidance has not been published since the time of writing in Spring 2012.

As with any relatively new legislation, until the regulations are thoroughly tested in employment tribunals and the courts, there is still room for further interpretation, and for some contractors this means ongoing uncertainty. Case law can also change how legislation is interpreted and applied.

Whilst the legislation provides a definition of an agency worker, BIS goes one step further and offers examples of the kind of individuals it sees as falling within the scope of AWR. BIS says that, for an individual, such as a contractor, to be an agency worker:

- There must be a contract between the contractor and the temporary work agency (BIS uses the abbreviation 'TWA' to describe contractor agencies)

- The agency supplies the contractor on a temporary basis to the client

- The contractor is under the 'supervision and direction' of the client. Note that this is not the same as 'control' in an IR35 context

- The contractor is not in business on their own account.

The guidance goes on to warn in its 'Out of scope' section (page 9), that:

*Simply putting earnings through a limited company would not in itself put individuals beyond the possible scope of the regulations.*

So it would appear that a limited company contractor could still be considered to be in AWR's scope if they fulfil the other in-scope criteria. The key to being in scope is the tripartite relationship between agency, client and contractor – without it the regulations can't apply. But according to BIS, genuine contractors should have few fears that AWR will apply to them

Umbrella company contractors are automatically considered to be in the scope of AWR, as umbrella solutions providers are classed as 'temporary work agencies' (TWAs); no exceptions are given.

Genuine contractors supplying their services via a limited company, partnership or as a sole trader, and not through an umbrella company, are out of scope, as BIS says:

*The definition of an agency worker excludes those who are in business on their own account where the status of the hirer is that of a client or customer of a "profession or business undertaking" (ie a genuine business to business relationship).*

The Guidance warns that if there is a dispute over status:

*The courts have devised a number of tests which examine the individual's circumstances and consider all aspects of the relationship, including what a contract might say or what it does not say, the expectations of the parties and their conduct, to establish the reality of the relationship.*

BIS provides an example on page 11 of its guidance of an IT contractor working on a typical 12 month contract, which suggests that, when finalising the guidance, BIS understood the mainstream contracting model and that genuine contractors are not intended to be in AWR's scope. The case study says:

*Given the absence of personal service and mutuality of obligation, the [hirer/contractor client] company is a client or customer of the individual, therefore the individual is out of scope. This must be a true reflection of the reality of the relationships between the parties involved and not simply a reflection of the contractual terms.*

According to BIS, genuine contractors should have few fears that AWR will apply to them. However, there is no definitive test for what constitutes 'being in a business undertaking'; until that is clarified by further testing of the legislation in tribunals and the courts, there remains uncertainty for contractors.

Despite its comprehensive and useful nature, the guidance from BIS is just that – guidance. When ruling during tribunal or in higher courts, a judge will always seek out and apply the source legislation.

## 9.6 Trading options for contractors

Contractors concerned that the Agency Workers Regulations (AWR) could impact negatively on their livelihoods have a number of trading options to choose from. These are discussed in more detail in Chapter 6, but this section details how they fit in with AWR.

The trading options available can establish your credentials as a genuine business undertaking or offer an umbrella solution that works alongside AWR to minimise or eliminate additional costs for clients. Fortunately there are trading solutions that will not result in increased cost and administration burdens for clients and that offer you the choice as to whether or not you want to claim the employment rights granted by AWR.

### 9.6.1 Umbrella company contractor trading solutions

The Guidance from the Department for Business, Innovation and Skills (BIS) is unequivocal about AWR's treatment of umbrella company contractors: they are in the scope of the regulations. That means clients using umbrella company contractors are required to offer day one rights and equal pay after 12 weeks, as the regulations demand.

However, an umbrella solutions provider operating compliantly and already putting into place best practice will already be most of the way towards offering a solution that complies with AWR. The two main options for umbrella companies are the:

- **Full employment model,** which provides contractors with pay between assignments. In theory, compliant umbrella companies should already be providing pay at National Minimum Wage (NMW) levels between assignments, so full employment is a relatively small step forward. This model uses the 'Swedish Derogation' to remove contractors from the scope of the equal pay requirements of AWR. In practice, the solutions on offer are likely to offer contractors a better deal than is strictly necessary under the Swedish Derogation. The client must also make day one rights available to contractors using this model.

- **'Match permanent pay' model**, which, as its name suggests, requires that the contractor enjoys the full benefits of AWR, gaining day one rights and matched pay after 12 weeks. This model is significantly more complex to administer than the full employment model, and will cost clients more after 12 weeks, but it does allow contractors to choose to accept the employment rights granted by AWR.

Not all umbrella companies will be in a position to offer both trading models, particularly as both require a high level of compliance. Contractors must ask their umbrella solutions providers what they are doing to trade compliantly with AWR.

Umbrella company solutions are described in greater detail in section 6.2.2.

## 9.6.2 Business undertaking trading solutions

Contractors genuinely in business who want to continue to trade without any AWR compliance issues can effectively continue as before. There are three main trading vehicles for contractors in a profession or business undertaking:

- Limited company
- Partnership
- Sole trader.

Although these are all legitimate trading vehicles, in practice the overwhelming majority of agencies and clients will insist that contractors use a limited company. By using contractors trading via limited companies, agencies and clients are able to minimise the risk of workers claiming employment rights. However, there are service providers that offer an intermediary for contractors trading as sole traders. That can work to both sides' advantages, because genuine contractors don't want employment rights.

The BIS guidance warns that a contractor trading via a limited company can still be in the scope of AWR. But it also makes it clear that contractors genuinely in business on their own account, "in a profession or business undertaking", and where the client is a customer and not an employer, were never intended to be the targets of AWR.

Limited companies, partnerships and sole traders are described in greater detail in sections 6.2.1, 6.2.3 and 6.2.4 respectively.

### 9.6.3 Offshore trading solutions

Since the December 2010 introduction of the Employment Income Through Third Parties legislation, also known as the 'disguised remuneration' laws, many offshore tax solutions – including the once relatively popular Employee Benefit Trusts (EBTs) – have closed. Others have developed to offer schemes based on currency arbitrage or other financial mechanisms. As existing schemes get shut down or lose their tax advantages as a result of anti-avoidance legislation, so new solutions will spring up.

The status of contractors using such schemes will depend on the individual scheme itself and the type of employment model it offers. Some solutions will undoubtedly fall into the exempt categories listed in the Guidance from BIS, but contractors from other solutions may be in AWR's scope.

See section 6.2.6 for a further explanation of how offshore solutions work.

Contractors genuinely running a business undertaking should be able to continue to do so. And umbrella company contractors will be able to choose between solution providers to find an umbrella trading solution that suits their AWR needs.

## 9.7 Recruiter contract wording solutions to AWR

You may find unexpected clauses regarding the Agency Workers Regulations (AWR) being inserted into contracts by your agency, but many such clauses should not give rise to any cause for concern. In fact, they could even help, albeit marginally, to strengthen your case for being seen as in business on your own account by HMRC.

The clauses vary from agency to agency, but typically say:

- "the contractor warrants that it operates on a business-to-business basis"

- "the contractor is operating a business undertaking"

- "services are performed by an independent consultant"

- "the contractor is not directed or supervised by the client"

- "the services are provided to [the agency] and the client as customers of the contractor's business"

- "the contractor shall indemnify [the agency] against any losses arising...from any claim that the contractor is entitled to rights according to AWR".

If you have made it this far through this chapter, you will quickly spot that all of these clauses relate to specific elements of the AWR legislation and are designed to give the agency, and possibly the client, comfort in establishing that you are not inside AWR, and that if you are subsequently found to be inside, any risk is passed from the agency to your limited company.

Despite the ominous nature of the wording, asking a limited company contractor to warrant that they operate on a business-to-business basis and that their client is their own businesses' customer are not necessarily bad things. Furthermore, the inclusion of AWR clauses has no relevance to your IR35 status. AWR and IR35 are separate and distinct pieces of legislation, and each should be considered in isolation. Either you are inside IR35, or you are not, and the same goes for AWR.

Despite their treatment in parallel and in isolation, the evidence used to determine IR35 and AWR status will be drawn from the same basic pool of facts. That means genuine limited company contractors are unlikely to come to any harm by warranting they are a business undertaking and indemnifying the agency against AWR.

## 9.8 AWR risk when hiring subcontractors

Contractors who are subcontracting client work to other contractors may find that their limited companies could be classified as temporary work agencies, which means that the Agency Workers Regulations (AWR) may apply to their businesses and the subcontractors they place. Under certain circumstances, if an individual or substitute you are supplying to a client does not satisfy the conditions of being out of AWR's scope, then that subcontractor could qualify for the equal treatment and employment rights granted under the legislation.

That's because the definition of a temporary work agency contained in the guidance for agencies and hirers published by the Department for Business Innovation and Skills (BIS) is very wide. As such, it could easily encompass a contractor supplying other contractors on a subcontractor basis or as substitutes.

The regulations state that a temporary work agency "is a person in business...involved in the supply of temporary agency workers". And an agency worker "is someone who has a contract with the temporary work agency but works temporarily under the direction and supervision of a hirer", or contractor client. If your client provides a contractor you supply with instructions, the client qualifies as giving "direction".

If your client also has the right to check what the subcontractor has done, and then to ask that subcontractor to make changes, this means your client is providing "supervision". So unless the contractor you are providing on a subcontract basis qualifies as fulfilling the criteria of being out of the scope of AWR, the regulations would apply and they could qualify for the rights granted under the legislation.

That means your subcontractor would be entitled to equal treatment of pay and basic working conditions after working on the same contract for 12 weeks. You might assume that someone you are subbing in gets paid more than the permies they sit next to, but this might not be the case. If one of your subcontractors discovers that the client's employee doing the same job gets paid an extra hour for lunch, they could decide that they deserve equal treatment.

For a contractor on £50 an hour, being paid an extra hour for lunch amounts to a lot of extra cash, especially over a three-month contract. There's nothing to stop the contractor you hired via your contractor limited company taking their case to an employment tribunal and insisting that they should be paid the same. Any settlement for non-compliance with the legislation and subsequent pay differential will be paid for by your limited company.

If you decide to go down the route of providing fellow contractors on a subcontract basis to clients, you should prepare for the worst and work backward. Assume your company is a temporary work agency and that your subcontractors are within scope and that AWR applies. Then seek expert help to determine exactly what action you should take as a result. The cost of legal fees will be far less than the cost of being made to pay a subcontractor more, or paying for representation at an employment tribunal.

# Contracting lessons from this chapter

- The better you understand AWR, the greater the chance you have of convincing clients and agencies that you present them with no AWR compliance risk.

- If you are trading as an umbrella company contractor, you are automatically considered to be in AWR's scope, but you can choose an umbrella company that operates a trading model designed to reduce or eliminate AWR risk.

- Contrary to common belief, if you are a limited company contractor contracting via an agency, you will not be automatically excluded from AWR's scope.

- The tests of employment used to define whether a contractor is a disguised employee for the purposes of IR35 are not relevant to a contractor trying to prove their status under AWR. Put simply, IR35 is irrelevant to AWR, although both may draw on the same pool of evidence.

- With a good understanding of AWR, you should be able to demonstrate that your limited company is a business undertaking, and that you won't be responsible for increasing your client's costs by trying to claim employment rights under AWR.

- Contractors who are subcontracting client work to other contractors may find that their limited companies could be classified as temporary work agencies, which means that AWR may apply to their businesses and the subcontractors they place.

- An agency worker in the scope of the Agency Workers Regulations (AWR) will qualify for a range of 'day one' rights. A further range of equal rights are granted after 12 weeks, including the right to equal pay.

# 10

# What to do when things go wrong

# 10.1 Contract search

The key to maintaining, enjoying and profiting from your successful contracting career – even when things might appear to be going wrong – is not to take anything personally.

Whether you are working for yourself through your own limited company or an umbrella company, there can be times when it seems like the agent and client are conspiring against you.

Remember, for them it is just business. And it is important that you stay focused on the fact that, for you, it is just business, too.

## 10.1.1 When an agent sends out your CV without your permission

Your relationship with an agency usually begins with you sending them your CV in response to an advertisement, or with the agency finding you from a job board listing.

An agent may send your CV to a client and then find that another agency has already sent it, even though you never gave them permission to do so. No one has the right to distribute your CV without your permission. If you do find out who was responsible – which may happen if, for example, the client tells your agent that they have already received your CV from XYZ agency – then you must call them and tell them you have not given your permission for them to use your CV. They will need to prove that you did, which of course they won't be able to.

Agencies cannot send your CV to a specific firm without your permission. So they cannot ask, 'Can I put your CV forward for a few roles next week for the banks in the City?'.

You are caught between a rock and a hard place because you need your CV to get maximum exposure, but you want protection from unscrupulous agents. It could lose you the contract, so you need to take action. Politely put in writing a request to the agency that you would not like it to happen again, and then move on.

## Been there, done that!

## Done over by the agent

**DAVE SAYS:** A friend of mine was interested in a contract role with a major healthcare insurance provider, and was surprised to find they already had his CV from another agent.

This was crazy, as he'd never even heard of the agency before. So he contacted them only to be lied to, with the agency claiming that not only had he given them permission, but also that if he wanted to take on the contract he would need to go through them!

Unfortunately, once a client accepts a CV from an agent, the agent's terms and conditions make it difficult or impossible for them to take on the contractor from elsewhere.

In this case, rather than slug things out with the agency, my friend just walked away from the position, even though he fancied it and would have been perfect for the client. So everyone lost out through the agency's unscrupulous approach.

Agents will send your CV to clients without your permission for two reasons:

- To demonstrate they can find really good candidates. Then, when the client wants to interview you, if you won't play ball the agent will simply say you have accepted something elsewhere; but it's given the agency time to be noticed by the client

- To be the first in the door.

This is totally illegal, very rare, but a pain to fight.

However, fight you should and if the agency refuses to take you seriously, your ultimate recourse is the recruitment agency industry body, the Recruitment and Employment Confederation (REC).

## 10.1.2 When an agent or client cancels your contract at the last minute

You have just signed a contract with an agency and cleared your calendar for the period when the agent calls and tells you that the contract is cancelled. The client had their budget cut or changed their mind.

You point out to the agent that you have a contract offer and acceptance, which you can prove because it is signed, and you've given up other work to take it. You expect some payment. You should certainly get the full value of the termination period, provided you can show that you actively sought work during the period as part of your 'duty to mitigate'. The client has to pay for the termination costs and any costs you incur to put you back where you started.

The approach to the agent should be a formal letter, preferably written by a lawyer, explaining the legal position, and that they have to pay you for the termination period. You should also explain you understand your duty to mitigate and that you are seeking further work, and would welcome their assistance.

You should tell them that once you have found further work you will bill them for the gap they need to pay you for. They may try to ignore this approach, or try to suggest they owe you nothing, but this doesn't comply with the law. You can then take the agent to the small claims court and, if you do things right, you will almost certainly win; but it is essential that you seek professional legal advice if you are forced down this route.

Unfortunately, most contractors don't take any action and the client and agent walk away without paying the contractor a penny. The sad truth is, that's because many contractors don't know their rights, won't stand their ground, or, to be frank, are simply too lazy to claim what's legally theirs. If the client had no termination clause, which is unlikely, then in theory the contractor should be able to claim the full value of the contract. In practice, though, they would be wise to focus on getting a new contract.

## Last minute cancellations

**DAVE SAYS:** Sometimes contracts can be cancelled at the last minute, before you've signed the paperwork. There's little point moaning at the agent, as they are going to be as upset as you – they've done lots of hard work to close the deal, and they're going to miss out on their commission. This is just one of the risks you take as a contractor, and, whilst it is very rare, it does occasionally happen. The important thing to remember is that if there is no signed contract, there is little you can do.

### 10.1.3 When an agent insists on you giving references before any interviews

Agents have a right to ask for references. Just like any other recruiter, an agency dealing in contractors has the right to be sure about whom they are sending to their clients. But they might just be 'phishing' for valuable information, including the names of people who will give you references and might therefore be in a position to make hiring decisions – such information is like gold dust to an agent.

It's not a good idea to keep giving out reference information all the time for the simple reason that your ex bosses won't take too kindly to being rung up all the time.

You do not have to give references before an interview if you don't wish to. There is no legal requirement for the agency to provide references to the client, and clients won't expect it. Agents are almost certain to put you forward even if you hold back on references. They make their money by placing you. Therefore, a good agent will get you the interview first and then, only if it is necessary, check your references when it looks like you'll get the contract.

Remember, you are a contractor and if you don't perform your contract is terminated.

As you don't want to offend legitimate agents while looking for contracts, here is an easy way to be diplomatic about not giving references. Say that your former clients and/or bosses have requested that you do not give reference information out until you have been offered a position, and you have to respect these wishes.

Tell the agent that if there is an interview and offer, you will provide not only references, but also the names of some firms that might be looking for contractors. They will be able to read between the lines. If they then put your CV forward without references, it is a real job. If you were suitable for the position, and they don't, then you can assume they were just on a phishing expedition.

## Been there, done that!

### No reference

**DAVE SAYS:** On one project with loads of contractors, things were coming to an end and people were slowly moving on whilst we handed over to a maintenance team.

One day the boss sent us all an email saying that he was happy to give references, but that he would no longer speak to agents unless the contractor had been offered a position elsewhere.

He'd been getting bombarded on the telephone by agents who kept asking him if there were positions available (which there weren't) and was getting tired of all the calls..

## 10.1.4 When an agent threatens to sue because you went to the client direct

If an agent reveals a contract opportunity that you subsequently win, but then go on to contract direct with the client, circumventing the agency, they can take action against you. But it depends on whether you opted out of the Conduct Regulations (Conduct of Employment Agencies and Employment Business Regulations 2003).

If you do not opt out, then the agency is required to disclose its terms of business to you, and these would generally stipulate that contractors should not approach its clients direct. In this case, it is likely you would be in breach of the agency's terms of business, and the agency would be within its rights to take action against you.

But if you chose to opt out of the Conduct of Employment Regulations, then there is no legal requirement on the agency to disclose its terms of business at the outset. Contract law says that undisclosed terms will generally not apply. Therefore, it might be that contracting direct with the client would not be covered by the agency's terms of business, and so there may be no contractual restriction to you contacting direct with the client.

But there is a catch. The agency may well be entitled to say that their disclosure of the client's details was made to you under conditions of confidentiality. If so, by contacting the client about the contract opportunity after speaking to the agency, you may be considered to have abused that confidence, and so there may be a liability on you to the agency in this respect. If you won the contract by going direct based on confidential information provided by the agency, whether you're opted out of the Conduct Regulations or not, the agency may well have grounds to sue you.

## 10.2 Contract terms

As indicated in chapters 7 and 8, it is very important that you get your contract right before you agree to it, either verbally or in writing. This sometimes requires negotiation with the agent. Once you have been offered a contract you are in a strong position and so should stick to your guns over the finer points of the contract – after all, it is very important to your earnings and IR35 status.

### 10.2.1 When the agent promises to make changes to your contract and doesn't

The interview went well, the client liked you and you've had an offer from the agent which you accept. Then you receive the contract to review and it is full of holes so large you could drive a coach and horses through them. You request changes, and the agent promises they will be made, so you start work. And then the agent does a U-turn, and claims that because you have started work, the implication is that you have accepted the terms of the original contract, as it was before you requested the changes.

Agents will not make changes to contracts for a variety of reasons, quite often because they don't wish to have to change their standard contract. This is because they don't have in-house lawyers and don't want the expense. The agent may also not wish to run the risk of a conflict between their contract with the client, known as the upper level contract, and their contract with you, the lower level contract. And there are a host of other issues that a contract review by a specialist legal adviser might identify.

Remember that the contract is not valid unless you have agreed, either verbally or in writing, to the terms. You can hold out for the agent to make the changes, and they may give in and agree to your terms to avoid upsetting their client and missing out on their margin.

Should they refuse, point blank, then you should be prepared either to walk away or to compromise on the contract. Should the agent agree to the change, though, you must ensure you get the agreement in writing, and that it is on the final contract.

If at all possible, don't start working without the contract finalised and signed. If you have started work, and have received a copy of the contract, you may find that you are stuck with it because it could be considered executed and 'live', unless you can categorically prove that the agent has been wilfully dishonest.

## 10.2.2 When the agent or client tries to change terms or rates during a contract

Some agents will always try it on with you and the most common way they do this is to try and change the deal mid-contract. Usually, any proposed deal would end up with the agent enjoying a higher margin. You have no obligation to accept any changes to a signed contract during a contract. Diplomatically, tell the agent not to try it on.

If you are contracting direct and the client comes up with a really good reason for a contract change that you are prepared to accept – perhaps relating to the evolution of the project – you might want to offer to renegotiate a new contract.

This is a perfectly reasonable scenario but you must be sure the new contract will work for you and does not place you at a disadvantage compared to the original one. If the proposed contract changes don't benefit you, you are perfectly within your rights simply to continue working to the terms of the original contract.

---

## Been there, done that!

### Client tried to demote me

**DAVE SAYS**: I was team leader at one client on an important project. One of their permanent employees wanted to be promoted to team leader, and they chose my project for him to 'take over'.

They couldn't just demote me, as it would have been breach of contract, but they needed me there to 'hand over' to this chap and show him the ropes on team leading.

I wasn't having any of that, so during discussions with the client I said, 'So, what you are saying is you want me to renegotiate my contract?' This put them in a corner, because if they wanted to change things they knew they had to terminate my contract and pay me four weeks money to leave, which wasn't really an option for them.

So they stopped their shenanigans and we carried on as usual. The other guy eventually went contracting.

---

### 10.2.3 When you sign a terrible deal and want to get out

You've signed the contract, you're on the job, and it's awful. You hate the client, you hate the work, and worst of all, you've discovered that you could have negotiated a much better rate with a contract on another client's project.

Can you get out of the contract? If your contract includes a termination clause that permits you to end it early, then you can give notice and leave. But if it doesn't, which isn't that unusual, then you are stuck unless you can replace yourself.

Assuming you used a lawyer to help with your contract it should include a substitution clause and you could try and bring in another contractor to replace you. You would be responsible for training and paying that person and that would cost you time and money. If they didn't perform, you would be responsible for putting right their failings.

So you might be best to see the contract through and put it down to experience.

### 10.2.4 When your client has been taken over and your agency tries to change the contract

This is a situation in which it is important to be clear about the difference between being an employee and a contractor whose limited company or umbrella company is involved in a business-to-business (B2B) relationship with the agency and end-user client. For those in employment, the situation is relatively simple. Because mergers and acquisitions are so commonplace, the process of transferring employees from the old business to the new one is generally quite straightforward, falling under the Transfer of Undertakings (Protection of Employment) Regulations, which are better known as 'TUPE'.

As a contractor, what happens when your end-user client is sold to another business depends entirely on what's in your contract. Because you're just another supplier, you get no protection under employment law. There is also the added complication of the agent. Technically, although you might provide your contractor services on your client's site and for your client, if your contract is with the agent, then you have no direct contractual relationship with the client.

If your client is bought by another company and becomes a different legal entity from what they were, then unless there are specific provisions for this in your original contract, the contract will need to change. There is nothing suspicious about the required contractual changes; it is simply because your contract is with a different business. The same sort of process can happen in the public sector, where the end-user client is not bought or sold, but might change from one government agency to another, or might be outsourced to the private sector. The key point is that the legal entity has changed, and this may affect your contract, particularly if it is direct with your client.

However, if your contract is with the agency and there is nothing in your agency contract about what happens if a client changes hands, then technically the agency has to stick to the terms of their contract with you. If it tries to change the contract to your detriment, then you can negotiate. But if the new terms offered are not to your liking, you may refuse to sign a new contract.

---

### Been there, done that!

## Dog ate my contract

**DAVE SAYS:** We had a couple of drop-outs on a really tough project. We were right on the bleeding edge of technology at the time, finding people was hard, and the hours were awful. Some people simply weren't happy. A couple of them left, giving the following reasons: "I'm not qualified for this, and you should find someone else," and "My relative has fallen very ill and I need to go back to Greece for a month to help out."

Neither excuse was true; neither was fair on the client or the people left behind; and in my opinion neither was morally right, either. But hey, that's business!

---

### 10.2.5 When you are asked to opt out of the Conduct Regulations

The Conduct Regulations (Conduct of Employment Agencies and Employment Business Regulations 2003) are designed to protect vulnerable agency workers from exploitation by unscrupulous agencies and gangmasters. Clearly, this is not of relevance to most highly paid limited company contractors with sought-after skills, so typically they choose to opt out.

Despite this, according to Regulation 32, the regulations still apply to 'work seekers who are incorporated', ie limited company contractors, which means you if you are trading via a limited company. The wording of the regulations is such that the work seekers (or contractors) are presumed to be under the control of the hirer (or client), which could have implications for your IR35 status.

Fortunately, the regulations allow you to opt out. But for the opt-out to be valid you (the 'incorporated work seeker' and/or the 'person(s) to be supplied to do the work') have to inform the agency or employment business that you are opting out before you are introduced to the hirer (the client). If you fail to sign the opt-out before the contract starts, this invalidates the opt-out, which introduces a variety of implications.

Under normal circumstances, most contractors would want the reassurance before the contract starts that they are legitimately opted out of the regulations and all the relevant paperwork has been done. Similarly the agency wants to be sure they can charge transfer fees if the contractor's status changes. But if the client wants to take you on as a full-time employee, and you are seriously considering the option, the exact timing of the opt-out becomes crucial.

If you started work on the contract before your opt-out was signed, then the opt-out is technically invalid and the agency would not be able to charge transfer fees to the client.

So, not having the paperwork signed can sometimes work in your favour.

## 10.2.6 When you start contracting without a signed contract

Contract negotiations that drag on towards the start date can place contractors in a difficult position, particularly if the issue is between the contractor and agency, leaving the client expecting the contractor on site on day one. The pressure on you to start work before contract negotiations have been concluded and a contract signed can be intense. But starting work without a signed contract is never a wise thing to do. If you start working for the client before the contract is signed you are potentially placing yourself at a commercial disadvantage.

The point of a contract is to make a record of the terms agreed at the outset, and as a point of reference for all parties. If you have a clear signed agreement in place, scope for subsequent difference of opinion is much reduced. A contract is also a form of 'insurance' that each party can turn to in the event of a dispute. In fact, the existence of a well-written contract generally prevents disputes between contractors, agents and clients.

Where a contract has not been agreed and signed, common areas of dispute can include such fundamental issues as rates, whether VAT is included in the rate, payment dates and payment periods. Clearly, starting work without knowing how much you're being paid and when is a very bad idea. Having a signed agreement also clarifies the expectations the client has of the contract, such as your role and responsibilities and what you are actually expected to achieve.

Starting work could very well amount to a sufficient act of acceptance of the contract. Or, if you start work while negotiations are still ongoing, you are in a significantly weaker negotiating position. If you have orally agreed the day rate, contract duration, termination conditions, project requirements and so on, then it is possible to start work, but highly unsatisfactory from your perspective. For example, what happens if a situation arises that has not been agreed orally, or if a disagreement arises about what exactly has been agreed? Resist the pressures and temptation to start contracting without a negotiated and signed contract being in place first.

### 10.2.7 When you sign a contract with terms you have not agreed

When negotiating and finalising contract, it is sometimes possible to make a mistake by signing a contract without spotting a clause you've not agreed, or thought had been deleted, or perhaps one has not appeared that you asked to be inserted. In some cases, the presence of the mistake invalidates the contract, but in others the contract is still binding. You are at most risk from 'standard' or generalised contracts offered by agents and clients who are unwilling to negotiate changes.

Generally, according to the system of common law used in the UK, if one party, such as the contractor or the agent, makes a mistake in the terms of the agreement or is mistaken about the basis of the contract, and the mistake is known by the other party, the contract is not valid. This is because although they appear objectively to have agreed terms, the parties clearly haven't, and technically the two parties are not really in agreement. Case law states that in this situation, there was never a contract to begin with. A court would look at the real situation, at what was known and understood to have been agreed by both parties, rather than just what is written in the contract, and rule whether the contract is valid.

A complication arises where the mistake is not in the actual contract terms, but forms part of your understanding of the agreement. In this case, it is possible that the contract could still be valid. If you made a mistake about a fact, which you then used to make the decision to enter into the contract, but the fact does not form a term of the contract itself, even if the client or agent knew about the mistake the contract would be binding. For example, you might have misinterpreted a discussion at the interview and assumed that expenses would be paid at a given rate. If, subsequently, you sign the contract without a term relating to expenses, the contract would still be valid.

The way around this is to invest in professional legal advice during the contract negotiation process. If your legal adviser spots a mistake before the contract is signed, you will almost certainly find the legal fee a small price compared to the consequences of the mistake.

## 10.2.8 When your client tries to sign you up to future rates

Should a client include a clause in your contract that in any way commits you to performing future work at the same rates as the contract you are currently negotiating, don't sign it – just strike out the clause. From a commercial perspective, clauses such as these are unreasonable. You are under no obligation to agree to such a clause, and should retain the right to negotiate the terms of any future work – and, if you prefer, to decline the future work.

That said, there is a possibility that you might have good reason for agreeing to such a deal. If you do, any clause covering future contracts and fees must be clear and without any grey areas, if it is to be enforceable. If the wording is imprecise or adds uncertainty, such as requiring you to provide an undefined amount of work in the future at the same rates with no time limit, the clause is likely to be unenforceable. If the clause is clear and certain, then it will be capable of being found to be legally binding if you sign the contract with it included.

Assuming you have signed a contract committing you to complete a future project at the same rates as the original project, then it may be possible to avoid it by exercise of a termination clause, if the contract has one, by giving notice to the client. But if there is no termination clause and the contract satisfies the principles of clarity and certainty, then it is likely to be legally binding. In that case, you could try and renegotiate the contract. However, if the client says 'no', then you must deliver what you agreed to or be in breach of contract.

## 10.3 Contract renewals

When you come to renew your contract, this can be both an opportunity and a threat: an opportunity because you can use the renewal as a chance to increase your rates; a threat because the agent may try and increase their margins by reducing your rates.

### 10.3.1 When the agent or client tries to renew your contract automatically

When you have questions about contractual obligations, the first place to look is your contract. And when it comes to renewals, the advice in chapters 7 and 8 is that you should not have renewal clauses in your contract, as it may affect your IR35 status by making you look like a 'disguised employee'.

If your contract does have a renewal clause, check it carefully. It should state that any renewals will be agreed in writing between you and the agency.

But, instead of taking the trouble to negotiate a renewal with you, some agencies try to economise on time by sending you a letter and by ignoring your requests to renegotiate. A letter with terms proposed unilaterally by one party to the contract has no legal standing, so don't be concerned by it.

Ideally you should handle renewals before they come due. Don't wait until after the contract period is over; get all the paperwork straight the way you want it well before the current contract is due to expire.

So, you do not have to accept an automatic renewal and you should dig your heels in if the agent stonewalls. If you don't have the paperwork in place before the contract ends, stop working. When your client asks why, you just tell them and, if they really want you to continue to complete a vital project, guess who they will call?

### 10.3.2 When the agent fails to have your paperwork in place by the renewal date

Following on from the previous section, if the agency does not send you the correct paperwork for signature before the contract ends and you get to the end date you must stop working.

If you continue to work, you have effectively agreed to the agent's proposal according to the terms of the original contract and extended your contract on the same terms.

### 10.3.3 When the agent tries to force a margin increase at renewal time

Contract renewals are a subject area that generates lots of difficult scenarios. The most typical of these is when the agent wants you to renew on the same terms, whereas you want different ones, including a rate increase. The agent will want a cut of the rate increase.

Sometimes the agent will try and force a rate decrease, explaining that they are not making enough of a margin on the contract. The agency will try to tell you that you have to accept their terms, or you won't be allowed to work at the client anymore under the terms of the restrictive covenant in the contract – this is a standard element in all agency contracts and entirely fair, until the agent tries to use it unfairly as leverage (see chapter 7).

If you want a rate rise you simply say, 'Pay it, or I will move on.' You cannot threaten to go direct because of the restrictive covenant in the contract. If you do they will sue you, and the judge will agree.

At renewal time, some agents may try and cut your pay claiming that they need to increase their margin of profit. Take the same approach and just say no. The restrictive covenant does not apply here, because it cannot be used as a bargaining tool.

Once the agency understands that you know your rights, they will become more reasonable.

### 10.3.4 When the client wants to bypass the agency and take you on direct

Another classic renewal scenario is when the client wants to renew, but does not want to use the same agency that originally found you, preferring to use a different agency or to renew your contract direct. In some cases, they may wish to change because they have been, or are, in dispute with the original agency.

Unless you have been released by your current agency, don't accept a renewal direct from the client or their new agency, as you will get in trouble. Both the restrictive covenant you have with the agency and the agency's terms and conditions with the client will place the agency in a position to sue both you and the client. Just don't do it.

### 10.3.5 When the agent insists you verbally agreed to a contract and threatens to sue

This situation can arise when you have talked to an agent about a contract, but you have accepted another one. The agent claims that you verbally agreed to the contract and insists you have to complete the contract they have negotiated.

Verbal contracts are, in theory, just as valid as written ones. The difficulty is in proving that there has been both an offer and an acceptance. If you have sent the agent an email saying you will do the job in exchange for payment at a specific rate that means you have accepted the offer and, because it has the elements required to form a contract (see chapter 7), it represents viable proof of the existence of a contract.

If you talk on the phone with the agent and say you'll think about it, that's not acceptance. Phone conversations would be very hard to prove without other evidence, and taped phone conversations may not be admissible in court.

Provided you've not signed anything you can easily get out of the contract, because you can argue that they have not sent the paperwork over. A deal isn't really done until the paperwork is signed, and neither contractors nor agents take each other to court based on claims of verbal agreements.

## 10.3.6 When your agent refuses to amend your contract

Agents occasionally show reluctance to change their standard contracts, as they are quite right to identify contractual changes as a potentially unnecessary legal expense. You have a number of options to consider in this circumstance.

The easiest, although potentially highest risk, option is for you to say to the agent that if the changes are not made to the contract, you won't sign it. However, you must be very sure of your negotiating strength before adopting this position, and must also be confident that you have a strong relationship with the end-user client. You should also be aware that your actions might result in the agent being in breach of contract with the client, if the agent has promised to provide your services, which are then withheld. That may work in your favour, but then again it might not.

Some recruiters may be receptive to an offer to 'buy-out' the contract, so that you can contract direct with the end-user client. The terms of the buy-out would make it clear that the agent could not enforce any restrictive covenant in the contract. But this is likely to be an expensive exercise. The agent is likely to calculate the buy-out price based on their margin times the length of the contract, to give an all-in lump sum for you to pay in one go.

You might also go to all the trouble of freeing yourself from the contract with the agency, only to find that the client adopts exactly the same attitude and refuses to change their standard contract. Clients are often significantly more inflexible than agents in this respect.

## CONTRACTING MINDSET TIPS:
### Agencies & clients can't change terms & conditions at will
As a contractor, you have a contract that details exactly what service you provide to your client. A contract is a legal agreement, so your client or agency cannot decide they want to change the terms and conditions at will – they must negotiate with you first.

### Does your electrician clean the toilets?
You've just hired a builder to install your new kitchen and you've signed a contract agreeing to pay her £1,000 a week for three weeks. But come week three, you decide that £800 is a better price. Is your builder going to agree to complete the kitchen and let you get away with it?

The contract with your nanny clearly states his working hours are nine in the morning until five in the afternoon. You tell him from now on he stays until seven each night for no extra pay. Is he obliged to agree?

The electrician you hired to re-wire your new home office turns up to start work and you insist he cleans the toilets every day, too. Do you think he should agree?

### A contract is a binding agreement and both parties must agree to change
How might this apply to contractors? Say you're just starting month three of your contract and your client insists you take a rate reduction. As with the builder you hired to install the kitchen, both you and your client have signed a contract agreeing a rate.

If you are paid by the day, with contracted core hours of nine to five, and then your client keeps insisting you stay until eight every night for weeks on end with no additional remuneration, your contract says don't have to accept the situation. The same applies to your nanny.

You are an accountant and you have been hired to develop a finance system, which is specified in your contract. Then, without consulting you, your client asks you to cover reception each morning. Your electrician's contract doesn't include cleaning toilets, and your contract specifies finance, not phones.

### Contract changes must be agreed or the other party is in breach
Contractors are called that for a reason. Because they work according to an agreed contract. So, if your client or agency unilaterally starts paying you less than was originally agreed in the contract, they have breached the terms of your contract. You could claim for any loss you experience as a result of such a breach and seek redress, if it comes to that, through the courts.

Contractors generally bill for services according to time spent delivering them. So if a client expects you to deliver in excess of what was agreed, you should expect your fees to increase and renegotiate your contract to reflect the longer hours and an increased day rate. Your client wouldn't expect its utility company to supply 20% extra fuel for free, would it?

Your contract stipulates the nature of the services you have agreed to deliver. If you are developing a new software system and then the client asks you to train its own developers, that's fine, as long as you draw up a new 'training contract' to replace your original 'development contract' and increase your fees accordingly.

**Contractors are expected to be flexible, but any changes to terms and conditions must be mutually agreed by all parties.**

# 10.4 Restrictions

## 10.4.1 When the agent insists you cannot work directly for the client

Clients may ask you to work directly for them in a permanent role. They may do this for a number of reasons, which often include the desire to save money and to have a leaner (ie cheaper for them) relationship with you.

If the client recruits you into a permanent role, they will be obliged to pay the agency a finder's fee. Depending on the volume of business the client has with the agency, the agency might let you become employed without the client suffering a penalty. But, it is down to the client to pressure the agency on this. You have no bargaining power as a contractor.

If the agency does agree, then you should get confirmation in writing from the agency that you have permission to work directly for the client in a permanent role and that the decision overrules the restrictive covenant in your contract.

Of course if you have not yet signed a contract with the agency, you do not have a restrictive covenant but the client will have terms and conditions with the agency that forbid them from recruiting you, if the agency introduced you, without the agency receiving a fee.

The restrictive covenant is designed for exactly these types of scenario, where you might be given the opportunity to work for the client direct. Quite rightly, agencies who have invested a significant amount in securing the client, marketing the role and identifying you as a candidate want to be sure they profit from the arrangement.

## 10.4.2 When you are told you cannot use client facilities

Believe it or not, even small things like using the canteen, or having a badge that allows you access to the building without signing in, can become hugely important in determining your IR35 status. HMRC and a judge might consider that you eating in the company's subsidised canteen, or having a company swipe card to enter the building, point to proof that you might be a 'disguised employee'.

As discussed in chapter 8, the case law governing IR35 includes a test of whether a contractor is 'part and parcel' of an organisation. Unfortunately, there are no clear criteria about what being 'part and parcel' actually means, and the case law on the subject varies greatly. But a rule of thumb is to try and not be, or behave like, the employees of your client, which of course will vary from one client organisation to the next.

So every little detail involved can be taken into account. In one case, a contractor was accused of being within IR35 because they had the same security pass that employees had and so could walk in and out of the building at will.

Other cases have included factors like eating at the company canteen, or sharing employee transport. Almost anything you do that makes you seem like an employee can be held against you, largely because the case law varies so much. This means that HMRC tax inspectors and judges will look at everything.

So if you're told that you cannot use the company canteen or aren't entitled to a security pass, or can't use the staff car park and don't receive a gym pass, be grateful. And if you're invited to use the canteen, or given that security pass that will make getting into the building so much easier, politely refuse and explain why.

As a contractor outside IR35, you must always distinguish yourself as much as possible from the permanent employees, and make sure that both your contract and your actual day-to-day activities show that you are an independent contractor and not a disguised employee. Even if it means missing out on delicious, subsidised lunches!

## 10.5 Termination and breaches

When a project doesn't go well, contractors are often blamed for the problems, even when these are not their fault. This can lead to unfair termination, when the client or the agency simply blames you and puts an early end to your contract.

But it can equally be the client or agency that is in breach of the contract; just by paying you later than the terms in your contract specify can lead to an agency or client being in breach, and this is a common occurrence. Other breaches of contract include the client failing to sign-off on timesheets, demanding services not included in the original contract and early termination without notice.

Although you could technically sue for damages as a result of breach of contract by the client or agency, in practice this may not be appropriate, because you want to resolve the issue and continue working. Late payment is generally a minor breach, where a negotiated settlement can be found. A major breach, such as non-payment, is grounds for immediate termination of the contract. It is also grounds for taking legal action to recover any debt and potentially for damages, too.

## 10.5.1 When your contract is terminated unfairly

There are several reasons that typically lead to unfair termination. A client can find that the original budget for a project has been drastically reduced, or that the original objectives have been changed. Your manager is now stuck with finding a way to make everything right, and blaming the contractor can provide an easy way out.

So the client's project manager calls you into the office, and says: 'You've made a right mess of this project, and you're terminated.' What can you do?

If you've done the work, and you are being falsely accused, you have a right to compensation for early termination and breach of contract. This should include payment for at least part of the contract time.

The key issue is proving what you've done. The best strategy is to pull together the best dossier of proof that you can, so that when your manager accuses you of making a 'right mess,' you can say: 'Not only is that statement entirely false, but I can prove it. And if you don't change your tune, my lawyer will call the tune in court with a demand for compensation.'

Very often a simple demonstration of strength on your part will make the manager think twice, or at least get the manager to see that a compromise with you on this is desirable. Because if you are obliged to seek legal redress, the issue will be the subject of a complex debate, and when lawyers say 'complex' what they really mean is 'costly'.

If you are going to be able to enforce your legal rights, you will need documentary proof, compiled as completely as possible. You should also ask fellow contractors to write statements on your behalf, and you should create a chart of progress, a kind of 'before and after' scenario.'

This is not as daunting as it sounds.

First of all, you should have been careful throughout the project to document what you've done. Keep all emails, indications of milestones reached or phases completed, and as many records of your work as you can.

Get as many of your colleagues on the project as you can to support you. If you are all being victimised in a group, that's likely to work to your benefit, because your combined testimony will be all that more damaging.

Use your own technical knowledge to explain what happened. You know what you were hired to do, and what the project was for. In the evidence, try to explain how things were at the start, what you did, and what was left to be accomplished. Use plain language. If the project's failure was due to negligence on the part of the client, explain what the client should have done and didn't do. Did the client fail to provide necessary materials? Were you given access to everything you needed? Do you have copies of the emails you sent warning the client that the project was on track to end badly?

Make the most convincing case you can. Then take it first to the highest-level manager you can reach, and lay out the case. Give them a good 'scare'. If necessary, you could consider paying the lawyers to contact them and help in the 'scare'.

It is of course frustrating to know that you are in the right but to accept less than all that you are owed. And, if the client refuses to negotiate, you should go ahead with the lawsuit if you've put sufficient proof together. But the best strategy is to get a reasonable settlement and to move on. Years of legal expense, frustration and health-damaging stress should be avoided if possible, even if you know you'll win in the end.

## Been there, done that!

## Getting terminated unfairly

**DAVE SAYS:** You get terminated unfairly, and the client is obviously making something up to get rid of you early. But they agree to pay you until the day you leave, which is today. Whilst you can sue them for the termination period, in reality this is going to be a major hassle for you. It's time consuming, costs money in legal fees and is very stressful. There's also no guarantee you will win.

Whilst this hasn't happened to me personally, I know contractors who've had it happen to them. The general feeling is that if you get dismissed on the spot, but the client agrees to pay up and not withhold any monies, then consider this a 'good result' and move on to the next contract. If they agree to pay you a month's money if you leave today, then get a signed agreement and skip all the way home. Or to the bank.

### 10.5.2 When you withdraw from a contract before it even starts

If you have signed a contract but decide to withdraw before the contract even starts, your agency may be entitled to compensation and could have grounds to sue you for breach of contract.

Should there be a termination clause in the contract and you provide sufficient notice as required by that termination clause, then it may be possible for you to withdraw from a contract before it starts without being in breach of the contract. But, even if there is a termination clause in the contract, the provisions of the contract might mean that time for the purposes of the termination clause would not start to run until the contract actually starts, so withdrawing would constitute a breach.

Penalty clauses are unenforceable, so that's not a route an agency can take. But if the contract contained a liquidated damages provision setting out a reasonable pre-estimate of its loss in the event of such a breach by a contractor, the agency might well be able to enforce such a provision. Where a breach of contract occurs, under English contract law, the agency has the right to be put in the position in which it would have been, had the breach not occurred. Having breached the contract, you would be the party responsible for paying such compensation.

However, the injured party, in this case the agency, has a duty to mitigate, so the agency cannot simply sit back and take no action in the expectation that you will make up the entire loss. Its duty to mitigate is likely, for example, to require the agency to seek a replacement. Even if the agency loses the client and the contract to another recruiter because of your withdrawal, your total liability for damages is likely to be limited to the earliest date that you could lawfully have terminated, according to the contract.

There is a principle of civil law practice requiring that parties must make reasonable attempts to resolve a dispute before resorting to legal action. Should all attempts to negotiate fail, the agency would be entitled to pursue you through the courts. A letter before action from the agency is the first step on this path, and the point when you will know the agency means business. The agency could eventually take you to court to secure compensation, although during this period it still has a duty to mitigate.

### 10.5.3 When your client breaches the contract

When agents or clients breach your contract, you should react with notification, and if appropriate and necessary, termination of the contract. You may also have the right to damages if your contract is breached, but these damages could be limited by your 'duty to mitigate' – you can't just sit around and collect damages, rather you have to make an effort to find a new contract and move on.

Remember that a contract is an agreement to provide goods or services in exchange for a 'consideration', which means money. This exchange is governed by terms: when will it take place, how will it take place, and so on.

Breach of contract occurs when one of these terms is not honoured by one or more of the parties to the contract. There are two ways in which this can happen: one party cannot do something they have promised to do; or one party can interfere in a way that jeopardises the completion of the contract.

There are two types of breach of contract: major and minor. A major breach allows you to terminate immediately, although this may not be your best option from a business point of view. If it's a minor breach, then you should certainly make a real effort to negotiate before pursuing damages.

For contractors, typical examples of major breaches of contract include:

- Non-payment or late payment
- Termination without sufficient notice
- Accusation of a breach on your part to justify early termination
- Cancellation of contract before work begins
- Client refuses to sign a time sheet when work has been completed
- Failure to provide materials or other conditions promised by the contract
- Demand for services not included in the contract.

The first thing to do if you are subject to a breach of this kind is to talk to the person responsible. Always try to avoid legal action in any case; going to court is a time-consuming, stressful and expensive process, and the results are never predictable no matter how certain you are of being right. Bring the matter to the person's attention, and see if you can work something out.

If that doesn't work, and you have to get formal, then notify the client or agent with a registered letter that you feel their action constitutes a major breach of contract, and that you will terminate and seek damages if they do not correct their actions.

The next step is either to take the matter to small claims court, if it involves less than £5000, or to seek legal advice. If the party in question settles with you, or if you win in court, you can expect to receive damages and any costs, in addition to the small claims court charges and fees, but these will be subject to what is called your duty to mitigate.

For example, if you have been terminated after three months for no justifiable reason on a six-month contract, you should be entitled to payment for any termination period. You have to show the court that you've made a real attempt to find more work after the early termination, which demonstrates your 'duty to mitigate'.

So the rule is discretion: you don't have to accept breach of contract, but don't just race off to sue without very serious thought, or without trying to negotiate. It's easy to threaten to sue when you are angry, but doing it is a lot more trying.

Understanding your rights and stating them clearly is the surest way to resolving most contracts disputes.

### 10.5.4 When you want to leave early and don't have a termination clause

The starting point is to have a friendly word with the client's project manager. They are unlikely to want to force contractors to stay who are unhappy and unmotivated. They could then terminate you early, assuming they have the option.

You could also offer to help find and fund someone to take over from you – a substitute. Incidentally, this would also help any future IR35 case, as providing a substitute is one of the factors that can help prove your limited company contracting business is a 'genuine' business. Your agent, if you have one, will not like you terminating as you are cutting off a source of income for them, potentially damaging their relationship with the client, and causing them additional work. However, if you provide a substitute, the agency will maintain their revenue stream and won't care who is providing it for them.

However, unless the agency, or client if you are contracting directly, agrees to terminate the contract early or accept a substitute, then you will have failed to deliver your services during the entire period you were contracted to, and will therefore be in breach of contract. The innocent party, in this case the agency or client, can claim for damages that would put them into the position they would have been in if not for the breach by you. That could be a lot of money.

The agency cannot physically force you to complete the contract, but it might sue your limited company or umbrella company for its losses – such as its loss of margin for the unworked period. Although it would not necessarily be entitled to do so, it might also withhold unpaid fees to compensate it for the financial loss. Should that happen, you would then need to sue the agency for not paying your invoices for work you have completed. When contracting directly with a client, a similarly messy situation could ensue, but the potential damages could be much higher if your departure puts at risk a project that could cause the client serious financial damage if not completed on time.

Clearly, it could all get very messy and expensive. Alternative solutions should be explored that would suit all parties and which might require both a substitute and you paying compensation to the agency, if there is one, for its lost margin.

### 10.5.5 When you are terminated and think you should have employment rights/compensation

It's simple: contractors do not have employment rights from their end-user client, even if they are within IR35. Any contractor who wants to make a representation to a client about employment rights is asking to be caught by IR35 and, as such, will potentially end up being targeted by HMRC for back taxes and penalties. So the strong recommendation to all contractors is not to even consider it.

You should also be aware that the courts have ruled that contractors do not qualify for employment rights even if they have been working for a client for several years.

### 10.5.6 When you disagree with your client over your contract's end date

It is possible for confusion to arise over the actual end date of a contract, particularly if there is an agency and umbrella company in the chain. What you agreed during discussions with the client might subsequently be changed during discussions between the client and agency, and agency and umbrella if there is one, but no-one thinks to tell you. Or sometimes a genuine mistake can creep into the paperwork.

The solution generally depends on the timing of the contract and the actions of the client. The contract will usually take precedence, so if you agreed with the client directly that your work ended on the 15th of the month, but a subsequent contract says the 10th of the month, then the contract ends on the 10th.

However, had the client acted in such a way as to suggest that you should have continued to work after the 10<sup>th</sup> then the contractor may have some options to take further action to recover fees for the disputed period. Did the client do anything from which you could reasonably have concluded that the contract was extended, such as send an email discussing tasks requiring completion before the 15<sup>th</sup>? If so, then that would constitute evidence you could use to seek payment.

If the parties in the chain, such as the agency and an umbrella company, made a mistake and put the wrong end date in the contract, and yet you still signed the contract, then you have no options. You should never assume what is in your contract – you must know.

### 10.5.7 When an agent tries to unilaterally cut rates mid-contract

Some clients – particularly those in the financial sector when facing difficult market conditions – have an unreasonable tendency to try and cut contract rates mid-way through a contract, and to threaten contractors with early termination if they don't accept. Unfortunately, some agencies have been known to attempt the same to increase their margin. They might, for example, put all their contractors on notice of termination and then blame it on the client. If your agency tries this on, the solution is to refuse to simply roll over; immediately seek professional legal advice.

If your agency has done this, it is potentially in a vulnerable position, particularly if you hold your nerve. This is because the agency is likely to have contract with the client to provide a specified number of contractors to perform specific roles. If it terminates you and your fellow contractors, the agency has put itself in a position where, within 30 days, it would be unable to honour its contract with the client for the supply of these contractors, and would therefore itself be in breach of contract with the client.

This situation of having rate cuts dictated is unfortunately familiar to many contractors. What is more unfortunate is that many have rolled over and accepted the rate cut because they lacked the confidence, based on sound legal advice, to tough it out. You don't have to suffer the same fate.

## 10.5.8 When you leave a contract early without notice

Under most circumstances, leaving a contract early without notice, even if there is a termination clause, will put a contractor in breach of contract, irrespective of the reasons. The action that an agency or client will take will depend on the circumstances, but could vary from being very understanding if the reason for the early departure was a personal tragedy to withholding money for time worked or even taking court action.

If you did not expressly opt out of the Conduct Regulations (Conduct of Employment Agencies and Employment Business Regulations 2003), then your agency cannot withhold payment for work that you've done. That is irrespective of whether you left the contract early or the client decides not to pay the agency money owned because you've left early. However, the Conduct Regulations would not prevent the agency from mounting a separate legal action to claim damages from the contractor for failing to complete the entire contract.

A contract creates mutual obligations, setting in stone what parties to the contract have chosen to agree. A contract creates expectations, and the expectation is that each party can put reliance on the commitment of the other party, and that the parties will fulfil their respective commitments. If one party fails to meet an obligation, the other party may suffer a loss as a result. Provided that loss is a reasonably foreseeable consequence of the breach, the innocent party can claim damages in respect of that loss.

That means if you fail to meet an obligation set down in a contract, then you, the party not fulfilling your end of the bargain, are in breach. In this case the other party who has been let down – the agency or client – could sue for damages. The basis for assessing damages for breach of contract is to put the innocent party into the position they would have been in if the contract had not been breached.

Damages are expressed in financial terms; so, if it cost the innocent party – the agency or the client – more to complete the contract, there is a case for the additional costs to be claimed from the party in breach – the contractor. Similarly, if the innocent party lost money as a result of the failure to complete the contract, there is a case for that loss to be claimed from the party in breach.

The measure of loss to the agency in this case would probably be the agency's margin on the work you should have completed – or, if it engaged someone else but at higher cost to complete your contract, the additional cost of hiring that replacement. The loss to the client, if you are contracting directly, could be substantially more.

### 10.5.9 When your agency tries to charge you a penalty for early termination

Assuming your contract is governed by English law, punitive penalty clauses in agency contracts would most likely not be enforceable. Under English law, a contractual provision which places a party *in terrorem* will generally amount to an unlawful penalty, and so be unenforceable. That legal term *in terrorem* means to intimidate or frighten a party to a contract into complying, and runs counter to general principles of contract law.

If your agency has offered no basis on which the amount of the penalty might reasonably be justified, then a court would be unlikely to enforce such a clause. That's because it has the appearance of being a penalty that would unjustly enrich the agency; it would not be a genuine assessment of the innocent party's loss.

When one party to a contract is in breach (which you might be if you terminated a contract early and did not adhere to the contractual terms regarding termination) the injured party can expect damages to put them into the position that they would have been in had the breach not occurred. But a penalty clause clearly does not fall into this category. If your agency attempted to enforce a punitive penalty clause in court, they would probably not succeed, because it has provided no basis for the amount of the penalty. It would, in the eyes of a court, appear as if the agency was seeking a bonus from the breach of contract, which is not allowable under English law.

What can be enforced are contractual provisions that are intended, in the event of a breach by one party, to give the other a sum that can reasonably be regarded as a genuine attempt to pre-assess the loss that party might suffer. So if your agency estimated its daily loss based on its margin and included a clause to the effect that you would pay the agency that amount for each day you fail to work, the clause may well be upheld by a court.

The courts are frequently asked to determine whether a clause providing for payment from one party to the other in the event of breach is an unlawful penalty, or a genuine pre-assessment of loss. If you are concerned about a penalty clause in your client or agency contract, you should seek professional advice to determine whether it is likely to be enforceable, should a breach occur. If it appears the provision is an attempt to intimidate you into not breaching the contract, then it may well be unenforceable

## 10.6 Difficult clients

Clients come in all shapes and sizes. Many are a pleasure to work with and provide years of stress free contracting, calling you up when they have moved on to see if you can come and work for them again. Equally, many can be a complete nightmare and are downright nasty. Some have simply never hired contractors before, so think you are an employee and treat you accordingly.

### 10.6.1 When you are asked to provide more services than you agreed

Often contractors are asked to provide more services than agreed, and this situation requires a business decision on your part. The law does not expect your work to conform strictly and absolutely to the letter of the contract description.

Reasonable allowances are made for the needs of the workplace, changes in demand and so on. You are expected to be flexible and reasonable, and, if there is a dispute that ends up in the courts, you will be sanctioned if you have been inflexible.

With that said, an agreement to perform service 'X' does not include your performing services 'Y' and 'Z' too. You should feel free to point this out to the client's project manager if too many demands are made. This can be quite important for your IR35 status: to retain your contractor status you must focus on your project and not just do whatever comes down the pipe, or you could easily be judged a 'disguised employee'.

## Been there, done that!

## You scratch my back, I'll give you champagne

**DAVE SAYS:** On one project, for which I'd been hired to do bleeding edge technology, a manager asked if I would spend a week with another team assessing how they could upgrade their ancient system to newer technologies.

I politely declined, saying: 'Sorry, I wasn't hired for that, but I could recommend someone you could bring in to do it.' So I did, and a colleague came, did the job for the client, and treated me to a decent case of champagne for the work I'd put his way. Everyone was a winner!

If the client threatens to terminate if you don't go the extra mile, you should point out that they are threatening a breach of contract, and that you will quit and demand compensation if they do not drop the unreasonable demands. If the contract is breached in this way, and you can prove it, you should notify the agency and client by letter that there has been a breach, or the threat of one.

Most of the time this threat will suffice to get the client to drop the unreasonable demands.

### 10.6.2 When the client won't let you take time off

Normally contractor contracts do not include time taken off from work except for standard holidays, and even these are not always included if the project is urgent. So, if your contract doesn't specify you can take time off, you can't.

If your contract does specify holidays then this would put you inside IR35.

The only way around this is to declare up front that your firm will not be able to provide services between certain dates and have those dates written in the contract. On the whole clients are pretty reasonable, and will let you take some time away, but they don't have to.

If you want to take off for extended leave, and not just a couple of weeks here and there then you need to substitute yourself. Holidays are covered in detail in chapter 11.

### 10.6.3 When the client forces you to take time off

Unless your contract specifies that you should expect periods of suspension, or that your period of assignment could be abbreviated, you are not obliged to take time off if you don't want to. This does not include time off for national holidays, like Christmas and New Year.

But for the rest of the year, if it's not in your contract that you can be suspended for periods of time, just say no. Your contract probably does include terms for termination, but if you are terminated, the client will probably want you back again when the project starts up again. You will be well-placed to demand a higher fee.

Should the client insist, point out that it breaches your contract and that you will take action. Warn the agency, and they will intervene. They should be made to understand that you will seek damages for the time lost on the contract.

If your contract does provide for such suspensions, obviously you are obliged to accept them. What would be perhaps the best solution is to talk the whole thing over with your client, and see if you can't find a compromise that works for you both. After all, you may want to work for the client again. But don't allow your rights to be impugned without a reasonable solution; ask up-front before signing the contract if time off is anticipated and get it confirmed in writing, at the very least in an email.

### 10.6.4 When the client threatens to terminate if you don't adhere to their unfair requests

If a client requires you to perform tasks that are well outside your remit, you always have the option of declining. If the client makes an issue of it, then you can remind them that you have a contract and what they are asking you to do is outside of the remit of the contract.

Should the client threaten you with termination the first step is to try and talk to them and negotiate a settlement. It might be that you can negotiate an additional contract to, for example, train the client's employees in a new skill. If the client terminates your contract unfairly, see section 10.5.1.

### 10.6.5 When your client decides to relocate and insists you must also move

You've been working on a contract for some months, based at a client's site within a reasonable journey from your permanent home. Then you learn that the client is closing down the site you work at, and relocating the project to another part of the UK, or even, in extreme cases, another country.

As a starting point, if you are being asked to move you should look to your contract paperwork first, reviewing the provisions both on the working location and on premature termination. Even if the specific address you work at currently is not specified in the original contract, what the client is proposing when asking you to move location is still a change. So, depending what other provisions have been made in the contract regarding your location, the client's request will still amount to a request for the contract to be amended.

Unless the contents of the contract say otherwise, the client cannot simply instruct you to start working from a different location. You might, though, consider it advantageous to move for other reasons, for example to maintain a temporary workplace and continue to claim for travel and subsistence expenses, rather than falling foul of the 24 month expenses rules.

If your contract requires you to complete the entire project, and the client is inflexible, then you might have to consider relocating. If you do, remember that as a contractor you will get no financial assistance from the client towards relocation.

In the unlikely event the client offers assistance, unless you can negotiate a higher rate as a form of indirect compensation, you have to decline it because to accept relocation expenses, or compensation for them, would immediately put you inside IR35. Don't let the client treat you like an employee.

The up-side is that, whether you are contracting through a limited company or an umbrella company, a significant amount of your relocation expenses, or extended travel and accommodation expenses if you choose a weekly commute, are tax deductible.

Some contracts specify the location where you will be working. This will give you the option of not completing the project and being able to claim a reasonable notice payment.

If you think this might be an issue from the start, say you heard that the parent company had been going through a major restructuring, then make sure there is a termination clause and that the location is written into the contract, with an exit option if this location changes.

### 10.6.6 When your client tries to force you to work fewer hours than your contract says

Strictly speaking, no contractor can technically be asked to take time off or a 'holiday' by a client, as the client does not employ the contractor, and instead has a contract for services with the contractor's limited company or umbrella company. However, you may be asked by clients to take breaks from contracts. And whether this is a breach of contract is down to what was agreed during the contract negotiations and what appears in the small print.

There are generally two possibilities for contractors in this situation. Your contract may be quite explicit and state that, for example, you must work 8 hours per day, 5 days per week for a contract lasting 3 months. Alternatively, you may have a less prescriptive contract, with little more than start date, end date and an hourly or daily rate. Your options will depend on which of these two possibilities applies to you.

If you have a contract that clearly states the start and end dates, the rate by the hour, hours to be worked per day and the days to be worked every week, then it is likely that not only will you be under the obligation to work for the periods specified, but also the client will have a corresponding contractual obligation to provide work for you for the periods specified, and to pay you for that work. Assuming you make yourself available and willing to work by turning up at the client's site every day, then you are not in breach of contract, but if your client fails to provide work then the client is in breach of contract.

Or, if there is an agency in the loop, then it would be the agency that is in breach of contract. That's because it has the contractual relationship with your limited company or umbrella company, and therefore an implied obligation to make work available for the period, and to pay you in any event.

Where you have a contract start date, end date, a rate and a payment date, but no specified hours or days to be worked, then there is no specific obligation for you to work on any particular day, and no corresponding obligation on the client to provide work on any particular day. Your client is fully within its rights to ask you to take a 'holiday'. The same is true if an agency is in the contract chain – the agency does not have an obligation to provide work either.

It is a judgement call as to whether you should take legal action over a client forcing you to take time off, if your contract allows. Many factors should be considered, including the loss of earnings for a fortnight versus loss of the contract entirely, especially if the contract has a long time to run. You may also wish to seek legal advice before taking any action.

### 10.6.7 When your client wants to move you to another project mid-way through your contract

Unless your assignment is specifically a troubleshooting role, or you have been hired to cover a role for a period of time rather than work on a specific project, there is no legal requirement for you to effectively move contracts and start a new project half-way through your current contract. Without your agreement, a client cannot simply decide part-way through a contract to unilaterally change contract terms, such as the specific outcome that you must achieve. Furthermore, for a client to be able to tell a contractor to do something different gives all the appearances of the client 'controlling' the contractor. Control is a key test of employment and could place you inside IR35.

You would be entirely within your contractual rights to respond to a client request to change company and job specification by indicating that you would prefer to continue with the contract as it is. If the client says this is not possible, then you can choose to negotiate a new contract with your client, or request that the current contract is terminated by the client, with notice.

The same is true if the client asks you to apply a different skill set to the one that you were originally contracted to deliver. You might have started on a specific copywriting assignment, and then be asked to provide strategic marketing consultancy on how the copywriting project is developing. By all means agree to supply your other skills, but under a different contract and at the market rates.

Of course, this might upset the client and so, in the interests of not burning bridges with a client who may provide future assignments, an option might be for you to compromise and suggest a reduced notice period. It is possible that the client could be requesting a change of approach, rather than a whole new project outside of the original project scope. But you would need to make that judgement call based on what is written in the original contract and what the client is asking you to do now.

## 10.7 Payment problems

Contracting is inherently different from permanent work in that there is more risk of not getting paid for the work that you do. Whilst this is rare, it does happen. Agencies and clients sometimes go bust and occasionally refuse or delay payment. However, in most scenarios, short of the agency or client going bust (which is covered in 10.7.4 below), there is something you can do to claim all or part of your fees.

### 10.7.1 When you don't get paid

In the event of payment being delayed by the client or the agency, then it is a breach of contract and you do not have to continue working. They will still owe you the money if you refuse to continue working. This is your legal right.

If this happens to you then the suggested course of action is to demand in writing that they pay you within three working days or you will terminate the contract. Your agency may counter this by saying they have not been paid by the client. However, this is not your problem, as your contract should not have a 'pay when paid' clause. Also, in practice, many agencies 'factor' their invoices so get the cash immediately anyway. When an agency 'factors' its invoices, a commercial finance company 'buys' the invoices from the agency for a discount. Although the agency won't receive the full value of the invoice, they will get paid faster and so should you.

If you are still not paid then simply withdraw your services. The more time you spend working for nothing, the more time you are losing looking for a new contract.

Having withdrawn your services, send them a letter explaining why and inform them that you have commenced legal action. Wait a week and if you still have not been paid then start legal proceedings. It rarely gets to this stage.

## 10.7.2 When you are consistently paid late

This is probably one of the most common 'when things go wrong' scenarios. Clients and agents often don't pay on time, even when the contract specifies that they should. Most small businesses have to deal with the problem of late payment every now and again.

It's an awkward situation: on the one hand, you need to get the money that you live on; on the other hand, you don't want to go overboard chasing agencies and clients so that you become known as strident and unreasonable. Nonetheless, it is wise to know your rights, and then to decide whether you want to play it soft or hard with a given agency or client.

Repeated late payment might well merit your attention for another reason, though. When it comes time to get the last payment under the terms of the contract, it may not just be late, it may never come. To remind the client or agency that you are very determined to receive what is due to you, a firm line on late payments can be useful. Or you may feel that repeated late payment is reason for terminating the contract. This is harder to do, but you may be justified in doing so under certain conditions.

If you have performed your contracting services exactly according to specification, the client has signed the timesheet, if required, and the invoice has not been disputed by the client or agency, there is no legal reason for you not to expect payment. If you follow the correct debt recovery procedure and process from the outset, that will maximise your chances of successfully obtaining payment from clients and agencies. It should also be borne in mind that, under late payment legislation, interest on overdue amounts can be charged at the current Bank of England reference rate plus 8% pa.

The debt recovery process is as follows:

- **Step 1**: Contact the debtor
- **Step 2**: Use a credit collection agency
- **Step 3**: Letter before action
- **Step 4**: Letter of intended proceedings
- **Step 5**: File claim with MoneyClaim Online
- **Step 6**: Alternative dispute resolution (ADR) [If debtor agrees]
- **Step 7**: Court ruling, bailiffs, forced liquidation.

You should assume from the outset that any correspondence, including notes of telephone conversations, may be subject to the scrutiny of a court. A judge will take a dim view of any contractor who did not follow due process and try every reasonable means to amicably resolve the dispute before seeking a legal solution. That means avoiding using phrases such as 'see you in court', no matter how tempting and stress relieving it may be!

So 'step 1' begins by emailing, sending letters by recorded delivery and then telephoning the client or agency, all the while explaining in reasonable terms why the client or agency should pay the invoice immediately. At this stage, you should give your client or agency seven days to respond with payment.

Bear in mind that some firms will have a strategy of fobbing off their creditors with lame excuses, or ignoring them, until they see that you are prepared to take legal steps.

So, if payment doesn't arrive after your initial attempts, and there are no other legal complications, then 'step 2' would be to use a credit collection agency, which in most cases will result in the client or agency paying. If not, then 'step 3' is a 'letter before action'.

The letter before action informs the client or agency that payment is overdue and that legal action will commence immediately if the debt is not paid within seven days of the date of the letter. If this letter is ignored, 'step 4', is to send a letter of intended proceedings.

If you are planning to use HM Courts Service's online service for recovering debts, MoneyClaim Online, then following HM Courts guidance, procedures and any pre-action protocols that apply is essential at this stage. Not to do so means that even should you win the case, you may end up having to pay your own costs, plus those of your client or agency. But the client or agency also has to abide by these protocols.

The letter of intended proceedings should offer the opportunity for arbitration ('alternative dispute resolution', or ADR), and your willingness to settle without going to court if the client or agency meets the required settlement amount. The settlement amount is the cash amount that you will settle for, which could even be higher than the original amount because of additional costs.

Having received your 'step 4' letter, the client or agency will typically respond in one of four different ways:

1.  The letter of intended proceedings is ignored, in which case you should proceed to 'step 5', which is to file a claim with MoneyClaim Online

2.  The client or agency dissembles without following pre-action protocols, in an attempt to make you delay legal action further. The response to such fobbing off should be a letter from you explaining that the response is not satisfactory, and why, and that court action will proceed within 72 hours unless payment is received. You should then proceed to 'step 5' if payment in full is not forthcoming

3.  The client or agency agrees to the offer of arbitration, or alternative dispute resolution (ADR), 'step 6' of the process

4.  The client or agency settles.

Should you get to the point of taking 'step 5' and filing with MoneyClaim Online, you must follow the instructions provided on the MoneyClaim website and wait for your court date. If the case is not straightforward, you may wish to consider professional legal representation. The fees for MoneyClaim online vary according to the size of your claim, but are in the hundreds of pounds, not thousands.

Assuming there are no complications or legal points to argue and you stay on top of your MoneyClaim Online case, then the likelihood of obtaining a ruling in your favour is high. However, if you receive a ruling in your favour and the client or agency still does not pay, the ruling remains on a public register for six years. This impacts negatively on the ability of the client or agency to secure business credit in the future. The threat of this 'damage' to their credit rating may well be enough to persuade the agency or client to pay.

You then have a number of options to extract payment, varying from sending in the bailiffs to preventing the sale of assets by the client or agency. As a last resort, if the amount owed is above a pre-set level you can apply to have the client or agency put into compulsory liquidation, but this can be expensive.

Ideally, you should attempt to resolve payment disputes amicably. And many such disputes can be avoided before you even sign a contract, if you undertake due diligence and also ensure all terms and conditions are clear. But if the courts become the final option, your adherence to process and protocols is essential to maximise the chances of securing the money owed.

But what if you want to terminate the contract?

It is possible to treat late payment as a breach of contract, but it must be of the essence of the contract. That means, for you, getting paid on time is absolutely essential, critical to the work you agreed to undertake when you signed the contract.

Some contracts have terms that make this clear in themselves. But if you need to prove that it is essential that you be paid on time, write a letter to the company and remind them that this is essential to the contract, and that you will consider it a breach of contract if they continue to pay late.

If the company still pays you late, you have the right to terminate without further delay, and you can seek to recover damages. If the amount is large, you should probably take professional advice at this point.

So know your rights, evaluate what you think is the most important aspect of the problem, and proceed accordingly.

### 10.7.3 When the agency or client withholds money from you, citing reasons

This is something that sometimes happens when, for example, a client claims that you have not returned a piece of equipment you have borrowed. Ideally, you should not use clients' equipment as this could be a contributing factor to putting you inside IR35. But if you do have to use your client's equipment, then you should always obtain a receipt on its return.

When a dispute arises and the client claims you have not returned equipment, the issue becomes a question of evidence. You must prove that you returned the equipment, which might require a statement from the person you returned it to.

Where it is not possible for you to prove you returned the client's equipment, then the client company has the right to 'set-off' the costs of the equipment. In other words, they can claim compensation from you for the cost of the equipment 'lost'.

However, this does not mean the client can withhold payment from you, which may amount to thousands of pounds in lieu of equipment worth a few tens of pounds. If the client withholds payment on the basis of equipment not returned and which is worth far less than the amount you are owed, then you are perfectly within your rights to take legal action to recover unpaid fees.

In this case, you should get in touch with a credit collection agency, or with you solicitor, or, if the amount of fees owed is less than £5,000, you could make a claim through HM Courts Service's Money Claim Online. Naturally, before taking such action, you should try all non-legal options by, for example, negotiating with the agency and/or client.

In a perfect world, contractors should not put themselves in the position of using client's equipment, because it could be used as evidence by HMRC that they are a 'disguised employee', which could put them inside IR35. But when a contractor really does have to use the client's equipment, they should ensure that there is a paper trail of receipts to account for that equipment's whereabouts.

## 10.7.4 When the agent or client goes bust

If your client or recruitment agency goes bust, this is not great news for you, as contractors tend to be fairly low down the creditor pecking order.

However, there are steps you can take to ensure you do receive any funds distributed by a defunct company, and how you go about it is different if you are working through your own limited company or an umbrella company.

An agency or a client is insolvent if they do not have enough cash to pay their creditors or their net assets are less than their net liabilities. This usually means one of three things happening:

- Appointment of an administrator
- Appointment of a receiver
- Appointment of a liquidator.

If an administrator is appointed, it is usually good news for you as you may see a small amount of your fee. The administrator is responsible for either managing the company out of its financial difficulties or realising as much value from the assets as possible to pay creditors.

Most agencies have factoring arrangements with a finance provider, which means they receive payment immediately from the factoring agent, less a commission. It is this relationship that can often determine whether an agency survives or not.

The receiver, or liquidator, would usually have the task of attempting to realise as much cash as possible from the failed agency or client to disperse amongst the creditors.

You should find out who the administrator, receiver or liquidator is, and ensure you register your debt with the right forms and proof of debt. You should keep in touch with the administrator, receiver or liquidator, but not hassle them as they have a statutory obligation not to favour one creditor above another except as laid down in statute.

If you are working through an umbrella company, you should not contact the administrator, receiver or liquidator at all, as technically is it not your problem but your umbrella company's.

You should make sure your umbrella company is aware that your agency or client has gone bust and ensure they are taking action. Some umbrella companies do not pay their contractors unless they get paid, but others do; therefore, you would be wise to ask the question when choosing which umbrella company to use.

From a practical perspective, there may also be many contractors who work for the same client and agency under one umbrella company. The umbrella company can manage the process better as a single point of contact and potentially a larger creditor.

The order in which creditors are paid in the UK is clearly laid down by statute and guidance from the Insolvency Service shows the payments made by an insolvent agency or client in liquidation are:

- The administrator's/receiver's/liquidator's fees and charges

- Preferential creditors, such as government departments like HMRC, employees wages owed in the four months before the insolvency and contributions to occupational pension schemes

- Secured creditors with a fixed charge over tangible assets, such as a bank lending money by a mortgage on land owned by the company

- Secured creditors with a floating charge, such as a bank that has lent money against assets such as stock and assets not included in the list of assets with a fixed charge

- General creditors, such as suppliers, which includes contractors, and lenders who have greater rights for recovering their losses than shareholders, such as preference capital holders

- Interest payable on any debts

- Shareholders in the agency or client, who in practice almost always receive nothing.

Remember, you are not an employee and are therefore counted as just a general creditor, or supplier, and as a result are almost at the bottom of the chain when it comes to payment.

If the worst has happened and your agent or client cannot pay, you should register your debt, then move on and focus on finding a new contract.

## 10.7.5 What to do when your umbrella company goes bust

Contractors should quickly cut their losses and move on if their umbrella company goes bust. However, they can and should be doing things well before their umbrella collapses to mitigate the impact on their personal finances.

When an umbrella solutions provider goes bust, it is usually because the business has run out of cash. So it is unlikely that you will ever see any monies owed, simply because there won't be the cash in the failed business to pay you. Just because umbrella company contractors are employees and not suppliers, which should in theory put you higher up the list of creditors, it makes no difference: if there is no cash in the business and no assets to liquidate, you're unlikely to see any money. It's tough, but if you're in this situation the sooner you deal with that fact, the better for your mental and financial wellbeing.

Umbrella companies' contractor clients are usually among the last people to find out that there is a problem. They typically find out when their umbrella company's customer services staff stop answering the phone. If you receive no response from your umbrella company, and you've checked with your agency and/or client with no positive news, you should not wait for any official confirmation but should switch umbrella company immediately. Waiting for the appointment of an administrator is leaving it too late. Resign from your existing umbrella company immediately and inform your agency or client of the situation, so that they can end their contract with the umbrella and stop making further payments to it.

It is those contractors who take steps to mitigate the impact and move on quickly who will minimise their financial loss. There can be warning signs, and one of the first of these is to look out for deals that look too good to be true. The government decides how much tax a contractor pays, not umbrella companies, so when you strip out fees and expenses, all contractors should take home pretty much the same percentage of contract value. So beware of umbrella companies making extravagant claims, as they may not be what they seem.

Another obvious warning sign is late or non-payment. If you don't get paid and the umbrella claims it is due to non-payment by the agency or client, this should set alarm bells ringing, because it suggests that the umbrella has a cashflow problem. You can easily check with your agency or client whether your umbrella company has been paid for work you have completed; and if the umbrella has been paid and is lying to you, this could mean the worst case scenario could be imminent.

By simply keeping on top of your administration, you can reduce to a minimum any losses you might suffer if your umbrella company goes bust. That means staying bang up-to-date with timesheets and submitting them regularly, so that the chances are the most you could lose is a week's or a month's pay.

### 10.7.6 When your client is taken over and the new owner won't approve your timesheets

When companies are taken over, employees usually transfer across to the new owner smoothly via the Transfer of Undertakings (Protection of Employment) Regulations, better known as TUPE. But being suppliers and not employees, contractors don't have this level of protection. If your contract does not include any clauses automatically transferring ('novating') the contract across to the new owner, you should be extremely wary of continuing to work without a valid contract. And if a new client project manager is appointed from the new owner's business who refuses to even sign your timesheets, it's time to take direct action.

Under normal circumstances, if no new contract has been sent and the original contract has expired and the client allows you to keep working, then you should be entitled to payment according to the contract previously in force. If you are working through an agency, if you have not opted out of the Conduct Regulations (Conduct of Employment Agencies and Employment Business Regulations 2003), then the agency should pay you, as it can't lawfully not pay a contractor for the time worked if the contractor has not opted out. However, you may have a fight on your hands to force the agency to pay, particularly if timesheets have not been authorised and the agency therefore can't invoice the client.

You need to sit down with the client and state that if you are expected to work, you expect a contract, so that you can be assured of payment. The agency should be willing and able to help with this, but if you let the situation drift, then there will be no urgency on the client to resolve the situation to your satisfaction.

### 10.7.7 When your agency refuses to pay an approved and signed timesheet

Unless there are specific provisions in the contract, which would be unusual, then the agency should not be able to legitimately withhold payment to a contractor once they have been presented with a timesheet approved by the client. A signed and approved timesheet will generally signify the client's acceptance of the time you have worked. In the absence of any qualifying note made on it by the client indicating any dissatisfaction, the approved timesheet would also generally constitute evidence that the client was satisfied that you had completed the work covered by the timesheet according to the contract.

If you have not opted out of the Conduct Regulations (Conduct of Employment Agencies and Employment Business Regulations 2003), then regulation 12 applies and the agency can't withhold payment if they have not been paid by the client.

So, if your client has signed the timesheet and accepted the work, then it's pretty clear that the agency is obliged to pay you. You should send a firm letter reminding the agency of its obligation to pay, and let it know that you will take legal action if payment is not forthcoming. It is probably also worth taking legal advice to confirm that there are no unusual provisions in your agency-contractor contract that might prevent payment, and then consider taking legal action to recover the unpaid fees.

### 10.7.8 When your umbrella company and agency change payment terms without your agreement

Contracting via an umbrella company can potentially place contractors at risk of losing control over the contractual relationship with their agency or client. Unlike when you contract via your own limited company, you are simply an employee of the umbrella company and have no authority to negotiate or make contractual agreements on its behalf.

Less scrupulous umbrella companies have been known to use this legal position to their advantage by negotiating contract terms with the agency that might be disadvantageous to the contractor. For example, perhaps in exchange for a reduction in timesheet levies, an umbrella might strike a deal with an agency to extend the agency's payment terms. The umbrella then passes these terms on to the contractor.

Should you find yourself in the situation of having your payment terms renegotiated without your agreement, you can take immediate action by changing umbrella company. The agency may try to put pressure on you by insisting that you stay, or that you use another of the umbrella companies on its preferred supplier list (PSL), but you may find exactly the same scenario then arises.

Under these circumstances, you may have to make a judgement call and call the agency's bluff, saying you won't use their umbrella and nor will you sign the contract or the renewal if the agency continues to insist on the unfavourable terms. Be prepared to follow through, but ensure the client knows exactly what has transpired and understands it is the agency's actions and not yours that have led to the contract or renewal falling through.

**CONTRACTING MINDSET TIPS:**
**If you don't like it, just quit and move on**
As an employee, employment law provides limited protection from bad managers and none against sheer boredom. Highly skilled contractors unhappy with their work associates or unfulfilled by their work, can simply choose to quit and find another contract.

**Would you hang around for more abuse from a bullying boss?**
You've hired a highly recommended local electrician to rewire your house. If you treat her like a skivvy, demanding she also cuts the lawn, do you think she'll complete your project?

As a highly trained 'big-four' forensic accountant, you can take your pick of plum jobs. So why would you hang around putting up with a boss who regularly yells at you and finds fault with perfect work?

Let's say you've few formal skills, you're on minimum wage and spent six months getting on the preferred temp list, only to find that each day your responsibilities increase but your pay does not. Are you going to sign up for another week's work?

**Employment is a double-edged sword**
Your employer can, within reason, pretty much tell you what to do, when to do it and precisely how. So if you are moved onto less important and interesting projects, but your job description does not change, then that's tough, and you probably aren't able to do anything about it.

Even highly skilled professional employees can find themselves saddled with an abusive manager and ironically, the higher up the professional and managerial ladder you are, the less likely it is that you'll be able to do anything about it.

As an unskilled or low skilled temporary worker, you are one among millions of UK workers from which employers can pick and choose. You might be expected to perform all sorts of additional tasks not reflected in your pay, but you have to accept that state of affairs if you want to keep the assignment.

**Contractors are highly skilled, in demand and can move on quickly**
But it's not like that for contractors, who run independent businesses, are not employees, and cannot be told what to do, or when and how to do it. As a contractor, you have invested in developing expert skills to enhance your contracting career and, when these are in greater demand, they often command high rates of pay.

If you are prudent, you ensure you earn more than you spend, which allows you to build a substantial buffer for downtime. That also means you can leave an assignment immediately if it is not working out, as you will have the cash to tide you over when finding new work, which will happen quickly with your highly developed skills.

And if you don't like the people you work with, or the nature of the assignment is less challenging than you had expected, just quit and go find another, better contract. Or alternatively, if the weather is nice, sit in the garden or on a beach counting your money for a few weeks.

**Contractors who invest to develop their skills can choose to quit and move on when a contract no longer meets their expectations.**

### 10.7.9 When your agency insists on paying you only when it has been paid

The arrangement between a contractor limited company, or an umbrella company, and an agency is a business-to-business transaction and not an employment relationship. So that means your agency can effectively put what it likes in the draft contract, including a clause saying you will only be paid when the agency gets paid by the client. However, one of the fundamental reasons that many contractors use an agency is so they don't suffer from payment issues relating to the client, so you don't have to agree and sign any contract you don't like the look of.

If you come across a clause like this, you should ask your agent about it at the outset – there may be a perfectly good reason, or the client may even require it. There could also be a perfectly sinister one, such as underlying cashflow issues with the agency or even the client. That's why you should address the issue as part of your negotiation process

In the event that you did not opt out of the Conduct Regulations (Conduct of Employment Agencies and Employment Business Regulations 2003), then it is unlawful for your agency to withhold payment on the grounds that it has not been paid. If a worker, ie you, is covered by the Conduct Regulations, then the employment business that is providing their services to the end client, your agency, cannot refuse to pay the worker, even if the client has not paid the employment business, as long as the worker has completed the assignment correctly.

### 10.7.10 When your client insists on paying only when it has been paid

If you are working as a subcontractor for another contractor, or working for a larger business delivering its services on a subcontract basis to its end clients, you may be told that you'll be paid when your client is paid by its client. Unless there is an express provision in the contract that states this, your client should still pay on time, or the provisions of the late payment legislation will apply.

If you find a 'pay when paid' clause in your contract, the advice would generally be to reject it. That's because a clause stating that the contractor will only get paid when their agency or client is paid means what it says, and most contractors probably would not want to accept that provision and suffer many months of waiting for payment, or of not being paid at all.

## 10.7.11 When your client tries to cut your rates during a contract

When economic conditions start to worsen, clients may try to impose an across the board rate cut on all their contractors. Clients with large contractor workforces, which can number in the tens of thousands, will typically send a letter announcing a 10% to 20% rate cut, and instructing contractors to take it or be terminated. Across the board rate cuts like these are particularly prevalent in the UK's financial services sector. When rate cuts like these first started happening in 2000, it was a take-it-now-or-be-terminated arrangement. More recently, it has been done less aggressively by giving people a notice period, or more commonly being told that at renewal time they have to take the rate cut.

Of course, contracting rates do fluctuate according to market conditions and the supply and demand for certain skills. When clients perceive supply exceeds demand, they may try to save costs with blanket cost-cutting measures. But contractors are not all commodities, and those who have invested in acquiring skills and experience in high demand can use their differentiation to their benefit. The bottom line is that you need not simply give in and accept enforced rate cuts when faced with clients who want to reduce their own overheads.

There are plenty of examples of how contractors have held onto or even increased rates during tough times. However, you should also be prepared to be flexible, particularly if the contract market for your skills is slow. You might feel, for instance, that a lower-paying contract is better than no contract at all.

If you are on the receiving end of a letter or email from your client demanding a rate cut you should:

- Not panic, or just roll over and accept the rate cut – keep calm and carry on!

- Not take it personally – contractors are business services providers and not employees; it's just business

- Understand that there is no loyalty in contracting; to the client contractors are suppliers and not employees; to the contractor, clients are just that – clients

- Understand that the email is the first stage in a business negotiation.

Under no circumstances should you 'shoot from the hip' with an immediate response. You should carefully consider the available strategies you can adopt to deal with a rate cut demand. The choice of strategy will depend on an individual contractor's skills, experience and circumstances. But, for most contractors, there are alternatives to simply accepting a rate cut. These include:

- **Calling their bluff:** If you have exceptional skills and experience without which the project might fail, or at least stall, you can respond with something like: "Thank you for your letter, but I am confident that the services I provide remain of excellent value. In addition, I have increased my skills base during the contract period, and we are not prepared to reduce our prices going forward. In fact, we were planning to increase rates by X% in line with inflation. However, as a sign of goodwill we will not increase our prices, but confirm that we will not be decreasing them either." When considering this strategy, you should also have, or be confident of quickly acquiring, a new contract.

- **Lining up another contract:** There is no need for you to be 'loyal' to your client and carry on working for it after the contract end date. Business is business. Do some market research about the buoyancy of the contract market and going rates for your particular skills and experience. Get your up-to-date CV out to agencies and work your online and offline networks. Gauge the level of interest and line up some alternative contracts. Then, if calling the client's bluff does not work, you can walk away into the new contract.

- **Letting the agency take the strain:** Agencies make margins on contractor day rates. It is possible the agency will take a cut in its margin if it keeps you in the contract. If you have another role lined up with a different agency, this can be a powerful ploy. However, some agencies have fixed margins agreed with the client.

- **Cut costs elsewhere:** There are other ways to make cost savings. If you are confident of your value to the project, you could suggest to your client project manager that costs are cut elsewhere. This could mean: suggesting a non-essential part of the project is scaled back; terminating another contractor on the team who is underperforming; or the entire project team reducing the number of days worked each month.

If you can foresee rate cuts on the horizon, which have yet to be enacted, you should consider pre-empting the cuts and putting into place some of the above strategies in advance.

Remember also that as a limited company contractor you are a small business and don't enjoy the benefits of employment rights. That means you can be vulnerable to sharp business practices that, in extreme cases, can devolve into dirty tricks by clients seeking to cut costs. You should beware of:

- **Client not signing the final timesheet:** If no compromise can be reached and you decide to leave, or are terminated by the client, pack your 'escape pod'. During the termination period, make sure you get the final timesheet signed, plus retain copies of any emails from client project managers confirming that any final work has been completed according to specification and schedule.

- **Beware breach of contract:** Having secured another contract, and having been terminated, beware of any attempts by clients to place you in breach of contract due to non-performance. This is a classic client tactic designed to save a month's worth of fees. Pay special attention to performing your duties exactly as requested and securing proof, such as project sign-offs and confirmation emails. If the client does try this on, you could make a counter offer to take half the termination period fees in exchange for the promise that you won't litigate against the client.

- **Contractors aren't in unions, so don't always share with other contractors:** Even though they don't have unions, contractors can effectively work together to combat a particularly unreasonable client. On smaller projects, where the rate cut is not organisation-wide, this can be effective. But in most large client organisations, it is every contractor for themself. One contractor's skill set might keep them out of pay cut territory, where the next ten on the same project will have no option because they are more expendable.

It is never pleasant for contractors to suffer rate reductions. But by adopting a rate reduction response strategy, you can push back and secure a good deal either with your existing client, or with a fresh one.

## 10.8 Finances, accountants and umbrellas

### 10.8.1 When your accountant (or umbrella) messes up and costs you money in fines

Your accountant can be your best ally in your contracting career. Much useful advice about how to structure and grow your business is to be gleaned from the accountant, particularly if they've dealt with lots of contractors in the past.

But accountants do make errors. For example, you might find that yours has failed to file forms in time and you've been fined for it by HMRC or Companies House.

If this is entirely the responsibility of the accountant, and in no way the result of your failing to supply information, then you have a right to compensation. The accountant knows this, so a little insistence will suffice in most cases.

If you work with a chartered accountant, and you're not happy with the result, you have an inalienable right to change accountants. Notify the old one with a letter, pay the last of their fees, and switch to the new one. The old accountant is obliged to provide the new one with all necessary information.

You are paying your umbrella company to process your pay efficiently and accurately – that is one of their major reasons for existence. Should you spot an error or if you attract the attention of HMRC, then ensure they correct it.

Reputable umbrella companies have a finance and HR department, like a regular employer, who exist to act on your behalf as a representative to HMRC. If you feel like they are not doing this, either tell them firmly you are paying for the service or vote with your feet and change umbrella.

### 10.8.2 When your accountant makes it difficult for you to stop using their services

This is a rare occurrence, but it does happen. Moving accountants should not be a difficult process, in fact accountants have a duty to ensure the process is as painless as possible, but sometimes your old accountant can make things difficult if they hold a grudge against you, or more usually if they feel you terminated their services unfairly and/or that you still owe them money.

As with every dispute, the first step should be to ask nicely and try to settle the issue amicably. However, all chartered accountants are governed by the code of conduct of their professional institute.

If the dispute cannot be resolved amicably, then you should find out which accountancy body your ex-accountant belongs to and contact them regarding their mediation services. The institute will investigate the circumstances and arbitrate, so you should be very sure of your position and that you are in the right.

## 10.9 Difficult situations in your client's workplace

### 10.9.1 When you are being harassed and threatened by one of your client's employees

Contractors are not employees and have no employment rights. This means that if you are being harassed, physically threatened by, or suffering abuse from one of your client's employees, you cannot use your client's employee grievance process; in fact any attempt to do so could put your IR35 status in jeopardy (assuming you are working outside IR35).

However, although you may have no employment rights and want to avoid any indications that you are an employee, you do have rights under health and safety legislation, which applies to all workers and does not distinguish between employees and contractors. Your client has a duty to provide a safe working environment for you.

You should detail the situation in writing to your project manager to inform the client about your concerns about health and safety. In the event anything should happen to you, the client will be liable and in default for not taking reasonable action despite being warned by you.

Many contractor and consultant contracts include clauses that place an obligation on the client to provide a safe working environment. Contractors can, and should, have an added layer of protection by including a clause detailing that the client, their servants and agents are responsible for maintaining a safe working environment.

If you are assaulted by a client's employee you must report the incident to the police immediately. Then you are in a position to make claims against both the client's employee who committed the assault on you, as well as against the client.

The assault is not just a criminal matter, it is also civil matter. You can, in effect, make a personal injury claim and, because you had warned the client in writing and they have not taken reasonable action to protect you following your warning.

Of course the hope is that you need not take any action apart from warning the client in writing. In most cases the client will deal effectively with your concerns.

## 10.9.2 When you suffer discrimination by one of your client's employees or another contractor

Limited company contractors encountering discrimination or harassment in the workplace unfortunately have few options. That is because, as a business-to-business services provider, you do not enjoy the same protection as employees. In fact, a limited company contractor taking action under equalities legislation via an employment tribunal or refusing to work alongside other workers because of discrimination would have to deal with the commercial repercussions, which could ultimately lead to a breach of contract, or make the claim worthless.

The equalities legislation in theory offers protection for all workers but it is not possible to discriminate against a limited company. So, if you chose to pursue a claim through an employment tribunal as an individual, because as a contract worker you have that right, it could call into question your status as a genuine business-to-business service provider, and therefore your IR35 status.

And whilst in theory umbrella company contractors should have a greater level of protection as employees of their umbrella companies, in practice there is little the umbrella company can do.

The first step if you are enduring harassment or discrimination on your client's site is to discuss the issue with your client project manager, with the aim of 'shutting down' any incidents before they escalate. Although discrimination and harassment are not acceptable in any workplace, the perpetrator may not realise they are harassing co-workers, or that their actions are having a negative impact. A quiet word with the client project manager, who can then have a quiet word with the offending co-worker, is frequently all it takes to defuse a situation. This typically also prevents escalation of the situation, ensuring that legal options are not considered necessary.

In practical terms, a large service provider that has workers who are being harassed can simply remove their employees from the end-client's location. The business itself can walk away from the contract and can afford to deal with the legal fall-out. But for small service providers, like you, this can cause commercial repercussions and even legal issues unrelated to equalities legislation. That's because it is unlikely that there is a termination clause between your limited company and the agency or end client that allows for termination on the grounds of your employees, ie you, being harassed.

So if you simply walked away and terminated the agreement on those grounds, your limited company would be in breach of contract for failing to supply your services as specified.

The 'nuclear option' is for you to take your discrimination or harassment case to an employment tribunal. But this option is fraught with risk – not only of failure but also of other repercussions. Contractors taking their clients to an employment tribunal for an alleged discrimination claim are likely to be terminated by their client, and the tribunal route also won't help when they try to find a new contract and have to rely on a reference from the client they just tried to sue. The reputational risk is significant.

The equalities legislation provides protection for all workers, regardless of their status. However, the realities for contractors tackling discrimination and harassment in their workplaces are tough.

## 10.10 When your personal life overlaps into your contracting

There are times when you can't help your personal life overlapping into your work life. When you were an employee, your employer would be obliged to be considerate to some of your personal problems, to varying degrees. But when you are a contractor, you are just another a business-to-business supplier, so if you fail to turn up and perform your duties as contracted, technically your client could take you to task for breach of contract.

### 10.10.1 When you become too ill to work

As a limited company contractor, you are a business supplier and not an employee. That means in the unfortunate event that you became too ill to work, you are not delivering the services as stated in the contract and you are technically in breach of contract. The client could sue your company for damages as a result of your breach of contract.

However, in practice, in the vast majority of cases a client would be more interested in finding a replacement to get the job done than chasing after an ill contractor for compensation. And because virtually all contractor limited companies will have limited liability, you will not be personally liable. The client could claim against your limited company's assets, which are likely to be simply cash in the bank, so you could still effectively walk away and start a new company for the next contract when you have recovered.

Most clients and agencies accept that people sometimes fall ill and that the contractor is not trying to deliberately sabotage a client's project, and so are unlikely to take a contractor to court for non-delivery. You would most likely find that your contract is terminated early and with immediate effect, while the client will work with the agency to quickly find a replacement to minimise any negative impact on the client's project.

## 10.10.2 When you have been chosen for jury service

Contractors can be chosen at random for jury service and, just like any other UK citizen, it is a statutory responsibility. If you are called for jury service, you are legally obliged to attend court.

You would normally be required to serve for ten days, or potentially even longer if a trial takes weeks or even months to resolve. During the period of jury service, you are likely to be unable to work, or can only work for part of your day. This not only results in a loss of earnings, but technically a client could claim breach of contract if you are unable to provide your services. Fortunately, such a claim would be tenuous and is unlikely to be well received by a court. So in most cases the client and agency accept that you are unable to perform your services for the period of service.

It is possible for you to be excused from jury service, or have your service deferred, but each situation is judged by the court's summoning officer and a request can be refused. However, you stand a good chance of being excused from jury service if you request it, particularly if you have a mission-critical role. For example, a specialist MoD security cleared contractor completing the final software patch on a vital weapons system who would be impossible to replace at short notice is likely to be granted a deferment.

The situation is different for umbrella company contractors, who have an obligation to inform their employer – their umbrella company – first. What happens next depends on the umbrella company's policies. If you are working for a compliant umbrella company with a full employment contract in place, and can call on its human resources professionals for support, the HR team will be able to advise on what relevant policies are in place.

It is also possible for workers engaged in jury service to claim a range of expenses back from HM Court Service. This might provide adequate compensation for loss of earning if you are on a lower hourly rate, but you are likely to be left well out of pocket if you are a higher earner. You can take out an insurance policy to cover loss of earnings during a period of jury service, but it probably won't cover the potential loss of earnings as a result of a long trial.

### 10.10.3 When you become pregnant

Pregnancy is a joyous occasion and not an occasion when something has gone wrong for a contractor, but it's included here as this section is the best 'fit'.

If you are a pregnant contractor you may face challenges you would not face if you were employed. And the situation for limited company contractors may be different than that for umbrella company contractors.

If you discover you are pregnant when you are in a contract, your pregnancy is unlikely to cause you any problems as long as the contract will be completed before your due date or the date when you are planning to start your maternity leave. Because you are a service provider and not an employee, your client has absolutely no obligation to you other than obligations under its statutory responsibilities, for example health and safety legislation.

Your client certainly does not have to provide you with any maternity benefits, and if your contract is not due to end until after you are having your baby, your company will technically be in breach of contract because you are failing to deliver the services you have contractually agreed to deliver.

This is also true if you want to start your maternity leave before the contract is complete. You agreed at the outset that your company would deliver your services for specified period. The fact that it can't complete the contract because you are pregnant is irrelevant to your client; your inability to complete the contract is what is important. If you have a contract termination clause, it should be exercised.

Furthermore, if you knew you were pregnant before starting a contract that will run beyond your due date, you are entering into an agreement that you have no intention of fulfilling, and so are potentially guilty of misrepresentation. The agency or client may have the right to seek compensation from you for failing to complete the contract.

But the reality is that your client is unlikely to sue for breach of contract and will be more interested in finding a substitute or replacement for when you start your maternity leave.

For umbrella company contractors, the contractual issues are much the same; but they will affect your umbrella company because it has the relationship with the client or agency, and not you directly. In fact, if your umbrella company is fully compliant, you will have a full contract of employment. This means that you may qualify for the full range of maternity benefits, which include time off for antenatal care, maternity leave, maternity pay and a raft of measures designed to protect pregnant workers' rights.

# Contracting lessons from this chapter

- The signed contract is king – don't work without one.

- If you enter freely into a contract with an agency or a client, you have an obligation to fulfil the contract. Avoid breaching contracts yourself, but make it clear when others have breached the contract.

- Contracts cannot be changed during the contract unless through mutual agreement with the contractor, agency and client.

- Although you do not have employment rights as a contractor, your business does have rights under contract law. Clients and agencies cannot unilaterally make changes to contracts. Learn the basics of contract law to help combat disputes

- If you are terminated unfairly, you can seek compensation from your agency or client for breach of contract.

- Learn to spot the warning signs of agencies or clients in financial trouble. Put into place loss mitigation strategies to combat payment problems early, and follow correct process when collecting debts.

- Agencies must abide by strict confidentiality rules and cannot share your details with anyone without your permission.

# 11

# Advanced marketing and sales

# 11.1 Marketing yourself

A new contractor often has red hot skills, and is in high demand, so even if they have objectionable personal habits someone is likely to hire them! The problem comes later when they have not kept their skills up to date and/or the market demand has dropped. An alternative scenario might be where there are plenty of contracts for everyone, but only a few plum contracts that everybody really wants.

In the run-up to the dot com crash, any IT contractor with experience was being hired. After the crash, there was a mass migration of contractors back to permanent roles; but many of the most successful survivors were those best at sales and marketing and not necessarily the most highly skilled.

The key to success in contracting is to remain as a highly paid contractor for the long term, preferably for your entire working life. How do you keep your skills updated? How do you manage your money? How do you secure contracts when demand falls?

The main message is to learn some business skills that might be outside your core expertise – typically, this means getting to grips with marketing and sales. They are invaluable skills that are likely to keep you in profitable, enjoyable and rewarding contracts for as long as you want them. It's about marketing and selling yourself better than anyone else. It's also about not joining the club of the most highly skilled contractors who seldom manage to secure the best contracts.

So you've started contracting, had your first or second contract, and you're beginning to appreciate your new lifestyle and earnings. But key worries never go away: will you always have enough work? Will you always make enough money? Being in business for yourself means that these worries are always there, especially in the early days. But your worst fears need never be realised if you market yourself well.

Contracting is a business like any other, in which you have to market your business, negotiate contracts, make sales and generally keep on top of many competing calls on your time. The contractors who learn these skills are the ones who stay in business, win the most contracts and have a choice of the best contracts. Those who don't often end up back in a permanent job, with the lack of flexibility and lower earnings that brings with it.

## 11.1.1 Your personal marketing plan

There is a discipline to marketing yourself. You need to constantly push yourself out into the marketplace, even when working on a contract, because that contract will eventually come to an end and you will need to have the next contract lined up. So here is a framework for your personal marketing plan:

**Network:** Keep in touch with your client contacts and other contractors you meet on the job, and make sure you add them to your networks on professional social media sites such as LinkedIn. You need to be the first person the client thinks of when they are looking to fill a role. Maintaining contact with other contractors can mean you have a sales force online and in the field doing your marketing and selling for you.

This works both ways, so if you can put in a good word for a fellow contractor that helps win them a contract, they will remember you and are likely to return the favour. After about five years, you will find you win lots of your contracts this way.

**Update your CV, LinkedIn and other profiles regularly:** Make sure you update your CV and social network profiles with your latest contract details and skills. Ensure that your updated CV is also visible on the key job boards on the internet. Even if you are in a contract, your profile should still be highly visible. This keeps the calls coming from agents and prospective clients, who increasingly look to LinkedIn and other online professional networks to find contract candidates.

**Meet with agents:** Most contracts are secured through agents, so it pays to maintain a relationship with key agencies. Be helpful to agents when you can; for example, if they call and you are not available, then refer them to a friend who may be. The agent might return the favour when you are looking for a new contract. It is also well worth creating and maintaining a list of agents you get on well with and emailing them close to the time when you will be looking for a new contract.

If you receive a 'Join my network' request from an agent, conduct a little due diligence to ensure they are bona fide and not just fishing for your contacts. If you do accept, you may find you are higher on their list of contractors to contact when they receive a relevant client brief.

**Market yourself via a website and white papers:** The cost of building and maintaining a website is small compared to the potential rewards of a new contract. In addition, having your own online presence reinforces your position of being in business in your own right, a strong factor in keeping you outside IR35. Take the opportunity to write and publish white papers on topics associated with your skill set. Many websites are desperate for good content and you can raise your profile by authoring thought leadership pieces. This will attract the attention of other people in your field who may contact you with work.

**Work on your publicity:** In addition to white papers, publicise yourself by writing articles for websites, blogs and trade media. Create work-related accounts on Twitter, Pinterest, etc and send out regular, relevant and informative links to useful business information. Also constructively interact with them online – they're called 'social' networks for a reason! Aim to become an industry commentator in your area of contracting and actively encourage journalists to contact you for expert opinion. The publicity will raise your profile and ensure your CV is top of the pile for agents and clients. You're also likely to be able to negotiate higher rates more successfully; after all, you're THE expert in the field!

**Market yourself on the job:** Make sure the client knows how much value you are adding to their operation and invest a little extra time in doing things that are not strictly in your contract – although not too much, for tax reasons that are explained in chapter 9. Let the client know what you are doing and blow your own trumpet, as no one else will; then ask for testimonials and LinkedIn recommendations. Don't forget that other contractors can be a valuable source of leads, so cultivate your colleagues. If you can do them a favour, do it, as it will be remembered and could work to your advantage.

**Look the part:** Appearance is a large part of the battle. Get the look, and you'll get the work. It involves some effort, but once you've done it, you'll be amazed how a smart suit and the other trappings of being a professional businessperson will help you win contracts.

The objective of your marketing should be to ensure you have a stream of contract leads ready for when you finish the job you are currently on.

### 11.1.2 What are your features and benefits?

You will often hear sales or marketing people talking about 'features and benefits'. As a contractor selling a 'product', your knowledge, you'll need to be aware of your own features and benefits and ensure you explain these to both the agent and client. You should also be able to recognise when sales or marketing people, like agents, are introducing features and benefits in an attempt to sell you something, such as a contract you wouldn't normally choose to take on.

Marketing and sales training allows people to use a process and a formula that provides the most effective way of communicating a message with a positive outcome. Part of this process will always include mentioning the features of a product or service and describing the benefits of each feature. This may sound straightforward, but a common mistake made by many salespeople is to mention the feature and to forget to mention the benefit, or vice versa.

Remember that features and benefits enable a clear description of a product, like you, in such a way that it allows potential clients to easily and quickly agree to offer a contract. If parts of the process are missed out, the client may be confused and will probably not buy.

Firstly, what is a feature and what is a benefit? A good example to use is a car. The features of this product would include:

- Power steering
- Electric windows
- MP3 player
- Liquid petroleum gas engine.

It is important to mention these features to a potential customer, as they may not be aware that the product they are thinking of buying has them. When they discover these new features, the customer might be tempted enough to buy. However, mentioning just the features is not enough and will almost certainly not make the sale.

This is where benefits come in.

For every feature, there is at least one benefit and generally many. Benefits may not always be obvious, and what is obvious to you (the salesperson) is not necessarily so to others (your customers). The basic benefits associated with the features listed above are:

- Power steering – the key benefit to the customer being 'it's so much easier to drive'

- Electric windows – the key benefit to the customer being 'you never have to wind down the windows manually'

- MP3 player – the key benefit to the customer being 'you can listen to all your own music'

- Liquid petroleum gas engine – the key benefit to the customer being 'it's much cheaper than petrol or diesel, so travel costs come down'.

Much of the above will seem quite straightforward and largely common sense. All the same, many salespeople neglect this area of their pitches and lose sales as a consequence. When you are being sold to and features are mentioned without the benefits – ask the salesperson what the benefit is. If you don't have the facts, you cannot make an informed decision and the salesperson is not doing their job!

Often when people are trained on this area of a pitch, they make a massive list of features and benefits and then do little more than list them to their potential clients. This is not the way to sell. One of the most fundamental parts of the sales process is the fact finding – doing some research and listening to what features and benefits the customer actually wants.

Before presenting any features or benefits, a good salesperson will have already asked many questions of the prospective customer. The answers to these questions will suggest to the salesperson which particular features and benefits are likely to influence their decision, or not.

So, when selling a car, the salesperson will try and find out what is most important to their customer. If the customer indicates that they are conscious of high travel costs, then a car that runs economically on LPG is worth pointing out. If the customer mentions they're looking for something that's easy to drive, then power steering and electric windows are good features to introduce.

In the contracting world recruitment agents will try to sell the contract to you by first establishing which of your buttons to press, and then by explaining the features and benefits of the contract that align with your magic buttons. Conversely, you should do exactly the same with both the agent and client. This is why you need to ask lots of questions and listen carefully to the answers, to find out what those buttons are.

Your sales pitch should always be tailored to each customer as far as possible, be they a client or agent. Find out what they need or desire, and why, then clearly match the answers they give you with the relevant features and benefits you offer.

## 11.2 Effective sales

Part of the effort to secure lucrative contracts – a crucial part, in fact – is learning how to sell. To a highly educated and skilled contractor like you, selling may seem 'demeaning'. Get over it! Because, on the contrary, selling is the best affirmation that you are good at what you do. All it involves is you learning how to convince people of what you already know: that you can do a good job.

So, as a contractor marketing your expertise, you are going to have to sell yourself. Unfortunately, sales as a profession gets a bad press. But there is a great difference between a professional salesperson and a conman. A salesperson knows how to best present what there is to sell; a conman lies about it.

You should not make the mistake of feeling bad about selling yourself, as all business depends on sales. Sales is the method of presenting a product or service in the most positive light, helping the potential customer see that the product or service meets or exceeds their needs, maintaining control over the 'sales process' and ultimately achieving the highest level of profit together with delivering the highest level of customer satisfaction.

Once you're in the game, the better you can sell yourself, the more work you'll win, the greater the number of contracts you can choose from, and the more money you will earn on each contract.

It's true that your skills are the principal selling point for your contracting. But there's no point having great cutting-edge skills if you're sitting at home waiting for an agent to call.

It sounds obvious, but is worth stating: the contractors who win the contracts are the ones who know how to find them in the first place and how to go about having them offered at a great rate. Something else to bear in mind is that these contractors are not necessarily the best candidates for those plum contracts; they're sometimes just the best when it comes to winning contracts. It's all down to their sales and marketing skills.

There are plenty of exceptional contractors who find it difficult to secure a regular flow of contracts, or are working for less than they are worth simply because they are unable to successfully sell their product – themselves.

Contractors with little or no sales experience often wrongly believe that competitive pricing is the sole key to securing business. This is untrue. Most clients will expect to pay the market price for the services they need, and they have budgeted for it, although bizarrely there are always a few clients who expect something for nothing. But that does not mean you have to behave like a monkey and get paid peanuts!

If you learn and apply sales techniques, you will maximise your chances of securing contracts and of making the most money. And in addition to the advantages of using a professional sales approach to your contract searches, you will also find the sales experience useful for other areas of your contracting career.

Being able to formulate and sell a winning argument will prove very useful for getting your ideas adopted. In addition, your sales knowledge will help you to build a good reputation and a network of contacts, which are invaluable in the long term for obtaining work directly or via recommendation.

## 11.2.1 Using a sales process

The sales process is a clear and structured way to introduce and to sell a product. It is a step-by-step approach that takes the seller from the introduction to follow-up on the sale. A typical sales process employed by recruitment consultants when selling a position to a contractor is as follows:

- The recruitment consultant will match a CV to a current position

- The recruitment consultant contacts the candidate and introduces themselves

- The introduction explains the nature of the call, the business of the agency and what the consultant is looking to do, to arrange an interview with the contractor for the position

- The contractor needs to be 'qualified' for the contract, which in the consultant's terms means: is the contractor looking for a new position?: are they qualified to carry out the work?: do they charge an acceptable rate?; and are they interested in the contract?

- The recruitment consultant then interviews the contractor, normally via phone and in the same call:

  - The recruitment consultant assesses the contractor's ability to carry out the work and how successful they feel the contractor will be at an interview

  - The recruitment consultant must 'sell' the position to the contractor

- The recruitment consultant must then 'sell' the contractor to their client. They will send over the CV for the contractor, which may well have been modified to represent the contractor in a better light for this position, and must convince their client that the contractor is worthy of an interview

- The recruitment consultant then prepares the contractor for the interview process. This will include providing background material for the contractor about the client and the role

- After being offered the position, the recruitment consultant will then attempt to negotiate the rate of pay for the contractor with the highest margin they can get for their agency

- The final job is for the recruitment consultant to further convince their client that the contractor is the best person for the job and that the rate is acceptable. At the same time, the recruitment consultant must also convince the contractor that this is the best role for them and at the highest rate of pay

- On agreement from both sides, the deal is closed and contracts are signed.

Of course, this simplifies a much more complex process. But the advantage of this model is that you can track each stage of the sale and ensure that the necessary action has been taken for each step.

You need to maximise your impact in each step of this process. All experienced and successful contractors have developed their own sales process when searching for contracts. They might not have formalised it and written it down, but over the years they will have fine-tuned a process that works for them.

The agent will try to sell you the contract and you are trying to sell yourself to the agent. So there are sales techniques employed on both sides.

## 11.2.2 Fact Finding

When you are being sold to, be aware that you are probably not being presented with all of the facts. It is not the job of the salesperson to tell you everything about what you are about to buy, it is their job to sell it. Don't be too alarmed by this, it is just business and quite normal.

So when you are being sold to, it is your job to discover the information the salesperson has not told you. Ask lots of questions and always question detail. The agent might not have too much detail about the contract and could over-promise. You should ensure you verify these facts at any subsequent interview with the client.

In contracting this works both ways. For example, the agent might not want to tell you that the last five contractors hired by the client left in disgust after the first day. Similarly, a contractor might not want to tell the agent how they totally messed up their last project and were escorted off the premises!

### 11.2.3 Buying signals

When you are being sold to, the salesperson is looking for buying signals. These are signals that you make, often involuntarily, that indicate that you wish to buy the product. The buying signal relates to the reason you may have for buying.

For example, when buying a new car, it may be the running costs that are most important to you or it could be the speed at which the car drives. The salesperson does not know why each customer is looking to buy and so needs to find out by talking to you.

Once they have found your touch point, you are likely to give off buying signals. To make life hard for the salesperson, practice dealing with salespeople and giving away none of your feelings. This can be quite difficult, but you will see the salesperson get frustrated.

This is actually a very useful skill to develop. When you're speaking to an agent after an interview, for example, it may not be wise to tell them how ecstatic you are about the contract and that you would love to start straight away. This is sending the agent clear buying signals, that may result in you being offered a lower rate, with the agent enjoying higher margins.

Like all salespeople, agents have targets to meet and so want you to sign the deal now. Never allow yourself to be rushed into signing up for a position you have been offered. Sophisticated closing techniques can often manipulate you into signing when you may not have been ready to commit. Take your time, digest the information you are receiving and try and take a balanced view. It is easy to be caught up in the moment and salespeople not only know it, but have also been trained to exploit it.

If you have been offered a position, agents will certainly try every trick in the book to persuade you to sign, as they are eager to earn their commission. You, of course, can use your own closing techniques to exploit their eagerness, and so obtain a higher rate or improved terms.

### 11.2.4 Body language

The majority of your discussions with agents will be over the phone, but body language will be important for you during the interview stage, when you become the salesperson. Body language can reveal much that is hidden, a fact that is widely understood in the sales industry and manipulated by salespeople to good effect. A salesperson is often taught to mirror the same body language that their customer is displaying, as this makes people feel more connected and eases the atmosphere.

Your body language also gives away a lot about how you are feeling. When you are being sold to, be aware of your body language and make sure that it is neutral. Neutral means not sitting forward, rubbing your hands and looking like you are just about to reach for your wallet on the one hand, and on the other not slumping back in your seat and looking like you are about to fall asleep. You want something in between that does not give anything away.

Despite how professional you may look when turning up for interview, if you yawn and appear like you are not really listening, you will not be taken seriously!

## 11.2.5 Open questions

As a contractor trying to secure a contract, asking open ended questions of your agent or client during an interview is key to your fact finding, so that you can tailor your sales approach accordingly. One of the most important aspects of sales is asking the right questions of your potential client. If you don't ask questions, you are merely guessing or assuming the needs and desires of the person you are selling to.

The answers will indicate which points to cover, and which to leave out. By asking the right questions, you can also control the dialogue and guide your customer into a closing situation, where you can ask for the business, having covered all the necessary points.

When you speak to agents over the phone you will quickly need to establish what the client is looking for and then convince the agent that you are perfect for the role. When you reach the interview you will need to do the same with the client.

So how do you do this? Well, in a selling situation, you need to allow your client to open up to you and give you the clues and insights into what will make them buy. This is achieved largely by using open ended, or open, questions. The opposite is a 'closed question'. Let's look at examples of both, from the situation when a recruitment consultant is pitching a new contract to you:

*Open ended question:* 'What type of role are you looking for?'

*Closed question:* 'Would you consider a role for £20 per hour?'

The major difference between these two is that one of the questions can be answered with a one word answer, or more dangerously in any sales situation, with the answer 'no'! That question was of course the closed question. The open ended question does not allow you to say 'yes' or 'no'; it prompts you to start opening up and providing the recruitment consultant with information that will enable him or her to sell to you.

With the closed question, the recruitment consultant may have lost the chance to place the contractor. It may have been the case that the contract being offered did not offer the best income, but perhaps the skills being used in this contract may have been of particular interest to the contractor, or the contract timings fitted in perfectly with a planned holiday. So, they may have considered the contract, but have already said 'no', and so the opportunity is lost to both parties.

You will almost certainly have experienced telesales representatives attempting to sell you all kinds of products over the phone. A well trained salesperson will always attempt to make you open up and start talking about yourself with open ended questions. A poor salesperson will simply ask something like 'are you interested in double glazing', to which you and 99.99% of the population will reply, quite simply – 'no'!

Understanding and recognising open ended questions can help you to make people open up, and as an added benefit can also help you to deal with irritating salespeople! The next time someone contacts you, introduces themselves as someone you don't know and then asks an open ended question, you have the ability to stop the salesperson from controlling the dialogue. Rather than answering the question (and of course there is no law that says you must answer questions at all), be direct and say: 'Please stop, and tell me what you are selling?'

This is likely to put the salesperson off their stride, as they won't want you to know the nature of the call at this stage. First they want to lure you in a little further before presenting their product or solution to a problem you were not even aware that you had! The salesperson's answer to the direct question of 'what are you selling' will often, again, not be a straight answer. So, ask again until the salesperson tells you what they are selling. Now, you have more control over the conversation.

As a contractor you will need to deal with open ended questions that the agent asks you, that perhaps you do not want to answer. For example, "what is the lowest rate you will accept?". You will also need to learn how to ask open ended questions to gain as much information as you can in order to tailor your responses to maximise your sales pitch, from securing an interview all the way through to negotiating the rate and the terms and conditions of your contract.

There is, though, an important place for the closed question. Once the salesperson has completed asking their open ended questions and extracted the information they need from you, they can then pitch their product and deal with any objections you might have, which is covered in the next section about objection handling.

It is then time for the 'close', which is covered in section 11.2.7. And here a close can certainly be a closed question like, 'would you like to order the product?', although more commonly the salesperson would use an "assumptive close" and ask, 'what quantity of the product would you like to order?'.

Open and closed questions are certainly not new and are found in many aspects of life. We have all attended dinner parties where you sit next to the boring guest who answers all of your questions with one word answers. The antidote to this guest is of course the open ended question. You can, with practice, learn to ask questions that do not allow a person to simply say 'yes' or 'no'. You can also spot an open ended question when you hear one and stop an unwanted sales pitch in its tracks.

## 11.2.6 Objection Handling

Inevitably you will come up against objections throughout the sales and marketing process. Good salespeople welcome these, because they are a very strong signal that the person is interested in buying from you, and giving you the opportunity to deal with their concerns. So you, as the salesperson selling your expertise as a contractor, need to recognise and handle typical objections that will be raised by both agents and clients during your contract search.

This is a well known and well studied area of sales. Anyone who has ever worked in sales will have had to pay attention to the typical objections found when selling their product or solution. For someone to be able to sell a product, they must engage the customer. For a customer to raise an objection, this demonstrates that they are considering the product for themselves.

Some common objections you will be faced with as a contractor trying to secure a contract are:

- "Send me your CV and I'll consider it"

- "I don't think you have the right skills for the role"

- "You're asking for too much money and the client will not pay that"

- "The client needs someone to start sooner than you're able to"

- "Your experience does not seem to be enough for this high-level role".

All objections can be distilled into two basic types: real objections and unreal objections. Let's deal with the latter first:

## Unreal objections
These are when the customer raises an objection that they may not necessarily feel, but they think the objection may get rid of the salesperson. This is the case when you have received three sales calls in a row and you just don't want to listen to another sales pitch. You might say: 'send me some literature in the post, I'll read it and get back to you'. Salespeople know that in most cases the customer is not going to read the literature, they just don't want to speak with you at that time.

As a contractor you will be faced with unreal objections when you are chasing positions with agents who might ask you to send your CV as a way of getting you off the phone.

Handling the unreal objection is reasonably straightforward. All salespeople are aware that they are often considered to be a pest.

They know that you are not likely to read the literature they send you, but out of courtesy will send it through to you anyway.

Indeed, in many cases it is often not until the second, third or fourth phone conversation that the salesperson actually gets to speak to their customer properly. That's why successful salespeople develop thick skins and remain patient when first speaking with prospective customers.

So the answer to an unreal objection is to be polite and friendly, to do as asked, and also to attempt to gain some kind of commitment to the next stage of the sales process. For example, a salesperson might say: 'I'll make sure your literature goes in the post today – after you've received it, would Friday afternoon be a good time for me to call so we can have a chat?' Often the customer will recall they have agreed to a follow up call and will feel in some way obliged to at least listen to what the salesperson has to say.

As a contractor, you are the salesperson, so you will need to be patient, do as asked, and ensure you get a commitment to the next part of your sales process. Typically, this will involve sending a CV, then arranging to call back in a few days.

**Real objections**
The other type of objection – the real objection, is an objection that actually needs to be overcome and should be viewed as a buying signal. Going back to our earlier example of a car, a potential customer might say: 'I've read that this model is extremely poor on fuel consumption, and my fuel costs are already too high.' This is a fact that the customer has stated. Be aware that for the car salesperson, this may be a good objection to be raised. The salesperson will now have a clearer picture of what their customer is looking for and can present a more suitable product. On the other hand, it is a problem for the salesperson if they only have one car to sell you. Here, they must find a way of demonstrating that the product is still the right one for the customer and make the sale.

You will be presented with many objections to overcome by both the agent and client. Typically these will involve your skills, experience, availability and rate. The real objection must be handled differently to the unreal one, described above. On this occasion, this is a real objection that must be handled appropriately. Be aware however, that real objections are not always seen as the enemy to salespeople. Indeed, this may be the first time that the customer is revealing what they truly feel, and the salesperson cannot sell effectively if they have no idea about what the prospective customer really wants.

A good salesperson will have pre-rehearsed answers to all objections that arise and will not be caught by surprise – they might even appear to have 'the gift of the gab', although this is often the result of days, weeks, months and years spent carefully rehearsing answers.

Your preparation before applying for positions and attending interviews should involve considering all the objections that could be raised and preparing answers for them in advance. As you gain more experience it is advisable to keep a document containing all these objections and how they are handled, as part of your sales process.

A problem does develop, however, if the product being sold is flawed and the objection raised by the customer has identified the flaw. On this occasion the salesperson may have been found out and there is no 'magic sales wand' available that can help, other than providing the prospect with false information. So, as ever, be wary of disreputable salespeople, and beware of being one yourself!

Objections are actually a very useful tool for customers and salespeople alike. As a customer, you should raise objections until you are satisfied that you understand the product or service you are considering sufficiently to make the purchase. From the sales perspective, objections reveal who the customer really is and what they are really thinking. As long as the product or service is good, the salesperson should welcome objections.

## 11.2.7 Sales closes: theory and practice

When contracting, there are two primary situations where you will need to close a sale. The first is when securing an interview via an agent, and the second to secure the contract when you are at the interview with the potential client.

For salespeople all over the world, closing is often the most exciting and daunting aspect of doing business. It is, in essence, when and how you ask for the business. For most accomplished salespeople, closing is the part of sales they look forward to the most and once you begin to enjoy closing – you close a lot more!

A simple truth to bear in mind is that, very often, those who don't close a sale don't sell anything. The difference between a successful salesperson and a lousy one often comes down to the fact that the successful one closes, whilst the poor one doesn't. The lesson is not to expect agents to put you forward for interviews, or clients to offer you a contract, unless you actually ask them to; in other words, it's up to you to close the sale.

Much has been written on the art of closing and there are many well known and effective techniques employed. Closes often work differently in different market sectors. In the domestic and consumer markets, the most aggressive and manipulative closes exist. These closes however do not often work in the high level commercial world as more often than not, the buyer is trained to recognise them and so they are likely to have an adverse effect.

The most common closes include:

**Assumptive close:** This close involves the salesperson never actually asking their customer if they want to buy the product. Instead, they appear to assume that the customer is going to buy and closes with a statement something like: 'OK, I'll send the order to our delivery department and your product will be delivered in three working days." It is now down to the customer to protest that they have not indicated that they are interested in buying.

You would be surprised by how easy it is to be caught up in the moment and carried along with the sale. This type of close can even intimidate or embarrass customers, who therefore don't feel like they can disagree with the salesperson's assumption. This close is all about manipulating you into buying – be wary of it!

An example of an assumptive close an agent might use on a contractor is: 'I've spoken to the client, he is happy for you to work on the contract, and I've agreed with him that you will start on Monday.'

An example of an assumptive close a contractor might use on an agent is: 'I'm happy to be interviewed for this role tomorrow at 9am.'

## Been there, done that!

### I'm not being pushy, I'm being 'assumptive'

**DAVE SAYS:** I often used the assumptive close with agents. I would first tell them that the role was ideal and exactly what I enjoyed doing, and then ask something like, "When are the interviews being done?". Once I had the answer, I'd follow up with, "I can do Thursday at 11am or Friday at 3pm. What's best for the client?".

This would sometimes raise a chuckle with the agent who obviously knew they were being sold to, and they might respond with, "Hang on, I've not said I'll put you forward yet!" I'd respond with, "I'm perfect for this role, I'm available, and I'm very good at interviews. If you put me in there, I'll get the offer and it will work out well for both of us. Can I go and see them this week?".

An agent is a professional salesperson, so will also recognise when someone else knows how to sell themselves. You've just demonstrated that you might have a better chance than other contractors being sent to the client from competing agencies. Boring the agent to death about the intricacies of the skills you have, which they don't really understand, is less effective than convincing them that you will be the person who will perform the best in the interview.

**Alternative close:** A close relative of the 'assumptive close', this close is often used alongside it. Again, the alternative close dictates that the salesperson never actually asks their customer if they would like to buy. Instead, they will offer an alternative such as: 'Would you like to pay for this by cash or credit card?'

Again, the customer is being manipulated into feeling that they have already agreed to buying, it is just the payment terms that are left to be discussed. As with the assumptive close – be cautious of any salesperson trying to use it. And don't feel it's so obvious that you would never be caught, because many are!

An example of an alternative close the agent might use is: 'I've spoken to the client, he is happy for you to work on the contract; would you prefer to start on Monday or Tuesday?'

An example of an alternative close the contractor might use is: 'I'm looking forward to the interview tomorrow; would you prefer the morning or afternoon?'

**Silent close:** This is a fascinating aspect of closing and, as unlikely as it sounds, it really works. There is a saying in sales that says, 'He who speaks first, loses'. The silent close is based on this kind of psychology.

When the salesperson has made their final closing statement, they are taught to be silent immediately afterwards. If an uncomfortable silence follows, the salesperson must remain silent. The theory here is that whoever speaks first will 'lose', although the ideal for a sale is that everyone gets what they want.

There have been many documented cases of sales where agonising minutes have passed on the phone before someone speaks, and it is at first not easy to hold your nerve in such situations. Should the meeting be face to face, the salesperson must continue to look straight at their customer, appearing neither too aggressive nor too passive.

Of course the silent close does not always work, but be aware that it exists and that it does have an effect. The next time you find yourself in negotiation and a silent close is used, you know the rules – do not be the one to speak first!

An agent might use a silent close on a contractor when asking what rate they would be prepared to accept. They will listen to your answer but remain silent afterwards, waiting to see if you crumble and offer a lower rate.

A contractor can use a silent close on an agent in a similar manner when asking what rate the client is prepared to pay. After the agent names a price, the contractor can remain silent, hoping that the agent will crumble and offer a higher rate.

**Refractive close:** This close is unethical, and you may have even come across it already. This is where the salesperson says, for example: 'Please buy the product, I have a family of eight and my boss will fire me if I don't make this sale.'

Of course, the salesperson's personal circumstances should have nothing to do with a sale and, if they are using this close, there is a good chance that there is no truth to the statement either. Be influenced by a balanced view of the product and your reasons for buying it; do not allow yourself to be manipulated in this fashion.

Within the contracting world it is uncommon to come across the refractive close. If you do, then be very cautious when dealing what that agency. Or avoid it altogether.

The closes described above are some of the most common and interesting ones used, but closing is an enormous aspect to sales and cannot be learnt overnight. Often good salespeople close well purely because they have good presence and communicate confidently and in an effective way. Confidence is really what customers, and this includes agents and clients, want to see. When you buy from someone who looks nervous, you feel nervous about the sale.

But the opposite is also true. Try to be aware of what closing is and know when you are in a closing situation. This will prevent you as far as possible from being manipulated or tricked. For salespeople, closing is fun. After all, it really is all about asking for the business, which is, at heart, what business is all about!

## 11.3 Interviewing

The interview is the make or break part of the sales process. Sometimes it may just be a formality, but more often it is the part where you win the contract. Chapter 5 provided an introduction to interview techniques together with some basic do's and don'ts. Now we'll move on to look at these in more detail.

### 11.3.1 Going to the interview

To reinforce the key points covered in chapter 5, there are some obvious things to remember about preparing for the interview:

- Dress properly
- Take an umbrella in case it rains
- Make sure you know where you are going and how to get there

- If you're driving, make sure you can park

- Make sure you have the names of the people you are to meet with. If possible, find out from the agency what their title is—Mr, Mrs, Ms, Dr

- Never be late for an interview. It is amazing how much executives hate lateness; it will probably cost you the contract. If you really must be late, call as soon as possible with a convincing excuse.

Your preparation will win or lose you the contract, so be thorough and professional about your research before the interview.

## 11.3.2 What the interviewer is looking for

In the IT sector, when demand for contractors was outrageously high in the late 1990s contractors were snapped up quickly for simply having the buzzwords on their CV and being available, irrespective of their ability to perform at interview.

When the smoke cleared after the dot com crash the market was left with a large surplus of contractors. Good old fashioned commercial reality kicked in and the survival of the fittest contractors began. It still continues and went through another particularly tough period during the post-2008 credit crunch, although some of the core contracting disciplines, such as IT and engineering, remained relatively unscathed. So one crucial element to bear in mind when attempting to find a contract is this:

*The contractor who wins the contract is the one who knows best how to win that contract, not necessarily the best contractor available for the role.*

To win the contract you first of all need to write a high impact CV that will get you put forward as a candidate – see chapter 4. You will then need to prepare for the interview and ensure you maximise your impact at the interview to ensure you are offered the role. Good interview technique starts by asking the question 'What is the client looking for?' Look at the interview process from the point of view of the interviewer and use that to guide the approach to being interviewed:

The interviewer will be looking at the following aspects:

**Likeability**
- Do I like this person? Will they fit into the culture within our organisation?
- Will they avoid causing me trouble and making me look bad?

**Specific skills**
- Does this person have the relevant skills and experience for the role, or is their CV a work of fiction?
- Have they successfully completed a similar project for a company like ours?

**Bonus skills and knowledge**
- Do they have additional skills that would come in useful?
- Do they follow the industry and keep up with the latest advancements?

**Initiative**
- Is this person proactive, able to work alone and use their initiative?

**Motivation**
- Are they a happy and keen person or a lazy merchant of doom?

**Communication skills**
- Can they communicate with other human beings?
- Do they have the humility and confidence to ask questions if they don't understand something; or are they arrogant or shy enough to simply pretend that they understand perfectly?

**Ability to listen and understand**
- Can they listen respectfully and really understand issues, or do they jump in before people have finished to present solutions to what they assume is the issue?

**Commercial awareness**
- Are they commercially aware or have they no understanding of cost versus benefit and business goals?

**Interest in company**
- Do they know anything about our company or have they been interested enough to find out?

During the interview you need to address all the points listed above to give yourself the best chance of success. Basically, go through the list and tick all the boxes.

Based on the interviewer's motivation, your killer interview technique should:

- Demonstrate your appreciation of their problems and needs

- Demonstrate you have previous experience that is directly relevant to tackling those problems and needs

- Demonstrate you have extra skills that they might find useful

- Demonstrate that you are keen and motivated

- Leave out anything that is not directly relevant

- Demonstrate that you can fulfil all of their requirements.

This is not rocket science, but it is amazing how bad some people are at dealing effectively with all these points in interviews. Don't be one of them.

Chapter 5 discussed the need to prepare your list of questions tailored to the role based on the aspects the interviewer will be looking for and the entire preparation process up until the time you leave the interview room. Now we're going to cover how you should 'drive' the interview to ensure you are able to cover all the points the interviewer/s will be looking for.

If you are collected from reception by the interviewer, your interview will start before you've even arrived in the interview room. By making casual conversation on the way you get the chance to tick the 'likeability' and 'has interest in company' boxes.

There might be more than one person interviewing you and it may not be the decision maker who picks you up. Still, establish straight away if they are going to be in the interview room with you. If they are then start making conversation by asking them questions about themselves – 'how long have you been working here?' and 'what do you enjoy most about working here?'.

If you are led into the interview room by someone who is not going to interview you then still go through the motions of asking the questions. You never know. They might be asked their opinion of you.

**Breaking down the interview:** An ideal interview has four basic sections:

- Chat about company
- Discuss and understand needs
- Sell your solution
- Close.

You might think this looks like the sections of a sales meeting. That is because it is identical. The whole purpose of an interview is for you to sell yourself to the client. You are the product.

**Chat about the company:** They ask you about the company and you tell them what you know from the research you did in your preparation *[Tick – Has interest in company]*.

They are impressed you know stuff, but tell you a bit more.

You listen, smile, nod your head, sound impressed and perhaps ask short questions. *[Tick – Likeability, ability to listen, has interest In company]*.

**Discuss and understand their needs:** Driving point: You take control of the conversation and ask them what the business problem is they are attempting to solve, and how they envisage you helping them to solve it. *[Tick – commercial awareness]*.

They will explain the business drivers, what the project is, and what they are hoping to achieve by bringing you in. Some might even ask you if that interests you. Whilst they do this you nod but don't interrupt, asking the odd short question to perhaps get clarification on some house jargon. *[Tick – Ability to listen and understand, good communication skills]*.

You tell them it sounds exciting and interesting. You then summarise exactly what they have just said to show you can listen and understand a problem. You could then perhaps ask further questions about return on investment, expected timescales and so on. *[Tick – Good personal skills]*.

**Sell your solution:** Driving point: Now for one of the most important parts of the interview: You then tell them what specific skills you have that will help them solve their problem, where you have used them before and the results that were achieved. You then summarise how you would tackle their problem. *[Tick – Specific skills, personal skills]*.

If possible you then go on and explain how they could perhaps enhance their existing planned approach and use further skills and expertise that you have. Make sure you also mention that of course you would need to evaluate the timescales of doing so and justify the extra effort, since there is no point doing stuff just for the sake of it. *[Tick – Bonus skills, general skills, commercial awareness]*.

After convincing them you are the person for the role you can go on to hammer it home by getting out your list of questions and asking them other questions that are more general to show that you have other areas of expertise. As an example, in IT you might ask about their project life cycle, testing approaches, methodologies, configuration management and so on. *[Tick – Bonus skills]*.

**Closing the interview:** Driving point: The next thing is to say you have no further questions and state that you would be really interested in the role to show you are keen.

Very important part – the close: Ask them 'Are you satisfied that I fulfil your requirements?' This gives them the chance to mention any areas they are unsure about, which you can then deal with to provide that reassurance. Leave nothing to chance here. You might not have covered all bases and there is no point missing the opportunity to deal with any nagging doubts they might have.

Finally, ask them when they are going to be making a decision. Unless you've had your eyes and ears shut the whole time you should be able to tell if they are considering hiring you.

In an ideal world you will work through each of the steps and secure the contract. However, sometimes everything does not go according to plan.

**Poor driving:** This means that the interview does not adhere to the format above because you failed to ask the correct questions at the right time and also steered away from some of their questions that were not on your ideal route. Notice there are some key driving questions that lead you into each section of the interview. If you don't latch onto these then you risk veering all over the place.

**Picking from the sweetie jar:** This is where you fall into the trap of allowing the interviewer to say something like, 'Please talk us through the previous roles you have done', before you have even established their need.

You then end up describing what you have done with no understanding of what their requirements are or if anything you are covering is relevant. You are literally inviting them to have a look in the jar and take out anything they might find useful.

If they ask you that question then you can respond with: 'I'm happy to do that, but first I'd like to understand a little bit more about your requirements so that when I explain what I've done in the past I can discuss the stuff that is actually relevant and interesting for you.' You then get back to the second stage of establishing the need.

## CONTRACTING MINDSET TIPS:
### You're responsible for managing your career, not the client
Contractors are business services providers and responsible for their own career management and skills development. Any attempts by clients to impose practices resembling human resources processes must be fiercely resisted, otherwise contractors start to look like employees, and could be caught inside IR35.

### Would your builder welcome a 'personal development review' from you?
The builder you hired to build the loft extension is on the National Register of Warranted Builders (ie well qualified and recommended). Are you really going to offer him a personal development review so he can put together a personal development plan whilst he's working on your loft?

Would you then request that the builder attends a short course on installing skylight windows, which were never a feature of the original design, at your expense, and expect your builder to meekly submit?

At the end of the job, once the extension has been completed, how do you think your builder would respond if you asked him to attend a performance review and exit interview to identify how he might improve how he builds future extensions, and to discuss whether he has the potential to do more than just build loft extensions?

### Employees have personal development reviews and planning meetings with their managers, contractors' don't
Clients sometimes forget that contractors are not employees; more often the human resources (HR) department gets involved, and insists that contractors undergo the same personal development and planning processes as employees.

Contractors are sometimes invited to join general business skills training sessions with employees, or are told by a client that they must learn specific new skills if they are to continue to work on a project that was not included in the original contract.

Because it's appraisal time of year, or because HR processes say so, contractors find themselves being invited to attend career development meetings, or exit interviews during the final week of a contract.

### Contractors are business services suppliers hired to provide specific deliverables for a fixed duration
You can reasonably expect, and can often benefit from, constructive feedback on how you deliver your services during project review meetings. However, you are not an employee to be developed but a service provider delivering a specific service for a fixed duration, so you should politely decline invitations to personal development meetings.

If a client requests a new skill not specified in the original contract, this is a variation to the contract, which you must negotiate into the original agreement as an addendum. If you need to learn a new skill, your contractor limited company must pay for your training. Then, you must ensure any new skills are reflected in a new, higher, rate.

If you've not delivered on your original contractual requirements, that's a contract issue, which you should rectify in your own time; it is not a performance management issue. And by all means conduct a project review on its completion, but you're not an employee, so you should not participate in an exit interview.

### Contractors are businesses delivering specific services for a fixed period, not employees with careers to be managed & developed.

**An equal trying to prove they are better than you:** This is where there is someone else in the interview who is supposed to have the same skills as you and will try to test you. Sometimes they have no sense of commercial reality and might even consider you a threat to their superiority.

They can mislead you by taking you on wild journeys into detail for ages just to prove they are better than you. Don't fall for this. Have a little bit of a detailed discussion to prove your worth, but don't go on for ages. Flatter them and tell them how much you would enjoy working with someone like them then get back on track to selling yourself to the person who makes the main hiring decisions.

**Timing:** You might be doing really well, but if you don't get to do your whole pitch you won't be able to sell yourself fully. Keep an eye on the clock and allow for a maximum of an hour. Ask how long they have for the interview when you arrive.

**Failure to take into account the client's capability:** You might be speaking to someone who is an expert in what you do, or they might not have a clue. However, there is bound to be a capability gap between yourself and the client, and you need to identify what that gap is. If you are clearly more capable than the client you need to establish whether it would be risky to let your 'capability cat' out of the bag. They might feel threatened that you could make them look stupid.

More likely they will be impressed by your knowledge. In this instance the advice would be to perhaps pop out the cat's tail to test their feeling then bring out the rest of the cat and her kittens if it is appropriate. Basically you need to avoid not being hired because you are too good.

If they are more capable than you then just smile and say how impressed you are. But, don't say things like, 'Great, I'd like to learn xyz.' Mentioning how the contract will benefit you is of no interest to them and is a common BIG mistake during an interview.

You are the product. Sell yourself.

# 11.4 Negotiating

When negotiating, the key is to pitch to the decision maker, and that's the client. The golden rule in sales is: 'Always speak to the decision maker'. The agent has played an important part in bringing you and the client together, but they have little part to play in the decision making process once you and the client want to close the deal.

However, once the client has decided to hire you, the agent then becomes hugely important when it comes to negotiating rates. Remember, this is business: the agent will want to maximise their commission and minimise your payment. Accept this fact and deal with it to your best advantage.

## 11.4.1 Negotiating with the agent

Always try to avoid committing yourself to a specific rate until you have to. When the agent asks your rate before you go for interview, just talk about accepting the 'market rate' and be as vague as you can. If the agent mentions a number, continue to be vague and say something about the figure they mention appearing to be in the right ballpark, but don't agree to a certain number and, if pushed, agree on a range. Remember, at this stage you're in a weak position and all you should be focusing on is getting the agent to put you forward to the client for a possible interview.

Bear in mind that agents will initially ask you to name your rate in the hope that your demand will be lower than the market rate. That gives them the opportunity to charge the client the market rate or above. If they can get away with it, they will pay you below the market rate and enjoy a greater margin and profit. And it's not because they're 'cheating' you, it's a result of them being a better business-to-business negotiator than you. So improve your skills!

Having 'secured' the contract at the interview, it's time for final negotiations with the agent. When the client has decided they want you for their contract, the game has changed and you now have the upper hand in the negotiation. It's up to you to close the deal. This is business, so whatever you've said until now doesn't really matter, although if you've made the mistake of agreeing to a certain rate, you really should keep to it.

If you are going to insist on a higher than previously agreed rate then the agent won't be happy – but don't worry, it's just business. Just make sure you give a good reason; this might be that you can get more elsewhere, or that the client is asking you to deliver some of your niche skills that were not originally in scope, and that you charge more for those. Just bear in mind that you're in a strong position: you've done the interview and you've either nailed the contract down, or you have a pretty good idea from the client's reaction that you will win it. So, ask for a good high rate and let the agent negotiate you down. The hard work will now be down to the agent.

For the agent the deal is almost done, and they will want your signature on a contract. But this is not something you should rush to sign immediately. Review the contract, and make sure it includes everything you expect. Check chapter 7 for the important clauses you want to include, and also those you want removed or altered.

At this stage, investing in a contract review, particularly from an IR35 perspective, can pay dividends. No matter how experienced you consider yourself to be, and no matter how much IR35 knowledge you have, it is best not to 'wing it' – a small fee invested now could save you a fortune in the future. Only after you've received the green light from the contract review should you agree the contract.

If you are a first-time contractor, then chances are that your sales and negotiation skills will be less developed. It takes time to learn how to do this. For that reason alone agents often enjoy securing contracts for first timers, since they can maximise their margins. Don't worry if you don't negotiate the deal of the century first time around and the agent secures a hefty, above-market-rate margin. You certainly wouldn't be the first contractor this has happened to and it is all part of the learning process of going contracting.

If you can, try to only commit to six months for your first contract, so you have the chance to renegotiate. If your agent has managed to secure a huge margin for themselves, they will want you to sign for as long as possible of course, but you can resist this by saying that you would prefer to try it for six months to make sure you and the client are happy.

## CONTRACTING MINDSET TIPS:
### Negotiation based on margins is futile
Contractors are small firms supplying their services in the business-to-business marketplace, which has none of the consumer protection or employment laws designed to protect the individual. And like any business, contractors negotiate rates with agencies and clients according to the realities of the marketplace and market forces, *not* some notional sense of fair play.

### Focusing on margins during negotiation is nonsense in the real world
Last time you bought a car, did you ask the salesman what profit the dealership makes on each car they sell, and then try to haggle based on your personal view of what should be a fair margin?

If you sold collectables online via an auction site like eBay, would you expect your buyers to demand to know the original prices you paid for your goods and expect them to insist they pay a margin they feel is fair?

When you go shopping for new clothes do you expect high street retailers to display their cost price next to the retail price they charge you?

### Client budgets and agency margins are normally confidential
Agencies are given a budget day or hourly rate by the end user client that is based on market forces. Either the agency has a fixed margin agreement or, being a commercial organisation in business to make money, they will try and negotiate the maximum percentage margin they can out of the client's budget.

Unless an agent or client accidently reveals the budget and margin, or they are unusually open, you won't know the total client budget, nor the likely margin the agency has agreed or will be targeting. This information is treated by most agency and client organisations as confidential, and rightly so.

### Contracting businesses price to market, not margin
The amount you can expect to receive from that budget set by the client first depends on whether there is a fixed margin agreement with the agency. If not, then you need to have a feel for the market rate for your services and the availability of other contractors with your skill set. Then it's down to how well can you can negotiate your contract.

If your skill is highly specialised and in great demand, you can call the shots in negotiations and demand a higher rate. But if your skill is very common and many of your fellow contractors are chasing a few contracts, then your negotiating position is weak.

**Basing your negotiating strategy on the possible margin an agency will receive and appealing to a notion of fair play is futile.**

## Been there, done that!

## Renewal ransom or new contract?

**DAVE SAYS:** I started working for a client after the dot com crash, and the rate was at rock bottom – half what it used to be. After a year the market had picked up, rates were 35% higher, and the project was going great, so I figured that asking for an increase to market rate would be fine.

At renewal time the agent phoned me and said, 'Great news, they want to renew, but unfortunately there are no rate rises.' This was hardly surprising, considering the agent was paid pretty much the same regardless of my rate. So I started negotiating directly with the client, and basically said I wanted to stay, but expected to be paid market rate or I would leave. I had a few interviews lined up and was confident I'd get something. At the same time one of my fellow contractor colleagues was doing exactly the same thing – pay market rate or I walk.

Well, the client did some research and seemed to think we were asking for more than the market rate (which we weren't), and felt that both of us were holding them to ransom over the project, which was not yet completed. It was a messy business and we were both reluctantly given the rise to market rate, as they didn't want to delay the project. But the deal was that once what we were working on was released three months later, we had to leave. And that's exactly what happened.

Six months later we heard they had increased the rates of all their contractors to market rate, but the bridges were burnt. It seems that some clients are more than happy to cut your rate when the market drops. But they have issues raising your rate when the market picks up. Their view is that they're simply having to pay more for the same thing.

If you are going to insist on a rate rise and claim the market rate is higher than you're getting, you'll need to have some pretty strong evidence and start negotiating early to avoid the accusation of holding the project to ransom. But personal experience tells me that to get a higher rate when the market increases, the easiest way – and the one in which you won't harm your reputation or burn any bridges – is to simply move on to a new contract.

## 11.4.2 Negotiating renewals

When you've completed your contract, you will often be asked by the client or the agent to sign on again for another period. This is called an extension or renewal. From a legal point of view, you have no obligation to do this. And, importantly, you have no obligation to accept a given rate, or any specific conditions. You can seek to change everything in a renewal if you want to. Whilst the client or agent may refer to a contract extension, this is just the same as a renewal and so you have no reason to accept any conditions you do not wish to.

From a business point of view, you are in a much stronger position than you were when you first started out. The client knows you, and if you're wanted back you must have made a good impression. A renewal can be a good thing for a number of reasons. It shows that you've done a good job and been seen as 'good to have around', so it looks good on your CV. It also means that you don't have to find another contract for a while and secures your income for another few months.

Furthermore, you can usually make your working conditions better when you renew, and you'll know the project and the client. All of these are advantages to renewals, but if you're not happy, don't feel obliged to renew. Just try to leave on good terms.

There are some key things to bear in mind when seeking or negotiating a contract renewal:

- **Blow your own trumpet – gently:** Discreetly remind the client of the value you've added to their business and what you can continue to offer

- **Judge the strength of your bargaining position if asking for a rise:** How keen is the client to keep you? Can they afford to lose you? Are you under-paid? Or over-paid if the market has dropped? Can the client afford to pay you more? Do you have other offers? What's the market demand for your skills?

- **Be realistic about agents:** Agents broker your services to clients and try to obtain the maximum margin they can. They earn significantly more focusing on new deals than renegotiating existing ones. They might not have your best interests at heart. The longer you've been with the client the more you can squeeze the agent's margin

- **Pitch to the decision maker:** The first thing professional salespeople learn is to pitch to the person who makes the decision and has the final say – the client

- **Appear indifferent to staying:** If you appear too keen to stay you will weaken your position

- **Timing:** Avoid getting into negotiations until four weeks before your current end date, otherwise you will not have a chance to line up alternatives

- **Avoid holding the client to ransom:** If your departure would damage the project then avoid holding the client to ransom by asking for a rise – "stick 'em up or the project gets it!". Burning bridges is not a good strategy – long term contractors get repeat business and referrals from previous clients

- **IR35:** If you are caught by IR35 then negotiating terms to place yourself outside IR35 will probably give you a better net return than negotiating a better rate. But remember, the project must be different; if it's more of the same, then IR35 will still apply

- **Don't continue without paperwork:** Don't continue working unless you have the contract terms agreed and the paperwork signed. There will be no legal recourse, and if you have a draft contract from the agent then they could argue that by executing the contract by starting it you have accepted the terms. This rarely happens, but is something you should be aware of

- **Renewal length:** When the market demand is high a renewal for six months ensures you'll have another bite at the cherry sooner rather than later. If demand is low then the longer the better (although bear in mind IR35 considerations, too, as you don't want to appear a 'disguised employee')

- **Do your sums:** Calculate the cost of downtime if you leave and have nothing else lined up – you might find the

cost of sales and time without a contract is more than the
rate rise you are pushing for

- **Don't burn bridges if you are leaving:** Ensuring a
  smooth departure will maintain a healthy client
  relationship. That's always advisable for providing good
  references and a source of future work. It will also help
  keep agents happy and, in most cases, they're the ones
  that help keep you in contracts.

Keep the client on side at all times, and the agent on side as much
as possible, because the value of having positive referrals and
testimonials could keep you in contracting for many years.

## 11.5 Evaluating your bargaining position

Maximising your return in negotiations is dependent on the strength
of your bargaining position, and your sales skills. The strongest
bargaining position for you to have is, 'I have other options, so I
will not renew unless you meet my demands.' This is a great position
to be in, particularly if you already have another tempting offer
elsewhere.

If you don't mind leaving the client and believe you can do better
elsewhere, then try and line up an alternative contract. You can
even hint to your existing client/agent that you are seeking
alternatives. This tends to get things moving! Seeking alternatives
to strengthen your position is not unethical, and not disloyal to
your existing client. It is simply business – playing the game and
looking after your own interests.

If you are happy to stay at the existing client for the same money
and terms, then avoid laying those cards on the table, otherwise
you can consider yourself trumped. There is no point holding a
begging bowl and entering into negotiations saying, 'I'll work for
the same, but please give me more money!' Understanding your
bargaining position and negotiating a contract renewal is all about
sales technique. You must know the strength of your position, play
your strategy accordingly, and finally – above all else – ensure that
you keep the client happy.

## Been there, done that!

### Strongest position is, 'I'm leaving'

**DAVE SAYS:** On my second contract it was renewal time and the market rates had not only increased, my skills had too – I had passed about 10 exams and was a Microsoft Certified Solution Developer. Market demand was red hot and I was getting plenty of phone calls each day.

So I requested a rate rise to the market rate of £50 per hour and stood my ground. Over the course of two weeks both the agency and the client kept refusing the full £50 but were creeping up slowly. With four days to go I received an offer elsewhere for £65 an hour. The original client finally agreed to the £50 but I was out the door. I did, however, arrange for someone else to replace me, and spent my own time and money handing over the system, which went down very well indeed.

Most clients will acknowledge commercial reasons for moving on, and are often frustrated when those above won't release budget to pay market rate. But, it's worth keeping them happy by making sure that if you do jump out during a contract you don't leave them in a hole. Burning bridges is a really bad idea.

Two key strategies to improve your bargaining position are:

- **Line up alternative contracts:** Applying for other positions gives you a chance to research the market and line up an alternative contract, which enormously strengthens your position during negotiations – 'pay me the market rate or I'll go elsewhere to get it!'

- **Buffer of money:** It is always useful to have a buffer of six months money in the business bank account in case of surprises or future periods without a contract. The alternative, being desperate for money, is not a strong bargaining position.

Then you need to consider the state of the market and your skills:

- **If the market has dropped** since your last renewal, or contract, then a rate rise is highly unlikely. After the dot com bubble burst and during the economic crisis that began in 2008, contractors found themselves negotiating rate decreases. If you are being paid over the current market rate, then your best strategy is to keep quiet and hope that you can renew at the same rate.

- **If the market has risen**, then the fact that you can earn more money elsewhere is a strong bargaining point and should be stressed. If the client is sensible they are unlikely to want to incur the cost of replacing you with someone who will, anyway, demand the same increased rate.

- **If the market is unchanged and you have not improved your skill set**, then the only justification for a rate rise would be the cost of replacing you. Taking this approach is not recommended at all – you should always seek to keep your clients happy and earn yourself good references.

- **If the market is unchanged but your skills have increased** and are worth more in the market, then you have good reason to request a higher rate. Tread carefully though, because from a perception standpoint clients are unlikely to agree with this. In this scenario, to achieve a higher rate might mean moving on.

The timing of your renewals also has a major influence over the strength of your bargaining position. Normally the contract renewal process is not started until one month before your current contract end date. If clients anticipate a risk that a contractor might not renew, resulting in a project schedule being affected, they might try to persuade a contractor to consider an early contract renewal.

If you have not heard from either the agent or the client at the start of that four week window then you should start the process yourself by asking both the client and agent if they are interested in offering you another contract. If the client is slow to respond, start making hints that you are leaving. If the client is not planning to renew your contract, they do not usually tell you, so you will know the situation from the negative response after chasing them.

## Been there, done that!

### Back pocket contract leverage

**DAVE SAYS:** If you're going to ask for a rate rise, then it's worth having another offer in the back pocket to a) justify your rate rise with real evidence, and b) strengthen your bargaining position – "pay up or I leave".

When sourcing a replacement position you need to make the right noises to the agent, who will try and establish if you are just seeking a new position to leverage a potential rate rise. So don't tell the agent the name of the boss you are currently working for, or even if you are in a contract. You don't want them phoning them up. If they know you are moving on, then offer to give details if they secure you a position elsewhere.

You can say that you are definitely leaving because the project is coming to an end. It could always end up having a 'surprise extension' if you stay on or the client could offer you another project. Don't let on that you're just considering alternatives. The agent wants to put forward his best candidates for the position, not ones who might let them down.

## 11.6 Seasonal factors

Like the best farmers, the best contractors know when to sow, when to reap, and when to stay indoors. The contract market has its own rhythms. A farmer knows when to plant and when to harvest. A contractor should know when to be looking for work and when to be safely in a long-term contract.

The contract market has seasons. Just as we know when winter is coming, contractors need to know when the market is slowing down. If you're reaching the end of a six-month contract, and your CV isn't generating the buzz it did before, you should focus on getting an extension rather than risk being left out in the cold.

## Been there, done that!

### Deal done on training

**DAVE SAYS:** I ran a team of developers at a bank in the late 1990s and trained everyone on some quality techniques for increasing productivity. We were the team that always delivered on time, and eventually the boss asked how I managed to do it – so I told him.

We then agreed that he would pay me the same rate to develop a training course. I would own the IP and deliver it to the other teams – 25 people. It was a great win/win as I was paid to develop a training course, and deliver it, and could then put training on my CV and website.

Although I had some enquiries from others wanting me to deliver the course, it wasn't something I had time to do as I was always contracting. I did, however, mention it in interviews and say that I'd be happy to impart some (not all!) of the knowledge to their workers. It had a proven value add, and helped me secure several positions.

If you're reaching the end of your contract, and you're getting lots of attention from agents, then you can probably find more money somewhere else. It's worth putting out the feelers every now and again to see what the market temperature is. It's not because you want to finish your contract early. You just want to know what the weather's like outside.

The most successful contractors have a market barometer. They keep one eye on what's going on out there. By doing this, they build a picture of the seasons and rhythms of the contract market. With the wealth of online resources available to contractors, it is not difficult to keep abreast of developments and the personal networks of friends and colleagues can provide excellent 'human intelligence'.

## Contracting seasons

Your own research will let you know what the 'weather' is like where you are. The range of sectors, clients and skills covered by contracting is so vast that it is impossible to give hard and fast rules; however, for many sectors, the seasonal pattern tends to be:

**Spring** – after winter, the market starts to warm up and flower buds begin to appear. Listen for the first cuckoos – your phone will ring just that little bit more often, and the rates on offer will be just that little bit higher. Keep your feelers out, as summer is on the way.

**Summer** – your skills are in demand and rates are looking better. This is the time to start a new contract, as for clients and agents it's all about finding the right people at this point.

**Autumn** – traditionally, this is harvest time. This is the best time to renegotiate. The highest contract rates are usually paid to people who've proven their worth. If your client sees you as too valuable to lose, you're in a strong negotiating position.

**Winter** – the best place to be in winter is indoors in the warm. Even if you're not 100% happy with your current contract, the weather outside can be far harsher. Hunker down and sit it out until spring comes round again.

## Contracting cycles

The contract market has short-term and long-term cycles. It also has two annual cycles, driven by the financial year and holiday seasons:

- **Jan/Feb** – after the Christmas holidays, clients start to galvanise into action. New budgets are approved and hiring starts. This is the equivalent of spring

- **Mar/Apr** – this is the equivalent of summer. Arguably the best time to look for a new contract

- **May/June** – time to bring in the autumn harvest. If you can secure a three-month contract in March, you'll be in a strong negotiating position in June

- **July/August** – Holidays break the rhythm of the market in what is effectively contracting winter, and hiring becomes a low priority. If you're not in a contract by the end of June, you could end up without a contract until September

- **September** –After the summer holidays, kids return to school and the HR department awakens from its slumber; it's contracting spring again

- **October/November** – another summer brings better paid contracts, making this a very good time to be on the market

- **December** – autumn and winter come around quickly. Many projects are scheduled to deliver in the week before Christmas, which means this is the perfect time to renegotiate. By December 24th, the market goes dead until the New Year, when contracting spring begins again.

There is a longer cycle that can last up to a decade. The demand for contractors can mirror the growth – or lack of it – of the economy very closely, as contractors are the easiest people to hire, and the easiest to get rid of when times are hard. You're probably best off watching the growth of the financial markets, and looking out for a plateau, the edge of the bubble after which it's likely to burst.

As the market nears a plateau, start making plans to become less easily expendable. This might be a good time to go permanent, or to start looking at secondary sources of income.

As things start to warm up again, you want to be in a position to take advantage. If you're in a job that requires six months notice to quit, getting back into contracting might be difficult.

Contractors tend to be very popular during times of economic uncertainty, as they offer clients exceptional flexibility. When business confidence is wobbly, contractors are used to focus on short-term projects designed to free up permanent employees. The contractor is essentially there to help with capacity management. But they are not employed, and so can be renewed or let go when the contract expires according to prevailing business sentiment.

So always aim to be in the best position for any of the short, medium or long term contracting cycles, and you'll always be maximising the amount you can earn. Even when the economy is at its lowest ebb, there is always a demand for contractors, so use the lessons in this book to make sure you're always ahead of the pack.

# Contracting lessons from this chapter

- One of the keys to long term success in contracting is getting to grips with marketing and sales. If you don't, you could be joining the club of the most highly skilled contractors who never manage to secure decent contracts.

- You need to constantly push yourself out into the marketplace, even when working on a contract. Your current contract will eventually come to an end and you will need to have the next contract lined up. Create a personal marketing plan. Follow it and refine it.

- Be aware of and understand your own features and benefits, and ensure you explain these clearly to both the agent and client.

- Don't despise sales. You are in business, and business revolves around sales. A good sales technique will ensure you stay in contract, that you get to choose from the best contracts, and that you are paid the most you can be.

- The interview is the make or break part of the sales process. Sometimes it may just be a formality, but more often it is the part of the sales process where you win the contract.

- Good interview technique starts by asking the question 'What is the client looking for?' Look at the interview process from the point of view of the interviewer and use that to guide the approach to being interviewed.

- Prepare for interviews and take control to ensure you win the business.

- Maximise your revenues by adopting effective negotiation techniques. Negotiation is about strengthening your own bargaining position and playing your hand accordingly.

- When selling, always make sure you are pitching to the decision maker, and that's the person that makes the hiring decisions.

# 12

# Managing holidays and absence

# 12.1 Taking time away from contracts

It is inevitable that at some point in your contracting career you will want to take some time away from a contract. There are any number of reasons to take time away, and specifics such as holiday, sickness and appointments are dealt with separately.

However, whatever the reason for taking time off, the process of arranging the time off with the client is going to be similar. Assuming your contract is outside IR35 and you work through your own limited company, it very important to ensure that at no time do you allow yourself to be under the control of the client.

Firstly, you must never ask a client's permission for time away. This is a fundamental point, because by asking the client for time away you are implying that the client can say 'no', that they therefore have control over you, and that your 'outside' IR35 status is on very shaky ground. However, you must agree in some fashion with the client that you need to take time off; for example, it could be that the project you are working on is at a crucial stage and you are needed to work for the next month without a break.

It is also a question of professional courtesy. How often have we all sat at home, having taken time off work to wait for a tradesman, only to have them not turn up? You need, in as diplomatic way as possible, to 'tell' your client that you are taking time off. The way to handle this is by using an alternative close:

*"I'm going to take half a day off next week to attend a medical appointment. Is Tuesday or Thursday better for you?"*

You have quite clearly demonstrated that you are taking the time off, and the client is not in a position to object. However, you stroke the client's ego and extend basic professional courtesy by choosing to accommodate the client's requirements.

If your contract is inside IR35, then it is less important to keep to the process of not 'asking' or 'requesting' time off, and you should judge your approach according to the relationship you have with the client.

As a contractor working through an umbrella company, you will need to inform both your client and your umbrella that you are planning to take time off, as many umbrella companies hold back a portion of your pay in anticipation of holidays and sickness.

You need to check with your umbrella company for the specifics of their scheme, or if choosing your umbrella company for the first time make sure you add sickness and holiday pay to the list of questions to ask when doing your research.

## 12.2 Occasional absence – doctors and dentists

As long as you give your client plenty of notice and try to work around the project schedules and deliverables, then taking time off for medical and dental appointments is rarely a problem. Remember, of course, to account for the time off on your timesheet as you will not get paid for and should not claim for any time you spend not working on your client's contract. Indeed, trying to negotiate pay for medical and dental appointments could make it look to a tax investigator as if you were acting as a 'disguised employee'.

It is best not to make a habit of taking too much time off as the client may get concerned that your frequent absences will impact on the project's timescales. Of course if you are unwell that cannot be helped, but as a contractor you have no employment rights and, technically, as your limited company is delivering a contract of services, if a client wanted to be awkward they could claim a breach of contract for your absence.

That is why it is important to have the client on-side and to arrange such appointments at the beginning or the end of the day to minimise the time you are not working on the client's project. Alternatively, if you have arrangements with the client to spend time working on a contract in your own office, which may be at your home, then try to schedule appointments on those days.

It is still important to ensure your time sheet accurately reflects the time you have spent; if you lost a half day for a hospital appointment some distance away, don't try and charge the client for any of the time you were away, even though you are working from home. Of course it's not just doctors and dentists you may need to see on occasion. You could also need to have optician appointments or sessions with a physiotherapist, chiropractor or other medical practitioner.

The same principle applies – give the client plenty of warning as a courtesy and ensure your absence will not affect the project timescales or clash with a crucial project team meeting you should attend.

## 12.3 Holidays

As a contractor, you may take holidays, but you should never use your client's holiday booking forms or systems; to do so could be taken as evidence that you are a 'disguised employee'. It is generally best, from both your and the client's point of view, to plan time off to take place during a future contract, during the contract renewal period, or before you start a new one.

Having said that, as a contractor working through your own limited company, you have the flexibility to take odd days off for holidays during the term of a contract. Naturally, though, such holidays mustn't adversely affect your work or the delivery of that contract. It is very rare that you will be required to work every day during the contract period, unless the contract length is less than one month.

If you take time off during a contract then it is very unlikely you will be allowed to take more than two weeks off at a time. If there are quiet periods during your contract then most clients will let you take ad-hoc days off at very short notice. This saves them money and does not affect project deadlines. But if you wish to take long periods away from contracting, one month or more, then this really is best done between contracts.

You are not limited to a certain number of days per year, because your time off is not paid by the client. You can take as many days off as you want, provided the client agrees that you do not need to provide your services during that time. Taking holidays in no way changes the length of your contract. Contracts have a fixed start and end date. If the client wishes you to extend your contract for a few weeks, to cover for potential holiday taken, then you would need to sign a contract renewal. This is extremely rare though.

There are no set rules for how to book holidays when you are a contractor, although the key is to ensure you keep your client happy. Guidelines for dealing with existing clients include:

- If you want time off during your existing contract, or an agreed renewal, then simply inform your project manager that you are taking a break

- If you strongly suspect you will be offered a renewal which you will accept, then again speak to your project manager

- If you do not think you will be offered a renewal, or don't want to renew then go ahead and book your holiday – you are the boss!

- But to stay outside IR35, you must avoid acting like an employee – so never use any of your client's holiday booking procedures and do not allow yourself to be controlled by the client.

When you are looking for a new contract you might have holiday already booked, which you would need to take during that contract. Best practice includes:

- Don't plan on any holidays for more than a week within the first month of a new contract. This could affect your chances of securing the contract

- Wait until you have received an offer before you mention that you have holiday booked. Having holidays booked might not get you chosen for interview by the agent and you will fall at the first hurdle

- After receiving a contract offer, if you have holidays booked then check with the client that you can take time off before signing the contract.

If you wish to take time off for more than three weeks then this will probably need to be done between contracts. Bear in mind that on your return from holiday it could take between one week and a month to secure a new contract.

For this reason, if your planned holiday is less than three weeks it is better to plan it during an existing contract, so that you have something to come back to immediately. If you did take holiday at the end of one contract you could attempt to line up a new contract ready for your return. However, most clients hire contractors on very short notice, usually less than one month, and the process can take a couple of weeks.

## 12.4 Sickness

If you develop a medical condition that means you are unlikely to make it into work with your client, then ensure you inform your project manager immediately. Most clients will be sympathetic for a few days absence but with any condition that requires you to take weeks off, you could be in danger of being in breach of contract.

### Been there, done that!

### No more Mondays off

**DAVE SAYS:** As a contractor who doesn't get paid when you are ill, you will find that you will recover from hangovers much more quickly, and rarely get 'man flu' on a Friday. Most contractors I know have a rule that says unless they've just broken both legs, they are going into the office!

It may be that you can exercise your substitution clause and find a replacement, but in many cases this might not be practical. However, to protect your status as outside IR35 it is good practice to have a pool of colleagues who could step into a position if your condition means you need to take more than a few days off. Naturally, you would have to cover the costs of any training and for their time spent working for you on your client's project.

Some contractors invest in a private health insurance policy, so that they have a little more control over their access to medical treatment. If you have a condition that is likely to result in a procedure that will require time off to recuperate, private health insurance will make it easier to plan your health needs around your contracting, or vice versa!

Should you require ongoing treatment, it might be possible to negotiate a reduced schedule with your client, for example only working four days a week for a period. As long as this will not impact on the deliverables of your contract, most clients will be amenable. After all, they don't pay you when you don't work.

## Been there, done that!

### Doctor's note

**DAVE SAYS:** A contractor friend fell quite ill and ended up taking two full weeks off work. The client asked him to provide a doctor's note. This isn't a contractual requirement, and if you comply then you'll be seen as being treated like an employee; that's not good for your IR35 status. In this case, he politely declined.

Under no circumstances should you imply that you should receive sick pay from your client, as this indicates you might be a disguised employee. If you are signed off by your doctor as unable to work, you may be eligible for statutory sick pay (see section 12.8). And you should not provide your client with a copy of your sick note as this implies you have an employee-employer relationship, which spells doom for your 'outside IR35' status.

If you are involved in an accident that was not your fault, then explore what options you may have for claiming loss of earnings from the party responsible for the accident. In addition to private health insurance, you can also take out policies that may provide you with income protection. Chapter 12 covers insurances in more detail.

## 12.5 Long term absence

Should you have a medical condition that means you will be unable to work for a year or more, it may be a good option to make your limited company dormant, a process described in chapter 6. Similarly, you need to inform your umbrella company (if you are using one as your trading vehicle), as you may have been paying into a scheme to provide you with some pay during extended periods of illness.

If you make your limited company dormant during a long spell of illness, you can always reactivate it at very short notice when you are ready to start work again. If you have dissolved the company you have to go through the time and expense of setting up a new business all over again. Making your company dormant is a last resort as it precludes you from earning any fees through your limited company. But the costs and time associated with keeping the company running may not suit your circumstances, and of course you may not be well enough to manage your limited company effectively.

Although not a topic many people would want to discuss before it happens, if you are seriously ill you should also make allowances for the fact that you may never return to work. This is where an income protection policy and private health insurance may justify the premiums you pay when you are well. Peace of mind comes at a cost, but it could be worth the investment, particularly if you have dependants.

Another worst case scenario is that if you do not have a termination clause, you may have to provide a substitute to take over from you. If the client insists, then this includes training them and paying them from your contract fee. The client is certainly within their rights to insist you provide a substitute if they want to; and if you don't comply they could sue you for breach of contract. If you are inside IR35, or working for an umbrella company, then you don't have to worry.

## 12.6 Compassionate leave

As a contractor, you are not entitled to paid leave of any kind. If the worst happens and you experience, for example, a close personal loss, then the same rules apply as for sickness – you don't get paid for time off. Most clients will be very understanding and pleased to allow you a day away from their project for you to attend a funeral. However, to cope with longer periods of grief you may have to tough it out at work as you won't get paid and the client will be concerned about project deliverables.

It's difficult, but try and minimise the amount of time taken off for compassionate reasons in the same way as sickness. Clients will be understanding about a day or so, but any longer and they will start asking questions that might lead to you being found in breach of contract.

## 12.7 Financial planning for time off

Many contractors work out the cost of their holidays by calculating the cost of the money they won't be earning if they go away. This is a scary route to go down, which could stop you from ever enjoying a holiday or taking the rest you need for the good of your health!

To plan accordingly, so you have money set aside for when you take time off, consider the following:

- There are eight public holidays in each year

- You will probably take fewer days off sick than when you were a permanent employee and received sick pay

- You'll want to take the same, or more, holidays than your entitlement when you were a permanent employee

- If you play your cards right you should have few or no gaps between contracts.

With the above in mind, you should typically plan to be earning for 44 weeks in the year. It is therefore prudent to estimate your annual revenue for 44 weeks paid contract work and then pay yourself a monthly amount that takes that into account. Don't forget to allow for savings for personal taxation. Your accountant or umbrella company will be able to advise on an exact amount to take each month.

Taking breaks for a few weeks holiday won't cause any problems, but if you spend many months or even years away from contracting you are likely to attract unwelcome attention from HMRC. You can continue to draw a salary and claim valid expenses for as long as you can justify that the costs are in the pursuit of trade; but as soon as it's clear that you are taking more than just a short break from trading, company costs can no longer receive corporation tax deductions. And, if you have built up assets in your company, the business runs the risk of becoming a Close Investment Company, which would result in a higher rate of corporation tax on any profits.

You may also fall foul of HMRC over your expenses claims. All business expenses to be offset against corporation tax must be incurred 'wholly and exclusively' for the purposes of trade. What could happen is that during a routine employer's PAYE inspection or Corporation Tax Enquiry, a tax inspector will spot a period of low trading activity, representing you having taken a long break. Plenty of companies have low levels of trading for quite long periods. However, if there is no corresponding drop in business expenses during the same period, the inspector is likely to ask why. You could have to pay additional corporation tax, which will have been underpaid because of the expenses claimed during your break, plus interest on the underpayment and possibly penalties, too.

## CONTRACTING MINDSET TIPS:
### Save money for sickness, holidays and time out of contract

As a contractor, you are a business-to-business service provider and you will only get paid for the services you deliver to your client. Unlike when you were an employee, you won't get paid if you fail to deliver your services for any reason – be it sickness, time off for holidays or when you're not working between contracts.

### Would you pay £300 to watch daytime TV?

If your gardener, who normally turns up once every week to mow the lawn, breaks a leg and can't work for a month, meaning you have to find a replacement or mow the lawn yourself, would you still expect to pay her?

Do you expect to keep forking out fares to the regular taxi driver who normally takes you to the station each morning and collects you each evening when he takes a two-week holiday on the Costa Brava?

Is spending eight hours watching daytime TV really so important to you that you'll spend £300 for the privilege?

### Clients only expect to pay for services delivered

When you go contracting, you become a service provider, just like your gardener or taxi driver. Once a client hires you, they pay for your specific skills and services to solve a particular problem. If you don't deliver your services, you won't get paid.

When you were an employee, you were paid holidays and sick pay. But as a service provider like your gardener or taxi driver, your client won't pay you to laze on the beach or visit the doctor.

And taking a 'sickie' becomes an expensive habit. If, for example, you are earning £400 per day and decide to take a 'sickie', this is likely to cost you approximately £300 from your own pocket in lost earnings, as employment legislation for sick pay and paid holidays doesn't apply to your relationship with the client.

### Be professional and make financial provision for time off

Taking long holidays is one of the benefits of a contracting lifestyle, as you can plan vacation breaks between contracts and factor the cost into your target earnings. Work out how much time you want to take off in a year, and make sure what you earn in the remainder covers your annual requirements.

Of course, sickness can't be predicted and, if you are genuinely ill and/or infectious, you won't be thanked for turning up. But several hundred pounds of lost income generally proves sufficiently motivating to most contractors to overcome minor ailments. More seriously, though, good financial planning and insurance are essential to ensure a more serious illness doesn't become a financial disaster.

In addition to holidays and sickness, there are times when you are likely to be involuntarily without work, even if it's only for the occasional week between contracts. So, having money saved up will not only provide you with a cash cushion, but will also mean you won't have to take the first offer that comes along. In other words, you should always be able to choose an assignment and rate that suits your requirements, not your bank manager's.

**Contractors don't get paid holidays, sick pay or for time off between contracts by their clients. So plan your finances carefully.**

## 12.8 Contractor eligibility for state benefits

Contractors are typically employees of either their own limited company or of an umbrella company. That means they are eligible for certain state benefits, just like any other employee. However, although you may be eligible to claim statutory sick pay (SSP) or unemployment benefit in the form of Job Seekers Allowance (JSA), you should not rely on these payments as a substitute for maintaining your six-month buffer of cash savings, or for taking out health insurance.

### 12.8.1 Job Seekers Allowance (JSA)

The Job Seekers Allowance (JSA) is designed to be a temporary measure to help people without work to get back on their feet and find a job. This is equally true if you contract through your own limited company or if you are in a partnership or self-employed. However, there are strict rules regarding eligibility for the JSA and you must meet a range of conditions before you qualify. The allowance is also counted as taxable income and so impacts on your tax affairs.

A limited company contractor who is a company director and shareholder can claim JSA. You must meet the eligibility requirements and ongoing conditions in the 'Jobseekers Agreement' that has been agreed with Jobcentre Plus, which administers the JSA scheme.

The key point for limited company contractors to bear in mind is that their limited company's business assets will be considered 'capital' and added to their personal assets and capital when they are means tested. Until combined funds and capital in your business and held personally fall below £16,000 (correct at the time of writing), you will not be able to claim JSA.

In addition, if you regularly pay large dividends, these and any cash in the business will be considered part of your savings limit of £16,000. So Jobcentre Plus will want to see detailed company accounts and financial records, and may wish to access your accountant when making any eligibility assessments. For contractors who are sole traders or in a partnership, business assets are not considered as part of their savings or capital.

Although it is a state benefit, JSA is still taxable income. But under some circumstances, not all JSA is counted as taxable income, and HMRC provides guidance on how to calculate how much JSA is taxable. You will find that having claimed JSA as a taxable income in a given tax year does complicate your tax affairs, but this need not cause problems as long as you ask your accountant to take JSA payments into account when completing personal tax returns.

The good news is that you don't have to shut down your limited company with all the attendant costs and hassle. That's because you can continue to earn a small amount in addition to your benefit payments, although earnings above a certain threshold will be deducted from your weekly JSA payment.

The scenario for umbrella company contractors can be slightly more complicated. That's because if you are trading via an umbrella company, you are employed by that business and have a contract of employment. To qualify for JSA, you must resign, which may not look great to the Jobcentre Plus staff reviewing your case, as to outward appearances you have made yourself unemployed. So, you may have to spend some time explaining to your Jobcentre Plus case officer how contracting works and why you had to resign. Persevere, and ask your umbrella company, or 'former employer', for assistance, and you will be able get the message across that you are legitimately unemployed and in need of benefits.

### 12.8.2 Statutory sick pay (SSP)

If you are forced to take time off work because of illness, as an employee of your limited company, you can claim up to £81.60 per week in statutory sick pay (SSP) from your company (figure correct at the time of writing). This can be paid for a period of up to 28 weeks if the condition is serious. And if you are entitled to recover SSP, it can be deducted from your payroll liabilities, or reclaimed from HMRC directly if there are insufficient Pay As You Earn (PAYE) funds to cover payment.

However, although SSP can be a welcome income during a period of no earnings, it won't financially support most limited company contractors through a long-term illness. So other financial provision is recommended, such as a healthy cash balance in the business and possibly income protection insurance.

To qualify, you must:

- Be off sick for four days

- Notify your employer (your company, not your client) according to the policy on sickness in your employment contract with your company, or if the contract does not specify a notification period, within a statutory seven days

- Earn above the lower earnings limit, which is £102 per week at the time of writing.

- Have at least one Qualifying Day in each week, ie these are the days you normally work. For most contractors this would be Monday to Friday.

The three days before SSP kicks in are called 'waiting days', for which workers never receive SSP unless consecutive periods of time off for sickness are linked. Linked periods of sickness are consecutive periods that occur less than 56 days apart, and where the second period is for four days or more. There is currently no requirement for you to produce a 'sick note' or prove a doctor's visit to justify a claim for SSP.

Should you qualify, you should pay yourself £81.60 per week pro rata – the daily rate of SSP is the weekly rate divided by the number of Qualifying Days in that week. So if, for example, you are sick for a full working week, the first three days are 'waiting days' and unpaid, and you would receive two-fifths of £81.60, or £32.64. If your working week is Monday to Saturday, then in this case you would be entitled to three-sixths of £81.60, or £40.80

Having paid your SSP as an employee, you then need to change hats and reclaim SSP from your company's payroll liabilities or directly as an employer from HMRC. An employer can only reclaim SSP if the SSP payments made to employees are greater than 13% of the company's gross Class 1 National Insurance Contributions (NICs) liability for that month. HMRC calls this the Percentage Threshold Scheme (PTS).

Conventional employers would normally recover SSP payments to their employees by calculating the PTS and total SSP payments on a monthly basis, and then claim the surplus of SSP above the PTS from their income tax and NIC liabilities under PAYE. This means that if you are inside IR35, or you've chosen to pay yourself a salary above the personal allowance, you can offset SSP to yourself from the money your company owes HMRC for income tax and NICs.

But if you are paying the more conventional low salary and high dividend, which may result in you having little or no payroll liability, you may actually have nothing to offset SSP against. In this situation HMRC's guidance on calculating and recovering SSP tells employers, ie you, to contact their HMRC Accounts Office directly.

In practice, if you are in the situation where you have a financial and health profile that means you might benefit from claiming SSP, you should ask your accountant for advice first, particularly if there are long-term implications for your contracting business.

## Contracting lessons from this chapter

- Contractors are not paid by their clients for time off for sickness or holidays. You must make your own financial provision to take time off.

- You must never ask permission for time away, because that implies your client exerts control over you – bad for IR35. Instead, simply inform the client you will be away.

- Breaks of three weeks or more are best done between contracts.

- In theory, you can take off as much time as you want, provided it's arranged with your client. In practice, it may interfere with your ability to complete your contract. Tread carefully and only take as much time off during contracts as you need to.

- You may be eligible for Job Seekers Allowance and Statutory Sick Pay, but these benefits are not really designed for contractors, so you will encounter obstacles.

# 13
# Personal finance for contractors

## 13.1 Why contractors are different

Contractors inhabit a space where they are not employed, yet they are not self-employed. For this reason, because they don't have the advantages that permanent employees enjoy, when seeking a mortgage, handling pensions, or considering how to make investments, contractors are different.

Because you are different, you must ensure you take proper advice from a qualified financial expert before making any decisions. The following chapter is only to be used as a general guide and is not to provide a substitute for professional advice.

Permanent employees rarely have a problem obtaining mortgages. They walk into a high street mortgage lender, show their pay slips and they are offered a mortgage based on the lender's standard, current criteria.

Contractors don't enjoy the same reception, even when they may be earning several multiples more than the permanent employee. When a contractor goes to a high street mortgage lender and tells them that they run their own business, they typically face demands to see accounts for the past three years, and then all sorts of references are taken, and calculations made, following which they are still unlikely to be offered a reasonable mortgage.

The whole process can be made worse because accountants, quite rightly in most cases, will advise contractors to maximise costs in the business and minimise profits. In this way the contractor's company is as tax efficient as possible and the contractor's net pay is maximised, usually because they take a fairly low salary and make up their earnings through dividends. This does not impress the banks and mortgage lenders, though, who like to see consistent healthy profits. This chapter will explain ways around what can sometimes seem like a 'Catch-22'.

Sometimes things work in favour of contractors, though, and not against them. For example, one of the pre-tax costs to a business can be payments into a contractor's pension fund – if the business invests in the contractor's pension, it can reduce tax to be paid and prepare the contractor for a flexible, early and comfortable retirement.

There are also financial services suppliers who have developed products specifically for contractors, for example by using multiples of the contractor's typical rate to calculate their borrowing limit. These types of suppliers have steadily increased as the benefits of lending to relatively solid, higher-income customers like contractors become apparent.

## 13.2 Mortgages

The problem for the High Street banks is that they lack the experience in understanding contractors. A typical contractor in IT, for example, earns close to £100,000 per year at the time of writing, so you would expect banks to be eager to do business with them.

But the lenders see only that it's not a 'regular salary' as they define them. Of course, job security even for permanent employees has declined to a point where many actually have less security than contractors, but the lenders do not yet acknowledge this.

Fortunately, the contracting sector is so strong that it has made the financial services industry recognise its profitability and adapt to serve it. There are now specialised brokers who work with contractors, and they are well equipped to handle contractors' mortgage requirements. They are used to working with the lenders

## Been there, done that!

## Make your piggy bank your friend

**DAVE SAYS:** Many contractors enter the market when things are red hot. They see all their friends doing it, and find it easy to secure a contract and double their income overnight.

But, the market doesn't perform like this all the time, so don't increase your lifestyle thinking you'll earn the same forever, otherwise you might be in for a rude shock at a later date when the market drops.

Pay off any credit cards and loans and then try and live off the same as you were doing before, or perhaps just a little bit more. Prudence is key and you have nothing to lose: either you'll find yourself with enough (or more than enough) to tide you over the quiet times, or you'll end up with a large stash of cash.

and to filling in the gap between permanent employees and contractors for them. Lenders will now base mortgage size on multiples of contractors' contract values.

Independent contractor specialist mortgage brokers, who are usually qualified and regulated Independent Financial Advisers, know from experience what questions the lenders will want answered, and they have the contacts among lenders to present your mortgage request. Brokers can also deal directly with the personnel at the lenders who actually make decisions about mortgages; these are the key underwriters within the lenders' centralised processing units. This avoids the involvement of high street branch employees, who are unlikely to have the right blend of knowledge and experience.

The broker will help you compile documentation to show that you have regular income and that you have contracts ongoing at a solid rate of pay. Obviously your personal credit rating, and your background have importance as well; but a good broker can even help you overcome obstacles like a poor credit rating. The one thing you must be able to demonstrate is a good hourly or daily rate of pay, as it appears in your actual contracts. This works as a kind of substitute for the pay slips that the permanent employee would be asked to present.

The lender will want to see a signed copy of your contract and will calculate an annual contract rate based on the hourly or daily rate and the number of hours and days worked in a year. The amount you can borrow is typically a multiple of around four times the annualised contract rate. This approach often means that contractors can borrow more than their permanent employee counterparts.

A good broker can also avoid schemes that have extended loyalty clauses and hefty associated fees, such as higher lending charges. And they can often obtain competitive rates, with smaller deposits required.

The growth in contractor specialist mortgage brokers means that you can generally access the same range of mortgage products as permanent employees. The major mortgage products available for contractors include:

**Fixed interest mortgage**: Also known as a fixed-rate mortgage, the interest is fixed for a specified period, after which the lender's standard variable rate (SVR) applies. The SVR could be greater or lower than your fixed rate, depending on the base rate trend. The advantage is that you know that their mortgage payments cannot go up during the fixed-rate period.

**Variable rate mortgage**: A lender's variable rate mortgages usually track the base rate. There are several variable rate mortgage products, chief among them:

- **Variable Rates/Standard Variable Rates (SVRs)**: usually higher than most 'tracker' rates, these generally fluctuate according to the base rate but can also be influenced by the commercial needs of the lender; they can be good when rates are high, as lenders will sometimes absorb some of a peak in repayment costs for borrowers. But they can be less good when rates drop dramatically, as the lender will try and preserve or increase its margin

- **Tracker rates**: will be set at a rate above the base rate, eg base rate plus 2%, and will track the base rate precisely; these are often lower than SVRs

- **Discounted rates**: the lender agrees to discount the SVR or tracker by a certain number of percentage points over a set period and then reverts to the SVR or a higher tracker when the term expires

- **Capped rates**: the rate can increase or decrease, but cannot increase over a set agreed level; this can be a useful tool to ensure your mortgage repayments don't go over the limit of what your budget allows.

**Flexible mortgage**: Flexible mortgages allow you to over-pay, take payment holidays and generally finance your mortgage according to circumstances. For example, if you are working on a contract with high rates, you can overpay, and then take a payment holiday between contracts. By regularly overpaying, you can significantly reduce the total amount of interest you pay and the length of the mortgage.

The key mortgage types mentioned above will also sometimes benefit from a degree of flexibility, but you should always ensure this is the case before taking out the mortgage – don't expect lenders to be on your side if you want to change the rules and ask for flexible terms after agreeing a mortgage contract.

**Offset mortgage**: Offset mortgages will take into account the balance of linked accounts, such as a contractor's savings and current account balances, when calculating interest on the mortgage loan. That means if you have significant savings, the 'negative' mortgage balance will be reduced by this amount, so interest on the debt balance overall will be lower. Contractors putting aside personal cash for income tax liabilities can use this money for an offset mortgage, but business funds cannot be used unless you are in the unlikely position of being a contractor trading as a sole trader.

Trying to use company funds to offset a personal mortgage can cause you all sorts of problems, ranging from a hefty tax bill to prosecution under the Companies Act, so just don't even try it. For example, if your limited company allows its money to be used by you to offset personal debts, it may be viewed as a beneficial loan for tax purposes. If the offset mortgage product that allowed you to use business assets to offset personal debts was termed by HMRC as a beneficial loan and the sum loaned was above £5,000, this would result in you incurring income tax on the notional rate of interest (4.0% at the time of writing) of the loan. In addition, your company would pay Class 1A National Insurance Contributions (12.8% at the time of writing), also based on the notional interest rate.

And although the mortgage provider's literature might say that the business's money technically remains in the business account, the shareholder – you – is deriving the benefit from the money, and the tax legislation is broad, saying transactions that are "arranging, guaranteeing or in any way facilitating a loan" would be considered beneficial.

In addition to the tax implications of using company money to offset personal debts, you may also be flouting rules introduced by the Companies Act 2006. Duties from 1 October 2007 include a requirement to promote the success of the company, and from 1 October 2008 not to accept benefits from third parties, plus a duty to declare an interest in a transaction. In extreme cases, breaking these rules can lead to prosecution in the courts.

## 13.3 Pensions

Often the same independent financial advisor (IFA) who helped with your mortgage can also advise on your pension. You might ask, particularly if you are younger and new to contracting, why you should set up a pension? Well, apart from the importance of providing for your future, it is one of the most tax-efficient ways of saving money. It makes no difference whether you are inside or outside IR35; either way, you can put money into the pension fund and see it start collecting interest, and you won't pay tax on it.

At the time of writing, the amount of tax relief can be as much as 58%, meaning that for each £100 invested you only pay £42, while the taxman pays the rest. The marginal tax rate is the highest percentage of tax you pay on the last bit of income you earn.

For example, if you are a higher rate tax payer using an umbrella company you pay £48 tax on every £100 you earn (or £58 tax if you earn over £150,000 per year). This is because you pay employers NI, employees NI, and income tax. If instead you put the £100 in a pension, you may consider that you are getting 48% tax relief. "Tax relief" is the percentage of tax you have not paid because you have decided to invest in a pension.

For contractors using limited companies, who are also in the higher rate tax bracket but not caught by IR35, the tax relief is approximately 38%. So, instead of paying £38 tax and taking £62 as net income, you can invest the full £100 in a pension, thus obtaining 38% tax relief. For those earning over £150,000 per year the additional rate means your tax saving is even more. And for earnings just over £100,000 per year the effective rate of tax is 60% due to the personal allowance reductions introduced in the April 2010 Budget.

For contractors who are not higher rate tax payers there are still large tax benefits to be achieved, because they avoid tax at the lower corporation tax bracket of 20%.

The rules governing pensions investment no longer fix a percentage of salary for investment. Now contractors can place up to 100% of their contract income into a pension. In addition the rules regarding funding a pension scheme direct from your limited company (or contractor umbrella provider) allow an investment of up to £50,000 per annum without regard to the amount of your earnings, with a lifetime allowance of £1.5 million. If you do not use your annual £50,000 allowance, perhaps because your income has fallen, you can carry forward the unused portion to a subsequent year when your income might be higher. The rules say you can use your last three year's worth of allowance in this way.

Many contractors are concerned that if they set up pension funds for their contracting business, they won't be able to access them if they go back to permanent employment. But by choosing the appropriate provider, one that permits the appropriate flexibility, you can resolve this issue. The pension fund you set up should be something that you can contribute to for your entire life irrespective of whether you're contracting, not working, or working for a permanent employer.

Any pension also needs to be flexible enough to reflect the fact that as a contractor your employment status is inherently changeable and you must have complete freedom to increase, decrease, suspend, restart and cease contributions completely, and on a month-by-month basis if necessary. Any pension must be versatile enough to allow contributions regardless of whether you continue to work through a limited or umbrella company, are between contracts or a permanent employee.

The scheme must also be with a financial institution that has the financial strength and backing to remain the steward of your fund for the long term. Whilst previous performance is not an indication of future growth, you are likely to be better off with a provider that has a long track record and solid financial strength.

The variety of pension fund structures is a complex topic best left to the experts; you should contact a well-recommended Independent Financial Adviser to discuss all the best possibilities. Of course you will probably be better served by an Independent Financial Adviser who works regularly with contractors and understands the characteristics of the contracting market.

### 13.3.1 Pensions for limited company contractors

The deregulation of the pension market in April 2006 and subsequent years has resulted in considerably more flexibility for contractors working through their own limited companies. The major difference is that there is no limit on the contributions you can make from your limited company, up to £50,000 a year without any tax penalties.

However, it is safer if the amounts you plough into a pension are not larger than your company's income for the year of the contribution, otherwise there might be questions from HMRC about whether the money was actually sourced from your trading activities.

Your limited company can contribute 'pre-taxed' company income to a pension. If you are a higher rate tax payer, instead of declaring the income as company profit and taking the income as a dividend, you can put the same sum straight into a pension.

For example, you have £100 worth of company income, and you are a higher rate tax payer, not caught by IR35. You can either put the £100 into a pension, or you can declare it as profit and take it as a dividend.

But if you choose the latter option and take a dividend payment, you pay £20 in corporation tax on your £100, leaving £80, 25% personal income tax on the dividend, which takes another £10. Your total net take home is £60.

Choosing to invest in a pension, on the other hand, means that the whole £100 goes into your pension fund and then has an opportunity to grow in a tax efficient environment. £25 of your contribution represents the part of the pension fund that you can draw tax free when you retire. A further £37 of your money goes into the pension fund, together with the £38 that would have gone to the taxman (quite a decent initial 'return' on your £60). This £75 can also grow and be used to draw down at a later date, or buy an annuity.

## 13.3.2 Pensions for umbrella company contractors

If you are using a contractor umbrella company to manage your contracting income, you can enjoy very significant tax advantages through pensions while at the same time building up a fund that you can start withdrawing from at age 55 for younger investors. The principle is similar to a limited company but with key differences.

Provided your umbrella company has a pension scheme in place you can use 'salary sacrifice' to contribute 'pre-taxed' income to a pension. Most umbrella companies do have a scheme in place, and this should be one of your questions to any prospective umbrella company. So, instead of paying employers NICs, employees NICs and Income Tax you can put the whole sum straight into your pension.

For example, you have £100 worth of income, and you are a higher rate tax payer. You can either put the £100 into a pension, or you can take it as salary via your umbrella company. But if you choose the latter option and take a salary, you pay £14 employers and employees NI, leaving £86.

A further £34 is paid as higher rate PAYE tax (Income Tax). Your total take home is £52. Choosing the pensions option means that the whole £100 goes into a pension fund and then has the opportunity to grow in a tax efficient environment. In reality £25 of your contribution represents the part of the pension fund which you can then draw out tax free when you retire. £26 of your own money also goes into the pension fund, together with the £48 that would have gone to the taxman (quite a decent initial 'return' on your £52). This £75 can also grow and be used to draw down an income at a later date, or buy an annuity.

### 13.3.3 Pensions for contractors caught by IR35

There are fewer financial benefits to contracting if you are caught by IR35. However, even if you are within IR35 your gross income can be invested into a pension scheme, before taxes are applied.

For someone caught by IR35 earning £40 an hour, each £100 drawn as gross salary (at the top end of their earnings) attracts £52 tax with only £48 ending up in their pocket.

Instead of drawing it as salary the whole £100 could be contributed to a pension. This reduces net income by £48, but increases a pension by almost double. This means contributions attract 'tax relief' of 52%.

### 13.3.4 How you can use your fund as you approach retirement

There is no longer a statutory requirement for you to purchase an annuity when you reach the age of 75. You can use drawdown to take a certain amount from your pension as income. Most annuities only pay around a 5% return, but remember if you've only invested £37 yourself and with the £38 from the taxman it is paying off as £75. So even with the choice of an annuity your overall return is much higher because of the initial tax savings.

When you retire, if you wish, you can take 25% of the money as a lump sum – completely tax free. With the rest of the money there are various options:

- Drawdown: you can take income from your fund based on specific limits each year relative to the size of the fund, leaving the remaining fund invested for future growth

- Inheritance: You can leave your pension to your heirs – it is not subject to inheritance tax if you die before you retire (if you die after retirement age, but before you take an annuity, you can still leave the funds to your heirs but there are taxes to pay.)

### 13.3.5 Pension drawdowns

Contractors aged 55 and over may find that a pension drawdown arrangement offers a flexible and tax-efficient mechanism for accessing some of their pension savings, at the same time as securing a pension income and continuing to grow their pension pot. A pension drawdown allows you to extract a tax-free lump sum, take an income and continue to invest in your pension.

For example, when you turn 55, you could adopt a phased retirement and potentially draw down 25% of your pension fund as tax-free cash, use a lump sum from the fund to purchase a smaller annuity to provide a fixed income for life, and continue to invest company profits into the reminder of the fund so the pension pot continues to grow.

A drawdown can be of huge benefit if you want to reduce your hours but not stop working altogether. But it can be a complex area that can potentially leave you much worse off in the longer term, so it is not something you should attempt without securing professional advice from your IFA.

## 13.4 Savings and investments

There are, of course, many sorts of savings and investments a contractor may make apart from pension funds. On this topic, one thing should be made clear from the start: you can generally invest through your limited company in anything (legal!) you want to.

You will hear, from time to time, that the small companies run by contractors should not be used as investment vehicles. This is entirely false. If you want to spreadbet your revenues, if you want to invest in stocks listed only on the Baghdad stock exchange, then go right ahead... at your own risk, of course.

Beware, though, of your company investments becoming more important than your trading activities or your fee-earning contracting. A contractor limited company classed by HMRC as an investment business attracts a higher rate of corporation tax under the Close Investment Company (CIC) rules. A CIC pays corporation tax at a higher rate than the 20% small company rate generally enjoyed by contractor limited companies. This could happen to your company if its activities are no longer wholly or mainly commercial activities.

If you are contracting through an umbrella company, you are limited in what options you have to save, because you take your income as pre-taxed.

### 13.4.1 Property

Contractors often find that they have to travel to a distant site on a regular basis for work. If this travel is prolonged, you may decide that it's easier to buy a place, through your company, to live near the site and to stay there during the working week.

You can do this and still retain your right to deduct travel and living expenses to the site for the first 24 months of work (until you 'know' that you are going to work beyond 24 months). You can, however, only do this so long as the property does not become your principal residence. If you move in full time, you have to stop claiming travel and living deductions, as no one gets to live free courtesy of HMRC (or at the expense of other taxpayers).

---

## Been there, done that!

## Don't withdraw everything

**DAVE SAYS:** In the early days I used to take as dividends everything I could out of the company, and spare cash was invested in shares. In hindsight I wish I'd left it in the company, since I had to pay higher rate tax on it to earn it as personal income. I would have been better off leaving excess in the company, putting it in a high interest account, and then taking dividends during my year off when I was no longer a higher rate tax payer.

If you do plan on taking time off then do chat to your accountant or tax advisor about planning for tax efficiencies. Of course, if you have other directors they may object, so that could be an obstacle. Plus, if you lose all your revenues and can't pay your corporation taxes or bills, that's still another, rather daunting, prospect. It is generally always wise to leave a sensible amount of working capital in the business, and not to risk money that is owed to suppliers or the taxman.

---

You can also buy the property through your limited company, and the maintenance is partly tax-deductible from your corporate profits. But be aware that any profit you make on any future sale is subject both to capital gains tax and to corporate income tax, and you could end up flouting CIC rules. Best check with your accountant from the start.

You can instead buy the property outside of your limited company with your own savings, and then it figures in your personal income tax. You will still have to pay capital gains tax on it if you sell it for a profit. Once again, check with your accountant early on, to find the most tax efficient way to proceed.

## 13.4.2 Individual Savings Accounts – ISAs

You can make significant tax savings by investing in Individual Savings Accounts (ISAs), especially if you take a long term view with your investments. ISAs are a highly tax efficient method of saving for retirement and you benefit from them in a number of ways. Unlike pensions, ISAs they don't attract the same upfront tax boost but are far more flexible in the way you can take out your money.

ISAs must be funded by your post-tax income so, unlike pensions, they cannot be funded using limited company income. However, there is no tax payable on the income received from ISA savings and investments.

You can invest up to £11,280 every year in ISAs (correct at the time of writing) and the total amount saved can mount rapidly. ISAs are offered by most major financial institutions and you can choose which option most suits you, although it is generally best to seek the advice of an independent financial adviser (IFA).

There are two main types of ISA you can invest your money into:

- Cash ISAs that generally have a variable rate of interest, with instant access and can run almost indefinitely. There are versions that have a higher rate over a fixed term, and some may have penalties for early withdrawal, or will revert to a variable rate at some stage in the future

- Equity ISAs, which can perform very well over the long term but have a risk associated because they depend on the performance of the financial markets.

Cash ISAs are like bank or building society deposit accounts, but tend to attract higher rates of interest because the financial institutions view ISA investors as long term savers.

Interest is tax free but the cash-based return can be low when compared with other options. The advantage of cash ISAs is that you can withdraw your money when you need it, although with some saving schemes this might result in a penalty.

With an equity ISA you can choose to invest your money in a managed fund or you can make your own choices about which companies to invest in. Managed fund ISAs invest in three broad areas:

- International equity funds
- Commercial property
- Corporate and treasury bonds.

You can specify which fund to invest in and can invest via a wrapper that allows funds from many different providers. Your money is actively managed by a professional and it is this manager's expertise that will aim to make money in both good times and bad, by selecting relatively high performing shares on your behalf.

It is also possible for you to have the option of investing in a tracker ISA, which benchmarks the FTSE 100 or some other share index, so the value of the ISA rises and falls accordingly. Alternatively you can have a self invested ISA, where you personally choose which shares to buy.

Stocks and shares ISAs are for contractors playing the long game, as the value of the investment can fall below the contractor's initial stake as markets fluctuate. Over time the markets rise again and the value of the ISAs will regain and surpass their initial value.

You can opt for investments managed by a number of different fund managers to maximise your investment and still remain within the tax free ISA wrapper. Using a range of fund managers within the tax free wrapper can also reduce your dealing costs if you opted for stocks and shares ISAs. Plus, you can choose to invest in other financial market items, such as gold, via specialist funds.

If you have the time and the skills, you can play the stock markets yourself within your ISA's tax free wrapper, using a fully self invested ISA. You can net a significant return, although there is also a significant risk of losing your cash, particularly if you are inexperienced in share dealing.

As their name suggests, ISAs are held by individuals; you cannot have a joint ISA with a partner in the same way that you can have a joint bank account. As a result you should do some inheritance tax planning because, over the course of your contracting career, the sums held in your ISA can mount up considerably; and as these accounts are held in your name, inheritance tax could become an issue.

The major advantage of ISAs is that you do not have to pay capital gains tax on the profits from your share dealing/dividends and interest. If you have consecutively saved over several years and worked the money hard on the financial markets, the profits could be significant, and the resultant tax savings could be considerable.

## 13.5 Insurances

Business insurances, such as professional indemnity and public liability, are covered in detail in chapter 6. However, there are other key insurances that you should consider to protect your lifestyle and as a safety net if things go wrong.

As a contractor, when you can't work because you've had an accident or are ill, you don't have the benefits permanent employees do. But you can easily and relatively inexpensively protect yourself against such financial hardship.

In your last permanent job you probably had 'death in service benefit' of something like up to four times salary. As a contractor your dependants have zero protection in the event of your death, unless you arrange for it yourself. If you have an outstanding mortgage then a policy covering you will ensure no debt is left for a partner, children or other family members should anything happen to you. And depending on the type of life assurance you take out, you may be able to make long-term provision for your loved ones after your death.

And finally, there is the risk that you are diagnosed with a critical illness, or that you suffer an accident, that prevents you from working. You can protect yourself from the potentially disastrous financial consequences of both of these scenarios.

There are a number of specialist companies that can offer a tailored range of specially selected 'contractor friendly' policies that reflect the unique way in which you work. This means that the protection can mirror that which is enjoyed by permanent employees.

The key insurances to consider include:

- Permanent health insurance, which provides a monthly income if you are unable to work

- Critical illness cover, which provides a lump sum on diagnosis of a critical illness

- Life cover, which provides a lump sum in the event of your death

- Death-in-service cover, which will pay out a multiple of your contract value in the event of your death.

In addition, it may be worth considering a private healthcare policy that provides you with a higher degree of flexibility over when and how you are treated.

### 13.5.1 Permanent health insurance

Most permanent employees have the benefit of at least three months pay in the event of accident or sickness. However, as a contractor you are exposed to financial loss from the first morning that you are unable to arrive on site, fit and ready to work. Fortunately, there are ways that you can protect yourself and your family against this loss.

You can preserve your current standard of living by setting aside a monthly figure towards permanent health insurance (PHI). These policies will support you financially if you are unable to work and can even maintain your standard of living through to retirement if you suffer a more serious illness or accident.

When considering different policies, it is important to compare and contrast the following key elements of the policy:

**Deferred Period:** The time delay before you are eligible to receive benefits, between one day and a year. The longer the period the cheaper the policy. If you have savings to pay your bills over this shorter term then you may choose to take a longer deferred period and have benefits starting after three or six months

**Protected Amount:** You can protect up to 75% of your income. The higher the percentage the higher the cost of the policy. Try to be realistic when considering a required figure. Some costs can be cut back, whilst others will be more essential

**Nature of Income:** It is vital that the financial advisor/insurance company understands the nature of your income. There are many policies that will pay out solely on salary. Check that dividends are covered if you are outside IR35 and running your own limited company

**Track record:** Check that the company has a good track record of meeting past claims. Delays in or attempts to limit or avoid payments of benefits in the event of a claim are frustrating and very unfair. Ask for evidence/statistics of previous payments to clients

**Occupation Type:** Ensure the policy will pay out benefits if you are unable to carry out your own occupation. This contrasts with a lesser definition that, if ill the claimant must be unable to carry out any occupation. This is an area that is often overlooked and could be used as a means of making a quote seem more reasonably priced

**Term:** Ensure that policies should cover you to your chosen retirement date

**Inflation Proof:** It is essential to inflation proof your benefit. £2000 per month today will have a fraction of the spending power in 10 years time

**Premium Payer:** This means the premium is personal or via your limited company. If you pay personally then benefits are tax free. If you pay via your company the benefits enter the company tax free but you pay tax and national insurance on any salary drawn. Paying into the company can help ensure executive pension premiums are maintained in ill health.

As with all complex financial products, you should consult an independent financial adviser who is experienced in dealing with the affairs of contractors before taking any decisions.

## 13.5.2 Critical illness cover

As a contractor you are at just as much risk from contracting critical illnesses, such as heart disease, strokes and cancer, as if you were a permanent employee, but you will have no benefits from an employer. You can protect yourself from the potentially disastrous financial consequences of critical illnesses that leave you unable to work, so that a lump sum is paid on diagnosis.

This can help pay for a period of convalescence, changes to your home or car to accommodate a reduced state of mobility and go towards maintaining your independence. Without, perhaps, the burden of your mortgage and with money in the bank, you can then decide whether and when you need to get back to work.

Critical illness cover pays out a lump sum on earlier diagnosis (rather than on death) for a range of serious conditions. It works well in tandem with permanent health insurance (PHI). However, note that whilst PHI pays a monthly income in the event of illness, it stops once you are deemed healthy enough to return to work.

A lump sum from a critical illness policy would be yours to keep, regardless of a return to some measure of good health and could maybe allow for some changes to your work pattern and lifestyle.

When considering different policies, it is important to compare and contrast the following key elements of each policy:

**Company Longevity:** will the company providing the cover be around in 10 years time to meet any obligations?

**Meeting Claims:** does the provider have a good track record of meeting claims?

**Conditions Covered:** medical definitions of what is covered are very important and vary considerably between providers. These must be comprehensive enough to be of practical use to you in the event of a claim

**Affordability:** premiums must remain affordable throughout, so that protection can be maintained as you get older and more likely to fall ill

**Term:** you can cover yourself for a fixed term – eg until children grow up or a debt is repaid – or for your whole life

**Amount of Cover:** you can choose 'level term', meaning the same amount throughout, or 'decreasing term', which reduces in line with a reduced liability, such as a repayment mortgage

**Payout Terms:** lump sum, or paid annually (called 'family income benefit', or FIB)

**Premium Waivers:** a 'waiver of premium' benefit is recommended to ensure premiums are maintained by the insurer if you suffer less serious illness that means you are unable to work for six months or more.

### 13.5.3 Life cover

Most permanent employees have some form of 'death in service benefit' of up to four or more times salary. However, as a contractor you no longer have this security and might want to consider arranging your own protection for your family.

If you have bought a property and have an outstanding mortgage this will need to be covered by life insurance, so that no debt is left for your family should anything happen to you. Ideally, there would then be sufficient left over to provide long-term security.

Policy aspects to consider are:

**Cover Type:** 'Term cover' or 'whole of life', which means protection for a fixed length of time, or your entire life

**Payment Type:** Lump sum or family income benefit (FIB) plan. Lump sum is paid in one go. A FIB plan pays a set income over a period of time

**Premium Waiver:** You could consider taking 'waiver of premium' as a low cost option to protect your payments against you being unable to work through sickness after six months.

Some reasons and uses for choosing term cover are:

- To provide a lump sum for those close to you to place on deposit and draw off the interest to make up for your lost income

- To cover your life for the time that your children will be dependents

- To protect an interest-only loan, such as an ISA mortgage, so that you leave no debts for your family to pay.

Uses of a decreasing term assurance include:

- To cover a repayment (capital and interest) mortgage or a similar reducing debt.

Reasons and uses for a 'whole of life' policy include:

- To provide continuous cover until your death
- To back up an investment plan that can be cashed at a later stage.

Certain life policies have an investment element. It is important to understand that these investments are longer term in nature and that the value of investments and income from them can fall as well as rise. So check with your independent financial adviser before making any decisions.

### 13.5.4 Death-in-service cover

As a permanent employee you will almost certainly have had a little-recognised employment benefit of death-in-service. Typically, this would have paid out three to four times your annual salary to the people of your choice in the event of your death. But on leaving permanent employment to become a contractor, you are suddenly without such cover.

The solution is the death-in-service insurance policy. This can be paid for by your limited company and, unlike products such as 'key-person insurance', there is a policy that pays out to spouses and family members tax free in the event of a claim, yet has no benefit in kind implications to the contractor. Furthermore, a death-in-service policy through a contractor limited company means your business pays the premiums, which are a tax deductible expense. In addition, as long as he or she is also an employee, your spouse could also be covered by a policy with the same tax benefits.

The cover takes into account all your earnings, dividend and salary, and you can take out cover up to a double figure multiple of the combined salary and dividend earnings that you take out of the company, although it is more common to insure for a lower multiple.

# Contracting lessons from this chapter

- Contractors often have high disposable incomes that can be used for savings and investments. Make sure you seek professional advice from a contractor specialist IFA before making decisions.

- The financial services landscape for contractors is not the same as for employees. Most mainstream financial services companies do not understand the contracting model, so you will need to speak to a specialist provider.

- Many specialist Independent Financial Advisers (IFAs) who understand the contracting model exist and have negotiated a wide range of financial services products, including mortgages, for contractors.

- Limited company and umbrella company contractors can invest tax efficiently in a pension, and should do so.

- Contractors don't receive sick pay, death in service or employer life assurance benefits, so you must make financial contingency plans for illness (even if it's just stashing some cash away), and may wish to consider making provision for your dependants.

# 14
# Contracting abroad

# 14.1 Advantages and disadvantages of working abroad

One of the great advantages of being a successful contractor is that you can find work almost anywhere. Your skills and experience are likely to be valued pretty much everywhere: Australia or the United States; China or the United Arab Emirates; Brazil or South Africa; Russia or India. Think of virtually any country, and there'll almost certainly be a thriving expat contractor community.

Many UK contractors go abroad – it's a great way to gain new skills, learn to approach projects in different ways, perhaps learn a language, or just experience all that another country can offer. It is not especially difficult for a good contractor to arrange to work in most countries. But there are some hurdles to be surmounted, even in the simplest of transitions.

If you are a European Union (EU) citizen wanting to work elsewhere in the EU, for example, you won't require a visa or work permit. But you may have to find the correct legal format to work in another EU country, which can vary according to member state.

As with many issues relating to contracting, this is an area where the use of professional support is likely to save you time and money in the long term. And because your net earnings should be so much higher as a contractor than a permanent employee, you should be able to comfortably afford the fees that professionals charge, even if they seem painful at the time.

If you have a transferable skill set, such as in IT, engineering or management, then there are many opportunities to work with client companies almost anywhere in the world. And it is now as easy to identify contracts in Australia, the Middle East or the USA, for example, as you can in the UK.

The downside is of course that you have to live apart from friends and family in the UK, but it's a judgement call you have to make. Some contractors choose to work abroad for three to five years to earn a substantial amount of money, sometimes paid tax free, that they will then invest on their return to the UK and possibly even semi-retire.

If you have a family, there are a great many logistical issues to consider, such as education and finding a family home, but none of these problems are insurmountable. And you could be offering your children the opportunity of a lifetime.

Just remember one thing – as a contractor abroad you are not an employee and thus have no safety net with the client company if anything goes wrong. Good planning is essential to mitigate any such risks.

## 14.2 Finding work abroad

It is possible to find work very easily using online resources and agencies that have international divisions. Most of the major agencies either have dedicated offices in key locations around the world, or they have reciprocal arrangements with indigenous agencies.

It is also possible to search online and apply for jobs directly in the country in which they are advertised. Language barriers aside, it is as easy to browse a foreign agency's contractor positions as it is a London based agency's ones. However, the caveat is that going for interviews with overseas clients could potentially be very expensive. Some clients will subsidise costs, which puts you at risk of being branded an employee by HMRC, even though you are travelling to interview for a legitimate 'outside IR35' contract in another country.

Embassies and consulates can be a very useful source of information for both contract work and regulations about working in the country in question. Major importers of UK labour, such as Australia, Canada and the USA, also have lists of skills shortages.

Another good source of information about the attractiveness of other countries as a contracting destination can be found in the World Economic Forum's (WEF) Global Competitiveness Report. The annual report profiles around 140 countries according to wide range of business, economic, societal and other factors. It can be downloaded for free from weforum.org/reports.

## 14.3 Factors to consider

### 14.3.1 Don't work through your own UK company

One thing is certain: if you are going for longer than five months, you do not want to work through your limited company in the UK. In practice, for short assignments you are likely to face no difficulties working through your UK company. But longer than five months means an effective change of corporate location; what that means is that your company goes where its controlling executives are, and that can have a tremendous impact on how you are taxed.

For most UK contractors working through their own limited company, the controlling executive is the contractor themself, and typically a partner or spouse, too. So, by definition, when you move to work in Brazil, your company moves there too. And it gets taxed there. As the tax system in Brazil is very different to that of the UK, and the corporate tax rate is higher, you may well want to make specific arrangements for your work in Brazil. Or wherever else you choose to work.

The bottom line is that it can be very complicated and is not a task you can take on yourself and hope to succeed at. International tax experts are expensive, but they are worth the investment as the money you stand to gain as a result of their expertise far outweighs their fees.

## 14.3.2 Visas and work permits

Such is the demand for skilled workers today, that nearly every country in the world offers a special visa to make it easier for their national companies to find such workers. This goes by different names depending on the country, for instance: in Australia, it's called a Skilled Australia Sponsored Visa; while in the USA, there's the EB-1, or the EB-2, or a myriad of others, depending on the skills required, the location of the contractor, and so on.

Staying with the Australian example, you should plan on spending a few months obtaining such a visa. Typically, an agency in Australia will make links with a client willing to sponsor you. Now the paperwork starts. You will have to provide extensive documentation of your work experience, your skills, and your education. You can do all this yourself, but it is a bit tricky, because the authorities demand very specific kinds of proof for all of this.

It is really well worthwhile finding a consultant or an agency that specialises in helping contractors who want to work abroad. A small investment will get you skilled help that tells you just how to apply for a visa, and what proof you need, and you'll save a lot of time and trouble.

You should be aware: if you are refused a visa for many countries, you will generally have to wait at least a few months, and sometimes a lot longer, before you are able to apply again. So expert help can really make a difference.

### 14.3.3 Fiscal systems and currency

Continuing with the Australian example, you will need to find a legal format for working there. Being self-employed is not an option, as most agencies and clients won't deal with you. You could start your own limited company in Australia, and if you do intend to stay for a long period, say five years or more, this could make the most sense.

Obviously starting a limited company in another country is time-consuming and complex, and you will of course have to handle all the administration and tax issues that arise from it. But, in Australia, you'll face another problem: contractors with limited companies may not enjoy all the same tax advantages as do those in the UK, so you may spend time and money setting one up to little result. Australia also has personal services income (PSI) rules that, when compared with IR35, are quite draconian, and there is little scope for contractors to work around the rules.

If you do plan to stay in Australia for a long time, and you are considering a limited company, you should consider contacting the Independent Contractors of Australia organisation for specifics, as these vary from sector to sector and depending on circumstances. Likewise, in many other countries there are contractors' organisations and labour bodies that are able to advise you.

### Using an umbrella

You will find that the simplest way to organise your work in Australia is to work with an international umbrella company. These are companies entirely dedicated to helping contractors arrive from abroad. Many will have offices both in the UK and in Australia and therefore can help arrange your visa and all your tax and administrative affairs to greatest advantage. Naturally there is a charge for such services, which will vary according to the location and local business practices.

## Fiscal matters matter

One area in which such an umbrella can be particularly helpful is in arranging a tax package. There are a whole series of tax reductions attendant on skilled migrants coming to Australia, but you have to know how to tap them. A local umbrella, or a good accountant, can help with this. Wherever you're planning to work, a good rule of thumb is to find good local advice.

## Currency risk

Whenever you work outside the UK, you work in a different currency. So if you plan on moving back to the UK, the worth of the currency you are earning becomes important. For example, if you were paid in US dollars, and you'd started work in January 2006 with the idea of returning to the UK in 2008, you'd have seen the value of your earnings with respect to the British pound decline by almost half. But choose a different set of dates, and the picture could be just the opposite.

Currencies work in what are called 'currency pairs:' the value of a British pound is determined with respect to the US dollar, or the Brazilian real, or any currency you care to name. Some countries have 'non-convertible' or 'blocked' currencies, which means they are for domestic transactions and not openly traded. If contracting in such countries, you are most likely to be paid in the convertible currency of another country.

Foreign Exchange (Forex) markets determine how much our money is worth, because money is traded in the same way that stockbrokers trade stocks. So you do need to watch carefully how the value of the currency you are working in is changing with respect to the pound.

Every major business newspaper will write endless commentary about these exchange rates, but you simply need to watch the major trends and make sure a major decline for the currency you are working in isn't in store with respect to the pound. If you think one is coming, try to beat it by changing your local currency into pounds before it hits.

It is also possible to hedge currency risk by changing your money into a variety of currencies, but this is fairly complex financial strategy, and you'll need to read up on it or work with an expert. A simpler strategy is to:

- Insist on payment in your own currency and push the risk onto the client

- Negotiate shorter contracts, which allows you to renegotiate if the currency rates move against you.

### 14.3.4 Different legal regimes

Different places, different laws. It is especially important that you find out about the legal regime in the country you are going to, the differences between its laws and the UK's, and how these will impact on you, your contracting and your life outside work, too. For example, the UK's legal system is very similar in many respects to that of the USA, as both are based on a common source; yet there are still vast differences that could get you into trouble if you didn't know about them, or chose not to respect them.

Similarly, our law is very different to the laws of mainland Western Europe, which is based on the so-called Napoleonic code. Even though we share so much in common – not least the legal structure of the European Union – there are significant differences that will affect you.

So the upshot is, even if you're just contracting on the other side of the English Channel in France, make sure you are aware of the legal system there and, best of all, always seek local, professional assistance.

### 14.3.5 Moving from the UK

You may still be liable for tax in the UK even though you have moved abroad, particularly in the first year after making the move to another country. In addition to using local experts to arrange your affairs in your new location, it is important to ensure your UK accountant has done everything possible to mitigate any residual tax liabilities in the UK.

In addition, you may continue to be taxed in the UK on income you receive from UK sources, such as investments. It is also possible, depending on how you manage your tax affairs and where you are working, that you may be taxed on your overseas income.

It is therefore essential that you plan the move and do your homework to ensure the most tax efficient arrangements. The complexities of international taxation treaties are such that you will need a professional to make sure you achieve the best deal. So assume that you will need expert help and source it accordingly.

## 14.3.6 The benefits and pitfalls of working 'offshore'

It is possible for contractors to spend their entire contracting career moving from a series of low or no tax regimes. Some do so by 'accident', because their contracting careers happen to take them to such locations; others do so by design, because they are unwilling to contribute to the general 'pot' that helps ensure good services for all UK citizens.

Some contracting sectors, such as engineering, oil and gas and offshore financial services, particularly suit an offshore lifestyle, because they have thriving contract markets in low and no tax territories.

If the idea of working and living variously in the Caribbean and Channel Islands, or off the coasts of Brazil or Tanzania appeals, and you have or can acquire the right skill sets, then becoming a 'tax exile' or 'tax nomad' may be for you. To maximise the benefits of working permanently offshore, a sensible move is to retain the services of a firm of international tax experts that can guide you on how and where to take your contracting income and where to invest. This is important if you plan to eventually return to the UK, as HMRC will want to know that your income has been legitimately gained whilst you have been domiciled outside of the UK.

Contractors who work predominantly offshore but with UK-based families should be extremely wary of claiming to be domiciled overseas, and should certainly take professional advice on making provision for any HMRC-led change of tax status. That's because HMRC has won tax cases against individuals claiming to be domiciled in low tax regimes outside of the UK who failed to make 'a distinct break' from the UK. This is a complex area of tax legislation, so if you think you might be affected, seek expert advice.

## 14.4 Working in the United States of America

For reasons of language, cultural similarities and, above all, because of the great opportunities for contractors in such a large economy, working in the USA remains very popular among UK contractors. But you do need to work your way through a very complex visa system.

More promising, of course, are the American versions of the skilled migrant visa, allowing foreign workers temporary residency so that they can live and work in the USA. Known as HB-1 and HB-2 visas, these are limited in number, and most of them are grabbed by certain companies – there is even an ongoing debate in the US about which companies should have most of them.

But there are other alternatives. It is possible to start a limited company in the US, and then to request a visa to run it. But this possibility, as well as some others, like short-term skilled migrant visas, involves going through a lot of very complex paperwork.

If you are determined to go to the US, and you can't find a company with an HB-1 or HB-2 visa for you, then your best bet is probably to start a US limited company. But you will almost certainly need the help of a US-based immigration lawyer if you are going to try it. There is good advice for this sort of thing to be had across the Atlantic. And, despite their perceived great wealth, American lawyers tend to cost much less than their UK counterparts.

## 14.5 Working in the European Union

For UK contractors who seek work abroad, the EU is entirely open and does not require any visas or permits. But you will need to look carefully at whether earning in euros or in the local currency changes your fee expectations. You should also consider your tax status carefully, as the entire system of taxation is different from country to country, and varies considerably once you are dealing with the EU countries of Eastern Europe.

What is important in working in the EU is to understand the specific regimes that govern contracting in each country. For example, agency work is closely regulated in Germany, while conditions for contracting in France are not too different from those of the UK, although you will not be able to work through a limited company in France unless you have more than one client.

Needless to say, you will want to find a local accountant, lawyer or umbrella company to help you deal with the vagaries of taxation and administration in the different EU member states. There are simply too many different variables, not only from one country to another, but sometimes even from one national province or borough to another within Europe.

# Contracting lessons from this chapter

- One of the great advantages of being a successful contractor is that, with your transferrable skill set, you can find work almost anywhere in the world.

- When considering contracting abroad, and when actually making the transition, the use of professional support is likely to save you time and money in the long term. It is worthwhile finding a good consultant or agency that specialises in helping contractors who want to work abroad.

- As a contractor abroad you are not an employee, and thus have no safety net with the client company if anything goes wrong. Good planning is essential to mitigate risks.

- International tax experts are expensive, but are likely to be worth the investment if the money you stand to gain from their expertise far outweighs their fees.

- In many other countries there are contractors' organisations and labour bodies that are able to advise you.

- Different places, different laws: even in the European Union, member states have local laws. Familiarise yourself with the local legislative landscape, use the UK embassy and consular network and consider using a professional advisor.

- Plan your move and do your homework to ensure you benefit from the most tax efficient arrangements.

- The EU is entirely open and does not require any visas or permits. But take the time to understand the specific regimes that govern contracting in each country, both within and outside the EU.

# 15
# Coming to
# the UK

## 15.1 Coming to the UK to work

The UK can be a great place to live and work. Like any country, it has its pros and cons and so it is largely down to personal preference as to whether it offers an acceptable alternative for the duration of a contract, or series of contracts.

The benefits of contracting in the UK are covered in detail in chapter 1. In addition to the greater earnings potential and flexible lifestyle, there are a huge number of other factors that make the UK attractive to workers from overseas.

For those looking to test their skills and further their careers, for example, the UK offers many of the world's most exciting and leading-edge projects to work on. And for those interested in 'seeing the world', the UK's tourism opportunities are equally exciting.

However, the UK's immigration landscape has changed significantly since a new coalition government was formed in May 2010. Although European Union citizens and those from Commonwealth countries can still come to the UK to work, virtually all of the previous immigration channels for highly skilled workers from outside of the European Economic Area, the Commonwealth and selected other countries are closed to contractors. In the main, only contractors from outside these areas who have a great deal of money to invest or have internationally recognised achievements in the arts, engineering and the sciences are being granted UK work visas.

These restrictions have been controversial. The UK suffers skills shortages in many of the core contracting disciplines, and there is pressure from employers who wish to have access to the brightest talent from around the world. Others believe that a free and open market is the only way for the UK to stay highly competitive and for its impressive skills base to remain at the cutting edge.

As UK businesses struggle to find suitably skilled candidates, pressure will mount on the government to relax immigration controls, and opportunities for expat contractors are likely to arise. So if you are determined to forge a contracting career in the UK, but currently don't qualify under any of the existing entry schemes, you should persevere. The visas and immigration pages of the UK Border Agency's website will let you know when immigration controls change.

### 15.1.1 Establishing whether UK contracting is for you

Doing your homework before starting the relocation process will really pay off. What you discover may heavily influence your decision to come, where you choose to accept a contract, and where you live.

For example, it may be that you live and work in a country with few business regulations and low taxation, and that you might find the situation in the UK less attractive from that point of view. Whilst the UK is not as heavily regulated as some European states, it does have its fair share of business red tape, and taxation rates for individuals and companies may be very different from those in your home country. Conversely, if you are coming to the UK from another European state, you may find the business environment much less regulated.

Across many sectors the UK is one of the leading nations in the world in terms of contracting opportunities, and this is certainly true in the IT, financial, creative, energy and engineering sectors, among others.

A vital task, if you are a non-EU or Commonwealth citizen, is to ensure you can qualify for a visa that allows you to work. Immigration has tightened up considerably and contractors who attempt to work in the 'black economy' without a proper visa will almost certainly be found out and may face fines, imprisonment and deportation. Section 15.2 covers visa issues and you may wish to consider enlisting professional help to ensure you can work in the UK legally. Professional immigration advisers are considered in greater detail in section 15.2.2.

There are many online guides and books about life in the UK. Again the key lesson is to do your research, which should include:

- Visa issues
- Other documentation, such as professional qualifications and health records

- Your financial arrangements, such as savings, banking and insurances
- Where in the UK to live and finding accommodation
- How you plan to get around
- Healthcare
- Education, both for school age children and if you intend to improve your own skills
- Starting a business and regulatory issues
- Finding a contract, preferably before you arrive in the UK
- Where to go for help if things go wrong.

The UK has a well developed public sector and this includes compulsory full-time education for all children and free healthcare at the point of delivery (although charges apply to overseas visitors whose countries don't have a reciprocal agreement with the UK). However, there are also many private sector options, which some contractors may wish to consider.

Your local British embassy or consulate is a good place to start your research. There are also numerous business and enterprise support agencies to assist companies from overseas who wish to relocate in the UK.

## 15.2 Visa issues and immigration advice

Contractors who are not UK citizens and who come from countries outside the European Union (EU), European Economic Area and the Commonwealth in the vast majority of cases have to apply for a visa in order to be able to work in the UK. Having a visa means they are classified as 'visa nationals' by the UK's Border Authority, which is the UK Government agency responsible for issuing visas. In addition, contractors from EU states that joined in 2005 and 2007 and contractors from the European Economic Area (EEA) may also have to register and request permission to be able to work legally.

Whether a visa is required, and the type of visa needed, depends on your financial assets, your personal circumstances, your qualifications and level of English, and the type of work you want to do in the UK. A contractor who speaks fluent English and has a significant amount of cash in the bank to invest in a UK business, or who is an internationally recognised leader in their field, will find it easier to get a visa; a contractor who doesn't have these attributes is unlikely to qualify.

A person with the typical profile of a contractor, who is highly skilled and educated and has a good command of English, will not need to use an immigration adviser, but would be well advised to do so. You could do a lot of the work yourself and probably succeed, but by using an adviser you are paying a premium to save your own time, buy the expertise of a specialist, and maximise your chances of success.

### 15.2.1 How the UK visa system works

The UK agency responsible for awarding work visas is the UK Border Agency (UKBA). It uses a Points Based System (PBS) to assess contractors' suitability to be allowed to enter and work in the UK.

Having established that you need a visa, you then need to decide under which of five 'tiers' and categories you will apply. These tiers were originally designed to allow workers from a wide range of backgrounds to apply for a visa to work and live in the UK, but at the time of writing many of them are closed to new applications. However, should immigration controls in the UK ease, you may find the rules are relaxed, so keep checking the UK Border Agency's website for the latest immigration information.

The tiers, or categories, include:

- Tier 1 High-value migrants, of which there are sub-tiers
- Tier 2 Skilled workers
- Tier 5 Temporary workers and youth mobility scheme
- Other categories
- UK ancestry for Commonwealth citizens.

The tier you will most likely be eligible for is Tier 1 for 'high-value migrants', which applies to contractors who are:

- "Recognised or have the potential to be recognised as leaders in the fields of science and the arts" (listed as Exceptional talent). To qualify, a UK learned society must endorse you and there are a limited number of endorsements available at any one time

- An entrepreneur or investor, with a substantial cash sum you will use to start a new business, take over an existing business or make a substantial financial investment in the UK under Tier 1 (Entrepreneur) and Tier 1 (Investor). The criteria vary slightly between the categories, but you'll need to have significant personal assets or funding from a UK seed fund or government grant to qualify.

The Tier 1(General) category has historically been the most appropriate tier for contractors since the points based system was introduced in 2007, but at the time of writing this tier is closed to new applicants from outside of the UK.

If you are a Commonwealth citizen, you may also be eligible to apply for a visa to live and work in the UK under the UK ancestry route. To be eligible, you must be a Commonwealth citizen, be able to financially support yourself and your family, and be able to prove that one of your grandparents was born in the UK, or on a British-registered ship or aircraft.

In the event that you are planning to apply for a visa under Tier 1, you then need to navigate the Points Based System (PBS). There is an interactive online points-based calculator tool you can use to establish where you are likely to score enough points for your application to be successful.

 homeoffice.gov.uk/pointscalculator

Before you start, bear in mind the following eligibility criteria:

- To apply as an investor you must have either £1m of your own money held in a regulated financial institution to invest in the UK, or personal assets totalling more than £2m and £1m loaned by a UK financial institution

- To apply as an entrepreneur, you must have at least £200,000 available to the business you are starting/planning to run or access to £50,000 from a venture capital firm, government-endorsed seed fund or funding from a government department. You must also have £2,800 in maintenance funds and be able to demonstrate your English language skills

- To apply as being an 'Exceptional talent', you must meet the criteria to be endorsed by a Designated Competent Body.

If you fail on any of the above criteria for the category under which you are applying, you will not score sufficient points and your will not even be able to start the visa application process.

In addition to scoring enough points using the UK Points Based System, if you are applying for a visa from outside the UK and EU, you will also need to submit supporting documentation, which can include:

- Your passport

- Certificates of professional and academic qualifications

- Documents to prove income, such as payslips, tax documents or bank statements

- Birth and marriage certificates of grandparents, as required by Commonwealth citizens

- Evidence of English language skills and UK experience

- Proof of financial assets, as required by Tier 1 applicants.

Full details of documentation required can be found on the UK Visa service website, visa4uk.fco.gov.uk, along with application forms and contact details of Visa Application Centres and UK diplomatic missions that can process visa applications. If you can't supply the relevant original documents, or certified copies in some instances, then the application will be refused.

If you are planning to bring your family to the UK, you should also be aware that entry for dependants, which generally means spouses, civil partners and children, is not automatic. Your dependants have to apply for entry clearance to the UK in their own right and with a separate dependant application form. In addition, there are conditions for dependants entering the UK, mainly relating to your ability to support them and the cash you have in the bank at the time of application.

There is a further category under which contractors can apply for a visa, which is Tier 2 Skilled workers, specifically the Tier 2 (General) worker category. The category is still open but there is a cap on the number of visas that can be issued under Tier 2. A condition of a Tier 2 visa is that you already have a job offer from a UK-based organisation, and that organisation, which becomes your sponsor, assigns you a certificate of sponsorship. That may limit your contracting opportunities, although it may equally lead to a succession of contract roles under the sponsorship of a client, or a string of clients.

Your sponsor should lead the visa application process, although you will still be required to make the application, so you should follow your sponsor's instructions. However, beware of 'scams', or tricks by dishonest businesses trying to cheat you out of supposed 'visa application fees' or 'immigration consultancy' fees in exchange for securing a Tier 2 visa.

## 15.2.2 Finding a contractor immigration adviser

Although for most workers who are non-UK or non-EU citizens, the visa application process should be easily undertaken using the UK Visa service website and Visa Application Centres (VAC), some contractors may wish to appoint an immigration adviser. There is no legal requirement or convention for anyone applying for a UK visa to use an immigration adviser. However, if your circumstances are less straightforward, an immigration adviser could mean the difference between being granted a visa or not.

Immigration advisers provide advice and a range of services on all matters to do with immigration in the UK. This means they may deal with issues such as:

- Visas

- Residence

- Nationality and citizenship issues.

These are all areas where contractors seeking to work in the UK may find the need for professional and specialist expertise and advice. Some immigration advisers also deal with other areas of immigration that you are less likely to be concerned with, including:

- Asylum claims
- Deportation, removal and deportation appeals
- Bail applications.

Most immigration advisers will charge fees for their advice and services, but there are some advisory services run by charities or other organisations that do not charge for their advice. These tend to focus their services on vulnerable migrants and asylum seekers.

You may want to use an immigration adviser for a number of reasons. The most obvious is that the adviser should understand the visa application process and how best to negotiate the process on your behalf. Typically, an immigration adviser is there:

- To assist with an application from outside the UK
- To assist with an application or extension when the contractor is already resident in the UK
- To help prepare the documentation, such as application forms
- To help build the dossier of supporting documentation that is essential to secure a successful application.

What an effective immigration adviser can do is speed up the application and minimise the chances of it being rejected on a technicality, for example, because a document is missing or hasn't been provided in the right format.

Take considerable care when looking for an immigration adviser, as some unscrupulous organisations prey on inexperienced migrants. It is always worth asking those who have succeeded in gaining a work visa for referrals, or your future client may suggest a source of help.

Most UK immigration advisers are regulated by the Office of the Immigration Services Commissioner (OISC). There is also a professional body, the Association of Regulated Immigration

Advisers (ARIA), and immigration lawyers/attorneys are regulated by the Law Society and other professional bodies. These organisations have databases of immigration advisers and their areas of expertise.

You should consider the level of advice you are likely to need. If you are applying for a Tier 1 visa as an entrepreneur or investor, the likelihood is that you will want an immigration adviser who is expert in dealing with high-net-worth individuals.

However, a regulated and reputable adviser should not take on a case they do not have the skills and experience to manage. Reputable immigration advisers should also provide a list of fees and schedules on request and should be able to provide an accurate estimate of likely costs. As with any professional service provider, it is advisable to get more than one estimate and to be very clear from the start as to what services might be required and what is included in the price. Once an adviser has been commissioned, keep track of costs on a regular basis.

## 15.3 Finding and securing a contract from outside the UK

If you have the right to work and live in the UK, by virtue of being a European Union, European Economic Area or, under certain circumstances, a Commonwealth citizen, you don't actually have to have a contract in place before you arrive. But you may wish to do so simply so you can start contracting and earning as soon as you arrive.

Before searching for a UK contract, you must ensure there is a ready market for your skills and expertise in the UK. By using websites such as contractorcalculator.co.uk, looking at job boards and the careers sections of industry and trade media (see chapter 2), it is possible to determine the likely demand for your particular skill. The research and preparation is not a 'one-off' task – it is an ongoing process until a contract has been signed and you have started work on it. Even then, there are ongoing actions, such as networking, that you should do to ensure you are always in a contract when you want to be.

The next stage is to prepare a UK style 'Curriculum Vitae' (CV) – this is the UK equivalent of a 'résumé' – the document that contractors and job seekers use to describe their skills, expertise, qualifications and past experience to a potential client, agency or employer. This is an extremely important part of the process, as successful UK contractors use a specific style and format of contractor CV that has been proven to attract interest and invitations to interview.

Section 15.3.1 provides tips on how to convert your existing résumé into a UK contracting format, and Chapter 4 takes you through the step-by-step process of producing a winning contractor's high impact, killer CV. Another important step is for the expat contractor to convert their academic and professional qualifications into the UK equivalent for inclusion in their CV. The objective of your CV is to secure you an interview which should then lead to you negotiating and signing your first UK-based contract.

Alongside producing your UK CV, you should also update your profiles on relevant social networking sites like LinkedIn. In addition, it is a good idea to find out which online professional networks and forums are most used in the UK for your area of expertise. Updating your profile on these and becoming active can be a good way to connect with potential future employers and colleagues, and to reassure them that you will be a good 'fit' in a UK organisation.

### 15.3.1 How to convert your résumé and qualifications into a UK contracting format

Contractors coming to the UK to contract for the first time and who want to get noticed by an agent, so they will then be put forward to a client for an interview, must first convert their existing résumé into a UK contractor Curriculum Vitae, or CV.

As a UK contractor you will be providing a business-to-business service to your clients, and like any business you need effective sales and marketing materials. For any contractor working in the UK, their sales literature is the high impact, or 'killer' CV, supported by matching profiles on professional social media sites, like LinkedIn.

Contractor CVs are very different from the CVs used by workers seeking permanent work as an employee. Agents who advertise for contractors to apply for contracts normally have to filter through tens to hundreds of contractor CVs, and if they don't instantly see exactly the information they require, your CV is quickly discarded.

So your CV must be structured to immediately display the information an agent and client needs to see. This should be in a standard format, so the agent and client know where to look for specific information about you. The key items to include are:

- Your contracting profile
- Your relevant skills and expertise – updated for each contract you apply for
- Your achievements that are relevant to contracting
- Previous relevant clients, with the skills used on that contract and the outcomes achieved (preferably including what commercial benefits these achieved)
- Confirmation of the right to work in the UK
- Relevant education, training and hobbies.

Your CV should be no more than two single-sided pages of A4. Your profile, skills, experience and achievements must be on the front page. Even with decades of experience and hugely impressive skill sets, unless you can communicate this information and sell yourself, you are unlikely to win any contracts. It's not the best contractors who win the best contracts; it's the contractors who are best at winning contracts who get the work. Chapter 4 tells you how to create a contractor CV in considerable detail, with examples.

Although qualifications become increasingly irrelevant as you gain greater experience, you will find that some agencies and clients want evidence of your academic credentials. If you are a professional, such as an engineer, architect, lawyer, or financial or healthcare professional, it is likely that your client or agency will require evidence that you hold the appropriate professional qualifications or certification. You may therefore have to 'translate' or validate your academic and professional qualifications before you can apply for, or be awarded the contract.

To validate your academic qualifications you can search the UK's National Academic Recognition Information Centre database

(NARIC). NARIC includes details of academic and professional qualifications from over 180 different countries, so you should be able to determine the UK equivalent.

 naric.org.uk

To compare professional qualifications, contact the relevant UK professional body. So, for example, if you have professional qualifications as a civil engineer, you would contact the Institution of Civil Engineers (ICE) in the UK, who are used to dealing with such requests. As professional and trade organisations frequently have international links, you should also contact your own national professional organisation for advice. It may be that a bilateral agreement is already in place recognising your professional qualification and status in the UK.

### 15.3.2 Agencies and interviews

It is estimated that approximately 80% of all UK contracts are found through and awarded by recruitment agencies. In some sectors, such as in IT contracting, it can be much higher. The remainder are awarded directly by the end-user client. Bear in mind, though, that a considerable number of the contracts awarded directly by clients are never advertised, because successful contractors tend to win them through personal contacts or referral.

You are at an automatic disadvantage with agencies when applying for contracts from outside the UK. This is because agencies typically prefer those candidates who will present them with the fewest problems and have the highest chance of quickly securing a contract offer. So unless your skills are highly sought after, an agent is more likely to opt for the easier option of a contractor who can attend an interview without having to fly into the country; who doesn't have to apply for a visa; and is instantly available by phone as they are not in a different time zone.

However, you may have highly sought-after skills, or be in an occupation identified by the UK Migration Advisory Committee, part of the UK's Home Office, as being on the recommended shortage occupation list, which means you are likely to be in great demand. Or you might find that something in your background, your experience or possibly a language skill, is attractive to the agency and the end-user client.

Once you have identified a contract and gained the attention of the agent, or end-user client, the next challenge is to impress them at interview. This may pose some practical problems, with logistics and travel arrangements, and you may require a visitor's visas for the purpose of interviews if you are a non-European Union, European Economic Area or Commonwealth citizen. Alternatively, of course, an initial interview might be conducted by phone or online. If contracting with the end-user client in a very international sector, like oil and gas, in which executives travel frequently, it is also possible that an interview might be set up outside the UK, perhaps in a third country.

Having secured an interview, you have the opportunity to sell yourself face-to-face to the end-user client. Agents and clients will generally make allowances for a contractor's past business background and for cultural differences, but there are still some business practices that do not cross international boundaries.

For example, in some countries it is expected that the start times for business meetings are approximate and it is normal that one party might arrive at another's offices within, say, half an hour of the agreed time. However, lateness is not acceptable in the UK and unless you have a very good reason, you are likely to have lost the contract before an interview even begins.

For that reason, and others, it is essential that you investigate and understand the UK interview techniques required to get a contract offer – see chapter 5.

### 15.3.3 Negotiation and contracts

Once you have impressed the client with your contracting skills at interview and been offered a contract, you then have the challenge of negotiating favourable and lucrative contractual terms, either direct with the client or, more often, with the agent. For a full explanation of how to negotiate a contract, either direct with a client or with an agent, see chapter 5.

It is very important when negotiating to understand the worth of the skills you are offering, and what that worth means in a UK context. Whilst on the face of it some salaries might sound low or high when converted into your home currency, it may well be very different for a UK contractor with those skills. The cost of living in the UK is also likely to be different to your own country, especially for those living and working in the major cities, so this needs to be taken into account.

Contractors by definition are reviewing, negotiating, agreeing and signing contracts all the time – that's why they are called contractors. So you need just enough knowledge about contract law to understand the basics and know when you should ask for professional help. Contracts are legal documents, so there is no substitute for taking professional legal advice – this is true for all contractors, whether they have lived and worked all their lives in the UK, or are newly arrived contractors from outside of the UK.

Lawyers' services can be expensive, but their fees are very cost-effective when compared to what it could cost contractors who don't seek advice and get it wrong. A basic knowledge of the law is also essential for when things go wrong, so you know when to try to solve a problem yourself and when to find a lawyer or other professional adviser.

A contract is a legally binding agreement between your trading vehicle (see chapter 6, section 6.2), which may be a limited company or an umbrella company, and the agency or, if contracting direct, with the end-user client. All contracts have two things in common:

- You exchange your services for a 'consideration', which is usually a cash payment (UK contract law goes back centuries to when a 'consideration' might, for instance, be a lamb)

- A contract is determined when an offer has been accepted, even if only verbally.

Why should these technicalities concern you? Because during disputes, which services were agreed to for a consideration becomes an important factor. So if you verbally accept an offer from a client or agent, even if perhaps you did not mean to, the contract has been formed and is legally binding.

There are other technicalities. For example, both parties must enter into the contract freely. And usually, but not always, an offer is accepted by a signature on a contract, which is described as a fully executed contract when both parties have signed. But it is important to note that a verbal agreement still constitutes a contract in UK law. Chapter 7 explains the basic principles of contract law in the UK and what you need to know to avoid the most common contracting pitfalls.

## 15.4 Relocating home and family to the UK

If you are single with no dependants, then coming to work in the UK could be as simple as packing a bag and getting on a plane. However, if you have a family coming with you, it is a major exercise in logistics to ensure everything goes smoothly. Good quality accommodation, and in particular family accommodation, is scarce in some parts of the UK. This is particularly true in the large capital cities, such as London, Edinburgh, Cardiff and Belfast, as well as other major cities like Birmingham and Manchester, where there are concentrations of contracting opportunities.

In such areas hotels and other temporary accommodation can be expensive, with prices driven up by a combination of under-supply and high demand from leisure, tourism and business customers. So the answer is to ensure you have, at the very least, affordable short-term accommodation in place before you get on the plane.

There are also significant regional variations in the UK, which impact on the availability of contracts and quality of life. For example, the financial sector is focused mainly in London and the South East of England, and the bulk of higher paying IT jobs in the financial sector can also be found there.

Oil and gas contractors will find work mainly in Scotland, particularly Aberdeen, and in Humberside and East Anglia. However, many oil and gas work contracts require offshore work, so it actually does not matter where the contractor is based as long as transport links are good.

### Housing
Before you arrive, it is important to at the very least have temporary

accommodation. Not knowing where you are going to stay (even if it's only a bed and breakfast) might even affect whether the immigration officer at your point of entry lets you into the country.

If possible, before you even arrive it is a good idea to have organised a permanent place to live. If you don't have a UK address very quickly, you will find securing a contract and accessing local services very difficult. There is a thriving and efficient private property market in the UK. This is subject to local and regional variation, so when buying or renting for the first time you should be able to find a suitable dwelling fairly quickly.

As with any country, rents and property prices are high in popular residential areas. Prices are influenced by access to transport links, the quality of local schools, and other amenities and attractions, which may be cultural, social or employment related.

### Healthcare
The UK has a single state healthcare provider called the National Health Service, or NHS for short. The idea is that all healthcare is free at the point of delivery, which means state healthcare is paid for by workers and employers in the UK via indirect taxation, called National Insurance Contributions (NICs), and other taxes.

But 'free at the point of delivery' does not mean 'free'. If your country of origin does not have a reciprocal agreement with the UK, then you will have to pay. Even if there is a reciprocal agreement, you might have to provide evidence of this, so should check on requirements with the relevant government department in your country, as well as with your local British embassy or consulate.

You may wish to choose to have private healthcare insurance for you and your family. The UK has a world class private healthcare insurance system that works closely with state healthcare providers, so comprehensive healthcare insurance provides you with access to the best of both the private and state healthcare.

### Education
Contractors with families and children of school, further education and university age have a huge amount of high quality choice in the UK. Full-time education for children is free. It is also compulsory

for children aged five to 16, who must follow a prescribed national curriculum. The upper age limit for compulsory education is rising from 2013, to ensure that everyone stays in education or training until they are 18. Further education for older teenagers up to 19 is mostly free, but some further education providers and all universities charge fees.

Most UK schoolchildren attend state schools, funded by the taxpayer. These include foundation and trust schools, community schools, voluntary-aided schools and voluntary-controlled schools. Some of these are specialist schools, which provide the full national curriculum, but also specialise in a particular subject, such as mathematics, humanities and the arts. To further confuse the state educational landscape, there are free schools (which are state schools that are not controlled by the local authority) city technology colleges, academies, grammar schools, maintained boarding schools, and faith schools.

All state schools are required to provide for the needs of children with physical disabilities and/or learning difficulties, but in addition there are community and foundation special schools (not to be confused with 'specialist schools') for children with special educational needs.

Parents everywhere in the world worry endlessly about their children's education, and will go to great lengths to ensure their child is educated in a particular school or type of school. But in the UK the state education system provides a generally excellent level of education. And, particularly in the areas near where you are likely to find your contracts, you will almost certainly have a choice of good state schools suited to your child.

Around 96% of all UK schoolchildren attend the taxpayer-funded state schools described above. The remaining 4% are educated by the private or independent schools sector, which includes day schools and residential boarding schools. The independent education sector also includes many international schools, most of which offer baccalaureates.

Although over half of these independent schools receive the equivalent of taxpayer subsidies through their charity status, they are largely funded by fees paid by parents and from investment revenue. So they are not free to attend: apart from a small number of parents whose children receive scholarships, full fees must be paid by all parents. These can be more than £30,000 each year, on top of which there are generally extra fees to pay for additional tuition, plus many incidental expenses to pay

Be aware that, through a historical quirk, even the most distinguished independent and private schools in the UK are called 'public' schools. The word public here refers to the fact that children are educated 'publicly', as opposed to privately in their own homes. So, when asking for information on schools, remember to be clear about the sort of school you would like to send your child to – fee-paying or state-funded.

Both the state and private sectors in the UK feature some of the highest achieving, and best known, schools in the world. But just because you may be paying for an independent school, don't assume it will achieve better results than a state school – that is often not the case.

Contractors with older children have an almost bewildering choice of tertiary and university education, with an enormous range of courses and locations to choose from, although most are fee-paying.

**Leisure and recreation**
The UK has something to offer everyone when it comes to leisure, recreation and vacations (typically called 'holidays' in the UK). As a contractor with a healthy disposable income, you will not struggle to find enjoyable and exciting ways to spend it!

You will have wonderful opportunities to travel throughout the diverse landscapes and cultures of British Isles. Because of their relatively small size and good transport links, most parts of the UK can be reached easily and quickly, so it's possible to enjoy a weekend away in even the furthest expanses of the UK.

As the UK is the European pioneer of low cost airlines, for contractors who want a short break away from contracting, there are hundreds of options as the rest of Europe is only a short flight, drive or train journey away. Be careful if you have a visa to ensure it allows you to travel abroad, and make sure you have the correct visa for the country you are travelling to.

# 15.5 Doing business and working in the UK

Winning a contract is nothing like getting a new job with a permanent employer. Contractors are normally expected to start work very quickly once they have been awarded their contract – an immediate start is one of the benefits contractors bring to clients. And, as you are providing a business-to-business service to your client, usually via an agency, you need to have a 'trading solution' in place so you can invoice the agency or client directly for their fees, sometimes in a matter of days or a few weeks.

A trading solution usually refers to the legal entity that you will use to trade with the agency or end-user client. In the UK, there are various legal entities available for a contractor to trade under, and these are described in detail in section 6.1.

The workplace for highly skilled and professional contractors is generally quite informal. Relationships between contractors and their clients tend to be reasonably relaxed, as long as everything is going well. Workplaces are heavily regulated, with much health and safety and employment regulation in place to protect workers. But remember that, as a contractor, you are not an employee of your client and do not have the same rights as your client's employees. This does not mean your client does not have to provide a safe environment for you to work in, but it does mean you will not be entitled to enjoy all the employment benefits and protection given to permanent employees you work alongside.

Although it has moved a little towards the litigious society prevalent in the United States, the situation in the UK has not reached the stage where every issue or conflict must be resolved in court. The UK courts are quite keen on Alternative Dispute Resolution (ADR), and if you end up in court without having exhausted non-litigious avenues the judge is likely to be unimpressed. This leads to a much more consensual workplace, where people and companies tend to work more constructively towards a solution that benefits all.

The major industry body that helps protect contractors' interests is PCG (formerly known as the Professional Contractors Group). Originally created as a single platform lobby group against tax legislation, PCG has become a fully-fledged industry body, although it is not a chartered professional institute. Having said that, the majority of its membership is made up of contractors running their own limited companies, rather than those working through umbrella companies. Nevertheless, PCG's activities are aimed at protecting and enhancing the working lives of all contractors.

## 15.5.1 Taxation for contractors coming to the UK

When you first start contracting in the UK you will rapidly learn that, as a contractor, you are under particular scrutiny by UK tax authorities. You must learn as quickly as possible how to effectively manage your UK tax affairs. So take advice from your accountant, umbrella company or offshore solution provider to stay within UK tax legislation

The government organisation responsible for collecting taxes in the UK is Her Majesty's Revenue and Customs, or HMRC for short. HMRC is also often called 'the revenue', 'inland revenue' or simply 'the taxman', and these names are frequently used by both contractors and contractor advisers. HMRC is an agency of the UK government department called Her Majesty's Treasury, which, as its name suggests, is responsible for controlling government spending and raising government revenues.

Employees in the UK are 'taxed at source' via a system known as 'Pay as You Earn' or PAYE. This means their employer automatically deducts income tax and other indirect taxes, known as National Insurance Contributions (NICs), when the employee is paid. The employer then pays the tax revenues directly to HMRC. But contractors who work through their own limited company don't pay tax like this, because they are not employees. They are likely to be employees of their own limited companies and pay themselves a small salary, but most of their income will probably come in the form of dividends. So limited company contractors pay tax based on their personal and company annual tax returns, which calculate their tax liability after deductions, expenses and a variety of other rules. Understanding these rules is central to understanding how, as a contractor, you can legally reduce your tax bills.

Where a citizen or organisation such as a limited company or partnership deliberately misleads HMRC to avoid paying tax, this is tax evasion and illegal. As such, it attracts severe financial penalties and can lead to imprisonment. However, it is possible and entirely legal to reduce the amount of tax that needs to be paid by being 'tax efficient' – in other words, understanding the tax system and ensuring you benefit from the rules, rather than falling foul of them.

Seeking professional advice from an accountant or tax adviser that specialises in contractor affairs can help considerably reduce the amount of tax you need to pay. In fact, seeking experts' help is highly recommended because, at the very least, they are likely to pay for themselves by ensuring you don't pay more tax than you should. Section 6.3 provides detailed coverage of what you need to know about taxation as a UK-based contractor.

### 15.5.2 IR35 – the 'contractor tax'

IR35, also known as the 'intermediaries legislation', is tax law aimed at charging contractors more tax if they are in reality 'disguised employees' of their client, rather than a genuine contractor. It is extremely important for you to understand this legislation, because by doing so you can expect to enjoy a much higher net income (the amount of money left after paying taxes).

So why does a UK tax law matter to you? Because if you find that IR35 applies to one or more of your UK contracts, you could end up being taxed as if you were employed. That could mean paying significantly more in tax, up to 25% more in some circumstances. To see what that means in practice, it could cost a contractor earning £40 per hour an additional £800 per month in tax.

IR35 applies to specific contractor contracts with an end-user client. So it is possible to have several contracts during a tax year, with some 'within' IR35 and others 'outside' it. The idea is to negotiate contracts in such a way that they are always 'outside' IR35. But it is important to note that what counts is how the contractor works and the working relationship they have with their client. The legislation is intended to identify 'disguised employees' who would be employees if they did not have an intermediary, such as the contractor limited company, between them and the client.

If the IR35 enforcement agency, HMRC, judges a contractor to be an 'employee' in every other way but name, then their contract is caught by IR35. That means they are judged to be working within IR35 and have to pay taxes as if they were employed. HMRC applies a number of tests to a contractor to determine if they are actually a 'disguised employee', and these are based on UK employment law.

But it is important to note that you must not assume you are working inside IR35 and that it's up to the taxman to let you know if you are not. You must be clear about your status and ensure that, if your contract is inside IR35, your run your tax affairs accordingly.

There is a long history of employment tests in the UK, because UK workers have generally been trying to prove they ARE employed, and can therefore claim potentially valuable employment rights from their 'employers'. IR35 is the reverse – contractors are trying to prove that they are NOT employees, and therefore do not have to pay tax as if they were.

As with all cases in UK law, each is judged on its individual merits and there is no absolute right or wrong answer. However, there are some broad indications of 'employment' that you can apply to check whether you should consult an IR35 expert. Chapter 8 explains in detail what you need to know and when to seek expert assistance.

You can start by assessing your own IR35 status using ContractorCalculator's free online IR35 test:

 contractorcalculator.co.uk/IR35_Test.aspx

# Contracting lessons from this chapter

- The UK offers many of the world's most exciting and leading-edge projects to work on.

- Although European Union citizens and those from Commonwealth countries can still come to the UK to work, virtually all of the previous immigration channels for highly skilled workers from outside of the European Economic Area, the Commonwealth and selected other countries are closed to contractors.

- If you are a non-EU or Commonwealth citizen, ensure you can qualify for a visa that allows you to work in the UK.

- By using an immigration or visa adviser, you are paying a premium to save your own time, buy the expertise of a specialist, and maximise your chances of success. If your circumstances are less straightforward, an immigration adviser could mean the difference between being granted a visa or not.

- Take considerable care when looking for an immigration adviser, as some unscrupulous organisations prey on inexperienced migrants.

- Prepare a UK style Curriculum Vitae (CV) – this is the UK equivalent of a résumé – the document that contractors and job seekers use to describe their skills, expertise, qualifications and past experience to a potential client, agency or employer. Convert your academic and professional qualifications into the UK equivalent for inclusion in your CV.

- It is estimated that approximately 80% of all UK contracts are found through and awarded by recruitment agencies.

- It is essential that you investigate and understand the UK interview techniques required to get a contract offer.

- It is very important when negotiating to understand the worth of the skills you are offering, and what that worth means in a UK context.

- A basic knowledge of UK law – especially contract law – is essential.

- Where a citizen or organisation deliberately misleads HMRC (the UK tax body) to avoid paying tax, this is tax evasion and is illegal. To avoid this, and maximise your legal tax avoidance, seek professional advice from an accountant or tax adviser that specialises in contractor affairs.

- Take the time to learn about IR35 tax legislation. You must be clear about your status and ensure that, if your contract is inside IR35, your run your tax affairs accordingly.

# 16

# Growing your business

## 16.1 Introduction

You can have a great time being a contractor, and many contractors take full advantage of the lifestyle: good money, work when you want to do it, time off to do the things you really enjoy, amazing flexibility, and few of the niggles, hassles and worries that permanent employees have to face every day. It all adds up to make contracting a hugely worthwhile choice. But inevitably, after a while, you start asking yourself, 'Where is all this heading?' Because, in order to enjoy the benefits of contracting, you have to work really hard, much harder than permanent employees do in many cases.

So sooner or later you come to ask yourself if you want to keep doing this same thing for the rest of your life. Some contractors are just fine with that. But many others decide that they want to build something more out of their contracting career.

---

### Been there, done that!

### Avoid monsters

**DAVE SAYS:** A friend of mine built a contracting business that was growing nicely after a year. But he was the business himself really, and needed to be working every day of the week. He'd not planned how it was going to run in his absence, which made taking holidays and sometimes even days off impossible. Be careful not to build yourself an uncontrollable monster!

---

They consider building a truly self-supporting business – one that doesn't depend on a single person. They want to escape the 'time for the money' equation that most contracting depends on, because you eventually reach the ceiling of earnings. This ceiling is your day rate multiplied by the number of days you are prepared or able to work.

For the typical UK contractor, the upper limit is likely to be around 220 working days.

## Been there, done that!

### Make sure it's yours

**DAVE SAYS:** When building a new business, make sure you're not basing it on someone else's intellectual property (IP). In one case, a contractor used techniques he had picked up at a bank to build a cutting-edge risk management system. When he then started selling that system to other banks in competition with the one where he'd learnt the technology, the original bank took him to court. He was found to have stolen the IP and the business was shut down.

Cases like this are difficult because, of course, most contractors' new business ideas are likely to be based on the knowledge and expertise they've picked up along the way. So if there's even the slightest doubt in your mind (and possibly even if there isn't), you should consult an IP specialist for advice. This might also help you hang onto your own IP, so that you have protection against others trying to copy or steal it.

You might find yourself wanting to build a self-supporting business after a couple of decades of contracting, or it might be your ambition from the start, and one of your reasons for going into contracting in the first place. Either way, you'll have to start thinking like an entrepreneur.

A typical example is a contractor who found that he really liked working with small businesses, and was able to add tremendous value to them. So he marketed his ability to work with such clients, then began hiring other contractors and later employees to undertake the actual projects for him. After a year, he had a full-scale dedicated consulting business up and running.

But consulting is only one obvious option. Another example is an engineering contractor who developed a patent for a drainage process and began to sell the rights to it. Before long, she had an industrial design business growing up around her.

There are plenty of opportunities if you have the motivation. And if you have been contracting through a limited company you already have a trading vehicle ready made for your new business.

## 16.2 Business development and strategy

Whatever your situation, and whatever your preferences, if you want to go down the route of building a business, you will need to do some serious business planning. A contractor can go footloose and fancy-free, as it were, from one contract to another. You can't do that if you're planning to build revenue dependent on multiplying sales, particularly if you might start employing people and taking on other overheads, like premises.

If you're ready to take this step, start by writing a business plan that will help shape your thoughts and provide you with some tangible actions and targets. But you may wish to put a bit more research into what is, after all, a major career step, and there are many business plan guides and plenty of planning software you can use to develop this.

In addition there are some publicly-funded support organisations, such as the online Business Link service, UK Trade and Investment if your business has export potential, or your Local Enterprise Partnership, which can provide independent, impartial and often free advice and support.

Whatever your approach to your new business, you will need to think about marketing it: who is your target market, how will you reach the largest possible section of this group, who else is competing for the attention of the same target group, how are you different to and better than them, etc.

In all of this, what you have learned as a contractor will be the best guide. You've seen what clients want most from you on the job, and you've seen how to get their attention. So use what you've learned as a contractor to build strong foundations for your business.

The principles are the same, only instead of the product being you and your skills/services, it's your new business model.

## 16.3 Diversification from contracting

Contracting is a very successful business model, but it does have limitations. Unless you intend to diversify, the business will always be limited by the maximum day rate you can command and the number of days you can work.

Top consultants and business gurus bill up to £5,000 a day or more, sometimes very much more. But the chances of you being able to generate such a day rate are limited. The number of working days in the UK is usually calculated to be around 220. So if you do the maths, and it's not likely you will be able to charge more than £1,000 per day, this limits earnings to about £220,000 per year.

This of course is a fantastic salary, but you will have to work extremely hard to sustain it and not take any time off. However, it is possible to change your business model to maximise your day rate and/or expand your revenue streams by charging out other contractors or developing products.

The three obvious options that may be relatively easily available to you include:

- Personal consulting, in which you do what you do as a contractor for a number of clients at the same time, and at a much higher rate

- Product development, in which you create some intellectual property and sell it

- Consultancy services, in which you hire out other people like yourself and manage and market their efforts.

These three routes are discussed below.

### 16.3.1 Consultancy

What's the difference between a contractor and a consultant? It's simple: a contractor builds something for the client, and the consultant tells or teaches the client how to build something.

Let's take an example from the experience of a corporate writer, who became an editorial consultant. When companies need content on their websites, they call in a corporate writer who writes something for them, gets paid for the piecework, and goes away. The contractor produces a product.

Or, the company could go to an expert on website content, and say, 'how can we build a team that will produce the content we need on the website whenever we need it?' The consultant helps hire workers with the right experience, finds a manager for the team, and provides the client with planning so that they can do the necessary research and produce the content themselves. The consultant shares know-how.

You will read endless jokes about consultants and their 'consultant-speak' in the business press, but the fact is that businesses need consultants to survive. They cannot possibly obtain all the know-how they need by hiring new people – the budget would burst at the seams!

Instead, they bring in a consultant who provides the know-how they need and shares it with the people they have. A good consultant saves money for the company, or adds value to it. The consultant's fee is therefore paid for out of the money saved or the increase in revenues and profits.

An obvious example where a consultant can save money is a good tax consultant, who will save a company 20% on its taxes, and then charge the company 10% in fees. In effect, the company hasn't spent anything on the consultant, but has saved 10% on taxes.

In your work as a contractor, you will often see knowledge gaps that you know you can fill yourself. If you have the motivation, there's your opportunity. Your great incentive is that consulting is highly paid: the best consultants earn upwards of £1,000 per day. And instead of being dependent on a single client, you'll build up a portfolio of clients who call you in again and again.

You will want to make yourself an acknowledged authority in your field, for example by publishing papers and 'working the conferences'. It's an extremely effective and quite agreeable way to market yourself, since you will often meet all your competitors at the same conference and you can enjoy the ensuing debates. More importantly, you will be meeting prospective clients, potential future employees or sub-contractors, and generally getting your and your company's name out there.

Consulting can have the added advantage of placing you well outside IR35, as you are clearly in business in your own right, are not controlled by your client, can supply a substitute and so on.

All in all, it can prove a highly profitable, enjoyable and satisfying way to earn a crust!

### 16.3.2 Product development

There is one classic story about a contractor who became a fantastically successful product developer. He worked in radio as a sound editor. When he edited tapes, he obviously made them shorter or longer as needed. This genius discovered one day that he could use the same techniques he used in editing to effectively get more 'stuff' (that is, more content) into the same time period. In other words, when an advertiser paid for a minute, the contractor could squeeze a minute- and-a-half's worth of content into it.

The contractor patented the process, and became extremely wealthy in the space of a couple of years. Every single advertiser on radio wanted to use this product. It's still being marketed more than a decade later.

All this sounds terribly unlikely and/or difficult; yet in fact, contractors see opportunities like this all the time. Going from contract to contract of the same type, you see each time that a certain kind of process, or a bit of code, or some very specific skill, resolves an important issue. You use it, you know it works and the demand for your services as a contractor proves that there's a genuine demand.

It's not really a great step from there to marketing that product yourself. You do need to think about how to reach the target market, and in some cases how to retain your hold on the intellectual property.

Build your business plan around those two aims, understanding the market need and creating a product to fulfil it, and you could create a thriving business.

### 16.3.3 Hiring contractors

This is an option for people who consider themselves good managers and who know how to delegate, explain, support and encourage. The basis of this business model is that if you can win work based on your skills and expertise, you can pay someone else to do that work and take part of their earnings. You find them work, you coach them on how to do it, and you get some of the money without spending a great deal of your own time.

With the advent of the Agency Workers Regulations (AWR), 'body-shopping' contractors into assignments may be used to categorise your business as a temporary work agency. So contractors you supply on a sub-contract basis, as opposed to those you employ, may be in the scope of AWR. See section 9.6 for further details about your AWR risk when hiring subcontractors.

Needless to say, a lot of hard work goes into building a consultancy of this type. Again marketing is the key, and you will benefit from what you've learned about the companies you've worked for yourself.

But managing people and marketing to companies are skills that do not necessarily come to all contractors, so ask yourself if you have what it takes, and even if the answer is 'yes', find ways to improve your management and marketing skills.

Obviously, there are many issues to be confronted with this type of business that don't really enter into contracting. Just because you are a good programmer or engineer, for example, you may not have the skills required for running a business that involves a whole host of specialist business skills: hiring, managing, administration, marketing, finance, etc.

But if you can make it through the skills gap, you will enjoy one advantage that contractors don't have: you'll have a business that is sustainable on its own, one that doesn't depend on you personally to generate billable hours. The advantage of each of these approaches is that you are adding value to the business – it is not just dependant on you personally.

That means you are not necessarily essential for its continued success, which means you have the opportunity to go through a transaction, which may be a trade sale of the business or floating in a financial market. And that's where you will really make your money.

## Contracting lessons from this chapter

- Some contractors are content with a simple contracting career. But many others decide that they want to build something more.

- When growing your business, be careful not to build yourself an uncontrollable monster.

- Whatever your preferences for business growth and development, if you want to go down the route of building a business, you will need to do some serious business planning.

- There are typically three options contractors choose to build their business: Personal consulting, Product development, or Consultancy services.

- Consulting, product development and hiring out other contractors can all have the added advantage of placing you well outside IR35, as you are clearly in business in your own right.

Lightning Source UK Ltd.
Milton Keynes UK
UKOW04f0458200114

224868UK00002B/13/P